# Markets, Politics and the Environment

*Markets, Politics and the Environment* answers three groups of overlapping questions:

- What is planning? And, as part of this, what are its key features as a style of social practice and action? And how does planning as a style of social practice relate to social and economic change?
- How, as part of the justification for planning, might claims of valid technical knowledge be constructed? What is meant by 'rational'? What is the contribution of pragmatism as a supplement or replacement to rationalism? How might rationality and pragmatism be adapted to postmodernism and the requirements of diversity?
- Finally, how may concepts of planning be reoriented towards sustainable development as a collective duty? How might sustainable development be reworked in relation to planning as a means of managing and stimulating change?

Each group of questions is discussed in a separate section chapter and is associated with different theories, debates and examples of practice. *Markets, Politics and the Environment* concludes that the full implications of sustainable development and climate change point in the direction of a different type of state—a green state whose future functioning can draw on planning theory but at present can only be conceived as a sketchy outline.

**Barry Goodchild** is Professor of Housing and Urban Planning at Sheffield Hallam University, UK. Over a long career, he has secured the publication of five books and 39 articles in refereed journals, and has worked for research clients in England, Scotland and France, including the UK Economic and Social Research Council.

# Routledge Research in Planning and Urban Design
Series editor: Peter Ache
Radboud University, Nijmegen, Netherlands

Routledge Research in Planning and Urban Design is a series of academic monographs for scholars working in these disciplines and the overlaps between them. Building on Routledge's history of academic rigour and cutting-edge research, the series contributes to the rapidly expanding literature in all areas of planning and urban design.

**Politics, Planning and Housing Supply in Australia, England and Hong Kong**
*Nicole Gurran, Nick Gallent and Rebecca Chiu*

**Sustainable Regeneration of Former Military Sites**
*Samer Bagaeen and Celia Clark*

**Place and Placelessness Revisited**
*Robert Freestone and Edgar Liu*

**Ideology, Political Transitions, and the City**
The Case of Mostar, Bosnia and Herzegovina
*Aleksandra Djurasovic*

**Placemaking**
An Urban Design Methodology
*Derek Thomas*

**Neoliberal Spatial Governance**
*Philip Allmendinger*

**Actor Networks of Planning**
Exploring the Influence of ANT
*Yvonne Rydin and Laura Tate*

**Territorial Governance across Europe**
Pathways, Practices and Prospects
*Peter Schmitt and Lisa Van Well*

'*Markets, Politics and the Environment* is an interesting and valuable attempt to connect some of the theoretical debates in planning to the examples from planning practice, and make them more accessible to a wider readership.'

—*Simin Davoudi, Newcastle University, UK*

'As English planning finds itself in a constant state of reform, it is more important than ever to step back and reflect upon where planning is going and what its future might be. This book provides a helpful and provocative stimulant to these and other questions, bridging the theory–practice divide and engaging with contemporary planning issues around sustainability, growth, complexity, the environment and the changing nature of space.'

—*Philip Allmendinger, Cambridge University, UK*

# Markets, Politics and the Environment
## An Introduction to Planning Theory

Barry Goodchild

NEW YORK AND LONDON

First published 2017
by Routledge
711 Third Avenue, New York, NY 10017

and by Routledge
2 Park Square, Milton Park, Abingdon, Oxon OX14 4RN

First issued in paperback 2018

*Routledge is an imprint of the Taylor and Francis Group, an informa business*

© 2017 Taylor & Francis

The right of Barry Goodchild to be identified as author of this work has been asserted by him in accordance with sections 77 and 78 of the Copyright, Designs and Patents Act 1988.

All rights reserved. No part of this book may be reprinted or reproduced or utilised in any form or by any electronic, mechanical, or other means, now known or hereafter invented, including photocopying and recording, or in any information storage or retrieval system, without permission in writing from the publishers.

Trademark notice: Product or corporate names may be trademarks or registered trademarks, and are used only for identification and explanation without intent to infringe.

*Library of Congress Cataloging-in-Publication Data*
Names: Goodchild, Barry, author.
Title: Markets, politics and the environment : an introduction to planning theory / Barry Goodchild.
Description: New York, NY : Routledge, 2016. | Series: Routledge research in planning and urban design
Identifiers: LCCN 2016012227 (print) | LCCN 2016020408 (ebook) |
ISBN 9781138658721 (hardback) | ISBN 9781315620640 (ebook)
Subjects: LCSH: City planning—Great Britain. | Regional planning—Great Britain.
Classification: LCC HT169.G7 G643 2016 (print) | LCC HT169.G7 (ebook) |
DDC 307.1/2160941—dc23
LC record available at https://lccn.loc.gov/2016012227

ISBN 13: 978-1-138-59512-5 (pbk)
ISBN 13: 978-1-138-65872-1 (hbk)

Typeset in Sabon
by diacriTech, Chennai

# Table of Contents

*List of Illustrations* — ix
*Acknowledgements* — x
*Summary* — xi

PART I
## Introduction — 1

  1  Interpretations of Urban Planning — 3

PART II
## Definitions, Styles and Forms — 39

  2  Planning and Urban Spaces — 41

  3  Political and Economic Planning — 77

  4  Styles and Forms of Planning — 96

PART III
## Applying 'Reason' to Politics — 125

  5  Rationalism and Pragmatism — 127

  6  Evaluation and Translation — 150

  7  Difference, Diversity and Dissent — 173

## PART IV
## Environmental Risks, Urban Transitions — 197

8 Managing Risks and 'Bad' — 199

9 Transition Management — 222

10 Sustainable Urbanism — 250

*Index* — 280

# List of Illustrations

## Figures

| | | |
|---|---|---|
| 4.1 | House Building Completions (England) by Developer | 109 |
| 9.1 | Transition Represented as a Simplified 'S' curve | 226 |
| 9.2 | Selected Trends in UK Energy Consumption | 230 |

## Tables

| | | |
|---|---|---|
| 4.1 | Types of Planning: From Management to the Promotion of Change | 96 |
| 4.2 | Styles of Allocative Planning | 99 |
| 6.1 | Applying the Logic Model/ Theory of Change | 158 |
| 6.2 | Including 'Reach' in a Logic Model | 160 |
| 8.1 | Managing Risk from a Socio-Cultural Perspective | 204 |
| 9.1 | Pathways for Environmental Transition | 236 |

# Acknowledgements

Many people have helped with this text, some without realizing that they were doing so. Specific contributions are acknowledged in endnotes. Otherwise, I must thank Aimee Ambrose and Katie McClymont for reading and commenting on different chapters and Sea Rotman for helping me understand the parallels between urban planning and energy policy.

# Summary

The aim of this work is to update previous accounts of planning theory, providing theoretical innovations as appropriate whilst restating the case for planning itself.

There are four main sections. **Part I**, 'The Introduction', comprises a single initial chapter that outlines the logic of theory, the relationship between theory and practice and the methodology of theory making. Theory is a device to make sense of the world and invariably involves relatively abstract ideas. Writing about theory is therefore about providing a store of knowledge or making a point or, most appropriately, a combination of the two.

Theory can take many different forms. An interpretative, hermeneutic approach, as is adopted here, has distinct advantages in breaking down barriers between disciplines, whilst also permitting the material 'turn' of recent theorizing in the environmental field. Issues of sustainable development, broadly defined, deserve in any case more prominence in planning theory. A further advantage of a hermeneutic approach is to enable analysis at different levels, including a consideration of power and the fragmentation of meaning.

Planning theory has international sources. At the same time, examples have to be given to provide evidence of 'real-world' situations to which the theory applies. The present work focuses on examples and applications from Britain, but provides as many international illustrations and international variations as possible.

**Part II**, 'Definitions and forms of planning', is about definitional issues and varieties of practice. The definition of planning rests on the interaction between two distinct meanings, between planning as:

- the preparation of plans involving representations of space as discussed in Chapter 2, 'Planning and Urban Spaces', and
- a series of deliberate, considered actions over time that are, in the case of urban planning, collective in character as discussed in Chapter 3, 'Political and Economic Planning', and Chapter 4, 'Styles and Forms of Planning'.

xii  *Summary*

Planning as the preparation of plans (Chapter 2) involves a series of further distinctions. Some distinctions are descriptive of spatial patterns, whether for example plans are characterized by hierarchical, tree-like patterns or by rhizomatic, cross-cutting patterns. Another distinction, between rules and models, is essentially cognitive, offering a means of organizing information and promoting social learning. Yet another, the distinction between Romantic and Baroque approaches, is essentially about dealing with complexity, with the nature of reality and with ontology. Finally, the distinction between use value and exchange value is about the epistemology of space. It offers a method for the analysis of political and ethical principles and conflicts.

Definitions of planning as a collective process complement and interact with notions of urban space. They rest on a series of ideal types, that is to say a list of characteristics all of which are not always present in a specific case and which draw on studies of economic and political planning.

The key themes in Chapter 3 comprise of:

- the distinction between justifications of planning as a broad necessity in modern society, as conceptualised by Mannheim and others, and neo-liberal justifications that limit the scope of planning to specific economic concepts such as externalities (or neighbourhood affects) and transaction costs;
- the historical and ongoing character of the debates that have moulded the scope and form of urban planning.

The key themes in Chapter 4 comprise of:

- the distinction between allocative planning (managing the status quo), innovative planning (marginal social change and product development within the status quo) and radical planning (transformation of the status quo into an alternative);
- the significance of housing land scarcities as arguably the most serious and long-term negative consequences of regulatory planning in Britain, together with the need for public intervention in land development and infrastructure as means to correct those scarcities;
- the logic of innovation as a cross-cutting exercise and of radical planning as an exercise that generally stands in opposition to or outside the state.

Part III, 'Applying 'reason' to politics', is about the methodology of planning and in particular those methodologies that are their own justification. This section is, in turn, divided into two chapters.

Chapter 5, 'Rationalism and Pragmatism', examines the main theories of decision making. Rationalism operates within a means/end framework and is commonly technical in its treatment of issues. The justification for planning is likewise technical. Planning is necessary to improve the information base and analysis for decision making. Pragmatism assumes, in contrast, that aims can be generated as analysis proceeds. Partly for this reason, pragmatism also offers a justification for planning as a means of promoting a democratically organised ethical debate about the future.

Promoting debate means evaluation and translation, the title and subject matter of Chapter 6. Various approaches are available, depending on the subject matter and timing. However, for the sake of clarity and simplicity the focus is on the distinction between methods in the evaluation of community initiatives and in plan making. The evaluation of community initiatives is best conceptualised through the application of the logic model/theory of change approach. Evaluation in the context of plan preparation involves a further distinction between methods that are about alignment with the political context and those that are about internal procedures.

Chapter 7, 'Difference, Diversity and Dissent', examines postmodernism and the various theories of how to handle conflict in planning, including questions of political legitimacy. Politics and technique are commonly intertwined in urban planning, suggesting that good practice involves a combination of more technical rationality and more democracy.

Part IV, 'Environmental Risks, Urban Transitions', returns to the distinctions between the various types of planning. The distinction between Chapter 8, 'Managing Risks and "Bads"', and Chapter 9, 'Transition Management', is a reworking of the distinction between allocative planning on one hand and innovative or radical planning on the other. The environmental equivalent of allocative planning seeks to sustain cities largely in their present form, dealing with risks and disamenities or 'bads' such as associated with poor living conditions and environmental degradation. The environmental equivalent of innovative and radical planning comprises the various forms of transition management and is, in contrast, about changing cities to minimise the impact of buildings, infrastructure and their users on the broader environment.

Chapter 8 involves a combination of socio-cultural theories of risk management, mostly concerned with social organisation, and risk society theory, mostly concerned with the impact of modernity and modernisation. Transition management, as discussed in Chapter 9, uses a multiplicity of different pathways and mechanisms for innovation and change. However, it remains an open question whether transition management in its present form is radical enough, whether it can change the practices of producers and consumers and whether policies will meet carbon reduction and other environmental targets. Moreover, the full realisation of an environmental transition depends on the use of physical and spatial planning techniques, the subject matter of Chapter 10, 'Sustainable Urbanism', and, in addition, on the emergence of a 'green state' that considers environmental issues as at least as important as finance and economics.

Taken together, the juxtaposition of different themes reveals a deep irony and contradiction in contemporary politics and practice. Just at the moment that neoliberal critics might proclaim victory in their campaigns to reduce planning practice to a minimal level, so concerns about the quality of urban environment and about environmental risks and climate change suggest a return to concepts of planning as a societal necessity, changing systems of production and consumption in a sustainable direction and changing, in addition, the physical fabric of cities. In this context, a re-examination of planning theory is justified, using relevant debates, methods and examples to formulate and assess directions for the future.

# Part I
# Introduction

# 1  Interpretations of Urban Planning

The aim of this book is, in the most general terms, to provide a new introduction to planning theory. The aim is to update previous accounts and, in doing this, to restate the case for planning itself.

As understood here, urban planning refers to the various arrangements that govern, shape and manage urban spaces and places. The subject matter is potentially very broad and, in principle, might include national or regional projects—for example, those dealing with airport capacity and expansion, high-speed rail lines and energy production (fracking, wind turbines, nuclear power and so on). These specific issues are not, however, the main focus. Instead, the focus is on urban planning as the various arrangements that govern, shape and manage the framework of daily life in towns, cities and communities and that, within variable limits, moderate or otherwise influence processes of economic competition and political conflict. The subject matter, as is indicated in the title, is the interaction between economics, politics and the environment in the formulation and implementation of plans and associated urban policies.

## Theory and Practice

How may theory help urban planning practice? The answer is deceptively simple in principle. The very essence of theory is to promote understanding and, depending on the subject matter, to go beyond understanding to explanations and predictions. Theory involves a set of linked ideas, a systematic conception or statement that is intended to make sense of the world (Beauregard 2012) and that enables critiques, understanding or application. Imagining alternative futures, imagining alternative ways to realise that future, notably future governance arrangements, and evaluating existing and previous measures are all necessary aspects of planning practice, where a consideration of theory can help clarify issues and specify rules of enquiry.

### A Store of Knowledge?

The usefulness of theory is related to its quality. Taking the discussions in business studies and psychology as a model, a high-quality theory might be defined in relation to a combination of three criteria—simplicity (a small number of elements), scope (its generalising ability) and accuracy (credibility of the account to those familiar with the object and situation being analysed) (Thorngate 1976; Weick 1999). The three criteria are demanding and not easy to pursue simultaneously. Yet other researchers, writing from a concern with qualitative research, are even more demanding. They would add that theories have to be related to described experience and that accounts of practice and accounts of human life should involve such criteria as 'vividness' (the ability of an account to draw readers in, generating a sense of reality and honesty) and 'richness' (the aesthetic depth and quality of the account that the theory generates) (Polkinghorne 1983, 45–6). A further complication is that the context of practice is liable to change and some forms of planning may even seek to change the context (Avelino and Rotmans 2011). And as the context changes, so may the most appropriate theory.

In response to a multiplicity of theories and equally to a multiplicity of criteria for assessing those theories, the metaphor of a 'store', as used by Healey (1997, 6–7) and Pallagst (2012, 37–72) is useful, in part. Planning theory is a store of knowledge—an apparently obvious phrase that has subtle implications. A store is a collection of valuables (goods, foods, knowledge and so on) accumulated over time. It is also 'a stock (of anything material or immaterial) laid up for future use' (Oxford English Dictionary online), for example a stock of tools or equipment that can be used for a variety of different purposes. A store does not therefore have to involve any degree of integration between its parts. Indeed a store of varied items (or theories) is likely to be more valuable than a store that only comprises a large number of the same items.

The metaphor of a store suggests, as Pallagst (2006) has also shown, that a specific case study of planning can be interpreted in a variety of different ways: as regulation (controlling development or other economic activities); as promoting investment decisions (for example, through the use of incentives); as design (as a means of shaping the urban environment); as collaboration (as a means of involving a variety of different stakeholders or interested parties); and finally as a means of monitoring change through the collection and analysis of data (as for example in Geographical Information Systems).

All these different interpretations imply different theories of how planning operates. Yet they can and do coexist alongside one another. The choice of theory therefore depends on which aspect of planning practice is to be examined. A variety of conflicting situations and conflicting pressures encourage both practitioners and researchers to 'pick and mix' ideas from different sources, accepting the possibility of a plurality of different ideas (Allmendinger 2009, 28). This being so, the aim of planning becomes about raising possibilities rather about providing prescriptive answers. Readers are left to make up their own mind about which argument and which theory provides the best insights and which methodology provides the most useful results in different situations.

There is a qualification, however. Merely presenting a list of items of knowledge is a recipe for confusion as it lacks direction. Raising possibilities and letting the reader go through a variety of different concepts and analytical frameworks is itself a worthwhile activity. However, theory also has to make a point, with appropriate lessons. Moreover, for planning theory, the basic point is the justification for planning, or its criticism as the case may be.

### *The Theory/Practice Gap*

Irrespective of whether planning theory is understood as a store of knowledge or as a means of justification and criticism, the assumption is that practice and theory go together. That assumption is not universally accepted. There is another meaning of 'theory', as an abstraction distinct from or in opposition to practice. And this less favourable meaning has also found its way into the planning literature. For example, Allmendinger comments (2009, 22) that 'to bemoan the theory-practice gap is now *de rigueur* for any exploration of planning theory'. Planning theorists in the US, for example Brooks (2002, 21–2) have also noted a gap. There is a variety of reasons for this.

In part, the theory/practice gap can be explained by specific historical factors that have influenced practice in Britain. For earlier generations of critics, such as Reade (1987, 156–62), the basic problem was that town planning in Britain acquired political legitimacy so quickly after World War II that it failed to provide a reasoned justification for its existence. The planning profession lacked a self-conscious awareness of its rationale and failed to undertake an evaluation of its economic and social effects and did not need to develop any such awareness to become established. The profession was, as a result, anti-theoretical. Reade's analysis has to be qualified in that there have been more attempts to undertake systematic policy evaluation since about 2000 than at the time that Reade wrote. Planning in Britain has come under far more party political attack than in, say, the 1960s. The point remains, however, that working out the preconditions and methods of plan and policy evaluation is one of the central tasks for planning theory.

In addition, in the period from about 2000 to 2007, a new anti-theoretical tendency arose in Britain in the form of a move towards skills-based practice and skills-based education. This particular period was one of a booming property industry, supplemented by publicly funded measures to promote urban regeneration. The demands of policy and practice ran ahead of the numbers of available professionals, but also, in the view of some, ahead of the skills available in the professional workforce. The assumption of a series of reports, notably the Egan review (ODPM 2004) in relation to urban regeneration, but also in relation to neighbourhood regeneration (NRU 2002) and urban design (CABE 2003) was that the 'good' professional was defined by their ability to work effectively in teams, with developers, the public and with one another. The assumption is sensible enough, but could also be interpreted, as was later made explicit in Kitchen (2007), as suggesting that professional education could proceed without theory, merely through the acquisition of skills to complete the task of making 'places better for people' (ibid., 1).

Issues connected to theory do not disappear, however. For example, the Egan review (ODPM 2004, 92–9) identified the creation of 'sustainable communities' as the fundamental aim of planning and urban regeneration and, on that basis, identified various statistical indicators of progress under a series of headings. However, there is no single technical answer as to the definition of either 'sustainable communities' or 'sustainable development', as different indicators can be given a different weight.

The distinction between practice and theory can, in part, be reformulated as a distinction between the world of work and universities. Writing mainly about the English-speaking world, Schön (1992, 119), suggests that in urban studies and urban policy there 'is a widening gap between thought and action, theory and practice, the academy and the everyday world' in most if not all forms of professional education. Likewise, in France, Ascher has noted that the world of research in urban planning is a world, with 'its paradigms, its timescales, its vocabularies and its rules, quite different from that of practice' (Masboungi 2009, 26).

To give an example: theory of the type that is linked to the social sciences is always in flux, always being defined and redefined and always being debated. In contrast, practice commonly requires that decisions are made within a short timetable. Practice assumes, moreover, that the knowledge base of those decisions can be treated as effectively closed so that action can go ahead (Gadamer 1975). Much of planning operates within public bureaucracies where closure of decision-making is particularly marked at lower levels in the administrative hierarchy. As a result, theory can raise problems and uncertainties that practitioners believe are either unimportant or even non-existent or that they have previously considered and discounted. Theory may also pose viewpoints with which practitioners may disagree or of which they may not be aware.

The very questioning of practice is therefore likely to involve some form of theory/practice gap. Though this may appear a contradiction from the viewpoint of some practitioners, the existence of some gap is also, to an extent, desirable as well as inevitable. Without any gap it would be impossible to retain a sense of critical distance. Enquiry would become immersed in the implications of the latest policy shifts or in the minutiae of the law and guidance. In Britain, the pages of professional journals give exactly that impression, as Webb (2010) has noted. Moreover, the unfinished character of theory is itself an advantage. Social theory, of which planning theory is, in part, a derivative, is unfinished partly because society is unfinished and partly because one of the educational functions of theory is to free minds from the acceptance of the status quo for its own sake.

A note of caution is, nevertheless, necessary. Even in the most favourable circumstances, theory alone is unlikely to change practice, because practice itself depends on routines, legal precedents and political opinions. Practice is embedded in a society that can be analysed and understood but has its own momentum.

A parallel can be drawn between planning theory and discussions of knowledge in sociology. Planning theory is analogous to the 'science of opinions', discussed by Durkheim (1964, 438 [1912]) in a study of religious life.

> The science of opinions does not make opinions; it can only observe them and make them more conscious of themselves.

Likewise, the preparation of planning theory does not of itself create practice; it is based on observations of practice, and seeks to promote new understandings of practice and make practitioners of all types more conscious of what they are doing. Planning theory can have an impact, most likely if theory is joined to a study of an issue of public concern. However, the impact always depends on acceptance by others and will most likely be tied to the specifics of a case or policy.

The reference to a science of opinions has to be linked to another aspect of Durkheim's sociology—namely a recognition of 'social facts', observable, secular trends and relationships that vary over time. For Durkheim, suicide rates were the social fact, *par excellence*. However, any number of trends and relationship are conceivable—migration rates, homelessness, levels of car use, rates of energy consumption and so on. Facts as well as opinions have to be considered in analysis and many social facts are likely to be relevant to processes of urban development, urban growth and decline. Discussions of planning theory, it should go without saying, do not preclude analyses of facts, including aggregate trends.

In addition, Giddens (1984, 221) has argued for a view of sociology as the interpretation of interpretations, or to be precise as an exercise in 'double hermeneutics', hermeneutics being the philosophy of interpretation. Single hermeneutics is about the interpretation of raw data such as texts or aspects of social practice or statistical trends or the visual impression of a landscape. Single hermeneutics therefore incorporates the interpretation of social facts, on the grounds that facts do not speak for themselves (Alvesson & Sköldberg 2008, 20–3). 'Double hermeneutics', the interpretation of interpreting subjects, is the study and interpretation of transcripts, qualitative and quantitative survey responses using a combination of the respondents' views and other evidence. Double hermeneutics therefore enriches the analysis of social facts, relating these to the motives and understandings of individuals

## 8  Introduction

and institutional actors and, in doing so, identifying contextual factors of which the actors may not be aware.

To give an example: it is possible to trace trends in the use of public transport through recording the number of tickets sold or the number of people recorded as passing through an automatic entry device. Interpreting these figures is practically impossible without also talking to a sample of passengers and understanding why they are travelling on a certain day and what factors discourage or encourage their travel.

The principle of double hermeneutics may likewise be applied directly to planning theory. Plans and planning involves the creative interpretation of places and their future. Planning theory is understanding the logic of plans and planning through their interpretation and application in practice.

### *Theory as Input or Output?*

How might relevant theory be constructed? Clearly, both the formulation and presentation of theory has to involve examples and, in particular, has to show how theory may be applied, either to test the theory itself or to indicate possible strategic choices and directions for policy and practice. The preparation and inclusion of examples means the use of case studies to generate and test hypotheses, to generate new interpretations and to provide illustrative demonstrations of how theories operate (Flyvbjerg 2006). The analysis of urban planning needs case studies more than most other fields of study, moreover, exactly because it is typically based on places, which is itself an integrating concept and because, in addition, attention to detail is necessary to draw out the full narrative of policy change and application (Flyvbjerg 2006; Watson 2002).

The use of case studies in social research has led to an approach that involves theory as an output rather than an input to research. The relevant approach is that of grounded theory, as outlined by Glaser and Strauss ([1967] 2012) and others. Grounded theory is one of the most commonly cited approaches to social research. Despite its name, it is not a theory as such but a methodology for theory construction. Grounded theory involves the researcher becoming immersed in the detail of a case study and undertaking a systematic classification of the data or coding of the comments of respondents. Hypotheses are then generated on the basis of the coded responses and refined as the project proceeds.

A study, undertaken by Innes and Gruber (2005), provides a relevant example. Through in-depth interviews, the study found the existence of four planning styles amongst those involved in strategic transport planning in the San Francisco area. These four styles comprised the technical/bureaucratic (based on conventional sources of administrative position and technique); the use of political influence (based on political leadership, deals and trade-offs); the promotion of social movements (based on promoting the interests of excluded groups); and finally collaborative (based on a search for a common position). Each style of planning coexisted alongside each other. The different styles were not mutually supportive, however. They involved differing and often conflicting assumptions about knowledge, participation and the nature of a good plan.

Another example of grounded theory is work undertaken by Jeannot and Goodchild (2011) in examining styles of professionalism in regeneration and local development. The work started in rural France where initial ideas became apparent and hypotheses were developed. The hypotheses were then refined and tested through the study of urban regeneration policies in France and Britain. The complexities of rural and urban regeneration were leading in both France and Britain to the emergence of poorly defined 'fuzzy jobs' in a way that echoed the Egan report. These fuzzy jobs tended to undermine the role of traditional professions, though they did not undermine professionalism understood as a commitment to competence and diligence. The crucial variation in urban regeneration did not lie, however, in the subjective orientation of the practitioners, as suggested by Innes and Gruber (2005). Instead, variations in work role depended largely on an external factor—the modalities of public finance.

Grounded theory has the advantages of flexibility and openness to specific situations. It suffers from the disadvantages of parochialism and over-specificity, though these can be overcome through repeated studies elsewhere or through comparisons with published studies (Mjøset 2005).

It is hardly possible to insulate oneself from previous ideas, however. In the case of Innes and Gruber, grounded theory is allied to complexity theory, a variant of socio-ecological systems theory (Connick & Innes 2003). Grounded theory becomes in effect an exercise in determining which style of decision-making is most effective in ensuring that urban systems and ecological systems function smoothly. In the work undertaken by Jeannot and Goodchild, grounded theory is allied to concepts and theories of professionalisation and professionalism. Grounded theory becomes an exercise in understanding and explaining how occupational groups cope with change and with challenging situations.

The inclusion of theory is, in any case, necessary for methodological reasons. In a qualitative case study, the coding of responses can be undertaken in a mechanical manner, through listing the number of similar responses under different headings. However, the responses depend on the questions asked. Moreover, the very selection of case studies and, within those case studies, of particular responses as significant itself depends on interpretation and the prior expectations of the researcher, based on prior experience or on understandings generated from the reported experience of others, for example from the mass media. And if it is impossible to escape prior conceptions, it is better to acknowledge them rather than ignore their influence, as is a central tenet of hermeneutics (Gadamer 1989, 269).

Prior conceptions are closely related to values and are inevitable in social research. They cannot be avoided, only controlled through a reflection of the aims of enquiry in the light of a distinct tradition of research or writing.

Theory alone is insufficient, but offers both a start and a reference point as research proceeds. Moreover, so long as theory is related to practice, theory can offer an initial overview and understanding of practice. Conversely, case studies without theory risk becoming descriptive and parochial, with little wider relevance or implication. Further, it is only through the discipline of grounding inquiry into a tradition of ideas and theory (and not just a specific situation) that the value assumptions of analysis and the expectations of the analyst can be brought into the open.

On a technical point, the same distinction between theory as an input or output arises in the distinction between hermeneutics and phenomenology, this latter being a philosophy of experience and consciousness, rather than interpretation. In some recent accounts, for example Lord (2014), recent trends in practice-oriented planning are said to imply phenomenology with little or no reference to hermeneutics. In other accounts (Seamon 1982; Wunderlich 2008) hermeneutics and phenomenology are treated as largely equivalent.

In the context of first-person accounts of places, the distinction between phenomenology and hermeneutics is indeed difficult to sustain, as both seek a subjective understanding of the relationship between people and urban environment and both generally focus on questions of social meaning and feeling. First-person accounts are, in any case, very varied. Norbert-Schulz (1980) has used an explicitly phenomenological approach to search for the '*genius loci*' or less evocatively 'local character' or 'character of a place'. Picon (1998) and Picon and Bates (2000) have used a mixed and more hermeneutic approach, drawing on the history of ideas as well as direct observation, to show why the contemporary urban landscape and in particular its disordered industrial fringe looks disconcerting.

In principle, however and in the context of the history of ideas, hermeneutics is distinct from phenomenology because of its rejection of the idea that a full understanding is feasible through personal intuition alone ('reduction', to use the phenomenological term). Equally, hermeneutics rejects an alternative idea that analysis can proceed purely at a linguistic level, using 'ordinary' language. Instead, hermeneutics involves a circle of understanding intended as a means of grounding understanding in pre-understandings and also a means of analysing the origins of these pre-understandings. Hermeneutics assumes an element of theory at the outset, albeit a theory that is open to modification as research proceeds.

Hermeneutics provides a broad framework for interpretation—a meta-interpretive framework—capable of application in a wide variety of different settings. However, the interpretive framework is also well adapted to specialist bodies of knowledge as it involves getting inside a tradition of ideas as a means of exploring assumptions, including value assumptions and asking questions. It provides a very general method without endorsing any specific approach or theory. Hermeneutics is not value free, however. Hermeneutics, and this is particularly clear for double hermeneutics, involves an interpretation of practice in a context and an acceptance that different forms of practice are appropriate to different contexts. As a result, hermeneutics treats both planning and the market as historical and social products and rejects any assumption of markets as the inevitable, 'natural' order of economic activity.

### Circles and Loops, Hermeneutics and Pragmatic Learning

Hermeneutics, like any process of acquiring knowledge, still presupposes that questions are posed and asked. A person who thinks must ask questions, must consider whether alternatives are possible and, if so, identify those alternatives so that they can be compared. Questions, or to be precise, a correctly posed question, open up an object or a practice to enquiry, enabling, for example, the application of theories from a variety of different disciplines, whilst also imposing limits on the search for an answer (Gadamer 1989 [1960], 367–8).

What, however, is a correctly posed question? Sometimes it is assumed that asking questions is a relatively simple exercise. Asking questions involves the familiar pronouns of 'what, who, when, where, how and why' and is therefore an easier exercise than providing answers, or so it might be argued. It is not easy, however. The lesson of grounded theory is that the exact form of the question or questions may become apparent only after analysis has continued for some time and the key issues are clarified. An open-minded enquiry proceeds, one might say, from the middle of analysis, rather than from either its start or end (Deleuze & Parnet, 2007 [1977], 94; Hillier 2008, 27). Starting from the middle is an obvious paradox, however. For the reader, the narrative is easier to understand, if questions are posed at the outset, as a means of framing and giving order to subsequent discussion.

Starting from the middle implies, in turn, continuity with previous accounts. The hermeneutic method is similar. Analysis proceeds from pre-understanding to a full (or fuller) understanding in a circular process that reflects on the original position in the light of subsequent analysis and its subsequent application. For Gadamer (1989, 308) application is 'just as integral a part of the hermeneutical process as are understanding and interpretation'. A full understanding of an idea only comes through a consideration of its actual or potential application—a position that makes both discussions with practitioners and knowledge transfer, the presentation of findings to practitioners, part of the research process.

The reference to application also means that hermeneutics has similarities with pragmatism, the philosophy of 'getting things done' in the words of Friedmann (1987, 187). Philosophical pragmatism of the type associated with Dewey is, moreover, a basic source of ideas for planning theory (Healey 2009) and, more recently, for theories of environmental management and planning (Maris & Béchet 2010). Pragmatism has been applied both directly to planning theory and, in addition, indirectly through concepts of social and organisational learning.

Both pragmatism and hermeneutics are concerned with interpretation and application as aspects of enquiry and understanding. Both assume that enquiry should repeatedly go forward and back in a cyclic process of enquiry. Both assume, in addition, that people commonly act through taken-for-granted assumptions and culturally determined background knowledge, but are not trapped by their assumptions. People can advance their practical understanding through a combination of reflective enquiry and trial-and-error activity (Polkinghorne 2000). Both suggest, therefore, that the capacity to learn and the methodology of learning should be central themes of applied knowledge, including planning theory.

Both hermeneutics and pragmatics may, moreover, be elaborated to show that the closely related and sometimes indistinguishable activities enquiry, research and learning take place and commonly should take place at different levels. For example, just as much as Giddens (1984, 221) distinguishes between single and double hermeneutics, so Argyris and Schön (1978, 18–26) have likewise distinguished between two types of social learning, 'single loop' and 'double loop' learning. Single loop learning is where an organisation or an individual makes a marginal adjustment to their working practices. It is about monitoring impacts and effects and 'accommodation' to new conditions, to use the terminology of Dewey (1934, 16). Double loop is where this initial stage of learning indicates the need to question, evaluate and adapt established working practices and strategies and to see them in context.

The parallels between hermeneutics and pragmatism may be extended, moreover, through the concept of triple loop learning as this latter term is also defined in organisation theory. Just as double loop learning involves correction of governing variables to a strategy, triple loop learning is concerned with change in whatever governs those governing variables. Triple loop learning, so understood, means any combination of a 'deeper' exercise in learning involving a review of values, an exercise in working out new methodologies to learn or, finally, political and policy evaluation involving empowerment and changes of governance (Tosey et al. 2011). It involves a process of 'adjustment' (Dewey 1934, 16), a change in the way that organisations relate to the world.

Triple loop learning is dependent on double loop as a precondition just as double loop is dependent on single loop. The assumption is of an organisation engaging in a process of multi-level learning to take control of its own destiny, whilst considering a wider range of variables and anticipating the future. (Tschakert & Dietrich 2010). Double and triple loop learning opens the way therefore to good practice in applied social research. For example Alvesson and Sköldberg (2008) argue that hermeneutic, interpretive social research should encompss considerations of power and be sensitive to its political implications.

Hermeneutics is not about organisation as such, however. It is about interpretation as an exercise in establishing truth and therefore valid knowledge as a precursor to social learning. Pragmatism, learning theory and its different levels are, in contrast, about the application of knowledge through experimentation and action.

The distinction reflects their origins. Pragmatism originated in discussions of the philosophies of science and education and is well suited to case study analysis and the analysis of public policy making, including the evaluation of impacts and outputs. Grounded theory may, for example, be regarded as a variety of pragmatism in assuming that 'knowledge is created through action and interaction' (Corbin & Strauss 2008, 2). In contrast, hermeneutics originated in the analysis of texts, including the analysis of religious and philosophical texts. It is more reflective and abstract and also more flexible in its ability to cope with issues of structure and institutional processes, rather than the micro worlds of personal action and interaction. Structures are open to interpretation just as much as texts as interactions. Prasad and Prasad (2002) have called the interpretation of structures and macro processes 'critical hermeneutics' as distinct from older, more micro-oriented approaches.

Partly because of its apparently exotic origins, hermeneutics has seldom been applied to planning theory and certainly not as commonly as pragmatism. Indeed, hermeneutics was once dismissed by Fainstein (2000, 456) as a 'thicket', by implication an impenetrable jungle of ideas that is worth avoiding. It is not necessary, however, to go far into the thicket to recognise that, at the most general level, planning theory is an exercise in interpretation. It is also possible that, as Gummesson (2003) has argued in the context of business studies, that all research, including quantitative research, is interpretive and that the explicit recognition of this merely serves to 'codify the best of common sense, insights, wisdom, sound judgment, intuition and experience'. However codification has its value, giving an investigation structure and a means of tackling the methodological issues that arise in any form of enquiry, including planning theory

## Defining the Questions

The hermeneutic circle suggests that, in any philosophical or practical enquiry, relevant questions have to be generated from those already asked, either explicitly or implicitly, in the relevant literature. In relation to planning theory, the number of potential sources is very large and both the number and diversity of sources has tended to grow over time as the subject has become more diverse (Allmendinger 2002; Klosterman 2011). For the sake of simplicity, therefore, only relatively broad reviews of the subject, rather than specific contributions, will be considered.

Two basic approaches are apparent:

- mapping exercises and guides where questions are derived from the theory or are implicit only; and
- accounts that start with a list of questions and then look to theory.

The former start from traditions of enquiry and ensure a degree of continuity of subject matter with the past (Friedmann 1995). The latter are more direct, enable more innovation and avoid the account becoming embroiled in the history and evolution of ideas.

### Mapping Exercises

In relation to the mapping exercises, the work of Friedmann offers a starting point. The work is represented by a summary guide to planning theory entitled 'Knowledge and Action' (Friedmann & Hudson 1974) and a much longer account entitled 'Planning in the Public Domain' (Friedmann 1987). Both define planning as a method of 'linking knowledge and organised action' and both focus on understanding the nature and origin of the knowledge that is tied to practice.

The definition of planning as 'linking action knowledge to organised action' is impossibly broad. The reference to organised action has to be specified to a particular field of action, for example that represented by the processes of urban development and management. On the other hand, on publication, the very generality of the knowledge/action framework had the merit of pushing discussions beyond technique and procedure and enabling a fuller exploration of the assumptions (Beard and Basolo 2009).

Taken together, Friedmann and Hudson (1974) and Friedmann (1987) involve five different intellectual traditions, namely:

- 'philosophical synthesis' and 'social reform';
- 'rationalism' and 'policy analysis';
- 'organization development' and 'social learning';
- 'social mobilization'; and finally
- 'empirical studies'.

'Philosophical synthesis' (Friedmann and Hudson 1974) is mostly concerned with the conflict between individual, market-oriented and collective perspectives as expressed in particular by the 'great debate' of the 1940s. This tradition is marked, above all, by the divergent views of Mannheim, an advocate of central planning, and Hayek, one of the key contributors to neoliberal approaches with their emphasis on the rights of private property owners and the primacy of the market. The great planning debate was about the level and form of public intervention necessary in a modern society. In 'Planning and the Public Domain', Friedmann shifted the emphasis and classified Mannheim as a theorist of 'planning as social reform' and a contributor to a tradition of ideas that predates the 'great debate' and has continued thereafter.

'Rationalism' (Friedmann and Hudson 1974) or 'policy analysis' (Friedmann 1987) is about planning as decision- and policy-making. This tradition involves a mixture of sources and subsidiary themes, notably quantitative systems engineering; management science; theories of self-regulating systems; and finally administrative science with its focus on extending the limits of rationality, all of which attempt to provide a technically valid basis for decision-making. Economic modelling of the type used to assess the impact of planning on land prices may also be added to the list of subtypes within rational analysis.

'A third stream', that of 'organization development', involves a blend of empirical studies and normative analysis dealing with the promotion of change in organisations. As Friedmann (1987, 181–224) explained later in 'Planning in the Public Domain', the tradition of organisational development also included theories of 'planning as social learning and, as part of this, theories based on the pragmatic philosophy of Dewey and others'.

The fourth tradition, discussed only in Friedmann (1987), is that of 'social mobilization' and is qualitatively different from the others. The first three 'streams' or traditions, namely those associated with the great planning debate, together with rationalism and organisational development are all about the management of society. Social mobilization is about promoting change from below. Social mobilization provides the basis for radical planning and has multiple sources in the various overlapping ideas of anarchism, utopianism and Marxism.

The final tradition comprises 'empirical studies' of national and urban planning and is mentioned only Friedmann and Hudson (1974). This tradition is more about answering than asking questions, Examples include the study of French national economic planning undertaken by Cohen (1969) and other, later studies, undertaken after publication of Friedmann's work, of environmental innovations by Callon (1999) and of urban regeneration by Flyvbjerg (2002). Empirical studies help generate and refine specific interpretations of practice and, in general, downplay rationality as a guiding principle in favour of politics.

The various traditions can be reworked to provide a series of questions as follows:

- The question posed by the tradition of philosophical synthesis: What is the justification for planning in relation to the rights of the individual, to economic efficiency and to models of democracy?

- The questions defined by the tradition of rational analysis: What is meant by rationality? What are the different varieties of rationality in relation to planning? What are the limits of rational analysis and what are the implications of those limits?
- Further, how might the pragmatic model of social learning best be reconciled with the more technical, rationalist approaches? What exactly is meant by learning as applied to planning and how may learning be operationalised through policy and plan evaluation?
- Finally, the questions raised by planning as social mobilization: What exactly is radical planning? How does radical planning manifest itself in the 21st century in contrast to the past?

'Knowledge and Action' is over forty years old. 'Planning in the Public Domain' is nearly thirty years old. Beard and Basolo (2009) have reviewed the subsequent evolution of ideas, mostly with reference to planning in the US, and suggested that ideas have mostly remained within the traditions identified by Friedmann. Some stability in the scope of planning theory is therefore apparent. They suggest two new areas of concern, namely 'the governance of common property institutions', covering the management of natural resources and the creation and delivery of public goods, and 'social movements and political opportunities', covering power and other forms of inequalities.

These apparently new categories are not wholly new either, however. Issues of common property and the tension between common property and private property are themes in the great planning debate of the 1940s and its successor political debates to the present, though usually articulated from a conservative, neoliberal or anti-planning rather than radical viewpoint. Webster (2001a, 2001b) has, in particular, argued for new forms of communal property arrangements that might offer an alternative to planned neighbourhood provisions. Further, references to social movements and to the political opportunities represented by those social movements are fully consistent with Friedmann's tradition of social mobilization. The main difference with Friedmann's classifications is an increased emphasis in later accounts on environmental issues, as the basis for both common property management and social mobilization.

'Planning Theory' by Allmendinger (2009) offers an alternative classification of ideas. It is less ambitious than 'Planning in the Public Domain', as it focuses on 'indigenous' planning theory, that is to say theories related directly to planning practice. Seven theories are identified as follows:

- systems and rational planning, concerned with decision-making procedures;
- critical theory and those approaches to Marxism whose 'essence' is 'to change rather than understand society' (ibid, 79);

- neoliberal planning associated with the idea of a market-oriented, competitive, but strong state (ibid, 107);
- pragmatic ideas that emphasise 'direct action regarding specific problems' (ibid 128);
- advocacy planning concerned with campaigning and representing the interests of different groups in a multi-centred diverse society (ibid, 148–71);
- 'after modernity' theories that emphasise that knowledge is a social construction and that favour the creation of 'cities of multiple faces and places' (ibid, 193); and finally,
- collaborative planning theory that seeks to redefine planning as an exercise in democratic social communication (ibid, 197–223).

The seven schools of planning of Allmendinger overlap the four main traditions identified by Friedmann some thirty years before. Again, some stability in planning theory is apparent. Systems and rational planning appear in both accounts. Critical theory and Marxism equates to Friedmann's tradition of social mobilization. Neoliberalism is one opposing half of Friedmann's great planning debate. Pragmatism, advocacy planning and collaborative planning are all variants of social learning.

There are contrasts, however, and cumulatively these amount to a greater sense of the limitations of planning. Mannheim's advocacy of rational planning is recognised, but the emphasis is mostly on how neoliberal ideas have worked themselves into and transformed practice. The reference to 'after modernity' is a reference to a feeling that the assumptions of modern town planning no longer work. Finally, the treatment of Marxism has a constraining, rather than liberating feel. The Marxism cited by Allmendinger (2009) is less about social mobilization and change and more about understanding the workings of capitalism and its implications.

*Questions-First Approaches*

A review by Yiftachel (1989, 24) offers a particularly direct and clear statement of the second, questions-first approach to planning theory. Three main questions are identified:

1  What is planning?
2  What is good planning?
3  What is a well planned city?

These questions inform the analytical, the procedural and the prescriptive (or urban form) debates. The analytical debate seeks 'to discover the nature of planning as a concrete social phenomenon and practice'. The procedural debate is about finding some way of combining normative theories of scientific decision-making models, the rationalist tradition of Friedmann and Hudson, with 'the insights of empirical research and the pragmatic lessons of real-life experience' (ibid., 25). Finally, the urban form debate is dominated by a choice between computerised modelling, as in traffic planning, and a search for urban sustainability with a strong emphasis on 'environmental protection, energy efficiency and urban consolidation'.

The analytical question is for Yiftachel the most important as it is about power. Here, Yiftachel departs from most previous assumptions of planning as a progressive, reforming force. Friedmann and Hudson (1974, 13–4), for example, see the task of planning theory and analysis as a means of promoting 'human potential' and, as part of this, a mediating process between the 'individual and social evolution'. Yiftachel (1998), in contrast, notes that planning is not always undertaken in a way that is inclusive of all groups in society and that, in some countries, planning operates in a way that amounts to outright discrimination. Planning is instead two faced, a means of promoting either reform or control and, in this latter respect, as an exercise in controlling minority groups. Planning therefore has a potential 'dark' side, associated with the repressive implications of power.

The distinction helps, in turn, Yiftachel (1995, 171) to pose a further question:

> Is control exercised through planning structurally different in pluralistic Western societies and in deeply divided 'homeland' states? (*I.e. those states divided on ethnic grounds*)

The way the question is asked also provides the answer. Planning in a pluralist society is assumed as more tolerant of dissent than one in a deeply divided, 'homeland' society. The question risks, however, labelling other countries as undemocratic, strange, 'homeland' countries whilst ignoring failings closer at hand. The term itself, 'dark side', implies a sharp distinction with a 'bright' or positive side. A continuum of greys from black to white might be a better description, with many different levels and types of control, each of which requires clarification and understanding.

'Readings in Planning Theory', by Campbell and Fainstein (1996, 5–11) and its subsequent three editions are probably the most widely used textbooks. The 1996 edition set the pattern for the rest. It identifies six questions, albeit with some repetition of the themes identified by others.

1 What are the historical roots of planning?
2 What is the justification for planning? When should one intervene?
3 Rules of the game: What values are incorporated within planning? What ethical dilemmas do planners face?

4   The constraints on planning power: How can planning be effective in a mixed economy?
5   Styles of planning: What do planners do?
6   The enduring question of the public interest: Is it possible for planners to serve the public interest and if so what is it?

This latter question, about the public interest, is the *'leitmotif* that holds together the defining debates of planning theory' (Campbell & Fainstein 1996, 11).

At the same time, for Campbell and Fainstein, the various issues have to subsumed under a broader, more fundamental question (ibid., 11), namely:

> What role can planning play in developing the good city and regions within the constraints of a capitalist political economy and a democratic political system?

This latter is also a question asked, in different ways, by the supporters and critics of planning in the so-called 'Great Debate'.

The 2016 edition again involves six, mostly similar, questions, within the context of the same fundamental question about the role of spatial planning in a democratic, political system and a capitalist economy (Fainstein & DeFilippis, 2016, 2). There are some differences. The reference to styles of planning disappears. Instead, a new question is inserted about whether planning is 'about means or ends, and which should it emphasise' (ibid., 6). Asking about means and ends means, in part, going over the strengths and weaknesses of the rational model as a set of procedures, but also whether it might be better start with concepts of 'equity planning' or the 'just city'. Definitions of the sustainable city would also fall into a discussion of the aims of planning, though sustainable development is not a central theme in 'Readings in Planning Theory.'

Two further statements of the scope of planning theory may be noted. Neuman (2005) identifies four uses or functions for planning theory, each with an implied associated question:

- 'Explanation': What do planners actually do in practice, and what is planning as a professional activity? What works and what does not?
- 'Prediction': What are the general principles that guide and circumscribe action?
- 'Justification': Why should we plan? Isn't the market better?
- 'Normative guidance': What is good practice? What are the underlying ethical principles?

This latter question about identifying relevant ethical principles has also been identified as relevant by numerous authors, including Campbell and Marshall (1999), Upton (2002) and by Allmendinger and Tewdr-Jones (2002) amongst others.

Finally, Connell (2010) suggests that different schools of thought in planning define themselves through how they answer the following questions:

- What decisions do planners make (i.e. what is their primary area of responsibility)?
- What is the role of a planner in the decision-making process?
- To what extent is a planner concerned with the future?
- What does a planner know about the future? To what extent is the future predictable? Or is it unknowable?
- Is there a (shared) public interest that guides planning? If so, what is it?

Connell's list of questions implicitly emphasises the technical aspects of decision-making. The planner seeks to understand and predict the future and is always constrained by limitations of knowledge. Like Campbell and Fainstein, however, the list also makes reference to the public interest.

*Excluding secondary concerns*

The list of possible questions requires a process of selection and refinement. For example, questions about what planners do on a routine basis in practice or about their primary area of responsibility tend to rely too heavily on local definitions of who is and who is not a planner. Identifying the different styles of planning, as suggested by Campbell and Fainstein (1996) but not Fainstein and DeFilippis (2016), is a different, broader question as it helps answer questions about the role of planning in managing or securing change in contemporary society. Identifying the styles of planning is not a trivial exercise once style is related to its aims and to considerations of power.

Analysing the historical origins of planning, as is also suggested by Campbell and Fainstein (1996), requires care. A chronological narrative, for example as undertaken for planning in Britain by Ashworth (1954), Cherry (1996) or Ward (2004), is likely to generate much detail, including detail of a type that is also not easily transferable to the present. Detailed histories of planning and urban development in particular cities at particular times have a similar implication. Relevant aspects of history may, however, be subsumed within answers to basic theoretical questions and approaches. History can be discussed as analysis proceeds, so providing a series of episodes, rather than through a single narrative or case study.

Conversely, to ask 'What does a planner know about the future?' (Connell 2010) is to go to the opposite extreme of asking an impossible, overgeneral question. The predictability of events varies enormously, depending in part on the length of the future horizon and the type of event being considered—for example, energy prices, consumer behaviour, the shape of a town or city and so on.

Reducing questions to a minimum also means avoiding overlap. Questions about the definition of planning and its justification merge into one another. The justification for planning defines its scope and the definition of planning clarifies its justification. To provide an example, limited justifications of planning favour narrow concepts of land use planning, whereas broader justifications encompass political and economic planning at a national level and community planning at a local level. The definition of planning is social and historical and varies over time.

In addition, it is impractical and probably unnecessary to define the 'well planned city' in the abstract, a concern of Yiftachel (1989). Theories of planning as a process commonly define the type of city that is to be created, even if they are not explicit on the point. Rationalist views of planning tend towards a technocratic functional view of cities as a system of land uses, movement patterns and energy consumption; communicative theories of planning tends to result in a vision of a city of decentralised communities and local interest groups; neoliberal views of planning favour a vision of the city as a marketplace and a place of personal consumption; and so on. Much the same can be said of the 'just city'. Different views of the planning process have implications for social justice and can be assessed on that basis. For example, neoliberal views implicitly favour property interests and say little about social justice, in contrast to theories that emphasise social rights and social protection.

The converse also applies. Visions of the city as a transport system favour rational planning; visions of the sustainable city favour socio-technical and socio-ecological views of the planning process; and visions of a socially just city imply a strong state capable of redistributing wealth, combined with a sense of collective responsibility. However, the emphasis in planning theory has invariably been to start with processes and practices, including in some formulations spatial practices, the main reason being that this enables a better grasp of change, including its economic and political aspects.

## Reworking the public interest and policy ethics

Some possible questions need to be broken up into separate parts. Defining the public interest is a case in point. The 'benefit of the public' is the stated object of the Code of Conduct of the Royal Town Planning Institute.[1] In the US, the concept of the public interest figures strongly in the statement of ethical principles of the American Planning Association and its professional institute. 'The planning process', it is said, 'exists to serve the public interest'.[2]

The public interest is not, however, a specific concept like an objective or aim. It is not a coherent body of knowledge or even an item in a store of knowledge. As Campbell and Fainstein (1996, 11) recognise, it is more like an underlying theme, a *leiftmotif*. Asking the question, 'What is the public interest?', is, therefore, to go over all the other questions of planning theory. The question cannot be isolated within planning theory.

In any case, in pursuing policies, planning is commonly dependent on the public interest as defined by the state, by relevant legal frameworks and sometimes by international agreements (Bengs 2005, 8). Where governments or the law are involved, asking questions about the existence of the public interest is pointless. The questions become those of how the public interest is interpreted in a specific case, how it is applied and to what effect it is implemented, including the identification of winners and losers.

Identifying the ethical principles of planning is likewise best conceived as a repeated, underlying theme, rather than posing a single, upfront question. Relevant ethical statements involve either workplace codes of conduct or broader policy principles. Both are 'public ethics' and can be justified in the public interest, but the emphasis of each is distinct.

Workplace ethics might involve any or all of the following: the requirement to declare any personal or private interests; the exercise of independent impartial judgement; a commitment to competence in the exercise of administrative or professional duties; honesty in dealing with colleagues and others; the elimination of all forms of discrimination; the proper use of confidential information; and so on. These codes define the ethos of public service in a public bureaucracy (du Gay 2000), but may also be extended to any organisation, public or private, that claims to work on behalf of the public.

Adherence to a workplace code of conduct is, in part, a personal commitment, depending on 'the individual morality and behaviour of all those involved' (Burley 2005). Adherence also depends on the extent to which it is institutionalised within an organisation, whether there are any other countervailing management principles (for example, serving a client irrespective of whether he or she is right or wrong) and, as part of this, whether it is supported by senior management (Schwartz 2004). The degree of management support is crucial in part because the employer is likely to become involved in enforcement for a breach of the code. However, enforcement action may also be initiated by external agencies, by the profession or, in the case of legal breaches, by police action.

Broader ethical principles involve statements of policy and values or 'aspirational principles', to cite the statement of the American Institute of Certified Planners.[3] Equivalent statements in Britain include the 'New Vision for Planning' (2001) and 'Shaping the Future' (2010), both of which outline policy aims to which planners might aspire and work towards.[4] The logic of aspirational principles is to provide direction beyond that incorporated into codes of professional conduct. These latter do not prevent poor decisions, as Marcuse (1976) has argued, and they do not encourage practitioners to think about the policy implications of their work, so suggesting the case for a broader alternative framework.

There is a downside, however. Though broad ethical principles help provide guidance for practice, they are seldom sufficiently precise or widely enough accepted to define clear cases of breaches that would trigger enforcement. Moreover, the very notion of aspirational principles suggests that these are optional. Relevant principles might cover, in the words of one account, by Bickenbach and Hendler (1994), the varied roles of planner as 'the environmental ethicist (land management); the mediator (of values, discourses and expertise); the advocate (of the disadvantaged); and the futurist (protector of long-term interests)'. As Bickenbach and Hendler go on to say, conflicts between these roles are inevitable and ensure that a statement of aspirational principles is unlikely alone to be sufficiently precise or universally accepted to define clear cases of breaches and so trigger enforcement.

In any case, it is difficult to see how the enforceable elements of professional codes could be easily extended, without implying an exaggerated belief in the authority of technical experts and professionals to resolve a multitude of political issues (Gadamer 1975, 312). Interviews undertaken in 2008 in nine different English local authorities found that elected councillors were already suspicious that workplace codes of conduct might undermine political discretion (Cowell et al. 2014), let alone broader aspirational or policy-oriented professional codes. Professional planners can get involved in politics, like any other citizen. They may have a particular expertise that is useful in specific campaigns. However, the role of the planning professionals, whilst employed as a professional, is distinct from that of a politician.

The planning profession, in any case, has no monopoly over urban development or urban management and the elaboration of enforceable professional policy codes would have only a limited or no impact. Members of other professions or other specialists would do the work instead. For this reason, planning theory is not about a specific profession. It is about interpreting practice and action. Moreover, though planning theory has specialist technical aspects, these specialist discussions invariably lead on to discussions about the organisation of politics and of the state—the welfare state in relation to social justice, the green state for environmental policy and sustainable development and the neoliberal state for the critics of planning.

Ethics are indeed central to planning theory and practice, but in a way that is always tangled up in social, economic and political processes and that means, in addition, that the issues involved are more than just professional. The principle of 'sustainable development' provides an example. Sustainable development has different dimensions and is itself subject to interpretations, but its roots involve an ethic, that of 'care for an endangered future' (Jonas 1977). Sustainable development also involves questions of workplace ethics and professional responsibility and competence, for example openness in releasing information and ensuring that all information and recommendations are based on valid knowledge. Caring for the future and caring for the environment is a stronger ethic than a mere aspiration, however. It is a collective duty.

## The Questions Restated

Bearing all this in mind, the following three groups of questions may be identified:

- What is planning? Also, as part of this, what are its key features as a style of social practice and action? What are the main varieties and subdivisions? How do these varieties relate to social and economic change?
- How, as part of the justification for planning, might claims of valid technical knowledge be constructed? What exactly is meant by 'rational'? What is the contribution of pragmatism as a supplement or replacement to rationalism? How might rationality and pragmatism be adapted to postmodernism and the requirements of diversity?
- Finally, on a different note, how may concepts of planning be reoriented towards sustainable development as a collective duty? How might sustainable development be reworked in relation to the varieties of planning as managing and stimulating change?

This last group of questions deserves a more central place in planning theory, linking the distinctions between means and aims as noted by Fainstein and DeFilippis (2016) and between analysis, procedures and prescription as noted by Yiftachel (1989). All the questions are open-ended and involve a considertation of the specifics of a case as well as theory. A full answer is unlikely, however, to avoid theory.

## Answering the Questions: A Note on Interpretative Methods

Identifying relevant questions defines the scope of analysis. Once the questions are defined, attention then has to turn to the assumptions of preparing an answer, that is to say the methodology of theory making and interpretation. The hermeneutic circle is itself a methodology, but it involves various complexities and qualifications.

### Positivism and Postpositivism

A consideration of methodology is, in any case, required by the claim of Allmendinger (2002) that planning theory has shifted from positivism to postpositivism. Positivism is about the analysis of the facts or data as these appear before the researcher. The task is to observe, measure and organise the data and, in doing so, to search for scientific laws and generalisations, above all statistical generalisations that predict the future course of events in similar circumstances. Postpositivism has more than one meaning. For Allmendinger (ibid., 87), however, postpositivism is a reversal of positivism and the abandonment of the rational model that dominated planning theory in the 1970s. Postpositivism is a recognition of the 'indeterminacy, incommensurability, variance, diversity, complexity and intentionality' of social knowledge. The result is an implied role for planning as a fallible exercise in the provision of advice 'in a complex world where there are no 'answers' only diverse and indeterminate options' (Allmendinger 2009, 33).

Dismissal of the positivist rational model is surely premature. Economic and financial models have grown in influence over the past few years, partly because they seem to offer definite, quantified estimates of the costs of planning control on property markets (Adams and Watkins 2014) or the viability of development projects (McAllister et al. 2013). Models of energy consumption have likewise started to be of increased importance in designing for sustainable development. And these use relatively simple physical measures of energy saved (kWh, mWh etc.) or carbon emissions reduced.

Indeed, for some (Rydin 2014, for example) planning theory has started to take a 'material turn', focusing mostly on the interactions between impersonal entities, such as technologies and social practices rather than focusing, as in the recent past, on social interactions and social construction. The exemplar of this is actor-network theory and its associated concept of a 'quasi-object', something that is 'neither object, nor subject', nor a mixture of the two' (Latour 1992, 11). Quasi-objects are, instead, a hybrid that may appear as either technological or social to different observers or that seems 'natural' and taken for granted. Quasi-objects proliferate in modern society and define the paraphernalia of modern daily life—for example in cars, buildings, transport systems, local energy networks and information technology.

An implication of the quasi-object is that accounts of policy innovation should place as much emphasis on the technological or environmental process as on the social or institutional. This particular criterion of 'generalised symmetry' (Latour 1997) is about the co-construction of products and objects by non-human and human forces, giving equal weight to each in a way that is drastically different from the usual accounts in the policy sciences and policy research. For Rydin (2010), the principle of symmetry is the distinctive feature of actor-network theory and the main way that allows a consideration of science and technology to be brought into analysis. For others, for example Boelens (2010), the principle of symmetry is rigid, unnecessary and a block on the use of actor-network theory (or actor-relational theory in Boelens' terms) to conceptualise the planning process. Likewise, Gunn and Hillier (2012) suggest that, even in the absence of symmetry, the use of elements of actor-network theory is justified because it clarifies the process of policy innovation and change.

Actor-network theory may show, for example, how policy is constrained or even distorted by information deficiencies and how, in addition, a lack of information may generate uncertainties. It also draws attention to how technologies and 'quasi-objects' are used, not just how they are designed, and so enables an appreciation of the non-technological obstacles—economic, social and political—that hinder the adoption of technological innovations and hinder, in addition, the achievement of energy savings targets. Resolving non-technological obstacles is almost always subject to qualifications and must of necessity take social constructions into account. Uncovering all these obstacles does not, moreover, require 'symmetry'.

The lesson is not to lurch from one position to another, but to accept a more differentiated approach that allows a combination of methods. Postpositivism, as defined by Guba (1990) for example, does not necessarily imply the end of positivist styles of research and theorising. It implies, instead, a mixed strategy where the distinction between methodologies is more complementary than contradictory. In the case of energy impacts, for example, a mixed approach would explicitly recognise the possibility of alternative scenarios of high takeup and low takeup of new technologies and of high behaviour change and low or no behaviour change. It would reflect on the conditions that would facilitate implementation and would ask, in addition, consumers and other end-users how they view and use energy-saving devices in various situations.

Analyses of the property market provide another example. Markets have an impersonal momentum of their own and set the context for the response of individuals and institutional actors. Markets are also easily converted into quantitative indicators of prices, transactions and building stocks. Equally, however, trends in prices or supply may be analysed through the institutional practices and policies that support, frame or undermine the market, as appropriate and, in addition, through the expectations of buyers and sellers. In property markets, the impersonal, objective and the subjective aspects of human action interact with one another (Guy and Henneberry 2000).

The same insistence on mixed methods means that it is unhelpful to make a sharp or fundamental distinction between positivism and interpretive methodologies. Interpretation can lead to explanation, for example if the same pattern is repeated in similar circumstances. 'Facts' and statistics, including energy and economic statistics, require interpretation. Likewise, causal reasoning persists in subjective accounts because analysis can pursue meaning and cause simultaneously. Accounts of how people create or construct social reality do not necessarily exclude the use of causal statements if these help make processes and relationships intelligible to relevant subjects (Giorgi 1994). Further, the reasons that people give for their actions may be treated as either equivalent to a cause or pointing to a cause (Sayer 2004, 12–3).

In addition, the use of statistical analysis and a search for trends can help correct a particular weakness of qualitative, subjective approaches, namely their tendency to focus on the micro-level of social and political relations. To grasp the bigger picture, for example to illustrate the effect of inequality or of social change or of environmental risks, the analysis of aggregate statistical and other patterns is commonly necessary. The interpretation of social facts goes beyond the statements of individuals or of plans and policies. It also goes beyond the observation of immediate events. Interpretation summons up a context whose effects can be revealed through description, explanation and redescription (Alvesson and Sköldberg 2008, 39–49; Bhaskar 2010; May 2011, 41–2).

Further, interpretation does not necessarily imply a search for a 'final', single answer. Investigation can continue and interpretation can remain open to new influences, observations and perspectives. The end result may be merely an agreement to disagree (Warnke 1987, 103) or in the case of policy evaluation an acceptance of different interpretations, criteria and situations.

## The Hermeneutics of Suspicion

Postpositivism raises questions about how planning theory and more broadly social research can incorporate concepts of power. Allmendinger and Tewdr-Jones (2002, 1) ask, for example:

> How does planning theory seek to expose and neutralise powerful interests and is it realistic to expect planning to achieve this?
>
> Will planning theory provide forms of rationality that can challenge powerful interests and provide a basis for collective action and understanding?

The questions are posed in a simple 'yes' or 'no' format. Yet, power is implicit in most analyses of policy making and planning because it is central to political decision-making and to the possibility for implementation. Governments cannot implement policies and plans unless they have the power to do so.

The analysis of power amounts to a further, third layer of interpretation that Ricoeur (2004, 327) and others call the 'hermeneutics of suspicion', where it is assumed some hidden and probably disreputable process operates in the background determining the outcome. Much as Giddens talks of double hermeneutics, considerations of power imply an exercise in triple hermeneutics (Alvesson and Sköldberg 2008, 20–3). Power is revealed through the practices, techniques and procedures that enable plans and policies (or indeed any other initiative) to have an effect.

Flyvbjerg's interpretation of the phronetic method provides an example. Phronesis for Flyvbjerg is not just the exercise of informed judgement or the clarification of political purpose, its original meaning in the work of Aristotle (Ruderman 1997). It is instead the analysis of power and, as part of this, the analysis of the way that power corrupts. 'Deception,' Flyvbjerg (1996, 392) writes, 'is part and parcel of the decisions that planners are involved in.' The aim of analysis is to reveal these hidden workings of power and, in the case of public policy and planning, to reveal the art and rationalities of government and the processes whereby governments ensure the cooperation of subjects. The method is that of a detailed case study of local planning policy.

Statements made by government, by politicians and by officials such as planners may well involve deception and dissembling. This is not to say, however, that deception is either universal or routine. Gadamer (1984, 65) suggests that the existence of a hidden political agenda cannot be resolved in any absolute theoretical sense. The hidden agenda can neither be assumed nor disregarded. Instead, attention has to be paid to the concrete details of each specific case.

There is another complication. Richardson (1996) and Flyvbjerg and Richardson (2002) follow the line of Foucault, saying that power and knowledge are fused together. Foucault ([1975] 1995, 27) states:

> … power produces knowledge … ; that power and knowledge directly imply one another; that there is no power relation without the correlative constitution of a field of knowledge, nor any knowledge that does not presuppose and constitute at the same time power relations.

Foucault gives priority to power over knowledge, saying for example that 'power produces knowledge'. Knowledge, according to Foucault's position, becomes impossible unless it is linked to and supported by power. Independent knowledge, criticism or policy evaluation becomes impossible. The opposing position that knowledge defines power is equally untenable (Avelino and Rotmans 2011). Knowledge is only one source of power, along with coercion, legal and institutional authority, the seductive quality of products and plans and so on (Allen 2003).

Knowledge and power have to be partially 'unfused'. They have to be conceptualised as partly, but not fully interdependent. Equally, the possibility of distorted knowledge must be acknowledged, whether the distortion is caused by the operation of power, for example through propaganda or ideology or for some other reason. Further, the possibility must be acknowledged that people do not necessarily know what is in their best interests, for example, in relation to public health, safety or long-term environmental impact.

In social philosophy, the notion of distorted knowledge is commonly traced to Marx's concept of false consciousness—a concept that is itself related to class and class consciousness. Later, the same theme arose through a distinction made by Lukes (1974, 37–8) between 'subjective' and 'real' interests. Lukes, like Marx, dwells on the way in which governments and other powerful groups shape preferences and expectations in ways of which people are unaware. The power of governments goes beyond the ability to make and implement explicit policy decisions. Governments construct a context or at least attempt to construct a context in which a specific decision or course of action appears inevitable and rational. However, in talking about 'real' interests, Lukes acknowledges that 'real' interests exist and that these may be analysed and determined in a way that is independent of existing power relations.

The hermeneutics of suspicion also arise in a different form in the psychoanalytical approach adopted by Gunder (2003) either writing separately or with Hillier (Gunder and Hillier 2004). The hidden processes in this case lie in the human unconscious rather than in the workings of power. Planning professionals, they argue, should look beyond the apparent rationality of its skills and techniques to the human personality and in particular to those personality aspects that are unknowable and that lead 'to disruption and a sense of insecurity and alienation' (Gunder 2003, 285). Planning is a counter to these disruptive elements. It offers 'a fantasy that ... successfully provides the answers necessary for certainty and harmony in our actions towards the future' (ibid, 286). Analysis should therefore look at practice from the outside as in a mirror and face up to the way that planning arises from and seeks to satisfy hidden psychological and psychoanalytical needs and processes

Those in charge of a planning office may sometimes produce plans that look more like an exercise in wishful thinking than a realistic assessment of options. Planning is a collective rather than personal activity, however. Even if wishful, proposals must have some type of cultural or popular appeal to be taken seriously. In any case, if hidden psychoanalytical processes are to be identified and interpreted, how might this be done? There are many competing theories of the hidden demons and fantasies of human life. Relevant theories include those of Freud, Jung and Lacan. Resolving their multiple disputes would take the analysis far from planning practice. Moreover, resolving the different approaches would have to be undertaken wholly in the abstract. These are hidden processes, mostly derived from childhood, about which people are unlikely to be able talk freely. In addition, empirical psychologists and social psychologists take a very different view of the determinants of the human personality and are commonly highly critical of psychoanalysis.

There is a further complication that the very process of enquiring into the possibility of a hidden agenda may involve the researcher imposing his or her own interpretation on the views of others. For example, even in an in-depth interview, it is not easy to ask interviewees whether they have acted in a completely open way or are imprisoned by some type of false assumption. Nor is a hidden agenda easily observed, through for example attendance at meetings (Alvesson and Sköldberg 2008, 162). Taking statements at their face value is the safest method of enquiry, unless there is credible evidence otherwise.

## Deconstruction

There is a further objection to hermeneutics and, in particular, to the hermeneutic or interpretive circle. Advocates of postmodern methods suggest that interpretation should seek to create difference through looking for breaks in the circle and through opening up the cracks in the apparent unity of texts and arguments. Deconstruction, the method of postmodernism, amounts to a further, fourth level of interpretation that sets different passages against each other, looking for hidden inconsistencies and contradictions and attempting to bring these into the open. In the words of one of the earliest discussions of postmodernism in planning, by Dear (1986, 375), 'the purpose of deconstruction' is said 'to turn reason against itself to bring out its tacit dependence on other repressed or unrecognised levels of meaning.'

The hermeneutics of suspicion reinforce a rejection of coherence. Foucault (1978, 98–102) would argue, in particular, that the fusion of power and knowledge in social practice creates meaning rather than the integrity of the text. Supporters of psychoanalysis in planning would add that the 'human subject is a split subject' (Gunder 2003, 284) and that the unknowable aspects of the human personality fragment social identities and undermine any sense of consistency, other than at the level of fantasy.

Some qualifications are necessary, however. Against the claims of deconstruction, Alvesson and Sköldberg (2008, 95–7) distinguish between two approaches to hermeneutics, each implying different conceptions of the hermeneutic circle and different degrees and types of coherence.

The first type, 'alethic hermeneutics', is concerned with resolving the tension between preunderstanding (in other words preconception and in extreme cases prejudgement and prejudice) and a fuller understanding. According to the Oxford English Dictionary, the term 'alethic', though not widely used in English, means 'relating to the truth' and comes from the relevant word in Ancient Greek.[5] 'Alethic' is used by Alvesson and Sköldberg (2008, 96) to indicate a process of uncovering the truth from multiple sources, alternating between different actors and alternating in addition from a combination of written sources, observations and interviews. The reference to observations means in turn that alethic hermeneutics covers the interpretation of statistical trends as part of a mixed strategy of research. Likewise, as elaborated by Ricoeur (2004, 163), alethic hermeneutics does not stop at texts, a term which is, in any case, generally understood in wide terms as any form of written or spoken statement or series of signs. Analysis also extends to 'arbitrating' between the plurality of experiences, that is to say interpreting and assessing differences in perceptions of events and processes. Alethic hermeneutics can, therefore, be adapted to considerations of power and fragmentation.

The second conception of the hermeneutic circle, 'objectivist hermeneutics', is, in contrast, only about the meaning of a text and the relationship between the whole and the parts in a text. 'Objectivist' hermeneutics as presented by Betti ([1962] 1990) involves looking at a document in its own terms as an autonomous object. A policy statement is therefore interpreted of itself, in its own terms, at its face value, albeit commonly in need of clarification and recognition of any obvious omissions. For example, if the aim of neighbourhood regeneration is to increase house prices, then this, rather than say housing need, is the focus of attention. In addition, to clarify meaning, objectivist hermeneutics accepts the principle of coherence and totality. Particular elements in a policy statement are clarified with reference to the full statement and often to other aspects of government policy that use the same terms. Conversely, to provide substance and clarity of meaning, the general direction has to be related to particular examples and instances.

The 'objectivity' of objectivist hermeneutics is based on the reconstruction of the meaning structures of what is stated (Mann & Schweiger 2009). Objectivity is not of a scientific character, but more of a legal and historical character (Palmer 1969, 243). Objectivist hermeneutics is therefore of relevance mostly to legal and quasi-legal analysis, to exercises in policy review where the exact meaning of the policy is crucial and to the analysis of historical documents where the validity and origins of the documentation is crucial. Alethic hermeneutics, in contrast, is more about recognising and controlling the subjective frames of meaning held by the researcher and others. The task in alethic interpretation is to use variations and oppositions in understandings to stimulate insights and understandings.

The preunderstanding/full-understanding circle and the whole/part circles are largely independent of another. They can be combined together, but they do not have to be so combined. Interpretation can cover the whole of a text or statement or situation, without assuming consistency or unity. The circle does not have to be closed. Instead, repeated, open-ended interpretation offers a means of recognising and testing inconsistencies, uncertainties and differences. The process of interpretive enquiry does not have to come to an end point. The outcome of enquiry may involve scepticism to that outcome, so triggering further enquiry. Moreover, neither complete fragmentation, the implication of postmodernism nor complete coherence and harmony should be anticipated at the outset. Instead, both possibilities should be admitted, with the possibility in addition of mixtures of the two (Alvesson and Sköldberg 2008, 139).

## Further clarifications

Planning theory is an international specialism whose origins lie in Europe and North America. To provide some examples: the basic philosophical debates about central planning became crystallised in Britain in the 1930s and 1940s, though both of the main protagonists, Mannheim as an advocate of planning and Hayek as a neoliberal opponent, came to Britain from German-speaking countries. Philosophical pragmatism originated in the US in the early 20th century. Finally, the most widely cited theories of environmental management and ecological transition mostly originated in northern Europe from the 1980s onwards.

In principle, irrespective of the country of origin, the various planning theories can be applied to a variety of countries in Europe, North America and also Australasia, all countries that, to cite Fainstein and DeFilippis (2016, 2) share basic characteristics of 'a capitalist political economy and a democratic political system'. To give an example, policies for carbon reduction in Britain can be examined through the lens of ecological transition management and criticisms of ecological transition management, even if policies in Britain depart from those elsewhere. Insights from one country and even from one local case study are possible if the practices are revealed in sufficient detail and if, in addition, any specific national and local features are recognised. Knowledge of the specific and the particular, it is assumed, is the only route to knowledge and the only route to effective learning (Flyvbjerg 2006). The specific and the particular do not prevent enquiries into the context or into general phenomena. They provide, instead, a starting point and a repeated point of comparison.

International examples remain desirable in presenting planning theory and in analysing its implications. However, given the complexity of the context, the account also has to draw on the local and national knowledge and experience of the researcher. To provide another example from Britain: the issues of land availability for house building and its impact on housing supply and affordability are central to neoliberal critiques of planning and have been taken up by government. As a result, they have been discussed so intensively that a narrative can only make passing comparisons to practice elsewhere. The comparisons are illuminating in showing the limitations of the domestic debate and, more generally, the limitations of the neoliberal critique, but the narrative itself has to be organised around the national policy discourse. There are differences in how capitalism and planning operate in different countries, say, between the Nordic countries of Europe and the southern states of the US. Most likely a concern with the general and the specific, the local and the international have to proceed together.

The origins of planning theory in Europe and North America nevertheless begs the question as to its applicability to non-Western countries where political and institutional arrangements are very varied and where material living standards are, on average, commonly less. The answer depends on the context and specific aspect of practice being studied. There are a few countries without a stable, functioning state and in these countries, planning is more or less impossible, as is equally impossible economic progress through the workings of capitalism. In addition, in some countries, for example sub-Saharan Africa, the majority of land is not subject to a formal system of property law, with specified boundaries, recorded titles and so on (Enemark et al 2014). Governments may still prepare plans but the implications for people living in informal housing areas, generally amongst the poorest, will be quite different. Western rules covering building regulations, design standards of housing and infrastructure are either inapplicable or, if implemented, are damaging to the interests of poorer households (Watson 2009, 178).

On the other hand, where living standards have risen, as in east and southeast Asia, issues related to liveability, pollution and carbon emissions have emerged similar to those in Western countries. The issues are similar, moreover, even if the system and assumptions of government are different or intolerant of democratic debate. As a result, it is as misleading to assume a sharp difference between Western and non-Western countries, as it is to assume homogeneity and continuity.

In any case, whatever the degree of difference, it remains relevant for all those involved in planning and urban policy to learn from each other, especially in a context where the international, global circulation of ideas has become ever easier and quicker (Healey 2012; McFarlane 2011). And if mutual learning and interpretation remain relevant in a way that crosses international boundaries, the theoretical aspects of planning also remain relevant. Indeed, theory is likely to become more relevant in the context of international comparisons, exactly because it offers a way of contextualising those differences.

## Notes

1 The Royal Town Planning Institute 'Code of Professional Conduct' as last amended by the Board of Trustees on 28 September 2011, consulted August 2012 at www.rtpi.org.uk/media/2269/Code-of-Professional-Conduct-Final-_2_Jan-2012.pdf.
2 American Planning Association 'Ethical Principles in Planning' (as adopted 1992), consulted August 2012 at www.planning.org/ethics/ethicalprinciples.htm.
3 AICP Code of Ethics and Professional Conduct, The American Planning Association, consulted August 2012 at www.planning.org/ethics/ethicscode.htm.
4 'RTPI Corporate Publications', The Royal Town Planning Institute, consulted August 2012 at www.rtpi.org.uk/knowledge/publications/rtpi-corporate-publications/.
5 From the Oxford English Dictionaries 'Pro', consulted May 2012 at http://oxforddictionaries.com/.

## References

Adams, D. & Watkins, C. (2014). *The value of planning*. London: The Royal Town Planning Institute.
Allen, J. (2003). *Lost geographies of power*. RGS-IBG Book Series. Oxford, UK: Blackwell.
Allmendinger, P. (2002). 'Towards a post-positivist typology of planning'. *Planning Theory* 1: 77–99.
Allmendinger, P. (2009). *Planning theory*. London: Palgrave Macmillan (UK original 2002).
Allmendinger, P. & Tewdwr-Jones, M. (2002). 'Introduction'. In: Allmendinger, P. & Tewdwr-Jones, M. (eds.), *Planning futures: new directions for planning theory*. London: Routledge.
Alvesson M. & Sköldberg K. (2008). *Reflexive methodology*. London: Sage.

Argyris, C. & Schön, D. (1978). *Organizational learning: a theory of action perspective*. Reading, MA: Addison-Wesley.
Ashworth, W. (1954 and 1972). *The genesis of modern town planning*, London: Routledge and Kegan Paul.
Avelino, F. & Rotmans, J. (2011). 'A dynamic conceptualization of power for sustainability research'. *Journal of Cleaner Production*, 19:8, 796–804.
Beard, V. A. & Basolo, V. (2009). 'Commentary: moving beyond crisis, crossroads, and the abyss in the disciplinary formation of planning'. *Journal of Planning Education and Research*, 29:2, 233–42.
Beauregard, R. A. (2012). 'What theorists do'. *Urban Geography*, 33:4, 474–87.
Bengs, C. (2005). 'Planning theory for the naïve?' *European Journal of Spatial Development* (Debate and Miscellaneous, July), [online] URL: www.nordregio.se/EJSD (consulted October 2013).
Betti, E. (1990). 'Hermeneutics as the general methodology of the Geisteswissenschaften' in Ormiston, G. L. and Schrift A. D. (eds.), *The hermeneutic tradition: from Ast to Ricoeur*. Albany, NY: State University of New York, 159–97 (German original 1962).
Bhaskar, R. (2010). 'Contexts of interdisciplinarity'. In: Bhaskar R. et al. (eds.), *Interdisciplinarity and climate change: transforming knowledge and practice for our global future*. London: Routledge, 1–24.
Bickenbach J and Hendler S (1994). 'The moral mandate of the "profession" of planning'. In: Thomas H (ed.), *Values and Planning*. Aldershot: Avebury, 162–77.
Boelens, L. (2010). 'Theorizing practice and practising theory: outlines for an actor-relational-approach in planning'. *Planning Theory* 9, 28–62.
Brooks, M. P. (2002). *Planning theory for practitioners*. Chicago: Planners Press.
Burley, K. (2005). 'Probity and professional conduct in planning: a personal perspective'. *Planning Theory & Practice*, 6:4, 526–35.
CABE—Commission for Architecture and the Built Environment (collective author) (2003). *Building sustainable communities: developing the skills we need*. London: CABE.
Callon, M. (1999). 'Some elements of a sociology of translation: domestication of the scallops and the fishermen of St Brieuc Bay'. In Biagioli, M. (ed.), *The science studies reader*. London and New York: Routledge, 67–83 (first published in English in 1986).
Campbell, H. & Marshall, R. (1999). 'Ethical frameworks and planning theory'. *International Journal of Urban and Regional Research*, 23:3, 464–78.
Campbell, S. & Fainstein, S. S. (1996). 'Introduction' to Campbell, S. and Fainstein, S. S. (eds.). In: *Readings in planning theory*, 1st Edition. Oxford: Blackwell.
Cherry, G. (1996). *Town planning in Britain since 1900: the rise and fall of the planning ideal*. Oxford: Blackwell.
Cohen, S. S. (1969). *Modern capitalist planning: the French model*. London: Weidenfeld & Nicolson.
Connell, D. J. (2010). 'Schools of planning thought: exploring differences through similarities'. *International Planning Studies*, 15:4, 269–80.
Connick, S & Innes, J. E. (2003). 'Outcomes of collaborative water policy making: applying complexity thinking to evaluation'. *Journal of Environmental Planning and Management*, 46:2, 177–97.
Corbin, J. & Strauss, A. (2008). *Basics of qualitative research: techniques and procedures for developing grounded theory*, 3rd Edition. Thousand Oaks, CA: Sage.

Cowell, R., Downe, J. & Morgan, K. (2014). 'Managing politics? Ethics regulation and conflicting conceptions of "good conduct"'. *Public Administration Review*, 74:1, 29–38.

Dear, M. (1986). 'Postmodernism and planning'. *Environment and Planning D: Society and Space*, 4, 367–84.

Deleuze, G. & Parnet, C. (2007). *Dialogues II*. New York: Columbia University Press (French original 1977).

Dewey, J. (1934). *A common faith*. New Haven, CT: Yale University Press.

du Gay, P. (2000). *In praise of bureaucracy*. London: Sage.

Durkheim, E. (1964). *Elementary forms of religious life*. London: George Allen and Unwin (French original 1912, English translation 1915). The Project Gutenberg EBook [online] URL: www.gutenberg.org/ebooks/41360?msg=welcome_stranger#FNanchor_1312_1312 (consulted June 2016).

Enemark, S., Hvingel, L. & Galland, D. (2014). 'Land administration, planning and human rights'. *Planning Theory* 13, 331–48.

Fainstein, S. S. (2000). 'New directions in planning theory'. *Urban Affairs Review*, 35:4, 451–78.

Fainstein, S. S & DeFilippis, J. (2016). *Readings in planning theory*, Fourth Edition. Chichester, West Sussex: John Wiley.

Flyvbjerg, B. (1996). 'The dark side of planning: rationality and *realrationalität*.' In: Mandelbaum, S., Mazza, L. & Burchell, R. (eds.), *Explorations in planning theory*. New Brunswick, NJ: Center for Urban Policy Research Press, 383–94.

Flyvbjerg, B. (2002). 'Bringing power to planning research: one researcher's story'. In: Thornley, A. & Rydin Y. (eds.), *Planning in a global era*. Aldershot: Ashgate, 117–42.

Flyvbjerg, B. (2006). 'Five misunderstandings about case-study research'. *Qualitative Inquiry*, 12, 219–46.

Flyvbjerg, B. and Richardson, T. (2002). 'Planning and Foucault: in search of the dark side of planning theory'. In: Allmendinger, P. & Tewdwr-Jones, M. (eds.), *Planning futures: new directions for planning theory*. London and New York: Routledge, 44–62.

Foucault, M. (1978). *The history of sexuality, vol. 1: the will to knowledge*. London: Penguin.

Foucault, M. (1995). *The birth of the prison system*, Second edition. New York: Vintage Books (French original 1975).

Friedmann, J. (1987). *Planning in the public domain: from knowledge to action*. Princeton, NJ: Princeton University Press.

Friedmann, J. (1995). 'Teaching planning theory'. *Journal of Planning Education and Research*, 14: 156–62.

Friedmann, J. & Hudson, B. (1974). 'Knowledge and action: a guide to planning theory'. *American Institute of Planners' Journal*, 40, 2–16.

Gadamer, H. G. (1975). 'Hermeneutics and social science'. *Philosophy & Social Criticism*, 2, 307–16.

Gadamer, H. G. (1984). 'The hermeneutics of suspicion'. In: Shapiro, G. and Sica, A. (eds.), *Hermeneutics: questions and prospects*. Amherst, MA: University of Massachusetts Press, 54–65.

Gadamer, H. G. (1989). *Truth and method*. London and New York: Continuum Publishing Group, Second English edition (German original 1960).

Giddens, A. (1984). 'Hermeneutics and social theory'. In: Shapiro, G. and Sica, A. (eds.), *Hermeneutics: questions and prospects*. Amherst, MA: University of Massachusetts Press, 215–30.

Giorgi, A. (1994). 'A phenomenological perspective on certain qualitative research methods'. *Journal of Phenomenological Psychology*, 25, 190–220.

Glaser, B. C. & Strauss, A. (2012). *The discovery of grounded theory: strategies for qualitative research*. New Brunswick and London: Aldine, Seventh paperback printing (US original 1967).

Guba, E. C. (1990). 'The alternative paradigm dialog'. In: Guba E. C. (ed.), *The paradigm dialogue*. Newbury Park, CA: Sage.

Gummesson, E. (2003). 'All research is interpretive!'. *Journal of Business & Industrial Marketing*, 18:6/7, 482–92.

Gunder, M. (2003). 'Planning policy formulation from a Lacanian perspective'. *International Planning Studies*, 8:4, 279–94.

Gunder, M. & Hillier, J. (2004). 'Conforming to the expectations of the profession: a Lacanian perspective on planning practice, norms and values'. *Planning Theory & Practice*, 5:2, 217–35

Gunn, S. & Hillier, J. (2012). 'Processes of innovation: reformation of the English strategic spatial planning system. *Planning Theory & Practice*, 13:3, 359–81.

Guy, S., & Henneberry, J. (2000). 'Understanding urban development processes: integrating the economic and the social in property research'. *Urban Studies*, 37:13, 2399–2416.

Healey, P. (1997). *Collaborative planning: shaping places in fragmented societies*. Basingstoke: Macmillan.

Healey, P. (2009). 'The pragmatic tradition in planning thought'. *Journal of Planning Education and Research*, 28: 277–92.

Healey, P. (2012). 'The universal and the contingent: some reflections on the transnational flow of planning ideas and practices'. *Planning Theory*, 11:2, 188–207.

Hillier, J. (2008). 'Plan(e) speaking: a multiplanar theory of spatial planning'. *Planning Theory*, 7, 24–49

Innes, J. E. & Gruber, J. (2005). 'Planning styles in conflict: The Metropolitan Transportation Commission'. *Journal of the American Planning Association*, 71:2, 177–88.

Jeannot, G. & Goodchild, B. (2011). "Fuzzy jobs" and local partnerships: case studies of urban and rural regeneration in France and England'. *Public Administration*, 89:3, 1110–27.

Jonas, H. (1977). 'Responsibility today: the ethics of an endangered future'. *Social Research*, 43:1, 77–97.

Kitchen, T. (2007). *Skills for planning practice*. Basingstoke, Hampshire: Palgrave Macmillan.

Klosterman, R. E. (2011). 'Planning theory education: a thirty-year review'. *Journal of Planning Education and Research*, 31:3, 319–31.

Latour, B. (1992). 'One more turn after the social turn: easing science studies into the non-modern world'. In: McMullin, E. (ed.), *The social dimensions of science*. Notre Dame, IN: Notre Dame University Press, 272–92, [online] URL: http://bruno-latour.fr/article?page=5 (consulted October 2013).

Latour, B. (1997). *Nous n'avons jamais été modernes*. Paris: Éditions La Découverte.

Lord, A. (2014). 'Towards a non-theoretical understanding of planning'. *Planning Theory*, 13:1, 26–43.

Lukes, S. (1974). *Power: a radical view*. London: Macmillan.

McAllister, P., Wyatt, P. & Coleman, C. (2013). 'Fit for policy? Some evidence on the application of development viability models in the United Kingdom planning system'. *Town Planning Review*, 84:4, 517–43.

McFarlane, C. (2011). *Learning the city: knowledge and translocal assemblage.* Chichester, Sussex: Wiley-Blackwell/John Wiley & Sons.

Mann, S. & Schweiger, J. (2009). 'Using the objective hermeneutics method in policy evaluation'. *Evaluation*, 15:4, 445–57.

Marcuse, P. (1976). 'Professional ethics and beyond: values in planning'. *Journal of the American Institute of Planners*, 42:3, 264–74.

Maris, V. & Béchet, A. (2010). 'From adaptive management to adjustive management: a pragmatic account of biodiversity values'. *Conservation Biology*, 24:4, 966–73.

Masboungi, A. (Direction éditoriale) (2009). *Organiser la ville hypermoderne: François Ascher Grand Prix de l'urbanisme 2009.* Paris: Éditions Parenthèses et Direction générale de l'Aménagement, du Logement et de la Nature (DGALN).

May, T. (2011). *Social research: issues, methods and research.* Maidenhead, England: McGraw Hill and The Open University Press.

Mjøset, L. (2005). 'Can grounded theory solve the problems of its critics?' *Sosiologisk tidsskrift*, 13, 379–408.

Neuman, M. (2005). 'Notes on the uses and scope of city planning theory'. *Planning Theory*, 4:2, 123–45.

Norbert-Schulz, C. (1980). *Genius loci.* New York: Rizzoli.

NRU—Neighbourhood Renewal Unit (2002). *The learning curve: developing skills and knowledge for neighbourhood renewal.* London: ODPM.

ODPM—Office of the Deputy Prime Minister (corporate author) (2004). *Skills for sustainable communities* (The Egan Review). London: ODPM.

Pallagst, K. (2006). *Growth management in the San Francisco Bay Area: interdependence of theory and practice.* IURD Working Paper Series, Institute of Urban and Regional Development, UC Berkeley, [online] URL: http://escholarship.org/uc/item/3w19r031#page-1 (consulted April 2012).

Pallagst, K. (2012). *Growth management in the US: between theory and practice.* Aldershot, Hampshire, England: Ashgate Publishing.

Palmer, R. E. (1969). *Hermeneutics: interpretation theory in Schleiermacher, Dilthey, Heidegger and Gadamer.* Evanston, IL: Northwestern University Press.

Picon, A. (1998). *La ville, territoire des cyborgs.* Besançon, France: Les Éditions de l'imprimeur.

Picon, A. & Bates, K. (2000). 'Anxious landscapes: from the ruin to the rust'. *Grey Room, 01*, 64–83, [online] URL: www.academia.edu/3482037/Anxious_Landscapes_From_the_Ruin_to_Rust (consulted May 2016).

Polkinghorne, D. (1983). *Methodology for the human sciences.* Albany, NY: SUNY Press.

Polkinghorne, D. (2000). 'Psychological inquiry and the pragmatic and hermeneutic traditions'. *Theory and Psychology*, 10, 453–79.

Prasad, A. & Prasad, P. (2002). 'The coming of age of interpretive organizational research'. *Organizational Research Methods*, 5:1, 4–11.

Reade, E. (1987). *British town and country planning.* Milton Keynes: The Open University.

Richardson, T. (1996). 'Foucauldian discourse: power and truth in urban and regional policy making'. *European Planning Studies*, 4:3, 279–92.

Ricoeur, P. (2004). *The conflict of interpretations: essays in hermeneutics.* London: Continuum Publications (First published in Britain in 1989, French original 1969).

Ruderman, R. S. (1997). 'Aristotle and the recovery of political judgment'. *American Political Science Review*, 91:02, 409–20.

Rydin, Y. (2010). 'Actor-network theory and planning theory: a response to Boelens'. *Planning Theory*, 9:3, 265–8.

Rydin, Y. (2014). 'The challenges of the "material turn" for planning studies'. *Planning Theory & Practice*, 15:4, 590–95.

Schön, D. A. (1992). 'The theory of inquiry: Dewey's legacy to education'. *Curriculum Inquiry*, 22:2, 119–39.

Sayer, A. (2004). 'Forward: why critical realism'. In: Fleetwood, S. & Ackroyd, S. (eds.), *Critical realist applications in organisation and management studies*. London: Routledge, 6–20.

Schwartz, M. (2004). 'Effective corporate codes of ethics: perceptions of code users'. *Journal of Business Ethics*, 55, 323–43.

Seamon, D. (1982). 'The phenomenological contribution to environmental psychology'. *Journal of Environmental Psychology*, 2, 119–40.

Thorngate, W. (1976). '"In general" vs. "it depends": some comments of the Gergen-Schlenker debate'. *Personality and Social Psychology Bulletin*, 2: 404–10.

Tschakert, P. & Dietrich, K. A. (2010). 'Anticipatory learning for climate change adaptation and resilience'. *Ecology and Society*, 15:2, 11.

Tosey, P., Visser, M. & Saunders. M. (2011). 'The origins and conceptualizations of "triple-loop" learning: a critical review'. *Management Learning*, 43:3, 291–307.

Upton, R. (2002). 'Planning praxis: ethics, values and theory'. *Town Planning Review*, 73:3, 253–69.

Ward, S. (2004). *Planning and urban change*. London: Sage.

Warnke, G. (1987). *Gadamer: hermeneutics, tradition, and reason*. Stanford, CA: Stanford University Press.

Watson, V. (2002). 'Do we learn from planning practice? The contribution of the practice movement to planning theory'. *Journal of Planning Education and Research*, 22, 178–87.

Watson, V. (2009). '"The planned city sweeps the poor away." Urban planning and 21st century urbanisation'. *Progress in Planning*, 72, 151–93.

Webb, D. (2010). 'The limits of associative democracy: a comment on an actor-relational approach in planning'. *Planning Theory*, 10:3, 273–82.

Webster, C. J. (2001a). 'Gated cities of tomorrow'. *Town Planning Review*, 72:2, 149–70.

Webster, C. J. (2001b). 'Contractual agreements and neighbourhood evolution'. *Planning and Markets*, 4:1, 7–13.

Weick, K. E. (1999). 'Theory construction as disciplined reflexivity: tradeoffs in the 90s'. *The Academy of Management Review*, 24:4, 797–807.

Wunderlich, F. M. (2008). 'Walking and rhythmicity: sensing urban space'. *Journal of Urban Design*, 13:1, 125–39.

Yiftachel, O. (1989). 'Towards a new typology of urban planning theories'. *Environment and Planning B: Planning and Design*, 16, 23–39.

Yiftachel, O. (1998). 'Planning and social control: exploring the "dark side"'. *Journal of Planning Literature*, 12:2, 395–406.

# Part II
# Definitions, Styles and Forms

# 2 Planning and Urban Spaces

Working out the definition of planning is to juxtapose all the various levels of hermeneutic interpretation—the search for coherence in meaning, the recognition of power as an influence on practice and the postmodern search for difference. To elaborate in more detail: searching for a coherent meaning involves relating the details of a definition in any given situation to a general principle. It is about working out the relationship between the word 'planning', or its equivalent in other languages, and its context, recognising that the meaning of words has a historical dimension and that meaning also implies some form of practice. Equally, interpretation means the deconstruction of meaning into its varied and sometimes contradictory implications and interpretation. Further, interpretation involves a recognition that meaning is not static, but subject to historical change. As society changes and also as cities change, so does planning.

As defined by the Oxford English Dictionary, online edition, the verb 'to plan' means, amongst other things, 'To arrange in advance (an action or proposed proceeding); to devise, contrive, or formulate (a project or manner of proceeding); to lay out in a plan.'[1] The definition involves two separate dimensions:

- the preparation of a design for something to be constructed, such as a building, district or town;
- an intention, especially one that anticipates some future event or time and an action to realise that intention.

The distinction between a plan as design and a plan of action and is not necessarily huge, however, as the different meanings share a common linguistic root. Planning comes from the act of making plans and this latter comes from the French '*plan*' and, in turn, from the classical Latin 'planum', indicating a flat area or ground. *Planum* and the general prefix 'pla' has entered the English language in numerous words indicating a flat surface such as plain, plane, plank, plate, plateau and platform.[2] The same prefix 'pla' is also present in 'plat' as in braided hair, a type of folded surface and in

## 42  Definitions, Styles and Forms

place (Skeat [1910] 2005, 396). Making plans is therefore is about making representations of spaces and places. Since plans as spatial representations help guide actions, whether in military campaigns or building, planning has also come to be associated with diagrams, programmes and possibilities for action.

## Mixing Design and Action in Space

The common root of design and action enables the terms 'plan' and 'plane' to be used interchangeably as both encompassing a logical or consistent perspective and some spatial representation of that perspective. Planning is about the exercise of some collective will and desire, either to promote or stop change in a specific direction. Deleuze and Guattari (1987) have explored the philosophy of desire at length and have as a result explored and brought together the themes of space and action, plane and plan more than most writers, as in the following example (ibid., 269):

> So the plan(e)—life plan(e), writing plan(e), music plan(e)—must necessarily fail for it is impossible to be faithful to it.

The plan strives for consistency, but generally fails to achieve complete consistency, either because of internal variations and contradictions or because of interaction with a 'real world' that is infinitely more complex and subject to a perpetual process of sometimes unpredictable change.

### *Spatial Assemblages*

The merging of plan and plane allows, in turn, the creation of a vocabulary that summarises and merges distinctions in spatial form and in the processes involved in changing space. Space, including urban space, is commonly conceived as something static—as an object, as a landscape or as a set of coordinated points. Equally, space may be conceived as a series of distinctions that imply a process of becoming as one type gives way and becomes folded into another. The work of Deleuze and Guattari (1987) is again a rich source of relevant concepts, including the following.

First, smooth space may be distinguished from striated or gridded space. The former is a fluid space of continuous variation, such as the open sea, where people can move around and come into contact with one another without obstacles. The latter is the space of fixed and variable elements, producing 'an order and succession of distinct forms' (ibid., 478). Striated space includes the space of urban areas, broken up by property boundaries, fences and walls and other obstructions, as well as by symbolic markers.

Second, territorialisation may be distinguished from deterritorialisation, as smooth space is converted into striated space and *vice versa*.

Territorialisation means the creation of space characterised by distinct qualities (ibid, 315), by markers of possession (ibid.) and by other fixed and variable elements such as colour, odour, sound and silhouette (ibid., 316). Deterritorialisation means the transformation of space into something unstable and is exemplified by processes of globalisation. Globalisation as deterritorialisation destroys established place identities, reducing territories to property rights of the type that can be bought and sold. Territorialisation and reterritorialisation are, in contrast, about local development, the maintenance and promotion of local identity and the mobilisation of local people and the local economy. Deterritorialisation and territorialisation may operate on the same place at different times, with the former breaking up former place identities before they are re-established, as for example in a redevelopment project (Wood 2009). Equally, they may operate on the same place at the same time as contradictory tendencies as local groups seek to defend local identities in the face of externally generated change.

Finally, rhizomatic may be distinguished from arborescent (tree-like) forms of growth. The former is 'a subterranean stem' (Deleuze and Guattari 1987, 6) that 'ceaselessly establishes connections between semiotic chains (*chains of meaningful signs and language*), organisations of power, and circumstances relative to the arts, sciences and social struggles' (ibid., 7). Rhizomatic growth, as Ingold (2006) has suggested, typically produces an entanglement of different lines issuing from multiple sources and intersecting one another, creating a bundle without clearly defined boundaries. As a spatial planning concept, it is exemplified by decentralised, multi-centred urban growth that, like an underground stem, is at first concealed from view (Ascher 1995, 282). Arborescent growth is, in contrast, represented by hierarchical systems with centres of significance (Deleuze and Guattari, 1987, 16).

Urban space is, therefore, a product of a repeated process of disassembling and reassembling of these and other opposites. The resulting 'assemblage' comprises different elements that may conflict, overlap, interact or merely coexist with one another in adjoining areas (Dovey 2012). An assemblage is not a functional system, like, for example, a land use/transport system or an infrastructure system, though it is likely to contain such systems (or machines in the language of Deleuze and Guattari) that interact with one another and these are also likely to be influenced by processes and forces beyond the immediate vicinity. An assemblage amounts to a juxtaposition of elements or 'interpenetrating multiplicities' (Deleuze and Guattari, 1987, 36) that are brought together by their proximity and have their own dynamic of change, their own collective history (McFarlane 2011a).

A typical urban street, for example, contains shops, houses, road, pavement, traffic flows, pedestrian flows, green landscaping and advertisements. Some of these elements are human, some are non-human and some, such as motor vehicles, involve a combination of human guidance and non-human technology. Some elements are part of a heterogeneous property market that itself counts as an assemblage of a multiplicity of human and non-human elements (Çalışkan & Callon 2010); some are outside the market economy and provided or managed by public agencies; and some are based on the most recent technology and others on old, possibly obsolete technologies. Some are coherently linked together, such as the existence of advertisements, shops and shoppers. Other elements, such as motor traffic and pedestrians, have no obvious functional relationship and conflict with one another. Yet they all coexist with one another in the same scene.

A spatial assemblage requires a degree of co-ordination, collective support and collective protection, whether this is against a disruptive threat, say an incompatible development proposal, or against an existential threat such as flooding or dangerous levels of pollution. The assemblage presupposes a degree of order as well as a continuing process of reordering as different elements change. Order and therefore hierarchy is an essential aspect of society and an essential aspect of territoriality. However, disorder has the potential for innovation and change and is not of itself undesirable (Douglas 1966, 95).

The notion of an assemblage leaves open the question of how change is initiated and also of how order is maintained, by whom and for whose benefit. Action may be initiated by a single, powerful actor or an elite group of actors, leaving others to adjust as a result. New actors may also enter from outside. Decisions made elsewhere may lead to more or less money flowing into the local economy, so stimulating a multitude of further adjustments. The non-human elements are also active. For example, buildings decay over time and rivers flood in ways that have their own logic. Otherwise change may be initiated by different actors working together or by one taking the lead or by some combination. The notion of an assemblage is therefore a warning against any temptation to treat individual, market-based and collectively planned change as necessarily opposing alternatives (Çalışkan & Callon 2010). The distinction between the two is analytical. Applied to specific places, to spatial assemblages planning and the market also take the form of 'interpenetrating multiplicities'.

## Planning as Drawing and Mapping

Where the operative method of change is through some form of collective action, plan preparation might likewise be conceived as a process of bringing together contrasting concepts of space and imagining how the might be related to one another. To use the terminology of Hillier (2007, 2008, 2010), planning is a flexible process of strategic drawing and strategic navigation 'concerned with trajectories rather than specified end-points' (ibid., 2008, 29). It is an exercise that, in responding to varied pressures and forces, weaves between multiple distinctions—between fluid space and stability, between the destruction of local established place identities and their reconstruction, and finally between the apparent anarchy of rhizomatic growth and the excessive order of tree-like hierarchies. Considered in the abstract, planning weaves between the various distinctions, but is neutral as to whether space should be organised in terms of any one rather than others. In any case, extremes in relation to the various distinctions, whether complete fluidity, complete territorial stability or complete conformity to the principle of rhizomatic change, are almost certainly impossible (Nyseth 2012).

At the same time, the existence of assemblages suggests another, more cautious reading of the various spatial distinctions involved in planning. 'Make maps, not photos or drawings.' Deleuze and Guattari suggest (1987, 12, 25). The map is an experiment in contact with the real; it promotes connections in all of its dimensions and is susceptible to constant modification, whereas the drawing simplifies the real and limits experimentation. Make sure, therefore, that planning as strategic navigation is grounded in reality, as this changes over time and is reflected in a good, up-to-date map. Make sure, in addition, that the plan does not get ahead of itself and acts as a constraint rather than a facilitator of change. For Deleuze and Guattari, therefore, mapping is a necessary precondition for effective action. It is the source of understandings of a reality that is always changing.

As an extension of the same assumption, mapping is also a historical precondition of planning. The first precursors of modern town planning emerged, according to Choay ([1980] 1996, 70), in the second half of the 18th century in the surveying exercises that portrayed urban areas in plan form. Prior to the 18th century and with the exception of maps of military fortifications, the representation of cities had been based on perspective views, rather than a plan or map.

Surveying is closely allied to the specification of property rights and this gives a hint of the way in which town planning emerged alongside the establishment of a formal framework of property rights and as both a support and a counter to property markets. Mapping is not just a product of an inquisitive mind and a desire to understand processes of change, as in the philosophy of Deleuze and Guattari. It is necessary for the buying, selling and development of property. Mapping offers a way of quantifying parcels of land, fixing them in space and transforming smooth, undifferentiated space into privately-owned parcels of land.

In addition, maps are a technique of governance, telling the authorities what can be expected in different locations and expressing the interests of different parties. A map is a space for work and activities of all types, including the work and activities of government, and its contents are influenced about expectations of how it will be used (Besse 2011). Once made, however, the map itself can be used in various ways. In this context, spatial planning becomes a means of coordinating and realising both the power and the possibilities implicit in maps.

The term 'town planning' only came to fore as a distinct form of public administration in the late 19th and early 20th centuries (Choay 1969), after the main mapping exercises had been completed and after a framework of local government had been established. It was literally a new word, invented to define the practices necessary to manage the rapidly growing industrial cities of the 19th century. The English term 'town planning' was paralleled by many other new terms that emerged at about the same time, including 'urbanización' (Spanish), 'urbanisme' (French) and 'Städtebau' (German), all of which reflected a search for new ways of administrative and political practice that would offer a better future and would deal with urban problems. The problems were, moreover, not just the practical problems of health, sanitation and congestion but also the cultural disruption caused by a rapidly changing urban landscape. Town planning grew, like the mapping exercises on which it was based, as a technique of government, albeit a technique that, through its focus on cities and spaces, also became implicated in hopes and fears for the future.

In Britain, the first town planning legislation was in 1909—the Housing, Town Planning, Etc. Act. This was also the year of publication of textbooks by Unwin (1909) and Triggs (1909), almost certainly the first in the English language. In addition, it was the year in which the Garden Cities Association and the National Housing Council added 'Town Planning' to their name. The professional institute, The Town Planning Institute, was established a few years later in 1914 (Cherry, 1996, 35–8).

## A Shift in Emphasis

At the time of its invention and for many years afterwards, planning remained marked by its origins in map-making, in surveying and in the related professions of architecture and engineering. However, the resulting style was the opposite of a fluid, mapping process implied by the notion of an assemblage. Instead, the map was conceived as a static representation of the present and the plan conceived as a static map of the future, or, as described by later theorists, as a blueprint of the future (Galloway and Mahayni 1977; Taylor 1998).

The Plans for Greater London (Abercrombie 1945; Forshaw and Abercrombie 1943) exemplified this tendency. The plans involved 'an evolutionary and corrective approach' (Forshaw and Abercrombie 1943, 145) that combined proposals for the spatial decentralisation of population to free-standing towns, planned suburban expansion and the redevelopment of almost the whole of the 19th century working class residential urban areas, all within the framework of a green belt that contained urban growth and retained London's traditional urban form. Modifications to the plan might be necessary, Abercrombie (1945, 185) admitted. 'These, however, will be made with understanding because there is a Plan and will not be the haphazard occurrences of the past.'

Large-scale blueprint planning collapsed in Britain once it was implemented after 1945 and once it faced the problem of coping with economic and political pressures in conditions of uncertainty. In areas where the public sector took the lead, for example in the new towns, fixed master plans continued to be used, much as they had been in the 1940s and earlier decades. A textbook, 'Principles and Practice of Town and Country Planning', by Keeble ([1952] 1969) is the pre-eminent statement of blueprint planning in Britain in the years after 1945. The cover is illustrated by the drawing of the centre of a theoretical new town. Elsewhere, in the body of the text, good practice is illustrated by a drawing, in plan form, of a fully worked out theoretical new town, with a full street layout, open space and neighbourhood centres (Taylor 1998, 3–14).

Elsewhere, where development was led by the private sector, the blueprint plans of the post-1945 era, including the local development plans prepared under the 1947 Act, were repeatedly criticised as being too rigid and too detailed (Taylor 1998, 51–4). In response, the government turned to new ways of providing a planning system that might meet the twin requirements of flexibility and certainty or, to use the language of Deleuze and Guattari, the contrasting characteristics of fluid, smooth space and gridded, stable space. These requirements are not easy to combine, however. The tension between them is inherent in any planning system that coexists with an unpredictable process of market-led development (Tewdwr-Jones 1999).

The search for some combination of flexibility and certainty has, moreover, continued to the present. A review of the planning system in England and Wales, undertaken by Barker (2006, 53), notes, for example, the existence of 'a key question' as to 'whether the planning system provides the right balance between certainty for those making long-term decisions and responsiveness for those seeking to respond to changing circumstances'. A further comment by Barker (ibid., 47) that economic change increases the importance of flexibility summarises the pressures on the statutory planning system since the early 2000s, from the viewpoint of the developer and, more broadly, from the viewpoint of governments seeking to promote economic growth. In contrast, environmental pressure groups do not generally welcome increased flexibility, for the obvious reason that flexibility may undermine established policies for environmental protection.

Cities have also changed in a way that has undermined large-scale blueprint planning. Just as much as the 19th century industrial city gave rise to modern town planning, so continued urban growth in the late 20th and 21st centuries has again led to new forms of practice and new words to describe that practice (Choay 1995). The use of the term 'urban', as reflected in urban design, urban policy and urban studies, is one indication of these new styles of intervention and practice. 'Urban' implies a relatively diffuse and dispersed urban area, commonly cutting across local government areas, as opposed to the more concrete and specific concepts of 'town and country'. The adoption of the term 'spatial' or 'territorial' planning from about 2000 onwards marks a further step in the same direction—one in which 'cities' have become so difficult to define that the object of planning merely becomes the space as defined by the relevant planning institution and the processes used in managing that space. Moreover, as cities have spread and in the context of growing commercial pressures and growing ethnic diversity, urban space has itself become more varied.

Planning practice has responded in various ways. Healey (2004, 267) writes on the basis of a series of case studies of planning in Milan, Amsterdam and Cambridge of a shift towards strategies that 'exist as revisable conceptions continually interacting with unfolding experiences and understandings, but yet holding in attention some orienting sensibility'. Strategic spatial planning so conceived is commonly diagrammatic and broad brush in character, but seldom exclusively so. Instead, strategic planning uses a combination of conventional fixed territorial boundaries, for example local government or national boundaries, fixed geographical features such as a coastline or rivers and diagrams or symbolic markers to indicate the planning content—for example, for movement patterns and for growth, restraint or regeneration.

The shift towards fluid space has weaknesses. Strategic plans can become so abstract and so diagrammatic that they fail to command either public interest or political support. Likewise, they can become so oriented towards fluid, 'smooth' space that they lack substance and lack, in addition, the ability either to control or direct change (Nyseth 2012). The so-called 'Northern Way' plan, published in 2004 as a strategic vision for the north of England, and now almost universally forgotten, provides an example of all this (Goodchild & Hickman 2006; Rees & Lord 2013).

Excessive abstraction is not a necessary consequence of strategic planning, however. Ascher (2001) and Albrechts and Balducci (2013) have independently argued for a project-based approach to strategic planning in which the project would itself provide substance and organisation. By project is generally understood an investment project, though a specific theme such as the adaptation to climate change or the protection of natural habitats and recreational spaces might also be sufficient.

The shift towards flexible, fluid space should not be exaggerated. Early blueprint town planning involved the use of diagrams where this would clarify the underlying ideas and proposals. The garden city, as proposed by Howard ([1898] 1985), included a social city diagram in which a group of freestanding new settlements are linked to another by a tram network. Conversely, design-oriented blueprint planning has continued alongside the growth of process theories and flexible strategy statements. From the 1990s onwards, concepts of sustainable development have inspired a revival of interest in long-term, large-scale physical planning, notably in the contrasting visions of the compact city and a revised version of the decentralised garden city (Breheny 1996). In addition, after about 2000 in Britain, a renewed emphasis on place making and the quality of places has led to the creation of a new generation of design-oriented or 'master' plans mostly at the level of a neighbourhood or district (Bell 2005; CABE 2008; Tiesdell and Macfarlane, 2007).

In the Netherlands, Faludi (2000, 303) has also noted the persistence of local 'project plans', namely 'blueprints of the intended end-state of a material object and the measures needed to achieve that state'. In France, blueprints persist in the form of the *Plan local d'urbanisme*, the main zoning plan, and in the plans that accompany the *Zone d'Aménagement Concertée*, a local action plan. Most likely, blueprint plans are likely to arise in any situation where developers, investors and property owners require clarity as to what they can and cannot do and where, in addition, development requires close coordination.

For all these reasons, it is difficult to accept the existence of a paradigm change, from plan to process, along the lines once suggested by Hall ([1975] 2002, 226) and implying a radical reinterpretation and reconceptualisation of planning practice and its relation to urban space. The emphasis has changed, but the notion of a paradigm change is too dramatic and, if accepted, would, in any case, rule out the existence of continuities between planning practice now and that in the past, say before 1960.

## The Multiple Distinctions of Blueprint Planning

Just as the terms 'plan' and 'planning' may be broken down into a series of different elements of space and action, so may blueprint planning. The multiple distinctions identified by Deleuze and Guattari (1987) offer a start, serving to animate concepts of urban space. However, they are only the start in the spatial distinctions that cumulatively define the scope and purpose of urban planning. Three further types of distinctions are apparent:

- A cognitive distinction between rules and models, meaning a distinction in how knowledge is organised, presented and used. Rules and models enable spatial assemblages to travel, to be applied elsewhere and applied in addition in new development.
- An ontological distinction between the Romantic and the Baroque, meaning a distinction about the character of reality and about the relationship between the observer (or designer) and reality. The Romantic and the Baroque define how rules, models and other elements are applied.
- Finally, an epistemological opposition between use value and exchange value. As epistemeology, the use value/exchange value distinction offers a method for the analysis of urban space and leads to further analytical distinctions about social rights, including the right to the city.

The first two distinctions—rules and models, the Baroque and the Romantic—can be traced back to the origins of modern town planning in the late 19th century and often to earlier periods. The use value/exchange value distinction also has 19th-century origins, but only became applied to urban space with the growth of Marxist urban sociology and geography from the 1970s onwards.

## Models and Rules

Planners, designers and other interested parties need some way of organising and holding knowledge and, in doing so, of determining whether proposals are potentially valid and suitable or not, as the case may be. The experience of living, of observing the world, of navigating around a city, of encountering diversity and 'otherness', is a basis for social learning, as the assemblage theory of McFarlane (2011a, 2011b) and others, for example Sennett (1992), suggest. Experience is also a source of empathy in design—the ability of the designer to put himself or herself in the position of a future user and so anticipate how well a proposal is likely to work in terms of convenience and feel (Lynch and Hack 1984, 98). Empathy originates in another form of spatial practice identified by McFarlane (2011a, 2011b) and derived from Hinchcliffe (2003), that of 'inhabiting', a process of interaction with the human and non-human world, of becoming sensitised to the materalities of that world and coming to appreciate its distinctive qualities. Inhabiting is also called 'dwelling' by McFarlane (2011a, 2011b) though the latter is commonly associated with a particular type of building and with residence. Inhabiting in contrast is an active form of learning about a place and environment.

However, the direct experience of urban space does not provide a single reading but 'multiple, overlapping, ever-changing and at times, simultaneous' readings (de Vega 2010). To be applied in the form of plan proposals, experience and equally 'inhabiting' needs to be elaborated, simplified and operationalised into an abstraction, pattern or 'mediating structure' (Hutchins 1997) that allows the communication of a common set of assumptions with other relevant actors. Knowledge needs to be delocalised and generalised so that it can be applied elsewhere. Deleuze and Guattari (1987, 7) put much the same point in asking for an *'abstract machine that connects a language to the semantic and pragmatic contents of statements, to collective assemblages of enunciation, to a whole micropolitics of the social field'* (italics in original).

The mediating structures that permit learning are, therefore not assemblages and likewise the mediating structures of learning in urban planning are not spatial assemblages, unless the term 'assemblage' is extended to the point that the term loses meaning. In a study of policy transfer and mobility, Peck and Theodore (2010) refer to 'models', understood as 'objects of emulation', in a way that has parallels in planning practice and history. However, planning does not rely only on models for the transfer of ideas and practices. It relies, instead, on a combination of rules and models, with the latter including a closely related concept in architecture of types—of buildings, styles, uses etc. (Schön 1988). Rules involve lists of criteria, whilst models (including types) involve images and forms. Both offer a means of constructing a representation (of a building, or group of buildings or an area) and therefore conform to the notion of a mediating structure or abstract machine. Neither rules nor models are, moreover, superior to or derivative of the other. They are instead interactive. In some cases, rules may be derived from models, but not as a generalisation.

Exactly because rules and models are fundamental to processes of designing and communicating concepts of space, they are recurrent in the history of modern town planning and its precursors, as has been amply shown by Choay ([1980] 1996). The traditional logic of urban development, Choay suggests, is informal and based on taken-for-granted assumptions. Modernisation involved the emergence of formal statements as individual designers and other interested parties started to think self-consciously about the principles of good design and sought in addition to adapt those principles in the light of considerations of nature, human needs and aesthetics. Rules and types in architecture may be tacit or unacknowledged, according to Schön (1988). For Choay, however, the novelty of modern town planning was the way in which rules and models became formalised and systematic in their application and in which therefore they acquired a life of their own, influencing practice through example, publications and professional education.

In relation to rules, arguably the first systematic, explicit written statement comes from Leon Battista Alberti's *De re aedificatoria* (On the Art of Building), first published in manuscript form in about 1452. *De re aedificatoria* discusses, in relatively simple language, good practice in architecture as it had accumulated from Ancient Rome, mostly through a comparison of different viewpoints rather than laying down hard rules. It comprises ten books, of which book four is the most relevant. This latter includes chapters dealing with public works, the situation of a city and the 'compass, space and bigness' of a city. The main concerns are aesthetics or 'visual delight', to use the original language, public health, the design of public buildings and defence.[3]

By the time modern town planning had fully emerged in the early 1900s, defence had largely disappeared as a relevant consideration. The explosive power and speed of movement of modern warfare had long made irrelevant town walls and other measures of external defence (Virilio 1984). Defence had been redefined as an exercise in maintaining security against internal threats, as was a theme in the rebuilding of Paris by Haussmann in the 1860s and remains a theme to the present.

Otherwise, a surprising degree of continuity is apparent, even in statements of 20th-century town planning. For example, in the standard British textbook of the 1930s, Abercrombie (1933) sought to simplify the aims of planning in the phrase 'Beauty, Health and Convenience in that order' (cited by Hall et al. 1973, 45). The planning and replanning of towns was therefore to be undertaken according to aesthetic and not just practical principles.

At the same time, listing a few apparently simple aims and criteria was not adequate to the task of replanning the industrial city. An alternative, forward-looking and more radical view came from the 'Athens Chart' of 1932—the manifesto of the modern movement in architecture and the manifesto of 'modernist' (as opposed to simply modern) town planning. Modernist is an exercise in glorifying the possibility of new technology and new ways of thinking, as opposed to 'modern', which is merely up-to-date and a product of its time. The Athens Chart declared that the city serves four functions: 'dwelling, recreation, work and transportation' (Sert, 1942, 246). Dwelling was 'the first urban function', primarily owing (though this was seldom stated explicitly) to the political priority of tackling housing shortages, and had to be analysed in terms of density and zoning. The task of planning was to ensure that the city was organised in such a way that all these four functions could be undertaken in the most efficient manner, both individually and collectively, as defined by technical criteria. Efficiency of design and planning also meant, in general, the allocation of different sites to different uses, so leading to land use separation as a typical characteristic of modernist planning.

Later, from the 1960s onwards, in a reaction against the initial, standardising wave of modernism, dissenting theorists redefined the aims and criteria of planning in ways that covered those aspects of city life that the Athens Chart ignored, so including aesthetic rules as well as function. For example, in 'Good City Form', Lynch (1984, 118) made reference to five broad performance dimensions in urban planning, including a reference to the sensed landscape, meaning the extent of 'match between environment, our sensory and mental capabilities and our cultural constructs'. Later, Sandercock (1998, 207-15) called for a culture change within the planning profession, with an expanded definition of aims, largely concerned with the social meaning of the urban landscape. The language of planning, it was suggested, should encompass 'the city of memory', concerned with conservation and identity; 'the city of desire' concerned with excitement and consumption; and finally 'the city of spirit', as represented by places that people can gather and relax and represented in addition by public art. In saying this, Sandercock called for planners to recognise the cultural richness that already exists in most large cities, with a variety of urban spaces.

The initial reaction against modernist town planning has, to an extent, been overtaken by the emergence of new ecological concerns. Yet ecological planning can also be understood in terms of the distinction between objective, 'modern' and subjective criteria. An eco-modernist approach substitutes ecological efficiency and carbon reduction instead of the principles of economic efficiency and functionality that preoccupied the first generation of modernists. In contrast, a subjective approach would promote a sense of appreciation and delight in the natural world (see, for example, Hester 2006). Another, pragmatic response would be to seek out the best of all worlds and use the various rules in combination with one another.

Models have almost as long a history as rules. For Choay (1996), the earliest proper, fully worked model is contained in Thomas More's 'Utopia' (Greek for 'no place'), first published in 1516. Models and utopian thinking are closely associated, as the search for utopia commonly leads to a consideration of ideal cities and ideal urban forms. However, before the 16th century, thinkers commonly treated a secular ideal as animpossibility, as perfection could only be achieved in heaven, expressed, for example, as the 'City of God' of St. Augustine (Akkerman 2000).

The industrial cities of the 19th and 20th centuries were, in any case, simply too different to permit direct continuity from earlier models. A range of new alternatives emerged as a reaction to the industrial cities of this time, from the extreme decentralisation and dispersal of Frank Lloyd Wright's Broadacre City, through the low-density proposals associated with the Garden City of Ebenezer Howard and finally the high-density, high-rise City of Tomorrow of Le Corbusier (Fishman 1977).

There were other proposals. In England, in the period before 1939, modernised terraces were occasionally suggested as a more practical and economic alternative to the low-density, low-rise garden city (Goodchild 2008, 33). However, the usual theme was a conscious break from the past, either opening up or abandoning the 19th century industrial city. Even the high-density proposals of Le Corbusier sought to open up the industrial city through building high, so freeing land at ground level and letting in air and sunlight. The proposals for modernised terraces never caught the public imagination, as they looked too much like the densely packed slums that modern town planning was intended to replace.

The ideal cities of the early 20th century also expressed slightly different ways in which a model might be used. For Frank Lloyd Wright, Broadacre City was an exercise in exploration and theory, worked out wholly through the human imagination rather than through local experimentation. Broadacre City remained a utopian project in the proper sense of the word—a 'no place.' For Howard, the Garden City was to be implemented on a flexible basis with local variations. Howard was mostly interested in the principle of joining town and country and, in addition, of finding a voluntary, non-governmental solution to the land and housing problems. In contrast, for le Corbusier and other advocates of modern architecture, the specification of models was an exercise in product development, similar to the production of a prototype for a mass-produced car. The model was a means of defining a standardised ideal that could be repeated over and over again and would lock standardised building types into a standardised urban form (Boudon 1985; Sert, 1942, 246; Tafuri 1976).

Models are, therefore, of varied novelty and ambition. Hoch (2009), whilst using slightly different terminology, has distinguished between models as 'precedents' and models as 'prototypes'. The latter are more innovative and generally seek to bring together 'a combination of ideas' about a city or other area. By definition, a prototype has no previous reference point, at least not a single reference point. Precedents, in contrast, involve the reuse of a specific example of urban design previously applied elsewhere. They may involve varied historical examples of design in an effort to promote tradition, local identity or popular appeal. In Britain, the garden city provides an example. The garden city, understood both as a city with gardens and a city set in a garden has persisted into the 21st century and continues to inspire new interpretations and applications. However, the garden city is also an example of a model that is open to different and sometimes conflicting interpretations, with a long running, continuing dispute as to whether garden suburbs and urban extensions can count as full garden cities and whether, in any case, they offer an acceptable planning solution. In the latest example of this dispute, the planning consultants URBED (2014) prepared a prize-winning proposal for the large-scale development of garden suburbs in England, only for this to be criticised by the relevant minister as 'urban sprawl'.[4]

Precedents may also be used because they have gained a reputation for excellence or progressive thinking—covering for example the use of green space, of public transport links, of commercial development or whatever (Ward 2013). In doing this, models allow planning in one area to 'catch up' elsewhere. To provide some examples: efforts made under the Urban Renaissance policy initiatives of the period from about 1997 to 2002 and intended to make planning more conscious of urban design made repeated references to Barcelona and, in particular, to the way that the local city council sought to improve and maintain the quality of public spaces.[5] Recent attempts to make urban planning more environmentally sustainable refer instead to the city of Freiburg in southern Germany, noted for the development of zero carbon residential areas and extensive traffic calming, or to Vancouver in Canada, a city with a reputation for liveability.

Planners, other professionals and students learn about practice elsewhere through making study visits. Leading practitioners from the model cities can also make presentations, drawing on their experience and providing relevant examples. However, what is being presented is not the full city. The study tours and presentations are selective. They involve a simplified model of the lessons to be learnt.

Judgements still have to be made, nevertheless, as to whether the models are too expensive, whether they are likely to appeal to a home audience and whether they can be adapted to local conditions, without diluting their distinctive, innovative contribution. The ability of a model to influence practice is based not so much on its intrinsic strengths, but its suitability to the circumstances. As such, the transfer of models from one context to another may itself change the model or more likely lead to a nuanced application with a different feel to the original (González 2011; Peck 2011; Peck and Theodore 2010).

There is nothing new in the application of models from one context to another. Early town planning, in the period before 1914, was characterised by international exchanges, notably between the US, Britain, France and Germany (Sutcliffe 1981). Models were also exported outside these four countries through the European empires and, later in the 20th century, through the desire of independent countries to modernise. The work of Le Corbusier in Chandigarh, India, undertaken between 1951 and 1964, is a notable example of the latter.[6] Increased international trade, increased travel, increased competition and the growth of international planning consultancies (Rapoport (2014) have, nevertheless, quickened the rate at which ideas and models circulate.

International circulation has provided the subject matter of most recent publications in urban planning and geography, mainly because this illuminates processes of globalisation. There is a countertendency, however, where local architects and planners have sought a revival of local and regional urban forms. In the Arab world, for example, a particular interest has emerged in favour of traditional, vernacular urban forms such as courtyard housing, rather than the modernist blocks of the colonial and immediate postcolonial eras (Al-Naim 2014).[7]

In any case, in many countries, 'home grown' models continue to have a larger impact on the urban landscape. The use of standard house types by volume house building in Britain provides an example (Nicol and Hooper 1999). Volume private house building may be regarded as the last bastion of modernism as mass production in Britain. Volume builders use models as precedents because all parties are familiar with what is involved, because buildings can be classified by use and functional requirements and, because if standardised to a single or limited range of models, development and building is generally less expensive. The result is a trend towards standardised architecture and urban spaces and a resistance to innovation, other than piecemeal, small changes stimulated by considerations of costs or consumer feedback (Ball 1999; Carmona 2001).

The green belt as applied in England is another example where adherence to a rigid spatial model, in this case for political rather than economic reasons, hinders innovation. Indeed the green belt model is so persistent and rigid as to constitute a 'planning doctrine', rather than a mere planning policy (Faludi 2000).

Blueprint planning does not necessarily involve an exclusive choice of either rules or models. Models and rules can operate at different scales, allowing flexibility in the details of development in the context of an overall plan. Cities can retain a green belt for example, whilst issuing a list of detailed rules for development elsewhere. Another possibility is the use of model-based projects, say an urban square borrowed from Barcelona, with a strategic plan whose contents are largely determined by site-by-site, rule-based assessments of development opportunities.

In addition, the rule and the model may be applied to the same area at different times and different stages of a development or redevelopment project. Moore Milroy (2009) provides an example from the regeneration of the Yonge/Dundas intersection in the central business area of Toronto. The first plan, published in 1996, adopted a rule-based approach, based on an appreciation of the potential of the area and its constraints. Within a few months, however, the local city council adopted a more radical redevelopment plan, based on the search for an alternative model of what this particular place might be. Once the city council adopted the alternative model, the potential for further innovation was closed off. Moore Milroy adds that, while the usual explanation of plan generation and implementation gives primacy to factors, notably economic and political factors, outside the planning process, the experience of Yonge/Dundas shows the 'cracks in planning itself'.

Once the plan is completed, the distinction between the model and the rule also influences its subsequent evaluation. For a model, the criteria for evaluation comprise the extent to which the location and form of a building or buildings as developed conform to the spatial arrangements specified in the plan. Evaluation is based on conformity to those arrangements or 'conformance', as this is also called. For a rule-based plan, evaluation is in terms of performance, measured through either the user response or a variety of specific measures of the quality of the built environment, including its 'fit' to its site and surroundings (Baker et al. 2006).

Rule-based planning is, in principle, more flexible than the use of a model. The use of standards allows designers and developers to use more than one layout or architectural form if they can demonstrate equivalent levels of performance. House builders can continue, for example, to use a variety of standardised street layouts and house types so long as these meet the specified criteria. The advantage of flexibility is not realised, however, if local rules are drafted in a restrictive way, intended to avoid every conceivable problem and risk. An example of such a tendency towards rigidity has been reported from the Australian state of Queensland (Frew et al. 2016).

Conversely, the search flexibility has disadvantages in that it may limit the effectiveness of plan implementation (Oliveira & Pinho 2010, 348) and complicate the application of performance criteria in plan evaluation (Baker et al. 2006). Evaluation is especially demanding if the performance criteria deal with user response and such matters as the assessment of the sensed landscape or the impact of urban design on human behaviour—for example reduced car use or reduced vulnerability to crime. Conformance is simpler. It can be assessed through the use of mapping techniques and an analysis of permit decisions to see whether these conformed to the pattern and use as intended (Laurian et al. 2004).

The evaluation of plans is made more complex by the existence of departures in plan implementation. Departures are common, partly because of changing, unpredictable economic circumstances and partly because deliberate exceptions may be introduced for specific purposes. Faludi (2000) argues that departures from the original provisions do not necessarily imply failure, but the plan itself should be known to and used by relevant stakeholders. The criteria for evaluation are the extent to which a plan provides a learning framework, facilitates choices and continues to be relevant over time. In saying this, Faludi shifts the notion of 'performance' away from the evaluation of the built environment as developed to the process and practice of planning. A plan still performs if it frames policy discussions and decisions and so facilitates collective learning.

Notions of a plan as a learning framework apply most clearly to strategic land use plans whose aim is to provide guidance to developers and institutional actors. However, it is difficult to see how the extent of implementation and the extent of departures can be disregarded in plan evaluation (Talen 1996). The scale and type of departure is also relevant, whether or not for example the departures amount to a breach of some fundamental principle or plan aim (Loh 2011) and whether, in addition, failure to implement part of a plan leads to a sense of unfairness or grievance.

Of course, once changed by the course of events or by conflicting priorities, the plan ceases to be a blueprint. It becomes, instead, an element in a process. Plans and processes are therefore closely related, more closely related than theories of paradigm change would suggest.

*The Baroque/Romantic Distinction*

Strictly speaking, the contemporary use of the Romantic/Baroque distinction is a metaphor—a figure of speech that guides reasoning—rather than a direct description. All metaphors carry meaning from one word or image to another. Used as a metaphor, the Romantic/Baroque distinction carries meaning from the world of art and architecture into other fields. As art and architecture, the Baroque refers to a distinct historical era in Europe and the Americas lasting from about 1580 to 1780. The Baroque was eventually overtaken by an era of revolutionary change, characterised by a different aesthetic, the Romantic. Whatever the precise dates, however, the use of an aesthetic metaphor is instructive. The Romantic/Baroque distinction is about a sensibility. It is an ontological concept that, as defined in the Oxford English Dictionary, relates to 'the nature or essence of being or existence', including the nature and essence of the landscape.[8] The Baroque is said to resist clarity, mastery and the single point of view. It is uncertain about scale, boundaries and coherence, favours the open-ended, and is apparently unfinished and therefore more likely to accept a loss of balance and order (Deleuze, 1993; Kwa, 2002; Law 2004). Applied to architecture, the Baroque favours theatricality (through the use of decoration on surfaces,

58  Definitions, Styles and Forms

sculpture and other artwork); monumentality (through massing and the use of large, often vertically oriented strictures) and a sense of surprise (through the use of *trompe-l'œil* or optical illusions whereby painting produces a feeling of three dimensions on a flat surface), concealment and the use of spaces of different sizes and shapes (MacLure 2006). Applied to urban design, the Baroque is defined with reference to two, apparently contradictory tendencies, the aesthetic and the scientific or geometrical. To use the words of Mumford ([1961] 1966, 402):

> First the abstract mathematical and methodological side, expressed to perfection in its rigorous street plans. ... At the same time, in the painting and sculpture of the period the sensuous, rebellious, extravagant, anti-classical, anti-mechanical side

The former, the abstract mathematical aspect, refers to axes and directed space, that is to say straight streets, avenues or boulevards that extend from focal points to focal points. The latter, the sensuous, rebellious side, covers the treatment of volumetric spaces such as public squares and courtyards (Zucker 1945).

The rebuilding of Rome in the late 16th century, notably under Pope Sixtus V, is the prototype for Baroque town planning. Pope Sixtus sought to integrate a number of apparently scattered monuments through demolition of the intervening buildings, the construction of linking streets and the provision of new points of interest such as fountains and obelisks (Bacon [1967] 1974, 126–34, 140–1; Zucker 1955). Wren's plan for the reconstruction of London after the Great Fire of 1666 is the most striking and ambitious attempt to apply artistic Baroque town planning principles in Britain. It was not implemented, however, due to opposition from property owners who after the fire started to rebuild within existing property boundaries.[9] Plans, as this example demonstrates, can become overtaken by events.

Baroque styles of town planning persisted into the 19th and even 20th centuries mostly because of a lack of alternatives for organising large-scale schemes. The reconstruction of Paris undertaken by Haussmann from the 1860s onwards and the City Beautiful movement active in the US in the first decade of the 20th century all used the Baroque principles of axes and focal points (Mumford [1961] 1966, 456–67). The use of axes and focal points continues moreover to the present. The redevelopment after 1990 of the commercial district of Pudong, on the right bank of the Shanghai River, provides a contemporary example (Xue et al. 2011). These later exercises were mostly about the application of the Baroque as a model, however, without the detail and complexity that characterises 17th and 18th century examples.

In addition, and this is the most distinctive aspect of the contemporary use of the term, the Baroque sensibility has come to include a specific philosophy of science. The main source, as Law (2004, 22) notes, is the 17th century philosopher Leibniz and his comments about the almost infinite complexity of the natural world.

> Every portion of matter may be conceived as a garden full of plants, and as a pond full of fish. But every branch of each plant, every member of each animal, and every drop of their liquid parts is itself likewise a similar garden or pond.

Commenting on this remark, Law (ibid.) goes on: 'Leibniz is telling us to look for a world of ponds within ponds and gardens within gardens. Such is the baroque sensibility.'

The Baroque philosophy of science as presented by Leibnitz is a positivist science in the sense that it relies on observation and seeks to make generalisations. Equally, however, it accepts that the observational field available is not the complete picture and accepts, in addition, that different mixes of variables operate in different situations to produce unique results and complex patterns of varied elements. As is also apparent in the quotation, the Baroque involves organic analogies. However, the reference to worlds within worlds (ponds within ponds etc.) suggests co-existence rather than tight integration.

Baroque philosophy has, in turn, enabled a reconceptualisation of space as including folded surfaces (Deleuze 1993). The fold is an aspect of Baroque art and architecture—in heavy curtains, at the top of pillars and in curved wall surfaces. At the same time, the analogy of the fold offers a means of understanding landscapes, both urban and rural. The fold is a reminder that nature holds surprises, that overall views cannot grasp details or enquire into concealed areas, that historical landscapes incorporate events and cultural identities and, further, that understanding the history of landscapes involves a process of unfolding, of stripping away layers to reveal relationships (Ingold 1993). The fold is therefore a reminder that space can be non-Euclidean, relational and variable.

Implicit in the folds of the Baroque is another spatial concept—the idea of heterotopia as promoted by Foucault ([1967] 1984). Heterotopia means literally an 'other' or a 'different' (*hetero* in Greek) 'space' (*topos* in Greek). Heterotopias are, for Foucault, a mirror to the world. They open up the self to somewhere that is real but exists as an inversion of the present place. They stand in opposition to their surroundings and involve therefore a system of opening and closing and by extension a means of controlling access. They are, moreover, distinct from utopias—a type of place that exists nowhere but the imagination. A heterotopia exists somewhere. However, they also stand outside conventional or normal time. Heterotopias include a single real place that juxtaposes different types of spaces in its interior—for example theatres, those types of garden that are subdivided internally into different areas and cemeteries of the type where each family has its own vault. Heterotopias may, according to Foucault, also include places of children's play and of institutions established to manage crises in people's lives and, increasingly in modern society, of institutions that manage various forms of deviancy. Each of these stand in contrast to their surroundings.

Interpretations of heterotopia are varied and numerous. Heterotopias include the virtual world of games where children and adolescents go to escape adults (McNamee 2000), urban wilderness areas where the usual principles of spatial order have been effectively abandoned (Jorgensen & Tylecote 2007), westernised 'Chinatowns' that include a disparate mixture of Chinese and Western cultural references, often behind an archway spanning a street (Lou 2007) and big city centres that combine a fluid juxtaposition of functional elements, cultural heritage and place for enjoyment and recreation and where again the individual may seek to escape normal social controls (Hatz 2010). One might also include the protected spaces and places or 'niches' that figure as a common theme in accounts of innovative and radical green initiatives (Seyfang & Smith 2007).

The Romantic, like the Baroque, combines architecture and the philosophy of science. Mumford ([1961] 1966, 551, 556–7) equates romanticism with escapism, a desire to escape from the frustrations of urban life and to embrace nature. The growth of suburbia, especially the growth of 19th century middle class suburbs in England, may be understood as an example of a Romantic sensibility, as wealthy householders sought to escape the disorder, dirt and pollution of the industrial city. Since modern town planning also arose as a reaction to the disorder of the 19th century city, the form of that escape—the suburban villa and country/city hybrid—proved highly influential.

The Romantic has other dimensions, however. Understood as a means of coping with complexity, the Romantic embraces nature, but only on the assumption that the apparent disorder of nature can be reduced to simple classifications and scientific relationships. The Romantic is constituted by the internal relations of different parts to other parts in the whole so expressing a degree of completeness and functional containment. Applied to the contemporary city, the Romantic favours those organic analogies that seek inherent wholeness, order, structure and form and that, therefore, support the search for ideal urban forms. All of these were common themes of modern town planning in the period from 1900 to about 1960 and they also supported the use of models of urban form, rather than rules (Eden, 1946; Herbert 1963). The Plans for Greater London again exemplify this tendency.

Since the parts amount to a coherent whole, Romantic approaches also assume the feasibility of understanding an object, including the city, through centralised modelling, control and the use of statistical indicators (Hillier and van Wezemael, 2008). The Romantic favours the big picture and in addition scaling up from the detail, according to invariant laws and models of those laws. Equally, the Romantic is about seeing the large scale as the product of outward expression of inner relationships that can be understood, explained and manipulated. Social learning, according to McFarlane (2011b) and Hutchins (1997), involves a stage of coordination in which ideas are crystallised and different elements, different interests and different actors are brought together. The Romantic is strongly about coordination, but is also about the internal coordination of the elements with an underlying rationale or aim rather than coordination with a context, as in the Baroque. The Romantic incorporates, therefore, the logic of ideal cities and utopian thinking, as opposed to the Baroque whose equivalent logic is that of the heterotopia.

Ideal cities and utopias portray an end state and so reinforce a sense of space as somehow static. Applied to existing cities, however, the Romantic is more radical and potentially disruptive than the Baroque as it seeks a new beginning, a complete replacement of the old. Admittedly, no plan, certainly no spatial plan, can or should specify every aspect of urban life. Decisions still remain with businesses and individuals and, as the critics of planning commonly argue, the creativity of cities largely lies with the spontaneous actions of people who live and work there rather than with land use or physical planning (Holcombe 2012, 200). In addition, to go beyond spatial planning, the urban environment itself provides the context for spontaneous action, for example in the arts, in decoration or in the creation of businesses. However, the Romantic approach would still seek to lay down an overall framework, specifying the main elements of a spatial assemblage.

A quotation from Unwin (1909) summarises the Romantic perspective, as applied to a self-consciously progressive and reforming view of modern town planning. The 'comprehensive and orderly planning of our towns' sought to bring the industrial city under control, from the inside outwards.

> In desiring powers for town planning our town communities are seeking to be able to express their needs, their life, and their aspirations in the outward form of their towns, seeking, as it were, freedom to become the artists of their own cities, portraying on a gigantic canvas the expression of their life. (ibid., 9)

Proceeding from the inside out in turn favours the large scale and comprehensive interventions rather than the selective interventions of the Baroque. The latter, as represented by Haussmann's rebuilding of Paris or the City Beautiful movement in the US did nothing, moreover, to tackle social problems, such as housing shortages and overcrowding.

Large-scale, comprehensive planning and building faced many constraints, however. Unwin's reference to 'town communities' is to local authorities. However, local authorities invariably faced financial constraints caused by their limited range of sources of revenue. In Britain, a Royal Commission on

Local Taxation (1901) had previously noted that the burden of the council rates, a form of property tax, had grown exponentially and had reached its limits in supporting even the limited range of social services, then available. Moreover, the garden city movement, of which Unwin was an influential participant, offered no effective alternative. Statistics prepared by the Garden Cities and Town Planning Association reveal that, by 1913, 10,045 dwellings had been completed in garden city and related housing societies in England—a number which represented less than 0.2 per cent of the inhabited housing stock (Calvert Spensley, 1918). Further, in seeking to maintain house building, the garden city societies had increasingly turned to the middle classes, owner-occupation and to an early form of shared ownership called co-partnership, rather than building working-class dwellings for rent (Purdom 1913).

After 1918, the central state assumed responsibility for planning urban development, rather than local authorities. Centrally funded grant aid was the only practicable way and effective source of relief to the rate-payers' burden and the only way therefore of establishing decent social provision, including housing. The alternative was a local income tax, but this was generally regarded as impractical, given the small size of local authority areas and the tendency even then for people to work in one district, for example a city, and live in another, a suburb.

However, the state faced a recurrent dilemma. Planning and building for the aspirations of a community implies a commitment to high standards. Yet building to high standards reduces the number of dwellings that can be completed in any single year and, as a result, fails to improve the living standards of those living in substandard or overcrowded conditions (Goodchild, 2008, 82). The Romantic leads, therefore, to a conflict between meeting needs in the short-term and raising long-term standards. Moreover, as construction and development proceeds, policy changes and technological changes risk making the initial plan obsolete, whilst decay triggers further inequalities. Exactly this tendency was apparent in the post-1945 London new towns, notably Crawley (Heraud 1968).

The limitations of the Romantic raise, in turn, the possibility of using Baroque principles to create the just city. The omens are not good, given the association between Baroque styles and both commercial urban design as in city centres and various heavy handed 20th-century conceptions of the city beautiful and monumental.

There is an exception, however. In the period between about 1905 and 1920, Geddes (1915) argued for a selective, flexible approach, based on the principle of survey before plan. Designers and planners could not assume *a priori* that they knew what was best for a locality. Plan preparation could only proceed after a survey, placing each settlement in its regional context, combining studies of nature with those of towns (ibid., 334) and covering the 'whole situation and life of a community in past and present' (ibid., 346).

The survey, as envisaged by Geddes, was, moreover, not just an exercise in statistical reporting and analysis. It was intended as an exercise in public education, including the mounting of exhibitions, with the hope of creating a 'social movement' in favour of 'civics', namely planning and urban improvement. The survey, therefore, would open up new possibilities, allow a mixture of proposals, models and rules in different contexts and so corresponded to the criteria of an open-ended Baroque method of research, as for example defined by Law (2009).

The survey method became widely adopted in plan preparation in Britain in the early 20th century, ensuring that plans would emerge from local circumstances and were more likely to respect previous patterns of urban development. However, the survey was generally used to provide background information for a process of comprehensive, orderly planning to paraphrase Unwin. In the words of Abercrombie (1916), the most influential professional planner of his generation, the survey allowed 'the systematic study which is necessary in order to ensure that a comprehensive treatment is being adopted'. The survey became professionalised and sought to provide the background for integrated, comprehensive approaches.

The open-ended Baroque approach remains, moreover, difficult to apply within government. Using surveys to reveal new possibilities requires in-depth qualitative interviews and a process of interaction between researchers and research subjects. Government departments and agencies typically do not do this, partly for reasons of costs, short time scales and administrative simplicity (Mason and Barnes 2007) and partly because they wish to control the policy agenda (Boehm et al. 2013). As a result, contemporary theories of social learning and open-ended planning emphasise consultation, political debate and involvement (Healey 1992) and improved democratic institutions (McClymont 2011; Mouffe 2000) rather than the survey method.

The assemblage theory of urban learning, presented by McFarlane (2011a, 2011b), and especially the concept of 'inhabiting' space is closer to Geddes' idea of survey. Geddes view of planning is likewise about the assembly of knowledge, through the 'accumulation of experience, from foreign travel or from observation at home', drawing on 'notes and impressions' as well as 'pictures, plans, models, and other graphic records (1915, 395). However, it was exactly the unspecific character of Geddes's method that worried the subsequent generation of social researchers. For Glass (1955), for example, the style of survey work associated with Geddes was hopelessly amateur, partly because it involved local volunteers rather than professionals. Undertaking surveys and accumulating experience looked too close to the 'unanalytical empiricism' of collecting information for its own sake (Abrams 1968, 120).

Apart from Geddes, two proposals are available to show how a Baroque approach may be applied to neighbourhood regeneration. One by a French architect, Le Dantec (1991) is an explicit attempt to apply Baroque urban design principles to the regeneration of the depressed suburban estates in Paris. The other by Boelens and Coppens (2012), while not explicitly referring to the Baroque, draws on very similar ideas of how to cope with complexity. This latter seeks the 'socio-spatial activation' of a deprived social housing estate on the western fringes of Antwerp.

For Le Dantec, a grid, say, of one-kilometre squares is laid across a map of the urban area. However, the aim is not to standardise urban space and not to create a dispersed American city. Instead, the aim is to bring out the distinctive qualities of each neighbourhood. Baroque urban design accepts the existence of multiple points and centres in a city. Baroque neighbourhood regeneration is similar in constituting an ethic based on the recognition of 'otherness', an ethic that seeks to express social and cultural differences and diversity, but that also seeks to promote the care of neglected places. Likewise, for Boelens and Coppen (2012), intervention is organised around a series of opportunity maps—sport and leisure, green space and work/centre—all of which are largely independent of each other but offer a promising future in the short, medium and long term.

To an extent, the two examples from Antwerp and Paris are distinctive only by virtue of their explicitness and awareness. It is difficult to see how any exercise in neighbourhood regeneration could avoid a Baroque approach, based on diversity and organised complexity, if that exercise is to retain the confidence of local people and businesses.

The Romantic approach is not obsolete, however. It is not obsolete partly because the process of plan preparation commonly involves the interplay between the two, between the Romantic and the Baroque, and seeks a combination of both internal and contextual co-ordination. In addition, specific ideas, theories and proposals are, on occasion, necessary to cut through a tangle of evidence. Internally co-ordinated proposals and ideal cities provide direction, at least in the abstract, and are particularly important in enabling different conceptions about hwo cities might develop in the future.

### *Use Values and Exchange Values*

The final distinction, between use value and exchange value, has an unusual history. Concepts of use value are implicit in the early critiques of the industrial city, including those associated with the town planning movement (for example the writings of Unwin) and are also implicit in Marxist critiques of capitalism. However, Marxist theory in the 19th century was dominated by attempts to construct a scientific socialism based on the labour theory of value and said little directly about the future of cities and urban planning (Benevolo 1967). In the 20th century, however, the labour theory of value has looked less credible. As a result, radical thinkers outside the Marxist tradition, as well as heterodox Marxists, have sought to apply similar analytical methods to other commodities such as land or natural resources, in the spirit of Marx's search for forms of exploitation (Keen 1993).

In particular, at the time of great planning debate in the 1940s, Polanyi (1957 [1944], 132) argued that the creation of a full-blown self-regulating market economy was itself a 'utopian' project, because any such theoretical market-based society would rely on the existence of 'fictitious commodities', that is to say commodities that serve basic social and ecological needs and that therefore cannot be subject wholly to the dictates of the market and 'commodified'. Fictitious commodities include money and land, as well as labour, with land being treated as an aspect of nature and the possession of the conditions for a healthy life. To cite Polanyi (1957 [1944], 178), land 'invests man's life with stability; it is the site of his habitation; it is a condition of his physical safety; it is the landscape and the seasons.' The distinction between the use value of space and its exchange value is therefore equivalent to a distinction between a 'real' aspect of life and a fictitious commodity.

Later, the concept of use value became embedded in a series of three-way oppositions or 'triads', presented by Lefèbvre (1985 [1969], 1991 [1974]). The classifications involve an opposition between different levels of reality, between the level of theory and ideology, that of practical application and that of urban practices, with the latter being equivalent to use value (1985 [1969]). The classifications also involve an opposition between types of space, between perceived space (otherwise called spatial practices), conceived space (otherwise called representations of space) and lived space (representational space), with the lived also being equivalent to use value (1991, 46, 38–9). So understood, use value is not just distinct from the exchange value of property on the market (Merrifield 1993, 522). Use value also expresses the concrete experience of space, the level of urban practices and local communities, as opposed to an abstract and mental conception of space, for example as promoted both by planning and by the market (Lefèbvre, 1991, 33, 39; Lehtovuori, 2010, 55–6; Simonsen, 2005, 7). As oppositions, these various types of space interact and change each other. They are intended, therefore, to be more than either distinctions or opposites that overlap and merge into one another.

The concept of lived space has echoes of the twin concepts of 'dwelling' and 'inhabiting' as presented in the assemblage learning theory of McFarlane (2011a, 2011b). The categories do not exactly match one other, however, despite their linguistic similarities. McFarlane's concepts of dwelling and inhabiting are closer to the concept of 'perceived space', as space directly experienced, as presented by Lefèbvre. In addition and more importantly, in the analysis of Lefèbvre, lived space is distinct from and in opposition to the 'conceived' spaces, the representations of space, models and rules, produced by planners.

Saying that lived space and conceived space are distinct from one another does not exclude planners and designers learning from experience and learning from residents and other potential users. A case study of the regeneration of Manchester from the 1970s onwards, undertaken by Leary (2013), provides an example, where repeated conflict and negotiation between different interest groups and agencies produced over time 'a range of spaces of representation and lived space in which a diversity of people feels comfortable'. Much depends on the specifics of the case, however. A study of strategic planning in New York state, undertaken by Buser (2012), suggests that a reliance on abstractions and economic factors may lead to a continued neglect of the material reality of 'lived space'.

Promoting use value in design implies flexibility in supporting local and changing lifestyles and circumstances, rather than following the dictates of a centralised building programme (Boudon 1985). Further, and more significantly for urban politics, use values imply the existence of a 'right to the city', that is to say the right of users to define urban space in opposition to the strategies of planners and developers. As presented by Lefèbvre (1998, 478), the right to the city is a 'right to a transformed and renewed urban life'. The right comprises the ability of all residents to participate in a renewed urban life and their right, in addition, to express their different identities, gained 'through practical action, through effective struggle' (396). In the broadest sense, the right to the city is therefore also a claim to cultural democracy in which the heritage of all groups is recognised.[10]

The right to the city is, moreover, not just a right to the city as it exists, but a right to participate in decisions that might change the direction of development and the priorities of urban policies (Harvey 2003). It is a claim for the recognition of 'the urban' as a locus for the operation of power and, as part of this, a claim to make social and cultural issues visible through campaigning activities and demonstrations in the street. The urban is therefore a product of and constituted by relationships of power and by the opposition between different forces of which the distinction between use value and market value is a product.

So understood, the right to the city supersedes the rights associated with property and property law. The right to the city is likely to limit property rights through prioritising the needs of the community over the rights of the individual property owner. Lefèbvre ([1974] 1991, 396) comments, for example, that the right to difference, itself an aspect of the right to the city, is 'diametrically opposed to the right of property, which is given validity by its logical and legal form as the basis of relationships under the capitalist mode of production'.

Opposing the right to the city and property rights is not helpful from a legal viewpoint, however. From a legal perspective, rights of use are themselves an aspect of property (Blandy and Goodchild 1999). Rights of use and, more generally, property rights are, moreover, a means of guaranteeing basic human rights—for example a means of guaranteeing that the state cannot evict someone from their home without due process, including the possibility of compensation. Basic human rights extend beyond property but property can promote social rights—for example in defining the rights of occupiers in low-cost housing. Property rights and social rights are not necessarily antagonistic to one another (Davy 2011, 40). The question, in relation to property, is whether the detailed allocation of rights in property supports or works against other sources of inequality.

In response the supporters of a right to the city would probably argue that this is also a social right and is not intended to interfere with human rights. Social rights are of various types, however. One way of conceptualising and operationalising the right to the city might be as a 'super right' that incorporates many social rights of diverse character. In part, the right to the city might imply participation exercises or exercises in community control where power is delegated to a varying extent to citizen groups or committees (Arnstein 1969). In addition, the right to the city may be operationalised through various social rights that guarantee minimum living standards for those living in cities and that, by implication, require adequate social expenditure.

Admittedly, the discourse of social rights is not the only relevant discourse. Another approach involves references to the promotion of human 'capabilities', namely what people are able to do and be (Bastia 2015; Nussbaum 2003; Sen 2005). The supporters of the capability approach would argue that the concept of capability is simpler and closer to everyday language than that of social rights. The idea of human capabilities is itself very close to social rights, however, and shares an interest in the definition of minimum standards, or 'entitlements' to use an equivalent, and, in doing this, providing the basis for social justice.

The discourse of social rights has the merit of international recognition. For example, the 'European Urban Charter', as agreed by the Congress of the Council for Europe in 1992, contains a list of twenty 'urban rights', including security, an unpolluted and healthy environment, employment, housing, mobility and health, as well as participation in government processes that involve 'pluralistic, democratic structures'.[11] In this context, recognition of social rights offers a means of promoting both social inclusion and social responsibilities on the part of the state. The rights included in the European Urban Charter are a restatement of the ambitions of a strong welfare state. Like the right to the city they are not legal rights. However, with the exception of the right to housing with its locational implications, they are more akin to a series of 'rights in the city', rather than the more general all-encompassing concept of a 'right to the city' or the pursuit of 'use value'.

In any case, the twin concepts of use value and the right to the city are more than a series of aims and ambitions. They imply a transformation in political values and organisation and, as part of this, the establishment of a self-managing society, based around a combination of industrial self-management and community self-management (Lefèbvre 1976, 120–1: 2003). Day to day political practice, according to Lefèbvre, is not a utopian state of itself and self-management is a political strategy rather than an end state. Even so, it is difficult to read Lefèbvre's concept of use value and right to the city as other than a utopian, rather than a conventional economic or structural reworking of Marx and Marxism (Coleman 2013). Self-management assumes the withering away of the state, according to the Marxist thesis and is utopian for that reason alone (Lefèbvre 1976, 125; Surin 1990). Or to put the same point in the language of Deleuze and Guattari, self-management assumes a society dominated by rhizomatic growth without the countertendency of arborescent, tree-like structures such as bureaucracies.

Whether self-management is consistent with the principle of social rights is another question, however. In a welfare state, as presented by Marshall (1950) or Esping-Andersen (2002) for example, social rights exist as part of an implied contract between the individual citizen and a legitimate political authority, the assumption being that societal well-being and individual well-being are mutually supportive of one another. A right implies a contract in which rights define a duty on another party to recognise that right. The social contract has wider implications than social rights in a welfare state, however, as it also offers a general means of conceptualising the relationship between the state and its citizens, albeit in a way that is variable according to the context. The 'social contract,' in this latter, broader sense, assumes that individuals give up a degree of freedom for the sake of order, including the maintenance of order on the streets (Tonkiss 2005, 24, 76).

Social housing provides an operational example of a social contract. Tenants agree to behave in a responsible manner (and, as part of this, pay the rent) in return for access to a decent home, built and maintained to adequate standards, usually with a public subsidy. The contract in a tenant/landlord relationship is usually a formal document which is signed by the parties and subject to legal interpretation and provides a series of specific rights and duties. Neighbourhood regeneration programmes, as these have been implemented in Britain since about 1990, offer an example where the contract is implied rather than formally stated. Here neighbourhood groups or local officials act as an intermediary between the state and the individual and the state recognises the right of a community to live in decent conditions and have a say in decision making (Flint 2003; Rose 1999), but again subject to certain conditions—to become involved in decision making, to attend job training sessions and to work with a variety of different agencies in the pursuit of common aims and objectives.

Finally, 'localism', as understood in England in the limited sense of giving local communities the right to prepare neighbourhood plans, offers another, more qualified interpretation of the social contract. Localism, so understood, amounts to a political right, rather than a social right, as it allows local communities to work out ways of adapting to development pressures but within the framework of national policies that encourage the continuation of those pressures. If, as has been the case since 2010, localism is accompanied by other measures that limit support to deprived communities and limit, in addition, the support for social housing, the effect is to undermine social rights and to weaken welfare provision (Flint 2015).

The concept of use value remains useful as a means of analysing local struggles as an exercise in negotiating or renegotiating the social contract. The opposition between use values and exchange values has been used in accounts of the right of all groups, including ethnic groups, to have free access to public space (Villa 2000), the right of existing local communities to retain or acquire local facilities such as community gardens (Schmelzkopf 2002) and the right of the poor to remain in central urban areas, for example in the face of gentrification and regeneration projects (Scharenberg and Bader 2009). In addition, the right to the city has been applied more generally to the policy dilemmas that arise in the modernisation of informal and self-built settlements (Roy 2005).

The application of the right to the city in case studies of community politics does not, however, invalidate the idea of a social contract. The promotion of a meaningful right to the city assumes an authority capable of enforcing that right. A purely horizontal, rhizomatic approach is impractical. Equally, a conceptualisation of community action as purely in opposition to the state is too simple. The relationship between the state and community groups is more subtle and varied.

To understand the various conflicting tendencies, it remains useful to return to the concept of land and, by extension, the environment as fictitious commodities as understood by Polanyi (1957 [1944], 132). Fictitious commodities are created as governments seek to extend market processes to all spheres of social and economic life and they are supported by neoliberal philosophies and ideologies that favour a minimal state and promote economic competition. However, exactly because fictitious commodities are essential to life and social well-being, they cannot be treated merely as market commodities without either provoking social disorganisation or encountering political opposition or a mixture of disorganisation and opposition.

The result is a 'double movement' where governments seek both to establish and open up markets and to ensure adequate social and environmental protection from the consequences of doing so (ibid., 132). The state does not disappear and cannot disappear. Instead, goverments implement different policies at different times, according to their economic and political interests, and these policies apply different frameworks for the interpretation of the social contract and its associated rights and obligations. For these reasons, conflicts will continue about the competing claims of use values and exchange values and the varied rights associated with these values.

## Notes

1 The Oxford English Dictionary, consulted February 2013 at www.oed.com.
2 'The Suffix Prefix Dictionary', consulted December 2013 at www.macroevolution.net/suffix-prefix-dictionary.html#.Ur3Jm_vuVeE.

3 The text used is a translation into English dated 1755, The Archimedes Project, consulted November 2011 at http://archimedes2.mpiwg-berlin.mpg.de/archimedes_templates/project.htm.
4 'Housing Minister Brandon Lewis blasts award-winning garden city plan as "urban sprawl"'. *Independent*, 04 September 2014, consulted September 2014 at www.independent.co.uk/news/uk/politics/housing-minister-brandon-lewis-condemns-awardwinning-garden-city-plan-as-urban-sprawl-9712801.html.
5 'Lessons from Barcelona Report of the Urban Task Force study tour, 30 October – 2 November 1998', Roger Levett, consulted September 2014 at www.levett-therivel.co.uk/Lessons%20from%20Barcelona.htm.
6 'Le Corbusier's Chandigarh: an Indian city unlike any other', *The Financial Times*, 03/07/2017, consulted December 2015 at www.ft.com/cms/s/2/2a194cb4-1a8d-11e5-a130-2e7db721f996.html#slide0; 'City of Chandigarh', consulted December 2015 at http://architectuul.com/architecture/city-of-chandigarh.
7 My thanks to Seham Elmansuri, a doctoral candidate at Sheffield Hallam University, for drawing my attention to this.
8 The Oxford English Dictionary, consulted November 2015 at www.oed.com.
9 'Sir Christopher Wren's plan for rebuilding London', consulted June 2011 at www.oldlondonmaps.com/viewspages/0345.html.
10 Thanks are due to Kerrie Smith, a former Sheffield Hallam University masters student, for this observation.
11 Taken from the website of the Council of Europe, consulted December 2009 at https://wcd.coe.int/ViewDoc.jsp?Ref=CHARTE/URBAINE&Language=lanEnglish&Ver=original&Site=COE&BackColorInternet=1EB1E9&BackColorIntranet=FFCD4F&BackColorLogged=FFC679.

# References

Abercrombie, P. (1916). 'Study before town planning'. *Town Planning Review*, 6:3, 171–90.
Abercrombie, P. (1933). *Town and country planning*. London: T. Butterworth.
Abercrombie, P. (1945). *The Greater London Plan, 1944*. London: HMSO.
Abrams, P. (1968). *The origins of British sociology: 1834–1914*. Chicago: The University of Chicago Press.
Akkerman, A. (2000). 'Harmonies of urban design and discords of city-form: urban aesthetics in the rise of Western civilization'. *Journal of Urban Design*, 5:3, 267–90.
Al-Naim, M. (2014). *Political influences and paradigm shifts in the contemporary Arab cities: questioning the identity of urban form*. Milano, Italy: EDUCatt-Ente per il diritto allo studio universitario dell'Università Cattolica.
Albrechts, L. & Balducci, A. (2013). 'Practicing strategic planning: in search of critical features to explain the strategic character of plans'. *disP–The Planning Review*, 49:3, 16–27.
Arnstein, S. R. (1969). 'A ladder of citizen participation'. *Journal of the American Institute of Planners*, 35:4, 216–24.
Ascher, F. (1995). *Métapolis*. Paris: Odile Jacob.
Ascher, F. (2001). *Les nouveaux principes de l'urbanisme*. La Tour d'Aigues: Editions de l'Aube.
Bacon, E. N. (1974). *The Design of cities*. London: Thames and Hudson (original 1967).

Baker, D. C., Sipe, N. G. & Gleeson, B. J. (2006). 'Performance-based planning perspectives from the United States, Australia, and New Zealand'. *Journal of Planning Education and Research*, 25:4, 396–409.

Ball, M. (1999). 'Chasing a snail: innovation and housebuilding firms' strategies'. *Housing Studies*, 14: 9–22.

Barker, K. (2006). *Barker review of land use planning interim report*. London: HM Treasury.

Bastia, C. (2015). 'From justice in planning toward planning for justice: a capability approach'. *Planning Theory*: Online first: [doi] 1473095215571399 (consulted October 2015).

Bell, D. (2005). 'The emergence of contemporary masterplans: property markets and the value of urban design'. *Journal of Urban Design*, 10:1, 81–110.

Benevolo, L. (1967). *The origins of modern town planning*. Cambridge, MA: M.I.T. Press,

Besse, J.-M. (2011). *Voir / Faire / Voir: la carte et le project de paysage*. Maison départementale de l'habitat de l'Essonne: Ressources Documentaires, [online] URL: www.essonne.fr/cadre-de-vie/habitat-durable/la-maison-departementale-de-lhabitat-mdh/ressources-documentaires/#.Ve2qBPSU0uU (consulted September 2015).

Blandy, S. & Goodchild, B. (1999). 'From tenure to rights: conceptualising the changing focus of housing law in England'. *Housing, Theory and Society*, 16, 31–42.

Boehm, M., Bowman, D. & Zinn, J. O. (2013). 'Survey research and the production of evidence for social policy'. *Social Policy and Society*, 12:2, 309–18.

Boelens, L. & Coppens, T. (2012). 'From spatial planning to socio-spatial activation: emerging new planning approaches in post war housing estates in Flanders – the case of Luchtbal'. Paper presented at the *AESOP 26th Congress* in Ankara, Turkey.

Boudon, P. (1985). *Pessac de le Corbusier* [*Le Corbusier's Pessac*]. Paris: Bordas (original 1969).

Breheny, M. (1996). 'Centrists, decentrists and compromisers: views on the future of urban form'. In: Jenks, M., Burton, E. & Williams, K. (eds.), *The compact city: a sustainable urban form?* London: E & FN Spon, 13–35.

Buser, M. (2012). 'The production of space in metropolitan regions: a Lefebvrian analysis of governance and spatial change'. *Planning Theory*, 11:3, 279–98.

CABE—Commission for Architecture and the Built Environment (collective author) (2008). *Creating successful masterplans: a guide for clients*, second edition. London: CABE.

Çalışkan, K. & Callon, M. (2010). 'Economization, part 2: a research programme for the study of markets'. *Economy and Society*, 39:1, 1–32.

Calvert Spensley, J. (1918). 'Urban housing problems'. *Journal of the Royal Statistical Society*, Vol. LXXXI, Part II.

Carmona, M. (2001). *Housing design quality: through policy, guidance and review*. London: Spon Press.

Cherry, G. (1996). *Town planning in Britain since 1900: The rise and fall of the planning ideal*. Oxford: Blackwell.

Choay, F. (1969). *The modern city: planning in the 19th century*. London: Studio Vista (translated from an unknown French original).

Choay, F. (1996). *La regle et le modele*. Paris: Éditions du Seuil (original 1980).

Choay, F. (1995). 'Le règne de l'urbain et la mort de la ville'. In: Roman, J. (ed.) *Chronique des idees contemporaines*. Bréal: Rosny, 366–8.

Coleman, N. (2013). 'Utopian prospect of Henri Lefebvre'. *Space and Culture*, 16:3, 349–63.
Davy, B. (2011). 'Property and the politics of belonging'. *FLOOR Working Paper No. 9*, [online] URL: www.floorgroup.raumplanung.tu-dortmund.de/joomla/index.php/working-papers (consulted October 2015).
de Vega, E. P. (2010). 'Experiencing built space: affect and movement'. *Proceedings of the European Society for Aesthetics*, 2, 386–409.
Deleuze, G. (1993). *The fold: Leibniz and the Baroque*. London: Athlone Press (French original).
Deleuze, G. & Guattari, F. (1987). *A thousand plateaus: capitalism and schizophrenia*. Translation and Foreword by Brian Massumi. Minneapolis, MN: University of Minnesota Press (French original 1980).
Douglas, M. (1966). *Purity and danger*. London: Routledge and Keagan Paul.
Dovey, K. (2012). 'Informal urbanism and complex adaptive assemblage'. *International Development Planning Review*, 34:4, 349–68.
Eden, W. A. (1946). 'The art of building cities'. *The Town Planning Review*, IV:2, 150–7.
Esping-Andersen, G. (2002). 'Towards the good society, once again'. In: Esping-Andersen et al. (eds.), *Why we need a new welfare state*. Oxford: Oxford University Press, 1–25.
Faludi, A. (2000). 'The performance of spatial planning'. *Planning Practice & Research*,15:4, 299–318.
Fishman, R. (1977). *Urban utopias in the twentieth century*. New York: Basic Books.
Flint, J. (2003). 'Housing and ethopolitics: constructing identities of active consumption and responsible community'. *Economy and Society*, 32:4, 611–29
Flint, J. (2015). 'Housing and the realignment of urban socio-spatial contracts'. *Housing, Theory and Society* 32:1, 39–53.
Forshaw, J. H. and Abercrombie, P. (1943). *County of London plan*. London: Macmillan and Co.
Foucault, M. (1984). 'Des espaces autres, Hétérotopies'. *Architecture, Mouvement, Continuité* 5, 46–49, [online] URL: http://foucault.info/documents/heteroTopia/foucault.heteroTopia.fr.html (consulted October 2010) (French original 1967).
Frew, T., Baker, D. & Donehue, P. (2016). 'Performance based planning in Queensland: a case of unintended plan-making outcomes'. *Land Use Policy*, 50, 239–51.
Geddes, P. (1915). *Cities in evolution*. London: Williams and Norgate.
Galloway, T. D. & Mahayni, R. G. (1977). 'Planning theory in retrospect: the process of paradigm change'. *Journal of the American Institute of Planners*, 43:1, 62–71.
Glass, R. (1955). 'Urban sociology in Great Britain: a trend report'. *Current Sociology* 4:4, 5–76.
González, S. (2011). 'Bilbao and Barcelona "in motion". How urban regeneration "models" travel and mutate in the global flows of policy tourism'. *Urban Studies*, 48:7, 1397–1418.
Goodchild, B. (2008). *Homes, cities and neighbourhoods*. Aldershot, Hampshire: Routledge.
Goodchild B. & Hickman P. (2006). 'Towards a regional strategy for the North of England? An assessment of the "Northern Way"'. *Regional Studies*, 40:1, 121–33.

Hall, P. (2002). *Urban and regional planning,* 4th edition. London and New York: Routledge (original 1975).
Hall, P., Gracey, H., Drewett, R. & Thomas, R. (1973). *The containment of urban England, volume two: the planning system.* London: George Allen and Unwin.
Harvey, D. (2003). 'The right to the city'. *International Journal of Urban and Regional Research,* 27:4, 939–41.
Hatz, G. (2010). 'Theorizing and evaluating Vienna's concepts and performances of quality spaces'. 24th *AESOP Annual Conference, Finland, 7–10 July 2010, Book of proceedings,* [online] URL: http://aesop2010.tkk.fi/index.html (consulted July 2012).
Healey, P. (1992). 'Planning through debate: the communicative turn in planning theory'. *Town Planning Review,* 63:2, 143–62.
Healey, P. (2004). 'The treatment of space and place in the new strategic spatial planning in Europe'. *International Journal of Urban and Regional Research,* 28:1, 45–67.
Heraud, B. J. (1968). 'Social class and the new towns'. *Urban Studies,* 5:1, 33–58.
Herbert, G. (1963). 'The organic analogy in town planning'. *Journal of the American Planning Association,* 29:3, 198–209.
Hester, R. T. (2006). *Design for ecological democracy.* Cambridge, MA: MIT Press.
Hillier, J. (2007). *Stretching beyond the horizon: a multiplanar theory of spatial planning and governance.* Aldershot, England: Ashgate.
Hillier, J. (2008). 'Plan(e) speaking: a multiplanar theory of spatial planning'. *Planning Theory,* 7, 24–49.
Hillier, J. (2010). 'Strategic navigation in an ocean of theoretical and practice complexity'. In: Hillier, J. and Healey, P. (eds.,) *The Ashgate research companion to planning theory: conceptual challenges for spatial planning.* Farnham Surrey: Ashgate, 447–80.
Hillier, J. & van Wezemael, J. (2008). 'Empty, swept and garnished: the public finance initiative case of Throckley Middle School'. *Space and Polity,* 12:2, 157–81.
Hinchliffe, S. (2003). 'Inhabiting-landscapes and natures'. In: Anderson, K. et al. (eds.), *Handbook of cultural geography.* London: Sage Publications, 207–25.
Hoch, C. (2009). 'Planning craft: how planners compose plans'. *Planning Theory* 8, 219–42.
Holcombe, R. G. (2012). 'Planning and the invisible hand: allies or adversaries?' *Planning Theory,* 12:2, 199–210.
Howard, E. (1985). *To-morrow: a peaceful path to real reform.* Eastbourne, East Sussex: Attic Books (first published in 1898, republished in 1902 as Garden Cities of To-morrow).
Hutchins, E. (1997). 'Mediation and automatization'. In: Cole, M., Engeströ, Y. & Vasquez, O. (eds.), *Mind, culture, and activity: seminal papers from the Laboratory of Comparative Human Cognition.* Cambridge: Cambridge University Press, 338–53.
Ingold, T. (1993). 'The temporality of the landscape'. *World Archaeology,* 25:2. 152–74.
Ingold, T. (2006). 'Rethinking the animate, re-animating thought'. *Ethnos: Journal of Anthropology,* 71:1, 9–20.
Jorgensen A. & Tylecote, M. (2007). 'Ambivalent landscapes—wilderness in the urban interstices'. *Landscape Research,* 32:4, 443–62.
Keeble, L. (1969). *Principles and practice of town and country planning,* 4th edition. London: Estates Gazette (1st edition 1952).

Keen, S. (1993). 'Use-value, exchange value, and the demise of Marx's labor theory of value'. *Journal of the History of Economic Thought*, 15:01, 107–21.

Kwa, C. (2002). 'Romantic and Baroque conceptions of complex wholes in the sciences'. In Law, J. & Mol, A. (eds.), *Complexities: social studies of knowledge practices*. Durham, NC: Duke University Press, 23–52.

Laurian, L., Day, M., Berke, P., Ericksen, N., Backhurst, M., Crawford, J. & Dixon, J. (2004). 'Evaluating plan implementation: a conformance-based methodology'. *Journal of the American Planning Association*, 70:4, 471–80.

Law, J. (2004). 'And if the global were small and noncoherent? Method, complexity, and the Baroque'. *Environment and Planning D*, 22:1, 13–26.

Law, J. (2009). 'Seeing like a survey'. *Cultural sociology* 3:2, 239–56.

Le Dantec, J. P. (1991). 'For a Baroque approach to cities and architecture'. *Architecture and Behaviour/Architecture et Comportement*, 7:4, 467–78.

Leary, M. E. (2013). 'A Lefebvrian analysis of the production of glorious, gruesome public space in Manchester'. *Progress in Planning*, 85, 1–52.

Lefèbvre. H. (1976). *The Survival of capitalism: reproduction of the relations of production*. London: Frank Bryant (French original 1973).

Lefèbvre, H. (1985). 'Introduction'. In: Boudon, P. (ed.), *Pessac de le Corbusier* [*Le Corbusier's Pessac*]. Paris: Bordas (original 1969).

Lefèbvre, H. (1991). *The production of space*. Oxford: Blackwell (French original 1974).

Lefèbvre, H. (1998). 'Le Droit à la Ville'. In: Ansay, P. & Schoonbrodt, R. (eds.), *Penser la Ville*. Brussels: AAM Éditions (extract from an original published in 1968).

Lehtovuori, P. (2010). *Experience and conflict: the production of urban space*. London: Ashgate.

Loh, C. G. (2011). 'Assessing and interpreting non-conformance in land-use planning implementation'. *Planning Practice and Research*, 26:3, 271–87.

Lou, J. (2007). 'Revitalizing Chinatown into a heterotopia: a geosemiotic analysis of shop signs in Washington, DC's Chinatown'. *Space and Culture* 10, 170–94.

Lynch, K. (1984). *Good city form*. Cambridge, MA: MIT Press.

Lynch, K. & Hack, G. (1984). *Site planning*. Cambridge, MA: MIT Press.

McClymont, K. (2011). 'Revitalising the political: development control and agonism in planning'. *Planning Theory*, 10:3, 239–56.

McFarlane, C. (2011a). 'The city as assemblage: dwelling and urban space'. *Environment and Planning-Part D*, 29:4, 649.

McFarlane, C. (2011b). *Learning the city: knowledge and translocal assemblage*. Chichester, Sussex: Wiley-Blackwell/ John Wiley & Sons.

MacLure, M. (2006). 'The bone in the throat: some uncertain thoughts on Baroque method'. *International Journal of Qualitative Studies in Education*, 19:6, 729–45.

McNamee, S. (2000). 'Foucault's heterotopia and children's everyday lives'. *Childhood*, 7:4, 479–91.

Marshall, T. H. (1950). *Citizenship and social class: and other essays*. Cambridge, UK: University Press.

Mason, P. and Barnes, M. (2007). 'Constructing theories of change methods and sources'. *Evaluation*, 13:2, 151–70.

Merrifield, A. (1993). 'Place and space: A Lefebvrian reconciliation'. *Transactions of the Institute of British Geographers*, New Series, 18:4, 516–31.

Moore Milroy, B. (2009). *Thinking planning and urbanism*. Vancouver: UBC Press.

Mouffe, C. (2000). *The democratic paradox*. London: Verso.
Mumford, L. (1966). *The city in history*. London: Penguin (US original 1961).
Nicol, C. & Hooper, A. (1999). 'Contemporary change and the housebuilding industry: concentration and standardisation in production'. *Housing Studies*, 14:1, 57–76.
Nussbaum, M. (2003). 'Capabilities as fundamental entitlements: Sen and social justice'. *Feminist Economics*, 9:2–3, 33–59.
Nyseth, T. (2012). *Fluid planning: a meaningless concept or a rational response to uncertainty in urban planning?* INTECH Open Access Publisher, [online] URL: http://cdn.intechopen.com/pdfs/33243.pdf (consulted December 2015).
Oliveira, V. and Pinho, P. (2010). 'Evaluation in urban planning: advances and prospects'. *Journal of Planning Literature*, 24:4, 343–61.
Peck, J. (2011). 'Geographies of policy: from transfer-diffusion to mobility-mutation'. *Progress in Human Geography*, 35:6, 773–97.
Peck, J. & Theodore, N. (2010). 'Mobilizing policy: models, methods, and mutations'. *Geoforum*, 41:2, 169–74.
Polanyi, K. (1957). *The great transformation*. Boston: Beacon Press (UK original 1944).
Purdom, C. B. (1913). *The garden city*. London: J. M. Dent.
Rapoport, E. R. (2014). *Mobilizing sustainable urbanism: international consultants and the assembling of a planning model*. Doctoral thesis, UCL (University College London), [online] URL: http://discovery.ucl.ac.uk/1449528/ (consulted December 2015).
Rees, J. & Lord, A. (2013). 'Making space: putting politics back where it belongs in the construction of city regions in the North of England'. *Local Economy*, 28:7–8, 679–95.
Rose, N. (1999). 'Inventiveness in politics'. *Economy and Society*, 28:3, 467–93.
Roy, A. (2005). 'Urban informality: toward an epistemology of planning'. *Journal of the American Planning Association*, 71:2, 147–58.
Royal Commission on Local Taxation (1901). *Final report*. England and Wales. London: HMSO, Cd. 638.
Sandercock, L. (1998). *Towards cosmopolis*. Chichester: John Wiley.
Scharenberg, A. & Bader, I. (2009). Berlin's waterfront site struggle'. *City*, 13:2–3, 325–35.
Schmelzkopf, K. (2002). 'Incommensurability, land use, and the right to space: community gardens in New York City'. *Urban Geography*, 23:4, 323–43.
Schön, D. A. (1988). 'Designing: rules, types and worlds'. *Design Studies* 9:3, 181–90.
Sen, A. (2005). 'Human rights and capabilities'. *Journal of Human Development* 6:2, 151–66.
Sennett, R., (1992). *The conscience of the eye: the design and social life of cities*. New York: WW Norton & Company.
Sert, J. L. (1942). *Can Our Cities Survive? An ABC of Urban Problems, their Analyses, their Solutions: Based on the Proposals Formulated by CIAM*. Cambridge, MA: Harvard University Press.
Seyfang, G. & Smith, A. (2007). 'Grassroots innovations for sustainable development: towards a new research and policy agenda. *Environmental Politics*, 16:4, 584–603.
Simonsen, K. (2005). 'Bodies, sensations, space and time: the contribution from Henri Lefebvre'. *Geografiska Annaler. Series B. Human Geography*, 87:1, 1–14.

Skeat, W. W. (2005). *A concise etymological dictionary of the English language*. New York: Cosimo (original published in London in 1910).

Surin, K. (1990). 'Marxism(s) and "the withering away of the state"'. *Social Text*, 35–54.

Sutcliffe, A. (1981). *Towards the planned City: Germany, Britain, the United States and France 1780–1914*. Oxford: Basil Blackwell.

Tafuri, M. (1976). *Architecture and utopia*. Cambridge, MA and London: The MIT Press.

Talen, E. (1996). 'Do plans get implemented? A review of evaluation in planning'. *Journal of Planning Literature*, 10:3, 248–59.

Taylor, N. (1998). *Urban planning theory since 1945*. London: Sage.

Tewdwr-Jones, M. (1999). 'Discretion, flexibility and certainty in British planning: emerging ideological conflicts and inherent political tensions'. *Journal of Planning Education and Research*, 18:3, 244–56.

Tiesdell, S. and MacFarlane, G. (2007). 'The part and the whole: implementing masterplans in Glasgow's New Gorbals'. *Journal of Urban Design*, 12:3, 407–33.

Tonkiss, F. (2005). *Space, the city and social theory: social relations and urban forms*. Cambridge, UK: Polity.

Triggs, H. I. (1909). *Town planning past, present and possible*. London: Methuen & Co.

Unwin, R. (1909). *Town planning in practice*. London: T. Fisher Unwin.

URBED (2014). *Uxcester Garden City: Wolfson Economics Prize Submission 2014*, [online] URL: www.urbed.com/wolfson-economic-prize (consulted September 2014).

Villa, R. (2000). *Barrio-Logos: space and place in urban Chicano literature and culture*. Austin, TX: University of Texas Press.

Virilio, P. (1984). *Speed and politics: an essay on dromology*. New York: Semiotext(e) (French original 1977).

Ward, S. V. (2013). 'Cities as planning models'. *Planning Perspectives* 28:2, 295–313.

Wood, S. (2009). 'Desiring docklands: deleuze and urban planning discourse'. *Planning Theory*, 8: 191–216.

Xue, C. Q. L., Zhai, H. & Mitchenere, B. (2011). 'Shaping Lujiazui: The formation and building of the CBD in Pudong, Shanghai'. *Journal of Urban Design*, 16:2, 209–32.

Zucker, P. (1945). 'The aesthetics of space in architecture, sculpture, and city planning'. *The Journal of Aesthetics and Art Criticism*, 4:1, 12–9.

Zucker, P. (1955). 'Space and movement in high Baroque city planning'. *Journal of the Society of Architectural Historians*, 14:1, 8–13.

# 3 Political and Economic Planning

Concepts of planning as a process may be either personal or collective. Individuals make plans, as do firms, governments and public agencies. In urban planning, however, the process is invariably collective, either in terms of agency or impact or both. Concepts of collective process planning and of blueprint planning run together and interact with one another and have done so since the 1930s. The history of planning as process is very different from that of blueprints, however. Concepts of planning as process stem from the great planning debate of the 1930s and 1940s (not from the pre-1914 era) and they were about central planning or political and economic planning as it was also called. Unlike blueprint styles of town planning, moreover, the idea of planning preceded its widespread application in practice. Planning represented both common sense and an aspect of modernity—a means by which governments could respond to the economic crises of the 1930s, improve the rationality of decision-making and increase the productive capacity of the nation (Marwick 1964).

By the 1950s, the crises of the 1930s had largely disappeared in most countries and governments were able to pursue full employment and the provision of welfare services, of varied scope and ambition, without the need for a full-blown central planning apparatus. The scope of planning, whether economic or land use, became more narrowly defined and ths narrowing of scope continued after the subsequent emergence of neoliberal and market-based critiques. Nevertheless, the earlier debates and, in particular, the work of Mannheim ([1940] 1971) remain important in setting a context. Most subsequent debates about political and economic planning amount to either an elaboration or refutation of Mannheim's ideas.

## Mannheim's 'Man and Society'

For Mannheim ([1940] 1971, 193), economic and political planning was:

> foresight deliberately applied to human affairs so that the social process is no longer merely the product of conflict and competition.

Planning, so defined, is a partial alternative to conflict and competition, but cannot wholly replace these. It is concerned with strategic or non-routine decisions, unlike administration, and concerned with the application of the techniques of social science, rather the ideologies of political parties.

Planning is moreover distinct from 'establishment', Mannheim's term for what later became called blueprint planning. Establishment deals with the preparation of an abstract artefact in the absence of an economic or social context. In addition, 'in establishment, the materials of construction are first brought together and then placed in a predetermined relationship with one another'. In contrast, 'planning', that is to say political and economic planning, deals with the use of 'what is immediately available' and with forces that are 'interacting on different levels' in society (ibid., 191–2).

Though Mannheim did not say so, planning and establishment are interrelated. For GDH Cole (1945), writing at about the same time, the relevant distinction was between economic planning and town planning. Economic planning and town planning could be undertaken separately but were best undertaken together as economic planning would help support and implement town and regional plans through stabilising the economy, through determining the form and timing of building programmes and through resolving issues relating to land values. Various reforms introduced by the post-1945 Labour government in Britain were intended to have exactly this effect. Moreover, if economic planning supported town planning, as GDH Cole suggested, the logical implication is that central planning would also support 'establishment', to use Mannheim's term. However, Mannheim was silent on this. Mannheim's concerns were not with a specific set of measures or with the organisation of urban space, but with the planning process as a technique of government.

Apart from clarifying the definition of planning, Mannheim is also helpful in identifying the conditions that would emerge. Planning was not an optional choice for governments. It was a functional necessity that stemmed from fundamental social changes.

In part, planning emerged from changes in the role of the state in the early 20th century, as was amply documented by later historians (Booth 2009; Wagner 2001, 44–8). The liberal state of the past, noted Mannheim, had gradually been transformed into a 'social service state'. A combination of measures—attempts to redistribute wealth, to provide national insurance, to provide social housing, to even out the trade cycle, to provide public broadcasting services—had ensured that the state was becoming more and more powerful, to the point that it was 'absorbing society' (Mannheim [1940] 1971, 336–7). Involvement of the state in social affairs implied, in turn, a greater role for social science in determining policy. Further, the principles of scientific management had started to be applied to mass industrial production in the private sector and had spread from the US to Britain and continental Europe. The scientific management of industry marked a new stage in the development of social technology. Political and economic planning meant the general application of similar principles, in a way that might benefit the population as a whole rather than benefit the operation of specific businesses.

The trends of the early 20th century were not sufficient to bring about a full framework of political and economic planning, however. The growth of state powers, even if supported by the growth of scientific management, could easily become dissipated in fragmented, uncoordinated initiatives. There had to be some sense of crisis to motivate concerted action. But what type of crisis? The 1930s were certainly a time of political and economic crisis. The analysis of Mannheim is notable, however, for its silence on the economy or on international instability, other than the risk that dangerous regimes might come to power owing to social conflict. Instead, the concern is to identify those social tendencies or 'points of departure' that might separately or together trigger a social crisis (Mannheim [1940] 1971, 39–75).

Planning, as conceived in 'Man and Society', is therefore not a utopian project that seeks to remodel society, as some critics, for example Popper (1944), have supposed. Planning, as conceived by Mannheim, is not even concerned with social reform, as suggested by Friedmann (1987, 87–105). Planning is, instead, a technique of government, concerned above all with the promotion of stability, but in principle also concerned with the promotion of change, if the latter is necessary for long-term stability. However, the very acceptance of planning was likely to prove radical at an emotional level. Central planning would not come about and would not last without changes in behaviour and expectations, this to be achieved through public education and the manipulation of the context through social controls (Mannheim [1940] 1971, 193–237).

Three tendencies and potential sources are identified, as follows:

1 'The disproportionate development of human capacities', with the growth of potentially destructive technologies
2 'The principle of fundamental democratization'
3 'The principle of increasing interdependence'.

The three tendencies merit a closer examination. The first, 'the disproportionate development of human capacities', would, from the 1980s onwards, be mostly about the risks caused by the impact of technology and human activities on the environment. The examples given by Mannheim are, in contrast, mostly about the destructive capabilities of weapons of war, such as bombs. Yet the avoidance of war depends on international co-operation and negotiations rather than planning. It is difficult to see how planning within a single country is relevant, except ironically for the mobilisation necessary to fight a war!

The second tendency, 'the principle of fundamental democratisation', expresses an internal contradiction in Mannheim's argument. Planning, as defined by Mannheim, involves the application of social science, technical skills and specialist knowledge. The logical implication of democratisation is therefore to raise further, open-ended, questions: about how planners and planning would be made democratically accountable (Friedmann 1987, 103). At the same time, democratisation implies that more people will want to have a say in decision-making and not leave events to chance or to the market. Planning, albeit an argumentative and democratically controlled planning process, is a suitable response.

The limitations of Mannheim's approach were recognised by other supporters of planning. For Wootton (1945), for example, planning involved a process of 'discovering' agreement (ibid., 148). In most countries, most people would agree on the need to eradicate mass unemployment, to improve standards of education or to make the best use of resources, even if they disagreed about the means to achieve those ends and even if, in addition, a minority of interested parties were to lose out from the relevant policies. Once, moreover, a planning framework is established, it would open up the potential for 'civic activity', that is to say public involvement in local government and the administration of local services (ibid., 173–4, 176). The introduction of planning would not, therefore, mean the end of politics or conflict.

Mannheim's third principle of 'increasing interdependence' was arguably the most persuasive. Mannheim ([1940] 1971, 50) argues that modern society is increasingly sensitive to accidents and unexpected events.

> In a well organised railway, for instance, the effects of an accident are more far-reaching than they were in the stage coach system of transport where accidents and dislocation were taken for granted from the very beginning.

The organisation of a railway system provides an example of functional interdependence, where different elements, both human and technological, have either a supportive or a destructive impact on the rest. Planning ensures that technological systems, including urban systems, work smoothly and efficiently, without risk of harm to residents. Moreover, planning becomes ever more necessary given the existence of conflicting public demands on those systems and given, in addition, the increasing sophistication of technology with all the various risks that this involves.

Functional interdependencies make some form of planning inevitable. Strictly speaking, however, the logic of functional interdependencies only applies to specific systems. It is not logical to jump from a railway system to the economy or society as a whole. Moreover, the degree of functional interdependencies varies. For example, the use of a railway system needs to be timetabled whereas a road system does not. To return to the concept of urban space as an assemblage of different elements: this involves a mixture of functional interdependencies and other elements that merely co-exist with one another. Writing from the perspective of actor-network theory, for example, Latour and Hermant (2006) suggest that the contemporary city is dependent on so many varied networks and systems—transport, energy, waste disposal and so on—that it cannot be viewed or understood as a whole. Each network has to be examined and planned separately, drawing out and making visible the interconnections and also the implications for the life of the city.

The implication is, therefore, for a relatively loose strategic planning framework, at the level of a city, a city region or a district, not the tightly organised centralised national system envisaged by Mannheim. Strategic planning is, nevertheless, likely to persist because the institutional actors, those who own or manage the networks, 'find it useful as a way of knowing what they should do, how they should do it, with whom, where, when, and why' (Bryson et al. 2009, 203).

The significance of functional interdependencies is recognised by neoliberal critics of planning. Moroni and Andersson (2014, 11-4), for example, argue that the acceptance of central planning in the mid-20th century was dependent on the existence of city-wide systems of infrastructure covering water supply, sewerage disposal and energy and that, in the future, these technological systems might change to allow ever more decentralised, flexible solutions. An alternative scenario is that new citywide infrastructures might emerge in the future, for example heat networks, and that these may also require a coordinated approach at the level of neighbourhoods and cities (Kelly & Pollitt 2010).

As an aside, infrastructure interdependence and planning are not directly related to ownership. Neither privatisation nor ownership by not-for-profit agencies necessarily mean the splintering of provision as was once postulated by Graham and Marvin (2001). Different privatised or nor-for-profit providers can be and are commonly required to work together through partnership contracts or regulatory mechanisms and may also be required to serve poorer districts, even if this is less profitable (Rutherford 2008). Indirect controls over economic actors is possible, as is also a theme in 'Man and Society'. In any case, coordination between different state agencies and not just private providers may prove problematic.

## Planning as an Ideal Type

Mannheim's definition of planning is only a brief, general characterisation. To provide detailed insights into the operation of practice—any type of planning practice whether economic, land use or environmental—the definition needs to be elaborated through the creation of relevant ideal types. 'Ideal' as used in 'ideal type' does not mean desirable; it has no relationship with ideal cities as these are used in blueprint planning and is not intended to provoke an instant evaluation. Ideal types can be constructed, for example, about criminal activities as well as charitable work. Constructing an ideal type of planning does not mean that planning itself is desirable. An ideal type is instead a method of analysis associated with Weber (1947). It indicates a social practice that is defined in terms of a general idea and a series of linked characteristcs rather than a single one. An ideal type is ideal because it simplifies and stands aside from the details of social reality, whilst also providing a bridge between theory and history (Rogers 1969; Watkins 1952).

Mannheim defined planning as a partial alternative to 'conflict', meaning politics, and to 'competition', meaning the market. Two ideal types are therefore relevant, dealing respectively with political and economic practice. Discussion will start with the economic as this has generated more subsequent discussion.

## The Economic Attributes

Economic planning is an exercise in allocating resources to different activities, groups and places and is generally associated with the specification of national and regional production targets. Land use planning, town planning and the various forms of environmental and urban planning may be understood in analogous terms as a specialised version of resource allocation dealing with land, property, infrastructure and the resources that constitute the human habitat and offer a place to live and work. This being so, the economic aspects of urban planning involve the same or a similar ideal type as economic planning.

A point of clarification is necessary. Saying that urban planning may be analysed through the same or a similar ideal type is not to say that urban planning is a mere subset of economic planning. If production is prioritised over everything else, as occurred from about 1950 to 1980 in the former centrally planned economies of Eastern Europe, the quality of life and environment issues will be neglected (Nedovic-Budic 2001; Pavlínek & Pickles 2000). The aims of economic planning, and its sensitivity to public pressure, as well as its relationship to the market, determine outcomes on the ground. The experience of central planning in Eastern Europe is also not popular in current discussions of either planning practice or planning theory, almost certainly because the governments then in power in these countries have long been discredited as both undemocratic and inefficient. Even so, the experience in Eastern Europe is useful in providing what would now be considered an extreme case of central planning and relevant, in addition, because it provides the context for the analysis of Kornai (1970, 1971, 336), probably the most authoritative analysis of its type.

Economic planning, suggests Kornai (1970, 3–4) is best understood as a form of collective intelligence: a process of 'cognition and compromise' whose 'main purposes ... are the collection and careful evaluation of information about the future'. The market also offers a means of collecting and assessing information, but the operating principles differ. To define the difference, Kornai uses the terminology of a 'pure' market economy and 'pure' central planning. However, the intention and the effect is to provide an ideal type understood as a series of characteristics linked to a central idea. Information flows in planning, suggests Kornai (1971, 336) have the following characteristics:

- the use of 'statistical reports: plan proposals and counter proposals', rather than offers and counteroffers or the use of contracts made between individuals;
- 'several transmissions' between relevant information and the real action and, therefore, a considerable time lag between the analysis of information and real action;
- a long-term memory and time horizon;
- 'Variables measured in both physical and value terms' with the former having an outstanding role;
- no exchange of money during the flow of goods; and
- vertical flows are dominant, from the top to the bottom of a bureaucracy.

So defined, economic planning is, in principle, independent of the characteristics of the actors involved in plan preparation and implementation. Planning may be undertaken by private agencies as well as by the public sector or public officials (see, for example, Lai 2014). Planning is unlikely to be wholly separated from the state, however (ibid.). The state has too much of an interest in the outcome and private power carries its own risks. In any case, it is difficult to see how an extensive, wide-ranging planning system, whether an economic or a land use planning system, could be either established or its legitimacy maintained by any institutional actor, other than the state.

An ideal type provides a unifying framework of elements that are associated with one another. All the different elements do not have to exist in any given example of practice, though the omissions are themselves of interest. In historical sociology, the ideal type is a means to an end, the end being an exercise in mapping institutional differences as these occur at different times and in different countries. The origins of Kornai's ideal type as an extreme or 'pure' case ensure, in any case, the likely existence of departures in countries where the government wishes to encourage private investment.

The possibility or likelihood of departures is, in turn, relevant to a claim by Lai (2014) that the plan–market dichotomy is fallacious. Lai (2014, 14) notes that development planning in Hong Kong and China has typically operated through the use of negotiated development contracts, undertaken within a policy brief and framework, and largely reliant on the powers of public land ownership. The contracts allow private developers a greater say than planning by decree and similar 'diktats'. Lai does not discuss the variability of practice in relation to an ideal type. Instead, reference is made to a conventional definition that, like Kornai's types, excludes the use of contracts. However, the existence of a departure does not undermine the ideal type, except as a descriptive classification. The departures merely suggest that the world is more complex than a simplified construction might suggest.

To provide a brief account of the historical background: in Hong Kong, development contracts originated under British colonial rule in a situation of extensive government land holding and where the law of leasehold could substitute and go beyond the powers available under a statutory planning system (Lai 2004). In China, the use of development contracts has enabled joint ventures between the state and private investors in the period after the reform of the centrally planned system of economic development. Criticisms remain, however, about the transparency of the decision-making process and about the dominance of market incentives and business interests (Heilmann & Melton 2013; Wu 2001; Wu et al. 2007; Yeh et al. 1999).

In Britain, negotiated planning agreements (known as Section 106 agreements in England and Wales) offer another example of a contract, in which a developer agrees to make certain public contributions in order to obtain planning permission. These break another characteristic of the ideal type in that, in a Section 106 agreement, money may change hands at the time that planning permission is agreed. As a result, for some critics, negotiated planning agreements introduce a commercial, market-oriented ethos in a system that is otherwise concerned with making decisions on the basis of plans, reports and physical criteria (Campbell & Henneberry 2005). The way that negotiations are undertaken in private is also of concern, especially for amenity groups concerned with the likely impact of the proposal. Section 106 agreements have nevertheless proved helpful in securing the implementation of development proposals and have also enabled the local authority to secure benefits for the local community.

The histories of development and planning contracts in Hong Kong, China and Britain have little in common with one another, except that in all cases governments have sought to combine elements of planning and the market in an effort to ensure better outcomes, as they would see it. Planning, understood as an economic ideal type, has a series of *prima facia* limitations and advantages. On the negative side, because it is hierarchical and top down in operation, economic planning is relatively remote from the pattern of costs, the wishes of consumers and the requirements of private investors—hence the introduction of compromises and market-oriented elements. On the positive side, planning enables a longer-term perspective, promotes the exchange of information and promotes coordination. Planning, considered as an ideal type, does not necessarily guarantee the pursuit of environmental and social aims, however, unless, of course, environmental and social criteria and their related spatial requirements are institutionalised within the system.

## The Neoliberal Critique

Merely listing the advantages and disadvantages of planning as an ideal type does not do justice to the arguments of the anti-planning critics. Planning is not just a neutral, analytical concept, as the concept of ideal type suggests. In Britain and other Western countries, planning and in particular planning by the state, has repeatedly raised ideological issues about the organisation of the state and society. Planning has, moreover, raised these issues since at least the time of the great debate of the 1940s.

The title of Hayek's 'The Road to Serfdom', published in 1944, summarises the anti-planning position as it first emerged. Planning would reduce or completely negate the freedom of the individual and in doing so would lead to economic failure. The complexity of the modern economy and society makes competition the only method by which the coordination of affairs can be adequately achieved (Hayek [1944] 2001, 59). Economic co-ordination depends on the operation of the price mechanism and this in turn means that the producers of all types should be free to set their own prices in competition with one another. Prices cannot realistically be determined from above by means of bureaucratic decisions. The information required for such a task is simply too great and, in any case, prices are inherently dynamic and dependent on trends in a multiplicity of different factors whose interaction is more or less impossible to predict in advance.

Hayek is an example of a neoliberal thinker who sought to defend and remake the economic liberalism of the pre-1939 and pre-1919 eras against the threat of central planning. The term 'neoliberal' itself was probably first used after a meeting of like-minded intellectuals in Paris in 1938 (Denord 2008, 48). In particular, Hayek is an example of what Moroni and Andersson (2014, 8–9) and others have called the 'classical liberal' variant of neoliberalism, concerned mostly with the clarification and demarcation of appropriate roles for the public and the private sectors and concerned, in addition, with the failures of government as well as the failures of the market.

Other even more radical or extreme, depending on one's perspective, variants of neoliberalism have subsequently emerged, including, according to Andersson (ibid), 'minarchism' and 'anarcho-capitalism'. The minarchist position is that the state should be reduced to the role of a policeman 'preventing and punishing force, theft and fraud'. Anarcho-capitalists believe that 'private planning is always and everywhere superior to public planning'. Anarcho-capitalism also goes by the name of libertarianism.

All these variants of neoliberalism have become more important, as governments have sought to promote national efficiency and competitiveness in the face of globalisation and international financial pressures. Neoliberalism has moved from a set of ideas, sometimes called 'proto-neoliberalism', to a policy agenda that governments could apply in apply in practice (Peck and Tickell 1992). As a set of ideas, neoliberalism is about the niceties of constitutional principles, as for example defined by Hayek amongst others. From the 1970s and even more so from the 1980s onwards, however, proto-neoliberalism has been accompanied and to an extent overshadowed by its application.

The movement from proto neoliberalism to its application amounts to a shift in the assumptions of analysis as well as a movement over time. Mannheim, in common with others in the 1930s and 1940s, saw modern society as moving along a path towards the welfare state, mass consumption and central planning. In response, proto neoliberalism emerged as a philosophy of protest that tolerated no ambiguities. Hayek ([1960] 1978) talks, for example, of the ideal of 'spontaneous' social growth that 'allows further experience to lead to modifications and improvements' (ibid., 63). The 'rationalist' is the enemy of spontaneity—the rationalist 'who desires to subject everything to human reason' and who 'aims at control and predictability'. (ibid., 38). Therefore rational planning is rejected out of hand. In proto neoliberalism, there is no middle position, no recognition that the contemporary economy and the contemporary city is likely to contain a mixture of planned and spontaneous elements and that, in any case, there are degrees of strictness in planning, from most prescriptive to the light touch.

In contrast, following recession in the 1970s, governments have pursued neoliberal strategies, removing constraints on business, cutting costly public services and introducing other measures to make local markets work in a competitive manner in the context of an increasingly global economy where distances measured in terms of time and cost have shrunk (Harvey 1989; Short 2004). Neoliberalism has been applied, but in a way that admits the messy world of political compromises.

The application of neoliberalism has been facilitated by the way that most neoliberals, Hayek included, came to accept that town planning was an exception to their preference for spontaneous action, a necessary evil. In doing this, neoliberal theorists also provided a market-oriented justification, albeit a narrowly conceived justification that has persisted and is widely accepted (Lai 2002; Sorensen and Day 1981). For example, Hayek (1978 [1960]) argued that, while economic progress depended in general on private property, freedom of contract and the price mechanism, these could not apply to city life.

> In the close contiguity of city living, the price mechanism reflects only imperfectly the benefits or harm to others that a property owner may cause by his actions. (ibid., 349)

Instead, a plan is necessary to establish 'the general conditions to which all developments of a district or neighbourhood must conform' (ibid, 350).

As is implied by the reference to general conditions, the plan itself should not be too heavy handed or prescriptive. The price mechanism, though an imperfect guide, remained 'an indispensable guide if development is to be left to private initiative' (ibid.). Planning, it was suggested, should not serve any other objective, apart from the promotion of competition. For Hayek ([1946] 2001, 43), therefore, 'Planning and competition can be combined only by planning for competition.'

The neoliberal rationale has been put a slightly different way. Planning, according to transaction cost theory, is justified when the costs of private management and private negotiation become higher than the costs of management and negotiation undertaken by a public agency (Alexander 1992; Dawkins 2000). Transaction costs refer to the costs of running a business or any other activity, including undertaking the development work associated with that business. The complexity and diversity of interests in towns and cities makes the use of some form of planning more efficient in principle than repeated private negotiation and the use of civil law remedies. In any case, civil law remedies such as the law of nuisance generally work after the event and matters relating to land and development are commonly difficult and expensive to reverse.

Even so, planning has administrative costs and, if confined to exercises in regulation, planning may also slow down private sector investment. The costs of planning are relatively easy to measure, in terms of staff cost and time (for both developers and government) and the finance costs associated with holding land while planning applications are being processed (Ball 2010). In contrast, the economic benefits of planning are elusive and largely hypothetical, as they are about avoiding the likely costs of a situation that does not exist. It is therefore in the interests of business and the state to determine whether planning itself can be made more efficient and effective.

Much depends on the context and the likely consequences of efficiency measures. Public administration of any type can be made more efficient through attention to the details, through the use of information technology and through outsourcing tasks to the private sector. It is difficult to believe, however, that attention to the details or the increased use of information technology will, of itself, lead to consistent, substantial cost savings. In Britain, as in the US, outsourcing has in any case already proceeded to the point that site planning is left to private developers, consortia of developers or private/public partnerships, with public planning agencies merely acting as regulators and laying down a broad policy framework (Fainstein, 2001; Lloyd and Black 1993; Weiss 2002). To ensure further substantial efficiency gains would, most likely, require drastic measures such as excluding elected politicians and the public from decision-making or a downgrading of quality in decision-making in favour of speed or a combination of both reduced quality and reduced democracy (Adams and Watkins 2014, 36;

Burgess 2014). Admittedly, the regulatory function of town planning might be contracted to a private consultancy, but, within the present arrangements for local government, the private consultancy will find itself subject to the same local pressures, the same local politicians and the same procedures as public officials.

Moreover, whatever the outcome of the search for efficiency, measures to deregulate the planning system are likely to run into objections exactly because of their potentially destabilising impact on property markets (even apart from separate amenity objections). The experience of the Conservative/Liberal Coalition government in power in Britain after 2010 provides an example. David Cameron, whilst Prime Minister, called in September 2012 for measures to get planning officers 'off people's backs'. Even so, the government only relaxed control for narrowly defined types of development (small-scale back house extensions for a three-year period) and land use change (offices into houses) (Goodchild and Hammond 2013). Political pressure from Conservative voters and the Conservative establishment were no doubt one reason for the lack of deregulation. The Conservative Party is divided between a free market, neoliberal wing and a conservationist, home owning and heritage minded wing. However, economic factors were also relevant.

A subsequent news item in the *Financial Times* (10/08/2014) illustrates some of the practical difficulties of deregulation, in this case arising from the deregulation of controls of changes of use from offices to housing. Quoting a property advisor, the report noted that the measure had caused a substantial loss of office space in the most prosperous areas in London, and that the loss of office space had started to disrupt local businesses and was having an unsettling effect on other property owners. In some parts of London,

> you can get office schemes sitting next to an industrial paint shop. ... Converting those offices would not create high quality residential homes. Then the residents would object to the paint shop next to them and get that closed too.

Some property owners had benefited from deregulation, but at the expense of small businesses. The existence of planning controls had previously brought some stability to the property market and this had been lost.

Despite variability in law and practice, land use planning is a ubiquitous exercise in economically advanced countries in a way that suggests its own justification. The only exception sometimes cited in the literature is the city of Houston in Texas where there is no zoning plan on the US model. Zoning is not only form of planning, however. The planning system in Britain does not rely on land use zoning, for example. Moreover, Houston possesses publicly provided infrastructure and various forms of land use and building regulation that together amount to a town planning system, albeit a minimal planning system (Buitelaar 2009; O'Toole 2014).

## Supply-Side and Demand-Side Interventions

The extent to which social objectives can be realised through planning overlaps another distinction, whether plans are implemented as an aspect of supply-side policies for the property market or in their absence. Supply-side policies mean direct intervention in the land market, through for example purchasing land, investing in infrastructure or investing in housing. Planning with the aid of supply-side measures involves an agency being able to initiate and implement a measure. In contrast, planning in the absence of supply-side measures is an exercise in regulation, with fewer means of implementation.

The neoliberal position favours 'light touch' regulation without supply-side intervention. Regulation is not the only issue, however. Governments currently use a range of demand-side techniques to influence property markets, including incentives or taxation concessions, in a way that amounts to intervention in property markets, but falls short of planning in any meaningful sense of the word. The treatment of housing provides an example. Supply-side policies in housing mean the active promotion of house building and the pursuit of programmes to modernise and improve the existing stock. In the absence of such measures, governments may still use and commonly do use demand-side subsidies, such as rent support, savings schemes for first-time buyers, income support and tax relief and so on in attempting to ensure that decent homes are provided for those in need and attempting, in addition, to support house building.

The main rationale for demand-side policies in housing is that, in the long term, this encourages recipients to move to higher quality accommodation, so driving up standards (Galster 1997). Other arguments are that demand-side measures enhance the locational choices of consumers (Galster 1997); that they encourage more varied, locally responsive forms of urban design and development (Savini et al. 2015); and, finally, that they reduce the financial risk to the public sector at times and places where the property market is depressed (ibid).

The disadvantage of demand-side measures is similar to the disadvantage of relying on any form of private planning to realise public policy goals. There is no guarantee that risk-averse and profit-minded private investors will respond to financial incentives in the same way that local authorities and other publicly funded agencies, such as social landlords, react to policy initiatives. In the absence of appropriate supply-side measures, moreover, governments are less able to intervene in the existing stock, tackling poor condition dwellings, and less able to pursue spatial objectives such as reducing social segregation (Yates and Whitehead 1998). Likewise, they are less able to improve the existing building stock and less able to stimulate demand at times and places of economic decline or recession.

Moreover, the very process of encouraging low-income households to move out, as is an apparent advantage of demand-side measures, can accelerate local population loss and decay. Elsewhere in higher demand areas, planners can still work with developers in improving design and making towns and cities attractive. However, in the absence of social housing, the clientele is likely to be those who can pay, rather than those in need. Moreover, if the various demand-side measures fail to stimulate supply, their impact may be merely to increase house prices, with negative consequences for affordability.

In Britain, negotiated planning agreements offer a partial exception where regulatory planning has been used to promote social objectives. In the early 2000s, the majority of new affordable housing in England was developed with the help of planning agreements (Whitehead 2007). In inner London, where property values are so high as to limit or preclude public property acquisition, Section 106 agreements have proved a particularly useful, though largely taken-for-granted, means of providing affordable housing. Here reports about their role in affordable housing provision only appeared after their use was curtailed by central government in a revised policy framework.[1] Section 106 agreements are dependent on the profitability of schemes, however. They do not offer a full replacement for supply-side intervention, for example in areas of economic decline.

Negotiated planning agreements are an unusual feature of the town planning system in Britain. Similar provisions do not appear in the housing and planning policy frameworks in the US or other European countries. In the US, for example, the imposition of social obligations is tied to the demonstration of a 'rational nexus' between a proposal and its public capital requirements intended to service that development (APA 1997). The criteria for imposing obligations on developers are narrower than in Britain, though it may be possible for local authorities and other public agencies to come to similar agreements through their power as landowners.

The mix of supply-side and demand-side policies is both part of the context of planning and also a policy choice that needs consideration and evaluation. It is part of the context because the weight given either to demand-side policies or supply-side policies varies over time and from country to country. Equally, the mix is generally not fixed. The likely and actual impacts of different policy mechanisms have to be anticipated and assessed in their context, rather than through the sweeping assessments that one approach is generally better than others. Much the same can be said of the choice between planning and the market and between the use of negotiated planning agreements and more formal and almost certainly narrower methods of charging developers. Given the specific advantages and disadvantages associated with planning, no sensible government would wish to rely wholly either on the market or on planning. Some combination of planning and the market is necessary.

*Ideal Type Political Planning*

Considered as an exercise in resource allocation, planning has political as well as economic characteristics. In general, however, these are subsidiary to the economic aspects, as intervention in the economy and in property rights is the starting point. Despite the reference to fundamental democratisation, Mannheim envisaged planning as essentially a task to be left to experts, subject to broad control by an elected body. The economic planning systems studied by Kornai (1970, 1971) were even less democratic as they operated in one-party states and was generally not amenable to grassroots influence. In contrast, later accounts of economic planning (Prosser 1988), environmental planning (Bulkeley 2006) and spatial planning (Healey 1992) have argued, more or less without exception, that effective learning is a precondition for rational planning and that effective learning requires openness in government. Learning may still proceed through technical devices, monitoring the outcomes of policies. Learning is not impossible in states without freedom of expressions, but is unlikely to be as effective as in states where an open democratic debate is possible.

The experience of indicative planning—economic planning by incentives and exhortation—in France in the 1960s provides an example of how planning as politics might be conceptualised in the context of an elected government, a mixed capitalist economy and a political system characterised by competing parties and few press restrictions. Here the lesson is not just that effective planning presupposes open government, but that the logic of planning, once institutionalised, is to push politics in the direction of openness. 'The plan', in the words of an account by Cohen (1969, 159):

> centralises both political time and space. It pulls a vast range of decisions into a single framework and insists that they be decided simultaneously. The politics of frequent, individual and partial decisions becomes a politics of simultaneous, interrelated and long term decisions. ... The politics (*of the plan*) are comprehensive, simultaneous and explicit. (*Italics added*)

These latter characteristics of a plan may itself be regarded as the statement of an ideal type. A fully worked out plan needs to comprehensive, in the sense of treating all the factors relevant to the plan outcomes and to the interests of those affected by the plan, simultaneous in ensuring that all relevant decisions are brought together at a single point in time and explicit about its effects. The attributes of being comprehensive, simultaneous and explicit are all aspects of co-ordination, not just spatial co-ordination but political and economic co-ordination.

Accounts of strategic spatial planning sometimes reject the principle of comprehensiveness as too demanding. Albrechts and Balducci (2013, 20) suggest that in 'strategic planning, the overall picture that inspires choices is not given by a comprehensive analysis, but rather by a synthetic long-term vision'. The objection is directed more at the technical and analytical implications of comprehensiveness, rather than its political implications, however. A 'synthetic long-term vision' is, in any case, still a broadly based exercise.

The attributes of planning ensure a degree of political autonomy. The preparation of plans is typically able to ask new questions about the direction of economic policy, as in the case study of national planning undertaken by Cohen. Equally, in the case of town planning, the process of plan preparation can ask questions about the shape of future cities and about local impacts on the quality of life, and is able through its own procedures, for example the use of local public inquiries, to generate a different perspective (Albrechts 2003; Owens and Cowell, 2011 [2002] 8).

Yet, as Cohen's analysis also makes clear, the autonomy of planning is only partial. The state and other influential political and economic actors have their own interests and may either conceal the implications of specific policies or fail to work out the possible implications. Effective social learning depends on openness in government with the logical consequence that much depends on the character of the relevant political system. In addition, even if a plan is prepared, with all the relevant consultation exercises, interested parties may not want to work within its fixed parameters. They may continue to campaign for piecemeal changes. Planning, according to such a view, is permanently stuck, in both theory and practice, in an intermediate zone between democracy on one hand and on the other the workings of power.

## Note

1 'London's planning regulations are weaker—and affordable housing has suffered', New Statesman, 27 January 2015, consulted June 2016 at www.newstatesman.com/politics/2015/01/londons-planning-regulations-are-weaker-and-affordable-housing-has-suffered.

## References

Adams, D. and Watkins, C. (2014). *The value of planning*. London: The Royal Town Planning Institute.
Albrechts, L. (2003). 'Planning versus politics'. *Planning Theory*, 2:3, 249–68.
Albrechts, L. & Balducci, A. (2013). 'Practicing strategic planning: in search of critical features to explain the strategic character of plans'. *disP-The Planning Review*, 49:3, 16–27.

Alexander, E. R. (1992). 'A transaction cost theory of planning'. *Journal of the American Planning Association*, 58:2, 190–200.
APA—American Planning Association (1997). *Policy guide on impact fees*, [online] URL: www.planning.org/policy/guides/adopted/impactfees.htm (consulted November 2015).
Ball, M. (2010). *Housing supply and planning controls*. Titchfield: National Housing and Planning Advice Unit.
Booth, A. (2009). 'A survey of progressive economic thought in interwar Britain: strengths and gaps'. *The History of Economic Thought*, 50:2, 74–88.
Bryson, J. M., Crosby, B. C., Bryson, J. K., (2009). 'Understanding strategic planning and the formulation and implementation of strategic plans as a way of knowing: the contributions of actor-network theory'. *International Public Management Journal*, 12:2, 172–207.
Buitelaar, E. (2009). 'Zoning, more than just a tool: explaining Houston's regulatory practice'. *European Planning Studies*, 17:7, 1049–65.
Bulkeley, H. (2006). 'Urban sustainability: learning from best practice?'. *Environment and Planning A*, 38, 1029–44.
Burgess, G. on behalf of the Cambridge Centre for Housing and Planning Research (2014). *The nature of planning constraints. Report to the House of Commons Communities and Local Government Committee*. Cambridge CCHPR, [online] URL: www.parliament.uk/documents/commons-committees/communities-and-local-government/Report-on-nature-of-planning-constraints-v3-0.pdf (consulted September 2014).
Campbell, H. & Henneberry, J. (2005). 'Planning obligations, the market orientation of planning and planning professionalism'. *Journal of Property Research*, 22:1, 37–59.
Cohen, S. S. (1969). *Modern capitalist planning: the French model*. London: Weidenfeld & Nicolson.
Cole, G. D. H. (1945). *Building and planning*, London: Cassell.
Dawkins, C. J. (2000). 'Transaction costs and the land use planning process'. *Journal of Planning Literature*, 14:4, 507–18.
Denord, F. (2008). 'French neoliberalism and its divisions', In: Mirowski, P. and Plehwe, D. (eds.), *The making of the neoliberal thought collective*. Cambridge, MA: Harvard University Press.
Fainstein, S. S. (2001). *The city builders: property development in New York and London, 1980–2000*, 2nd edition. Lawrence: University of Kansas Press.
Friedmann, J. (1987). *Planning in the public domain: from knowledge to action*. Princeton, NJ: Princeton University Press.
Galster, G. (1997). 'Comparing demand-side and supply-side housing policies: submarket and spatial perspectives'. *Housing Studies*, 12:4, 561–77.
Goodchild, B. and Hammond, C. (2013). 'Planning and urban regeneration since 2010: a recipe for conflict and dispute?' *People, Place & Policy*, 7/2, 82–90, [online] URL: http://extra.shu.ac.uk/ppp-online/wp-content/uploads/2013/10/planning-urban-regeneration-2010.pdf (consulted December 2015).
Graham, S. & Marvin, S. (2001). *Splintering urbanism: networked infrastructures, technological mobilities and the urban condition*. London: Routledge.
Harvey, D. (1989). *The condition of postmodernity*. Oxford: Basil Blackwell.
Hayek, F. A. (2001). *The road to serfdom*. Abingdon, Oxon: Routledge Classics (original 1944).

Hayek, F. A. (1978). *The constitution of liberty*. Chicago: University of Chicago (US and British original 1960).

Healey, P. (1992). 'Planning through debate: the communicative turn in planning theory'. *Town Planning Review*, 63:2, 143–62.

Heilmann, S., & Melton, O. (2013). 'The reinvention of development planning in China'. *Modern China*, XX(X), 1–49.

Kelly, S. & Pollitt, M. (2010). 'An assessment of the present and future opportunities for combined heat and power with district heating (CHP-DH) in the United Kingdom'. *Energy Policy*, 38:11, 6936–45.

Kornai, J. (1970). 'A general descriptive model of planning processes'. *Economics of Planning*, 10:1–2, 1–19.

Kornai, J. (1971). *Anti-equilibrium*. Amsterdam: North Holland Publishing.

Lai, L. W. -C. (2002). 'Libertarians on the road to town planning'. *Town Planning Review*, 73:3, 289–310.

Lai, L. W. -G. (2004). 'Spontaneous catallaxis in urban & rural development under planning by contract in a small open economy: the ideas of Hayek and Mises at work in town & country planning in Hong Kong'. *Review of Austrian Economics*, 17:2/3.

Lai, L. W. -C. (2014). '"As planning is everything, it is good for something!" A Coasian economic taxonomy of modes of planning'. *Planning Theory*, online in advance of publication.

Latour, B. & Hermant, E. (2006). *Paris: invisible city* (virtual book) (French original 1998), [online] URL: www.bruno-latour.fr/node/95 (consulted October 2013).

Lloyd, G. & Black, S. (1993) 'Property-led urban regeneration and local economic development'. In: Berry, J., McGreal, S. & Deddis, B. (eds.), *Urban regeneration: property investment and development*. London: E & FN Spon, 144–60.

Mannheim, K. ([1940] 1971). *Man and society in age of reconstruction*. London: Routledge and Kegan Paul (first published in English in 1940, partly based on a German original of 1935).

Marwick, A. (1964). 'Middle opinion in the thirties: planning, progress and political "agreement"'. *The English Historical Review*, 79:311, 285–98.

Moroni, D. E. & Andersson, S. (2014). 'Introduction' in Andersson, D. E. and Moroni, S. (eds.), *Cities and private planning*. Cheltenham, UK: Edward Elgar.

Nedovic-Budic, Z. (2001). 'Adjustment of planning practice to the new Eastern and Central European context'. *Journal of the American Planning Association*, 67:1, 38–52.

O'Toole, R. (2014). 'Houston's land-use regime: a model for the nation'. In: Moroni, D. E. and Andersson, S. (eds.), *Cities and private planning*. Cheltenham, UK: Edward Elgar, 174–98.

Owens, S. & Cowell, R. (2011). *Land and limits: interpreting sustainability in the planning process*, 2nd edition. London: Routledge/RTPI.

Pavlínek, P. & Pickles, J. (2000). *Environmental transitions: transformation and ecological defence in Central and Eastern Europe*. London and New York: Routledge.

Peck, J. A., & Tickell, A. (1992). 'Local modes of social regulation? Regulation theory, Thatcherism and uneven development'. *Geoforum*, 23:3, 347–63.

Popper, K. (1944). 'The Poverty of historicism, II. A criticism of historicist methods'. *Economica, New Series*, 11:43, 119–37.

Prosser, T. (1988). 'Markets, planning, and socialism'. *Journal of Law and Society*, 15:1, 42–57.

Rogers, R. E. (1969). *Max Weber's ideal type theory*. New York: The Philosophical Library.

Rutherford, J. (2008). 'Unbundling Stockholm: the networks, planning and social welfare nexus beyond the unitary city'. *Geoforum*, 18:6, 1871–83.

Savini, F., Salet, W. & Majoor, S. (2015). 'Dilemmas of planning: intervention, regulation, and investment'. *Planning Theory* 14:3, 296–315.

Short, J. R. (2004). *Global metropolitan: globalizing cities in a capitalist world*. London: Routledge.

Sorensen, A. D. & Day, R. A. (1981). 'Libertarian planning'. *Town Planning Review*, 52:4, 390–402.

Wagner, P. (2001). *A History and theory of the social sciences*. London: Sage Publications.

Watkins, J. W. N. (1952). 'Ideal types and historical explanation'. *The British Journal for the Philosophy of Science*, 3:9, 22–43.

Weber, M. (1947). *The theory of social and economic organization* (Henderson, A. M. & Parsons, T., eds. & trans.). New York: Free Press.

Weiss, M. A. (2002). *The rise of the community builders: the American real estate industry and urban land planning*. Washington, DC: Beard Books.

Whitehead, C. M. (2007). 'Planning policies and affordable housing: England as a successful case study?'. *Housing Studies*, 22:1, 25–44.

Wootton, B. (1945). *Freedom under planning*. London: G. Allen & Unwin.

Wu, F. (2001). 'China's recent urban development in the process of land and housing marketisation and economic globalisation'. *Habitat International*, 25:3, 273–89.

Wu, F., Xu, J. &. Yeh, A. G. (2007). *Urban development in post-reform China*. New York and London: Routledge.

Yates, J. & Whitehead, C. (1998). 'In defence of greater agnosticism: a response to Galster's' comparing demand-side and supply-side housing policies'. *Housing Studies*, 13:3, 415–23.

Yeh, A. & Wu, F. (1999). 'The transformation of the urban planning system in China from a centrally-planned to transitional economy'. *Progress in Planning* 51:3, 167–252.

# 4  Styles and Forms of Planning

The ideal types of planning can be further subdivided and extended into a series of styles. The 'bulk' of public planning, according to Friedmann (1987, 17) is of a modest variety and is mostly concerned with guidance, management of change and the allocation of resources according to a plan or policy framework. Environmental planning is admittedly, in part, about the allocation and control of 'bads', that is to say disamenities, nuisances and risks rather than goods or resources (Beck 1992, 3). In allocative planning, however, as this modest interpretation of planning may be called, the allocation of 'bads' is also about maintaining some type of balance, between the environment, its users and residents, as well as between various policy aims.

Innovative planning, in contrast, is about the promotion of social and economic capacity of some collectivity such as a city, region or government to anticipate and cope with change of all types. In innovative planning, plan making and implementation may become 'coterminous' (Friedmann 1987, 60) in a way that departs from the economic ideal type. Finally, radical planning is a more comprehensive process and involves either political change or changes in values and lifestyles or both.

Taken as a whole, the distinction between planning as guidance and radical planning and, within guidance, between allocative and innovative planning represent different points in a continuum. The maintenance of the status quo as represented by allocative planning is one end of a spectrum. Radical planning is at the other end, with innovative planning as an intermediate case, as shown in the Table 4.1.

The various types of planning are not necessarily exclusive, as one may be necessary to enable another (Avelino and Rotmans 2011). A stable society is necessary to establish the possibility of innovative and radical change, at least in a predictable direction. As a result, allocative planning is likely to

*Table 4.1* Types of Planning: From Management to the Promotion of Change

| Allocative | Innovative | Radical |
| --- | --- | --- |

continue alongside innovation and the promotion of change. Conversely, either innovation or radical change may be necessary to maintain stability in the long term.

To give an example from the field of sustainable development: a working economy is almost certainly necessary to enable a government to promote change in how goods and services are produced and consumed. Policies to promote sustainable development generally involve public expenditure (and therefore a regular supply of income) and require, in addition, a degree of stability amongst relevant institutional actors. Conversely, radical change may be necessary to maintain healthy cities and so maintain, in the long term, a stable pattern of social and economic relations. The styles of intervention are therefore simultaneously both antagonistic to and supportive of one another, in a way that mostly precludes either a clean break or complete stability.

## 'Allocative' Planning

To take each style of planning, in turn, allocative planning implies a process of balancing different aims and criteria against social and economic trends. Sometimes the aims of planning are simplified into a straight choice between environmental protection on one hand and neoliberal, market-oriented private sector economic development on the other (Raco 2005). Planning is then defined as an exercise in balancing development and the environment. Sometimes, and this is the most common interpretation, the aims of planning are conceptualised as an exercise in a process of sustainable development that rests on the 'three pillars' of economic growth, social equity and the environment (Campbell 1996; CLG 2012; INFRAS, 2004). The three pillars interpretation of sustainable development (and by extension of planning) was endorsed by the United Nations in the Johannesburg Declaration of 2002 (Robinson 2013a).[1] It is a reworking and, from an environmental viewpoint, a dilution of earlier definitions of sustainable development and environmental care such as stated in 'Our Common Future', the Brundtland report (WCED 1987). Brundtland was about prioritising the care and conservation of the environment for future generations. In contrast, the three pillars interpretation gives no indication about priorities, so suggesting either a series of mutually reinforcing priorities or an exercise of balancing one priority against another.

Yet neither the notion of mutually reinforcing 'pillars' nor the pursuit of balance provides a full account of the principles of sustainable development, even as currently interpreted. Robinson ([1982], 2013b), a US environmental lawyer, notes that some places are 'critical' to individual well-being or to cultural heritage or to both, that the law in every single US state recognises the concept of a critical area and that, where applied, critical area controls and conservation criteria take priority over the rest. Critical areas include sites whose physical characteristics pose a risk to health or safety, ecosystems that support human life and places of cultural significance. Planning in Britain operates according to different legal principles and offers more scope for local discretion. Even so, it is possible to identify *de facto* critical areas such as parks in urban areas, the highest grade of listed buildings and areas of scientific interest. The advocates of environmental care would want similarly stringent levels of protection more widely applied. Placing an overarching priority on a single, specific theme or objective is not an exercise in allocative planning, however, falling instead into a style of either innovative or radical intervention.

### The Main Variants

Balance also implies coordination. However, the extent to which coordination is possible varies according to the distribution of power, understood as the ability of one party to have an effect that conforms to the plan. Friedmann (1973, 71) distinguishes between four styles of allocative planning, depending mainly on the extent to which power is centralised in the planning agency, but also the degree to which it is concentrated or dispersed elsewhere. The styles are worked out for national economic planning, but given that land use planning deals with a particular type of resource, that of property, they may be suitably adapted.

The four styles identified by Friedmann (1973) are strongly centralised, weakly centralised, fragmented and dispersed. For the sake of simplification, Table 4.2 has ignored the possibility of strong centralisation. The most strongly centralised form of planning, 'command planning', is, in any case, largely obsolete, other than in the specific case where a state undertakes a large scale infrastructure project such as a new rail line, high speed road or flood defences and is the clear director of that project.

Once command planning is set aside, the table recognises three (rather than four) different distributions of power, with each distribution implying a particular method and style of planning and role for the professional planner. Friedmann's classification also uses some terms, notably 'policies planning' and 'corporate planning', that are odd in the context of urban planning, but these are retained for the sake of consistency. As is typical in tables such as this, the different styles may be mixed in practice.

To summarise each style: Relatively centralised forms of planning involve a single hierarchical organization and are characterised by a reliance on professional or technical knowledge. This type of planning seeks to 'shape' markets, rather than be wholly determined by markets and, in principle, involves four main, overlapping devices to secure change (Adams and Watkins 2014, 21–30; Hopkins 2001, 36):

- the preparation of broad policy statements and agendas that provide information about the future actions of government;
- the preparation of regulatory policies that specify the conditions under which privately financed development will be supported, including

Table 4.2 Styles of Allocative Planning

| The Distribution of Power | Relatively Centralised | Fragmented | Dispersed |
|---|---|---|---|
| Method of implementation | Targets, rules, inducements, *incentives* and information | Bargaining amongst a limited number of parties. Inducement, *incentives, charges* and information | Participation in decision making |
| Predominant form of control | Sanctions: restructuring of the context | Normative compliance: *the balance of costs and benefits* | Voluntary compliance |
| Role of technical experts | Specialist and adviser | Negotiator and broker: *deal marker* | Organiser and advocate |
| Style of allocative planning | Polices planning: *planning as the shaping of markets* (Adams and Watkins 2014) | Corporate planning: *co-operative private/public planning* (Denman 1978, 99); *co-operative conflict* (Sen 1987) | Participant planning: collaborative planning (Healey 1998); co-operative conflict (Sen 1987) |

Source: Adapted from Friedmann (1973, 71); italics refers to added or replaced text.

- conditions about the participation of developers in infrastructure provision;
- the preparation of visions and designs that show, in varying levels of detail, the intended outcome; and finally
- strategic interventions that transform property markets in places where markets are weak or otherwise not working well or where development will not take place without some form of coordination.

Each of these devices involves a different means of exercising power. Policy statements shape markets through the exercise of legitimate authority, the authority that is vested in government and its agencies, as well as through provision of information and education. Regulation shapes markets through enforcing or changing property rights and the value of land: regulation therefore carries the potential threat of police action. Visions and design shape markets through motivating investors, mobilising political support and seducing potential consumers who otherwise have choices in where to live or visit. Finally strategic interventions work through restructuring the context in which development takes place, for example by means of public investment in the urban infrastructure. Strategic interventions therefore depend on the existence of supply-side planning, at least at the local level.

Market shaping is a slight misnomer. Plans still have to be prepared and implemented in the context of wider market forces and implementation is likely to be less expensive to the public purse and more likely to proceed if the plan is in accordance to the general direction of the market. The persuasiveness of the plan to investors is therefore likely to depend, in part, on the ability to reveal an understanding of how markets operate (Adams and Watkins 2014, 28), including the likely preferences of potential users and consumers. In addition, because planning as the shaping of markets involves government, the persuasiveness of the plan also depends on the way that it fits into existing policy discourses and avoids political opposition. For this reason, the process of plan preparation is likely to involve extensive consultation with different groups.

'Corporate', as used in Friedmann's concept of corporate planning, means belonging to a single body politic. Corporate planning does not mean therefore complete fragmentation. It means, instead, an effort to undertake co-ordination in a fragmented context where operational power is held by a number of corporate agencies. The role of the planner is to negotiate possible means of resolving conflicts and, as part of this, to make deals between the various parties and to ensure that the costs of development are allocated through various forms of charges (negotiated agreements and fixed changes as laid down in a plan or policy statement). Enforcement is 'normative', involving voluntary compliance to a plan prepared in the interests of the relevant participants. Denman (1978, 99), a critic of public land ownership, once used the term 'co-operative planning' to summarise a similar arrangement in relation to the planning of urban development. Co-operative planning involves a combination of planners, developers and landowners coming together for their mutual advantage.

Concepts of corporate or co-operative planning can found in Britain in the writings of Conservative reformers, such as Nettlefold (1908), before 1914. They remain a persistent theme amongst those who dislike a strong state and especially amongst libertarians or 'anarcho-capitalists' (Moroni and Andersson 2014, 9). Sometimes, as in the work of Rothbard (1978, 27–30) voluntary action is preferred for ethical reasons as a means of avoiding aggression and coercion of any kind. In other accounts (Foldvary 2009), the voluntary principle is derived from the practical workings of the market, as the latter depends on the voluntary buying and selling of goods and services. Applied to urban development, therefore, the focus of libertarianism is strictly speaking not on the distinction between planning and the market, but between 'voluntary', or bottom-up private planning and top-down, 'governmental public planning' (Moroni and Andersson 2014, 8) or between contract and consent and 'planning by edict' (Lai 2004, 161).

The references to planning through voluntary action, co-operation and consent are, however, oversimplifications, as corporate planning is also likely to involve conflict, for example in bargaining between the various parties.

The modalities of corporate planning fall into a situation intermediate between co-operation and conflict and naturally called 'cooperative conflict' (Sen 1987) or 'pragmatic acceptance' (Mann 1970) where a person or a group accepts an arrangement for want of anything better. A person or a private firm may, for example, consent to a contract, not because of a positive acceptance of the terms, but because they know they are unlikely to obtain anything better. Top-down planning and planning by edict may involve unequal power relationships, but so does so-called 'voluntary' planning.

In any case, the only style of planning where power lies unequivocally with government is command planning and this is rare. Even in the context of planning as regulation, and this is itself a form of 'planning by edict' to use the words of Lai (2004), developers are able to influence decision-making. Admittedly, town planning systems generally possess strong legal sanctions to prevent unauthorised development. Banks and other financial institutions are unlikely to lend financial support without the security of a planning permission. As a result, clear breaches of a plan or local policy are mostly confined to small-scale developments, such as a single house or more commonly still extensions to or modifications of an existing building. However, planning as regulation has no means of enforcing compulsory production or building targets. Achievement of any development target is the responsibility of developers who are relatively independent and who can and commonly do offer economic benefits to a locality, either directly to a local authority (increased revenue from local taxes) or more broadly to a community (for example improved facilities or increased employment). These potential benefits offer a bargaining asset that developers may use to argue either for a modification to the plan or an exception after plan approval. Moreover, the larger the developer and the more the developer commands a monopoly in a particular situation or area, the more power they are likely to possess. As a result of these pressures, planning as regulation, including the statutory planning system in Britain, is likely to vacillate between policies planning and corporate planning, to use Friedmann's labels, or between the shaping of markets and private/public co-operation to use alternative terms.

Finally, a dispersed power situation refers to large number of actors, as for example in exercises in public consultation, and is best represented where the power to implement decisions resides with community organisations, especially in the context of a neighbourhood regeneration exercise involving a wide range of public and private institutional actors. The task in such circumstances is commonly to assess the feasibility of plans and policies in advance in the light of the availability of resources and to work out some acceptable compromise or consensus on which action can proceed. Such a style of intervention implies 'collaborative planning', as defined by Healey (1998) and 'transactive governmentality' in which community groups acquire a legitimate role in urban management (Certomà and Notteboom 2015). The operating principle is again co-operative conflict. Participation in policy debates and regeneration is voluntary. However, community groups and others may have to go along with a particular view or strategy because they know that raising fundamental issues about broad policy aims would lead nowhere and might, for example, lead to their exclusion from a policy-making forum (Shin 2010).

## Non-Residential Property Markets and Allocative Planning

Despite references to balance and sustainable development, routine planning practice commonly operates in a political context with a strong presumption in favour of economic growth. The technical measure of economic growth is the Gross Domestic Product, adjusted for inflation. Its popular and political meaning is more about general economic expansion, and about the benefits that accompany expansion, notably improved job opportunities, improved opportunities for local businesses, increased property values for local property owners, including home owners, improved tax receipts for local government and so on.

For US analysts in particular, the presumption of growth comes from a redefinition of the modern city as a 'growth machine' (Molotch 1976, 1993). Growth for private landowners and developers means capital gains. Growth for local government means increased revenues. As a result, all parties, whether in the private sector or local government, have an interest in promoting growth.

The financial gains to be made from allowing development are relatively less important for local government in Britain than in the US, given a context in which local authorities receive extensive financial support from the centre—a point that Hilber and Vermeulen (2012, 63–4) and others suggests is a key reason why local planning practice in Britain is less growth oriented than elsewhere. In Britain, encouraging further population growth in cities that are already growing is commonly unpopular owing to the congestion and urbanisation that this brings (Longlands 2013). However, the dependence of local authorities on central government for finance in Britain also means that they are susceptible to being influenced by central policies. And growth is equally important for central government in raising revenues and keeping down unemployment. As a result, in Britain, the pursuit of growth has become mostly associated with central government, as is apparent in the titles of policy statements, for example 'Local growth: realising every place's potential' (HM Government 2010) or 'Regeneration to enable growth' (CLG 2011).

Putting aside the objection of amenity groups, the pursuit of growth has raised two separate questions about land use planning in Britain:

- In regions with relatively depressed property markets, the desire of local authorities to promote urban regeneration provokes the question as to whether good planning or good quality urban design can, of itself,

increase land values, especially the value of commercial and industrial projects.
- In the more economically buoyant areas, in contrast, the question arises as to whether planning controls might, to the contrary, restrict growth.

The latter question about the impact of planning on growth overlaps issues relating to the provision of housing. For the sake of simplicity, however, the impact of planning on house prices is treated separately.

In relation to the first question, the possible use of planning to promote commercial property values, the former Commission for Architecture and the Built Environment (CABE 2008, 18) is apparently authoritative. The CABE guide to master planning states that 'Good design adds economic value by producing high returns on investments (good rental returns and enhanced capital values)'. CABE had an interest in finding any argument that might promote design quality, as this was its brief. Even so, similar arguments are implicit in most urban regeneration programmes where public investment is allied to attempts to promote the private sector. A report titled 'Competitive Cities' by the OECD (2007, 35–7) likewise sees a good quality environment as an essential aspect of city branding and marketing, whilst also admitting that this is not easy in the context of long-term industrial decline.

Are such claims justified? The answer is surprisingly elusive. A key justification of planning is that this leads to a higher quality of life and a higher quality of environment. However the link between a high quality of environment and property values is not exactly clear. Quality of life indicators are not always incorporated into economic data. The very inability of economic data to cover quality of life is the basis of critiques of uncontrolled growth, as well as the distinction between use value and exchange value.

Much of the claims about enhanced value are, in any case, about a narrower issue—that of design. At a technical level, the quality of design may refer either to the quality of building design and its materials or the quality of external spaces or a combination of the two. If building design is the main concern, the definition is likely to escape many of the key aspects of the quality of external spaces. If the quality of external spaces is included, the definition is likely to include many factors over which a developer and designer has little control, other than in schemes sufficiently large to cover a series of streets or a neighbourhood.

In any case, who is to judge good and bad design? For example, a study of landscape quality in South Yorkshire and similar, 'post-industrial' areas in Belgium and Germany repeatedly refers to low expectations as a constraint on the achievement of quality in design (Project Team 2008). In such a context, variations in quality are only likely to have an impact if the expectations of the public and investors are raised. Yet the very language of the project report raises further questions. If expectations are low, are they necessarily wrong? Developers would, in any case, argue that they have a more reliable understanding of what their clients want, within a fixed budget, than architects or planners. They would probably also insist on the importance of easy traffic access and extensive car parking—against the usual dictates of good quality urban design and sometimes of road safety. Raising property values is not the be-all of policy.

Even if good design is likely to raise values, investors and developers are likely to consider the impact of any associated added development costs and the time-scale in which the increased values are likely to be generated. The usual economic assumption is that private developers would not consider any increased costs, for whatever reason, if the increase in costs is not commensurate with the increase in value. Otherwise, the profitability of the scheme is endangered. In the case of high quality, but unprofitable development proposals, a typical developer would either not undertake the project or would use reduced, basic standards (Henneberry & Halleux 2008). This being so, quality in design, as reflected in the time spent by architects and others in preparing alternatives and in the quality of street furniture and of building materials, is more likely to follow the anticipation of higher land values in specific sites and locations and would not promote higher land values in depressed areas. In seeking higher design standards, therefore, planning authorities have to judge what the market will bear.

Quality as reflected in the provision of external green space is slightly different, as greenery is generally expensive in terms of land consumption and, as a result, the costs of providing greenery tend to increase in places with the highest property values. The relationship between quality and land values is therefore the exact opposite for green space provision than for architecture and building design, High land values are likely to work against green space provision even as this may favour high quality architectural design. Studies that show a correlation between greenery and high land values (for example Budinger and Gruehn [2012] in Germany) are commonly misleading as they focus on private property and the greenery is located on publicly owned land—in the street or in adjacent parks.

Even so, a planning agency may still deem external spacing standards as necessary for amenity reasons and may also specify public access requirements as being in the interests of an area, its visitors and residents. Harvey (1989), in analysing the entrepreneurial city, suggests that the promotion of amenity is itself an aspect of a neoliberal growth strategy, attracting people and investments. Perhaps so, but in the short term, the promotion of amenity, at least green space amenities, may work against commercial interests.

In relation to the second question, the impact of planning controls on economic growth, US studies, as summarised by Kim (2011), suggest little impact so long as sufficient development sites are allocated in aggregate. In such circumstances, the benefits of planning in the sense of providing information for developers, laying out transport infrastructures and conserving local amenities outweigh the costs. The US evidence also suggests that uncontrolled sprawl leads to diseconomies in the provision of public services, that in the context of a growing economy, the specification of greenfield controls encourages economic activity in central urban areas and, finally, that some planning controls such as an insistence on low densities and large scale zoning can cause increased travelling time (ibid.). The US experience is valuable because it covers a wide variety of different situations and policies. Much depends therefore on the exact character of the policies being pursued, not on planning *per se*.

The proviso is of course whether sufficient sites are allocated in aggregate. If they are not, the likely effect is inflation in land values and the imposition of additional costs on consumers and non-residential users. In principle, land scarcities apply to all forms of use and types of development. However, the debate in Britain has focused almost wholly on housing land. There are good reasons for this. Barker (2006, 35) noted that local authorities tended to use relatively crude methodologies in the allocation of employment land, but that in general they tended to err on the side of overoptimistic, overgenerous assessments of land needs.

There are dissenting voices, however. Cheshire et al. (2011) have expressed concern about the additional costs caused by restrictions on out-of-town retail parks. However, this latter is less important now than in the past as retailers have faced more and more competition from online sales. Moreover, as is a recurrent theme amongst neoliberal and similar critics, the criticism is mostly about how the planning system has been used, rather than about planning as such. Cheshire et al. (2011, 2–3) show, for example, that the development of retail parks has faced fewer restrictions in France than in England.

In addition, Cheshire and Hilber (2008) have argued that planning restrictions impose an unacknowledged 'tax' on commercial property and cite in this context the difference between marginal building costs of an additional storey and the consequent additional value in a heavily regulated area (for example the West End of central London, represented by the Borough of Westminster) to that of a relatively unregulated location (for example Newcastle). The figures provided by Cheshire and Hilber show that the West End and to some extent the City of London are outriders in terms of the cost/value patterns in both Britain and Europe. In the West End, the value of blocks was over 800 per cent of the marginal cost of building an additional story. Outside the West End and the City, the rate is less than 400 per cent. Even so the scale of the difference is sufficient to suggest that planning regulations are indeed costly for the economy.

According to the authors, the basic assumption of the 'planning tax' is as follows:

> in the absence of restrictions on heights, buildings should rise to a point where the marginal cost of adding an additional floor equals its market price. (F189)

Developers seldom add floors to a building. Most likely, they would have to replace an existing building of a given height with another—a much more expensive proposition, whilst also respecting the risk to damage to local services and to other nearby property. They would also have to purchase the site at its existing value and undertake building at prevailing labour rates (which are also more expensive in central London). The expense of replacing blocks means that, once completed, they are, moreover, likely to last many years. As a result, the landscape of offices in any city, like the urban landscape in general, is a reflection of economic conditions in the past, not just the present.

The 'planning tax' model also assumes that the value of property is a 'material' good, that is to say it is dependent on the volume of production, given roughly equal patterns of demand. In 'Social Limits to Growth', Hirsch (1977) makes a distinction between material goods, whose price is determined by the balance of supply and demand, and positional goods of the type whose value lies in its social scarcity. Positional value is usually considered in relation to housing and to the way some neighbourhoods become more expensive than others. The same principle is application to offices, however, or at least to part of the office market—the most upmarket, prestigious part. In any case, in high-demand areas, housing and commercial uses are in competition with one another and the high value of housing is itself likely to push up the value of non-residential sites, unless these are protected through enforced zoning policies or other planning policies. The West End of London is likely, in other words, to stand out from other office markets through virtue of its positional character that it is the interests of all parties—existing owners, developers and the local authority—to respect. This being so, unregulated development could indeed lower office rents, but only by destroying the unique character of the area. However, any such hypothetical reduction in rents would count for little as the commercial property market would create another exclusive area elsewhere.

Planning controls have an economic function. The very intensity of development in inner London requires more intensive regulation than elsewhere—for example to manage fire safety, traffic, overshadowing, the protection of existing services, including underground services, the preservation of greenery and the preservation of heritage, which is an essential aspect of any city's marketing image.

Moreover, planning is not just about controls. Planning is organised intervention, and organised intervention can shape and open up markets. The interventions by the London Dockland UDC in the 1980s and the development at Canary Wharf provide an example, as they served to ease market pressure on the City and the West End. They were not presented as planning by the government of the day, but they still amounted to an expensive programme of organised publicly funded action. The activities of the London Docklands UDC were at the time extensively criticised for ignoring the needs of established local communities (Brownill 1990). Ironically this very criticism suggests that planning can be pursued to promote the market, indeed ruthlessly so.

*Impacts on the Housing Market*

The impact of planning on house prices and housing supply has been discussed for many years and, contrary to the position for commercial property, the existence of a negative impact is supported by consistent, convincing evidence. In 'The Containment of Urban England', the first detailed study of the impact of the post-1945 statutory planning system in England, Hall et al. (1973, 404) argued that 'the crucial weakness of the post-war planning system was the failure to control the price of land.' The increase in the price of land immediately available for residential development had been of the order of ten- or twenty-fold between the late 1930s and 1960s, whereas the general rate of inflation was only about four times over the same period. The increase in land prices had been caused by a failure of the planning system to enable sufficient land to be developed in areas of demand. The increase was, moreover, passed on to consumers. The consequences were to disadvantage lower income first-time buyers who had to purchase a more expensive home on a smaller site, in the suburbs rather than the countryside, as was their likely first choice.

Why the failure to allocate enough land for new housing? Hall et al. (1973) put the blame on the history and ideology of town planning in Britain. The system was based on the principles of rural conservation and urban containment and after about 1950 had lost its countervailing emphasis on public sector development. Kornai (1979), in analysing the differences between planned economies and market economies, offers a complementary and more general explanation, one that has international rather than just British implications. Planning systems are resource constrained, whether this is land or some other resource; they are not in close contact with consumers and, in a situation of economic growth, have few mechanisms to respond to demand. Conversely, market-based, capitalist systems are constrained by demand, but have a system of production that works towards the satisfaction of demand, subject only to the limitations of prices and not the physical characteristics of resources.

Planning and market-based systems of allocation therefore have contrasting limitations. Planning is likely to remain necessary to manage resources. However, given the tendencies within planning systems, institutionalised arrangements are also necessary to counter persistant shortages.

To extend Kornai's analysis to land use, land is a distinct type of resource in that the amount is more or less fixed. Planning is justified for this reason alone, as would be the usual argument in central economic planning. Land use planning is also justified for varied, contrasting reasons, identified by Mannheim ([1940] 1971), for example system coordination, and by neo-liberal economists, for example the avoidance of negative neighbourhood effects and other externalities. For local residents, the development of new housing may itself offer a negative externatility, with few obvious economic advantages, certainly compared to industrial and commercial development—so reinforcing the case that institutional mechanisms are therefore necessary to prevent the emergence of shortages in housing development sites. The institutional mechanisms can take various forms, but in general may either represent a weakening of the planning system, through the relaxation of control, or its strengthening through the provision of additional powers and responsibilities.

The analysis undertaken by Hall et al. (1973) did not lead to extensive public debate. The lack of response was, moreover, later cited by Reade (1987, 76–83) as an example of the complacency and uncritical acceptance that surrounded the planning system. Times change, however. By the early 2000s, further house price inflation and the dictates of global competition led the UK Treasury to take a sceptical interest in town planning and in particular its impact on house prices.

The causes of house price inflation in the UK were analysed most thoroughly by the Barker review of 2003 and 2004. The review argued that house price inflation was caused by a lack of building supply and in particular by the apparent inability of house builders to vary their output to cope with periods of increased demand. House building had declined in the 1970s owing to the withdrawal of local authority subsidies, but the private house building industry had failed to respond and continued not to respond even at the time of house price inflation from the late 1990s onwards. Lack of supply was, in turn, caused by a lack of development sites and therefore by the rigidities of the planning system. For Barker (2004, 6), 'Central to achieving change is the recommendation to allocate more land for development'.

Barker made few recommendations about how to encourage house building, other than through the release of more development sites. Regional spatial plans, introduced by the Labour government of the time but subsequently abolished, put Barker's recommendations into effect. Regional planning amounted to an institutional mechanism to promote land release within the planning system, rather than a mechanism that sought to relax

## Styles and Forms of Planning 109

planning controls. The regional plans took the assessment of housing land requirements out of the control of local authorities and was, as a result, more amenable to central influence. However, the hope for an expanded building programme was soon overtaken by events, as is shown in Figure 4.1.[2]

The decline in house building was mostly caused by the recession of 2008 and by the way that the recession led small developers to go out of business. The larger house builders have subsequently increased their share of the market and expanded their output, but have not fully made up for the decline in completion rates, even though the market has allowed the achievement of relatively high profits (Archer and Cole 2014; *Financial Times*, 2/6/2015). House building by social landlords (local authorities and housing associations combined) has, moreover, stagnated, its scale limited by a lack of public finance.

The drop in house building has meant that land allocation through planning is no longer the constraint that it was formerly, say before 2008. A relaxation in planning control, from 2010 onwards, has had the same effect. Planning authorities typically monitor plan outcomes against population and household projections and their associated estimates of housing requirements. Under national guidance, they are required in addition to show that they have allocated a sufficient amount of available and suitable sites to cover house building over a defined period of time. The period itself has varied. However, the present rule in England is that land allocation should last up to 15 years and this is an ample guarantee of land availability in the context of a fluctuating, but not growing number of completions.[3]

Developers still sometimes argue for more and more housing sites, even if they have substantial land banks, as is commonly the case (*The Guardian*, 30/12/2015). As reported in the *Financial Times* (17/04/2015, 20), the

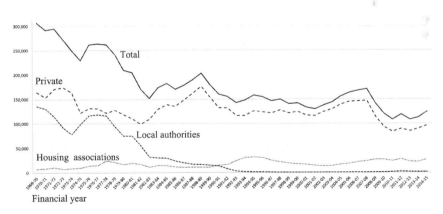

*Figure 4.1* House Building Completions (England) by Developer

developers 'seem not to be suffering any material impact from planning delays'.

In any case, pointing to land and planning constraints underestimates the way in which the financial strategies of housing developers limit expansion. Development companies make annual targets based on previous experience and expectations. In making these annual targets, companies are sensitive to price signals that might indicate a downturn in profitability (Barker 2003, 42; Pryce 1999). To this extent, increased house building is a response to anticipated house price inflation, rather than a means of reducing house prices. If prices decline, so does the rate of house building.

It is, nevertheless, conceivable that a lack of planning permissions could re-emerge as a constraint in the future. It remains of interest therefore to ask about the exact impact of planning restrictions in the past. It is only possible to give approximate measures, subject to numerous qualifications. However, two items of evidence may be cited, the first a local study of trends in a highly restricted planning situation and the second a national modelling exercise.

The experience in Cheshire in the period from 2003 to 2008 provides the local case study. During this time, the former Regional Planning Agency for the North West imposed a complete moratorium on the granting of planning permission for housing in selected areas of East Cheshire, on both greenfield and brownfield sites. The rationale was overprovision of new housing against previous plan targets and a desire to encourage house building in regeneration areas in Greater Manchester. Subsequent interviews with developers showed that the moratorium had the desired effect of diverting the interest of developers into urban regeneration (Levis 2008).

A five-year moratorium on house building might be expected to accelerate house price inflation in the areas subject to the policy. What therefore is the evidence? In August 2003, just before the moratorium first took effect, the average selling price in Macclesfield, one of the local towns affected, was £140,437. In May 2008, when the policy ceased, average selling prices in Macclesfield had risen by 37 per cent to £189,317. During the same period, the Cheshire average had increased by only 25 per cent (from £156,429 to £195,254). So one might conclude that the house price moratorium has put on an extra 12 per cent to house prices in the area affected, compared to Cheshire as a whole where a mixture of policies were in place. Yet house prices in Crewe, a town unaffected by the moratorium and a focus for much building activity, increased by 37 per cent over the same period (from £93,772 to £128,449). (the data has been obtained through 'Home.co.uk').[4]

If the time span is extended for a further two years to May 2010, assuming that there is a delay in the ability of house builders to respond, the pattern of results is more consistent in suggesting a house price impact. By this time, the average selling house price increases, compared to August 2003, were as follows: Macclesfield 42 per cent, Cheshire as a whole 33 per cent and Crewe 35 per cent. House prices had continued to increase in the area of the former moratorium, whereas in the growth area they had slipped back. The average relative increase in Macclesfield was of the order of just over one per cent per annum, so indicating a substantial inflationary uplift were the policy were to persist over, say a decade or two decades.

Very few local authorities have been either permitted or required the imposition of a complete moratorium on planning permissions for housing. The variations in local policy in East Cheshire may be regarded as an extreme test of planning control. That said, the data from East Cheshire is not of itself conclusive. Local peculiarities, short-term changes and the erratic character of house price data can easily overwhelm the specific impact of planning policy in any single year, especially if the policy difference between one place and another is not great.

The experience in East Cheshire is also not to be interpreted as supporting the use of price data as a general guide for the allocation of land for housing, as was once proposed by Cheshire and Sheppard (2005) and by Barker (2006, 6). The data is simply too crude and erratic for the purpose. Elsewhere, in a study in Greater Boston, Glaeser and Ward (2009) have argued that, faced with local housing scarcities within a city region, consumers may simply substitute living in one town rather than another, with the effect that local variations in house price inflation would not arise.

Most estimates of the house price impact of restrictive controls rely on counterfactual simulations of the housing market, based on the estimated economic impact of refusals of planning permission. The most detailed recent study is undertaken by Hilber and Vermeulen (2012) who used a panel of data combining house price and income information, spanning 35 -years and covering 353 local planning authorities in England, with direct information on regulatory and physical supply constraints for these locations. The comparisons were therefore regional and national, rather than local. They were also over a long, 30-year time span.

The results suggested that house prices in an average local planning authority in England in 2008 would be 'between 21.5 to 38.1' per cent lower if the planning system had been completely deregulated over the previous 30 years (since 1979). Complete deregulation was impractical, but substantial house prices would be achieved if planning in the most restricted areas of the south of England were relaxed to the level in operation in northeast England.

The pattern of results again suggests an average inflationary penalty of about one per cent a year. Again, however, health warnings are in order. Simulations are less credible than 'real' data because they refer to hypothetical situations. In doing this, moreover, the modeller commonly has to make many methodological assumptions and simplifications. For example, the estimation of the hypothetical costs assumes that in the absence of a planning system, house prices (together with the difference in land price between undeveloped greenfield and urban sites) would converge towards an equilibrium, subject only to physical constraints, and that this equilibrium is most closely approximated by the house prices in those regions, such as northeast England, where planning control is relatively relaxed. There is, of course, no way of knowing whether house prices would have tended toward an equilibrium over the intervening 30-year period, but that is the assumption.

The assumption of a unified national housing market is, in any case, open to objection. The housing market in central London is partly detached from the rest of England and, given the scale of international investment, also partly detached from the local labour market. Releasing land and building homes in or beyond the London green belt would, probably, only have a minor impact on demand in the upmarket fashionable neighbourhoods in central London. In any case, house prices and rents in London and increasingly in much of southeast England are so high that it is difficult to see how affordable housing could be provided, other than through social housing.

Conversely, in a context of regional low demand, the housing market is likely to become a patchy combination of high prices in some neighbourhoods and localised collapse elsewhere. Continued house building in the context of a depressed regional or urban economy (low population growth or decline, with above-average unemployment) may still lead the lower average house prices. However, the regional or citywide average is also likely to include very low prices in unpopular neighbourhoods (Bramley et al. 2008; Goodchild 2008, 244–6).

A further and final complexity arises from likely changes in the behaviour of developers in the absence of planning controls. In general, high-priced dwellings have higher profit margins, so encouraging developers to move upmarket until the local demand for higher priced houses is satisfied. That tendency is itself justification for policies to encourage the development of starter homes or social housing. However, it also changes the form and size of new homes. Modelling by Bramley (1993) suggests that the removal of controls on greenfield sites would lead house builders to change house type and to move upmarket, building larger dwellings in larger garden sizes. Gains in affordability would be less than suggested merely by an increase in the number of housing development sites.

International comparisons offer another way of imagining a counterfactual situation. House price inflation in the countries of the near continent has been lower than in Britain. Barker (2004, 5) noted that:

> Over the last thirty years UK house prices have risen in real terms by around 2½ per cent a year. This stands in contrast to some other countries, such as France, Sweden and Germany, where real house prices have remained broadly constant or even declined.

In the period from 1971 to 2001 house prices in the UK had risen to at least 170 per cent of those in these nearby countries, where house building rates per head of population were substantially higher. Barker's estimate of the variation in house price inflation refers to total differences in prices, not just the difference attributable to planning and is, for that reason, higher than that by Cheshire and Sheppard (2005) or the experience in East Cheshire in the period from 2003 to 2010. Whatever the exact estimate, however, the reference to France, Sweden and Germany does not support the case for deregulation. Effective planning systems exist in all these countries. The difference is that local authorities in continental European countries generally have a better record of using positive planning powers such as land acquisition and investment to work with private builders in creating new communities (Falk 2011; Studdert 2009).

Public sector involvement provides a way of bypassing the obstacles of the market or of private owners reluctant to sell. As is the usual effect of supply-side measures, direct intervention would also serve as a more effective means of securing spatial objectives. In addition, direct intervention might also have a subtle political advantage. The discourse of amenity and rural conservation groups is commonly directed at profit-minded developers. That discourse would lose credibility, if the profit from development were recycled within a local community.

For local authorities or any other agency to bring land onto the market in the UK, however, would require encouragement from government and perhaps also a simplification of existing legal procedures. The legal powers exist, but are not commonly used. Local authority land holdings have, in any case, tended to decline over the years. Moreover, as a result of financial pressures, they typically use their property holdings as a tool of short-term asset management rather than for planning and infrastructure provision (Adams and Watkins 2014, 39).

Barker's analysis stopped before the financial crash of 2008 and the consequent fall in house prices. The experience of the crash is itself of interest, however. Behavioural economics, of which Shiller (2005) is an exponent, differs from the neoclassical assumptions of house price models in assuming an element of irrationality in the determination of prices and that this predisposes markets towards occasional irrational booms or 'bubbles', followed by an inevitable bust. Others (Kyung-Hwan & Renaud 2009) suggest that, in addition, a cycle of boom and bust is not inevitable; they explain that the easy availability of housing credit was a decisive factor in permitting a house price bubble in the US and that the bubble would not have taken place if mortgages had been less freely available. After the financial crash, banks and other lenders have indeed tightened their requirements in Britain, the US and elsewhere.

In Britain, the experience of the short-lived city centre living boom, in the period from about 2000 to 2008 in Leeds, Manchester and other cities in northern England, provides an example of a local property bubble (Goodchild 2013). The experience in the Irish Republic provides another example, at a national rather than localised scale. Kitchin et al. (2010) write:

> ... during the Celtic Tiger period (*1993-2007*) a laissez-faire approach to planning predominated at all levels of governance that was insufficiently evidence-informed ... and ignored more cautious voices. Both the fiscal and planning levers of development were overly pro-growth. As a result, not only was there an unsustainable growth in property prices, but this was accompanied by a property building frenzy that led to a significant oversupply of housing (as well as offices, retail units and hotels) in almost all parts of the country. (Italics added)

Barker, in common with the conventional economic wisdom on Britain, argued that planning policies should anticipate demand and should allocate land for development in response to short-term fluctuations in housing demand. The Irish experience suggests, in contrast, that once the psychology of a housing bubble is established, allocating more and more land for new housing will have little or no impact. Demand proved insatiable, at least in the short term. Instead, Kitchin et al. (ibid.) argue that 'in a housing boom planning should act as a counter-balance to the pressures of development in order to maintain a stable housing market and try to prevent boom and bust cycles.' In terms of physical planning, providing a counterbalance means an exercise in securing stability in house building rates or an economically sustainable increase.

Neoliberal critics and like-minded economists sometimes complain that policies can be captured by specific pressure groups to the detriment of the public good (Fischel 1978; Pennington 2002). The experience of planning for housing in Britain bears out their complaints, but in the direction of intervention in the land market rather than further deregulation. Local amenity groups have no interest in promoting house building, whatever the means of doing so. Private developers operate on a business model that relies on inflation and on maximising land values within the constraints of the existing planning system. That desire, together with the same desire amongst landowners, creates the risk of 'bubbles' and also means that they oppose significant changes. Local authorities have, in the past few years, been weighed down with financial issues and have few resources to use for investment in land purchase or infrastructure in a context where the financial benefits would take some time to materialise, say at least five years after the initial expenditure. Finally, central government has little interest in stimulating actions by local authorities that, in the short term, would increase public expenditure.

Public, supply-side planning remains a realistic alternative as a supplement to and a means of guiding the housing market. Supply-side planning means either the direct provision of housing, as was the model before about 1980, or the provision of equipped sites for private house building or some combination of the two. The main issue, and this is a repeated theme once planning and the market are distinguished from one another, is how to ensure that they are mutually supportive and complementary.

## 'Innovative' Planning

A peculiarity of neoliberal and similar theoretical positions is a failure to recognise governments as a source of innovation. Governments are invariably seen as a break on 'spontaneous change' stimulated by private actions. Friedmann (1966), in contrast, suggests that innovatory planning is a necessary aspect of any state that wishes to embrace new ideas and new values. Innovation is about, in the words of Friedmann (1966), 'translating general value propositions into new institutional arrangements and concrete action programs'. Innovation does not necessarily have to succeed, as it is likely also to encounter resistance. Instead, innovative planning is marked by its intention and desire for change.

The examples provided by Friedmann (1966, 1973) draw in particular from the experience of economic development in Chile in the 1960s. Innovative planning in this case sought to bypass existing bureaucracies in an effort to modernise governmental responses to rapid social change. Crozier (1965) and Nizard (1973) have reported a similar example from France from about the same time. Economic planning in France was simultaneously a means of 'institutional apprenticeship' and institutional development. It involved a small group of officials who were able to work outside and alongside long-standing bureaucratic structures in an effort to promote economic growth. Existing bureaucracies were overloaded with information and a multiplicity of different demands. The economic planning process provided a stable, common reference point for joint action across different sectors of the economy and a base from which different initiatives could develop, so stimulating bureaucracies to change.

Since the 1970s, national economic planning has become less ambitious, less fashionable and in some countries such as Britain has disappeared completely from the political discourse. Yet the very absence of a national framework has placed more onus on local authorities to work out their own future. Local development and urban regeneration has, of itself, stimulated innovative planning, though the initiatives do not always go by the name 'planning'. In particular, in the period from about 1997 to about 2005, the Labour government then in power in Britain actively encouraged local authorities to innovate their practices under the name of 'modernisation'. Healey (2004) provides a case study of this particular era, based on the experience in the northeast of England. Innovation, in this case, was predominately stimulated by a search for economic regeneration in the face of industrial decline. Innovation partly involved a search for newness—'new', 'new policies', 'new projects', 'new practices' and 'new people' (ibid., 12). In addition, innovation involved efforts to promote cultural events and cultural activities on the assumption that this would enrich the lives of the local population and expose them to new ideas. There was, however, no 'recipe' for successful innovation as the process itself depended on experimentation and the ability to draw together varied and otherwise disconnected initiatives. Moreover, the scope for experimentation was limited as efforts at local modernisation became incorporated into a centralised procedure with an emphasis of maintaining control.

To extend the analysis, innovative local development is inherently transversal, breaking down professional and administrative barriers. Innovation occurs through creating multiple links between and across different entities—between public bureaucracies, across public bureaucracies, from the bottom to the top (for example linking the demands of communities to the leadership of a local authority) and between the public sector, business and voluntary agencies. Public sector bureaucracies still remain, however, so contradicting claims about the emergence of a full-blown 'network society', as suggested for example by Albrechts and Mandelbaum (2007). Instead, networks and bureaucracies interact with one another in a way that is partly in opposition, given the rigidity of bureaucratic structures (Jeannot 2005, 107–14).

More recently still, governments in Europe have sought to promote innovation through the national energy action plans prepared in European Union countries, including in this context the UK carbon delivery plan (DECC 2011). The energy action plans are part of a co-ordinated European response to the prospect of climate change, as stated in the relevant European Union directive, and seek to achieve a series of ambitious national carbon reduction targets.[5] In doing so, the plans seek to change the practices of many different agencies and actors, including manufacturers, property developers, local authorities and consumers. In the UK, the national energy action plan is also backed by legal targets in the Climate Change Act and by associated requirements for five yearly progress reports (Stallworthy 2009).

In seeking change in social practices, the energy action plans have implications for the institutions involved in urban development. The introduction of zero carbon heating networks provides an example where technological innovation and organisational innovation have to proceed together. Zero carbon heating is best organised through the provision of heating networks, as this enables a variety of different renewable heat sources. Heating networks are common elsewhere in Europe, but uncommon in Britain outside social housing. To ensure their widespread adoption requires a series of steps that amount to institution building—persuading energy consumers of the advantages and acceptability, specifying new legal obligations (Callcutt, 2007, 54, 91), working out models of financing (ibid., 54) to cover the high initial capital costs, setting up management companies and so on.

Innovative planning, as described by Friedmann, is about planning without plans. It is about action only and a process of trial and error seeking to establish new practices and institutional arrangements. The example of climate change shows that innovation can use a plan as a vehicle for implementation. Implementation through a plan has the disadvantage that the plan has to be prepared and agreed, but it also has advantages, however. The existence of a plan, especially a formal plan with a legal status, acts as a means of locking in those policies and reducing (though not eliminating) the likelihood of a policy exhaustion or reversal (Briatte 2011). The plan therefore offers a means of institutionalising innovation rather than relying on the leadership of individual politicians or public officials.

## 'Radical' Planning

Innovative planning is intermediate between allocative and radical planning, with no absolutely clear boundaries on either side. Radical planning differs from innovation in the extent of its ambition and its more overtly political character. It seeks to transform existing social practices and structures into something different, often in the face of opposition.

In some ways, radical planning is an impossibility—a contradiction of terms. Beauregard (2005) writes, for example:

> Planners are not revolutionaries. Trained to understand how the world works and to intervene to make it better, they operate within, even as they critique and act to change, existing institutions.

Planning, as Mannheim noted, typically operates from the centre or from within an established government agency.

Nevertheless, radical concepts of planning are possible. Radical measures are possible through seeking to apply political ideologies in circumstances where they had not been applied. Radical change can come from the Right as well as the Left, moreover. The market-oriented, neoliberal policies of the 'New Right' government elected in 1979 in Britain, for example the Enterprise Zones and Urban Development Corporations, provide an example, as these broke a political consensus that dated back to the 1950s (Allmendinger and Thomas 1998; Thornley 1991).

Radical planning is also possible at times when large-scale institutional change is likely anyway. For example, theories of state regulation interpret these same policies of the New Right as a necessary consequence of the emergence of a new era of globalised competitive capitalism, together with the decline in the British economy in the preceding decade. The policies of the New Right may have depended initially on political will and leadership, but their implementation and persistence thereafter would not have been possible without the existence of a competitive globalised economy and in Britain, without a legacy of decline that governments wished to reverse (Brenner and Theodore 2002; Peck and Tickell 1992).

Further, radical planning is possible if attention is directed towards social movements outside existing institutions and if, in particular, practice is based on the principles of social rights and empowerment. Radical planning in this second sense is, therefore, an ethical exercise, initiated from the margins by and for protest groups and excluded minority groups, the assumption being that resistance loosens rigid top-down structures and opens the way to change (Clough and Blumberg 2012; Sandercock 1995). So conceived radical planning is an exercise in preparing counterproposals, working out illustrative alternatives and reaching out to other potentially sympathetic groups and individuals.

A related radical strategy is an exercise in what might be termed democratic and political apprenticeship. A case study of an urban settlement in Indonesia, undertaken by Beard (2003), illustrates the point. Autocratic regimes such as that in power in Indonesia at the time of the study provide few opportunities for political debate. Participation in conventional physical planning and in local improvement exercises enables local groups to learn how to articulate demands. It is a precursor of more radical measures, first to prepare community plans, based on the expression of needs and then to mobilise support for a broader social and political transformation that would ensure that those needs would be realised, whilst safeguarding local identities and interests. In the context of an authoritarian regime, Beard adds, these latter stages are likely to involve covert political activities.

Not all radical change involves political resistance or gaining power. Another type involves groups that stand outside the mainstream and that seek to work out and undertake new forms of social practice. Such groups are very diverse and include those with religious motivations. However, they also include community groups that have sought to promote alternative models of sustainable living, building and transport, independently of the state and outside the conventions of commercial industry and corporate urban development. The global Eco-Village network is a specific example. It seeks 'a more sustainable future on Earth', characterised by 'mutual respect, sharing, inclusiveness, positive intent, and fair energy exchange'.[6] Other networks include the international transition towns movement (Scott-Cato and Hillier 2010), the slow cities initiatives (Mayer and Knox 2006) and those based on various experimental 'green builders' and 'green architects' (Lovell 2004, 2009; Smith 2007). City farms and community garden organisations are another source of alternative practices.[7] These have older origins in the provision of allotments for workers and are also an aspect of contemporary collaborative, transactive styles of allocative planning. Nevertheless, in promoting green lifestyles and products, community groups have the potential to offer an alternative form of social and spatial organisation and qualify, therefore, as an exercise in radical planning. Even if their efforts are not taken up by mainstream firms or public agencies, they are still likely to provide a political example and demonstration. The groups are about making small changes in favour of sustainability, even if large changes are out of reach and would in any case raise other potential difficulties.

## Notes

1 'Johannesburg Declaration on Sustainable Development', World Summit on Sustainable Development, 26 August–4 September 2002, the United Nations, consulted February 2015 at www.un-documents.net/jburgdec.htm.
2 Adapted by the author from raw data available in the UK government housing statistics, consulted March 2016 at www.gov.uk/government/statistical-data-sets/live-tables-on-house-building.
3 Smith, L. 'Planning for Housing', House of Commons Library Standard Note SN/SC/3741 (last updated November 2013), consulted February 2014 at www.parliament.uk/briefing-papers/sn03741.pdf.
4 Consulted August 2014 at www.home.co.uk/#tab-prices-and-rents. The analysis follows that undertaken by Levis (2008). However Levis used local authority data that cannot be verified and that stops in 2008. The data from from home.co.uk is, in contrast, publicly available and continuous to the present.
5 Official Journal of the European Union, 5.6.2009: Directive 2009/28/EC of the European Parliament and of the Council of 23 April 2009, consulted March 2015 at http://eur-lex.europa.eu/legal-content/EN/TXT/PDF/?uri=CELEX:32009L0028&from=EN. 'National Action Plans', the European Commission, consulted March 2015 at http://ec.europa.eu/energy/en/topics/renewable-energy/national-action-plans.
6 From the website of the Eco-Village Network, consulted March 2012 at http://gen.ecovillage.org/.
7 The website of the UK Federation of City Farms, consulted January 2014 at www.farmgarden.org.uk/.

## References

Adams, D. & Watkins, C. (2014). *The value of planning*. London: The Royal Town Planning Institute.
Albrechts, L., & Mandelbaum, S. (eds.) (2007). *The network society: a new context for planning*. Abingdon, Oxon, England: Routledge.
Allmendinger, P. and Thomas. H (eds.) (1998). *Urban planning and the British New Right*. London: Routledge.
Archer, T. and Cole, I. (2014). 'Still not plannable? Housing supply and the changing structure of the housebuilding industry in the UK in "austere" times'. *People, Place and Policy*, 8:2, 97–112.
Avelino, F. & Rotmans, J. (2011). 'A dynamic conceptualization of power for sustainability research'. *Journal of Cleaner Production*, 19:8, 796–804.
Barker, K. (2003). *Review of housing supply: securing our future housing needs. Interim report – analysis*. London: HM Treasury.
Barker, K. (2004). *Delivering stability: securing our future housing needs. Review of housing supply – final report – recommendations*. London: HM Treasury.

Barker, K. (2006). *Barker review of land use planning: final report – recommendations*. London: HM Treasury.

Beard, V. A. (2003). 'Learning radical planning: the power of collective action'. *Planning Theory*, 2:1, 13–35.

Beauregard, R. A. (2005). 'Introduction: institutional transformations'. *Planning Theory*, 4:3, 203-7.

Beck, U. (1992). *Risk society: towards a new modernity*. London: Sage Publications (German original 1986).

Bramley, G. (1993). 'Planning, the market and private housebuilding'. *The Planner*, January.

Bramley, G., Leishman, C. & Watkins, D. (2008). 'Understanding neighbourhood housing markets: regional context, disequilibrium, sub-markets and supply'. *Housing Studies*, 23:2, 179–212.

Brenner, N. and Theodore, N. (2002). 'Cities and the geographies of "actually existing neoliberalism"', *Antipode*, 34:3, 349–79.

Briatte, F. (2011). 'La mise en plan de l'action publique: planification et instrumentation des politiques de santé publique', presented at an international conference. *Les instruments d'action publique: Mise en discussion théorique*, Paris 6–8 janvier, [online] URL: http://hal.archives-ouvertes.fr/hal-00675782/ (consulted November 2015).

Brownill, S. (1990). *Developing London's dockland*. London: Paul Chapman

Budinger, A. and Gruehn, D. (2012). 'Increasing land value through open spaces – new options in brownfield redevelopment', a paper presented at the *International Academic Association on Planning, Law, and Property Rights, 6th International Conference*, Belfast, 7–10 February 2012, [online] URL: www.plpr-association.org/index.php/papers-publications (consulted June 2016).

CABE—Commission for Architecture and the Built Environment (collective author) (2008). *Creating successful masterplans: a guide for clients*, 2nd edition. London: CABE.

Callcutt, J. (2007). *The Callcutt Review of housebuilding delivery*. London: Department for Communities and Local Government.

Campbell, S. (1996). 'Green cities, growing cities, just cities?'. *Journal of the American Planning Association*, 62, 3.

Certomà, C. and Notteboom, B. (2015). 'Informal planning in a transactive governmentality: re-reading planning practices through Ghent's community gardens'. *Planning Theory*, online first: [doi] 10.1177/1473095215598177 (consulted October 2015).

Cheshire, P. C. & Hilber, C. A. (2008). 'Office space supply restrictions in Britain: the political economy of market revenge'. *The Economic Journal*, 118:529, F185–F221.

Cheshire, P., Hilber, C. A. L. & Kaplanis, I. (2011). *Evaluating the effects of planning policies on the retail sector: or do town centre first policies deliver the goods?* SERC Discussion Paper SERCDP0066, [online] URL: www.spatialeconomics.ac.uk/SERC/publications/default.asp (consulted December 2014).

Cheshire, P. & Sheppard, S. (2005). 'The introduction of price signals into land use planning decision-making: a proposal'. *Urban Studies*, 42, 647–63.

CLG—Department for Communities and Local Government (2011). *Regeneration to enable growth; what Government is doing in support of community-led regeneration*. London: DCLG.

CLG—Department for Communities and Local Government (2012). *National planning policy framework*. London: DCLG.
Clough, N. & Blumberg, R. (2012). 'Toward anarchist and autonomist Marxist geographies'. *ACME: An International E-Journal for Critical Geographies*, 11:3, 335–351, [online] URL: www.acme-journal.org/Home.html (consulted June 2013).
Crozier M. (1965). 'Pour une analyse sociologique de la planification française'. *Revue française de sociologie*, 6:2, 147–63.
DECC—Department of Energy and Climate Change (corporate author) (2011). *The Carbon Plan: Delivering our low carbon future*, Presented to Parliament pursuant to Sections 12 and 14 of the Climate Change Act 2008, Amended 2nd December 2011 from the version laid before Parliament on 1st December 2011, London, Crown Copyright.
Denman, D. R. (1978). *The place of property*. Berkhamsted: Geographical Publications.
Falk, N. (2011). 'Masterplanning and infrastructure'. In: Adams, D. & Tiesdell, S. (eds), *New communities in europe: urban design in the real estate development process*. Oxford: Wiley Blackwell, 34–53.
Fischel, W. A. (1978). 'A property rights approach to municipal zoning'. *Land Economics*, 54:1, 64–81
Foldvary, F. E. (2009). 'Urban planning: the government or the market', In: Holcombe R. D. & Powell, B. (eds.), *Housing America: building out of a crisis*. Oakland, CA: The Independent Institute, 323–43.
Friedmann, J. (1966). 'Planning as innovation: the Chilean case'. *Journal of the American Institute of Planners*, 32:4, 194–204.
Friedmann, J. (1973). *Retracking America*. Garden City, New York: Anchor Press/Doubleday.
Friedmann, J. (1987). *Planning in the public domain: from knowledge to action*. Princeton, NJ: Princeton University Press.
Glaeser, E. L. and Ward, B. A. (2009). 'The causes and consequences of land use regulation: evidence from Greater Boston'. *Journal of Urban Economics*, 65:3, 265–78.
Goodchild, B. (2008). *Homes, cities and neighbourhoods*. Hampshire: Aldershot.
Goodchild, B. (2013). 'Flats, higher densities and city centre living: a response to Evans and Unsworth'. *Urban Studies* 50:14, 3036–42.
Hall, P., Gracey, H., Drewett, R. & Thomas, R. (1973). *The containment of urban England, volume two: the planning system*. London: George Allen and Unwin.
Harvey, D. (1989). 'From managerialism to entrepreneurialism: the transformation in urban governance in late capitalism'. *Geografiska Annaler, Series B, Human Geography*, 71:1, 3–17.
Healey, P. (1998). 'Building institutional capacity through collaborative approaches to urban planning'. *Environment and Planning A*, 30:9, 1531–46.
Healey, P. (2004). 'Creativity and urban governance'. *disP-The Planning Review*, 40:158, 11–20.
Henneberry, J. & Halleux, J. M. (2008). 'Effects of landscape quality on property and land values'. In: Project Team (corporate author), *Creating a setting for investment: project report*. Interreg IIIB - Europe du Nord-Ouest, [online] URL: http://orbi.ulg.ac.be/bitstream/2268/64180/1/CSI6%20(1).pdf (consulted March 2015), 26–37.

Hilber, C. & Vermeulen, W. (2012). *The impact of supply constraints on house prices in England*. Working Paper. London School of Economics & Spatial Economics Research Centre, [online] URL: www.gov.uk/government/publications/impact-of-restricting-housing-supply-on-house-prices (consulted August 2014).

Hirsch, F. (1977). *The Social Limits to Growth*, London: Routledge and Kegan Paul.

HM Government (2010). *Local growth: realising every place's potential*. London: The Stationery Office, CM 7961.

Hopkins, L. D. (2001). *Urban development: The logic of making plans*. Washington DC: Island Press.

INFRAS Research and Consulting, von Stokar, T. & Steinemann, M. (2004). *Sustainable development in Switzerland: methodological foundations*. Berne: Swiss Agency for Development and Cooperation.

Jeannot, G. (2005). *Les métiers du flou. Travail et action publique*. Toulouse: Octarès Éditions.

Kim, J. H. (2011). 'Linking land use planning and regulation to economic development: a literature review'. *Journal of Planning Literature*, 26:1, 35–47.

Kitchin, R., Gleeson, J., Keaveney, K. & O'Callaghan, C. (2010). *A haunted landscape: housing and ghost estates in post-Celtic Tiger Ireland*. National University of Ireland, Maynooth, Co Kildare, NIRSA Working Paper 59.

Kornai, J. (1979). 'Resource-constrained versus demand-constrained systems'. *Econometra*, 47:4, 819.

Kyung-Hwan, K. & Renaud, B. (2009). 'The global house price boom and its unwinding: an analysis and a commentary'. *Housing Studies*, 24:1, 7–24,

Lai, L. W. -G. (2004). 'Spontaneous catallaxis in urban & rural development under planning by contract in a small open economy: the ideas of Hayek and Mises at work in town & country planning in Hong Kong'. *Review of Austrian Economics*, 17:2/3, 155–86.

Levis, D. J. (2008). *What affect have the housing restraint policies adopted by some Cheshire local authorities had upon provision of new housing in Cheshire?* A dissertation submitted in partial completion of a M.Sc in Urban and Regional Planning at Sheffield Hallam University.

Longlands, S. L. (2013). 'Growing nowhere: privileging economic growth in planning policy'. *Local Economy*, 28:7-8, 894–905.

Lovell, H. (2004). 'Framing sustainable housing as a solution to climate change'. *Journal of Environmental Policy & Planning*, 6:1, 35–55.

Lovell, H. (2009). 'The role of individuals in policy change: the case of UK low-energy housing'. *Environment and Planning C: Government and Policy*, 27:3, 491–511.

Mann, M. (1970). 'The social cohesion of liberal democracy'. *American Sociological Review*, 35:3, 423–39.

Mannheim, K. ([1940] 1971). *Man and society in age of reconstruction*. London: Routledge and Kegan Paul (first published in English in 1940, partly based on a German original of 1935).

Mayer, H. & Knox, P. L. (2006). 'Slow cities: sustainable places in a fast world'. *Journal of Urban Affairs*, 28:4, 321–34.

Molotch, H. (1976). 'The city as a growth machine: toward a political economy of place'. *American Journal of Sociology*, 82:2, 309–32.

Molotch, H. (1993). 'The political economy of growth machines'. *Journal of Urban Affairs*, 15:1, 29–53.

Moroni, S. and Andersson, D. E. (2014). 'Introduction' in Andersson, D. E. and Moroni, S. (eds.) (2014), *Cities and private planning*. Cheltenham, UK: Edward Elgar.

Nettlefold, J. S. (1908). *Practical housing*. Letchworth: The Garden City Press.

Nizard, L. (1973) 'Administration et société : planification et régulations bureaucratiques'. *Revue Française de Science Politique*, 23:2, 199–229.

OECD (2007). *Competitive cities: a new entrepreneurial paradigm in spatial development*. Paris: OECD Publishing.

Peck, J. A. & Tickell, A. (1992). 'Local modes of social regulation? Regulation theory, Thatcherism and uneven development'. *Geoforum*, 23:3, 347–63.

Pennington, M. (2002). *Liberating the land: the case for private land-use planning*. London: Institute of Economic Affairs.

Project Team (corporate author) (2008). *Creating a setting for investment: project report*. Interreg IIIB - Europe du Nord-Ouest, [online] URL: http://orbi.ulg.ac.be/bitstream/2268/64180/1/CSI6%20(1).pdf (consulted March 2015).

Pryce, G. (1999). 'Construction elasticities and land availability: a two stage squares model of housing supply using the variable elasticity approach'. *Urban Studies*, 36:13, 2283–2304.

Raco, M. (2005). 'Sustainable development, rolled-out neoliberalism and sustainable communities'. *Antipode*, 37:2, 324–47.

Reade, E. (1987). *British town and country planning*. Milton Keynes: The Open University.

Robinson, N. A. (2013a). Environmental principles & norms amidst the Anthropocene. *Nordic Environmental Social Science Conference*, Copenhagen, 11–13 June.

Robinson, N. A. (2013b). *Environmental regulation of real property*. New York: Law Journal Press (first published in 1982 and updated periodically, with revisions by K. A. Reilly).

Rothbard, M. N. (1978). *For a new liberty: the libertarian manifesto*. Auburn, AL: Ludwig von Mises Institute.

Sandercock, L. (1995). 'Voices from the borderlands: a meditation on a metaphor'. *Journal of Planning Education and Research*, 14:2, 77–88.

Scott-Cato, M. and Hillier, J. (2010). 'How could we study climate-related social innovation? Applying Deleuzean philosophy to transition towns. *Environmental Politics*, 19:6, 869–87.

Sen, A. (1987). *Gender and cooperative conflicts*. WP 18. Helsinki: World Institute for Development Economics Research.

Shiller, R. J. (2005). *Irrational exuberance*, 2nd edition. Princeton, NJ: Princeton University Press.

Shin, H. (2010). 'Can one actually say what one wants? Adaptive preferences in the negotiation process', *Planning Theory & Practice*, 11:3, 339–57.

Smith, A. (2007). 'Translating sustainabilities between green niches and socio-technical regimes'. *Technology Analysis & Strategic Management*, 19:4, 427–50.

Stallworthy, M. (2009). 'Legislating against climate change: a UK perspective on a Sisyphean challenge'. *Modern Law Review*, 72, 412–36.

Studdert, P. (2009). 'Building new communities through local partnerships'. In: CABE (collective author) (ed.), *Who should build our homes?* London: CABE, 32–55.

Thornley, A. (1991). *Urban planning under Thatcherism: the challenge of the market*. London: Routledge.

WCED—World Commission on Environment and Development (1987). *Our common future*. Oxford: Oxford University Press.

# Part III
# Applying 'Reason' to Politics

# 5 Rationalism and Pragmatism

Planning may be conceived in part as a method that is its own justification, independent of the substance of policy. So conceived planning is a means of improving the quality of the decision-making process, of improving the capacity of governments to make decisions and of society to learn and finally of improving policy integration and co-ordination. The rationale is not so much a set of specific methods, but the application of reason to a political process, in principle any political process, whether this involves economic planning, spatial planning or environmental planning or some combination. Reason means, as stated in the Oxford English Dictionary, 'a view of things or manner of proceeding which seems wise, logical, or correct'.

Applied to planning, appeals to reason involve two main discourses and philosophies of knowledge—pragmatism and rationalism. Pragmatism shares, in the words of, Hoch (1984), a common belief in 'doing good' and 'being right'. Doing good means some practical action to achieve the public good. Being right means ensuring that the actions are based on a sound analysis of the situation of diagnosis of the problem at hand. Pragmatism is about a world where idealism, the hope for a better future, interacts with realism, the sense of what is possible in any context (Hoch 2007). Pragmatism is also about a world in the making, rather than a world determined from above (Shalin 1986), a world, to use the language of Deleuze and Guattari (1987, 39–59), determined by molecular rather than molar processes, a world where individuals and social groups continue to possess the capacity for creative action (Joas, 1993, 4).

Rationalism is distinguished from pragmatism by a more formal character and is often more technical. Rationalism is, as a result, arguably even more limited in its ability to justify planning as a social or political programme. For example, the 'systems' variant of rational planning, developed in Britain by McLoughlin (1969) amongst others, is explicitly said to depend on a prior 'decision to adopt planning' (ibid., 96). Rationalism is a means of justifying or rejecting a specific alternative, as the case may be, within the framework of a policy commitment.

The distinction between rationalism and pragmatism is not huge, however, as both are concerned with how to create and apply valid knowledge and both raise questions of the scientific method. They are also both normative in character. In seeking to define valid knowledge, they also define how planners and policy ought to make and defend decisions. Rationalism and pragmatism may and commonly do coexist together. Wang and Hoch (2013) have examined the assumptions of practice in Chicago and Shanghai. Despite very large institutional differences, professional planners in both cities articulated their decisions with reference to notions of rationality, whilst they also made pragmatic, practical decisions as necessary.

Of course, to say that planning practice can be interpreted as a combination of 'rational' and 'pragmatic' thinking itself begs the question as to the exact character and implications of these concepts. For pragmatism, the origins comprise a particular American school of philosophy associated with C. S. Peirce, William James, George Herbert Mead and John Dewey, all of whom were active in the late 19th or 20th centuries. The very word, 'pragmatic', acquired its modern meaning from Peirce and James. The Oxford English Dictionary gives numerous example of how the adjective 'pragmatic' has been used. The definition derived from pragmatic philosophy means 'concerned with practical consequences or values'. However, the examples show that pragmatic came from mediaeval French and originally meant 'relating to the affairs of a state or community'. As a result, before the mid-19th century, to talk of someone being pragmatic commonly suggested that he or she was officious, interfering, conceited or dogmatic—this latter being the very opposite of its modern meaning.

Rationalist theories of knowledge and planning have more varied origins and also have varied names, including not just the rational model and the decision model, but systems approaches and positivist models. Rational planning involves systems because it involves the guidance or design of either land use/transport or other urban systems, as was argued by McLoughlin (1969) and Chadwick (1971) in Britain, or other types of socio-technical systems, for example systems that link the urban infrastructure and the various activities that take place in an area. Finally, rational planning is sometimes called 'positivist' because it has generally assumed the ability of social science to predict the future, often using quantitative models.

## Rationalist Logics

According to Friedmann (1987, 89, 421–27), rational planning theory originated in part in the US in the 1920s and 1930s in theories of scientific business management, before becoming the dominant model of decision-making in the US in the 1950s and 1960s. Given that rational planning theory was also the source of the earliest theories of the planning process elsewhere, rational planning may be discussed first. US rational planning theory provides, for example, the basis of most of the readings in 'Planning Theory', edited by Faludi (1973), the first publication of its type in Britain and almost certainly the first in Europe.

The reliance on US sources should not be exaggerated. The origins of rational planning theory also lie in early 20th century European sociology, notably in the work of Simmel ([1903] 1997, 13), Weber (Lassman and Speirs 1994) and Mannheim ([1940] 1971). Simmel argued that 'the modern mind has become more and more a calculating one', partly as a result of the pressures of city life and partly as a result of the growth of a money economy. Weber identified 'rationalisation', the growth of rational organization, as a basic tendency of a modern society and linked this to the growth of economic calculation, bureaucracy and legal institutions. For Simmel and Weber, therefore, rationalisation is grounded in processes of economic and institutional modernisation that are international and worldwide—an interpretation supported by contemporary similarities between rational planning in Chicago and Shanghai. Mannheim took the ideas of Simmel and Weber further. Mannheim saw central planning as a further stage in the rational organization of society. Planning would coordinate bureaucracy and the law and promote rationality in the face of contrary tendencies. Whether of US or European origins, however, rationalism as applied to urban planning was indeed largely a US innovation. The advocates of planning in the US in the early 20th century were more concerned with urban governance than their British and European equivalents and were more inclined to see physical planning as only acquiring meaning in a social and political context (Faludi 1970).

The multiple origins of rational planning reflect different definitions of rationality. Mannheim ([1940] 1971, 52–8) distinguished between two types, functional and substantial rationality, the former being a narrower, business management and bureaucratic approach. The two approaches are, in part, complementary. A narrow approach can, in principle, proceed within a long-term political strategy. However, for Mannheim, the risk also existed that the repeated pursuit of narrow business and bureaucratic rationalities could crowd out broader, strategic thinking. Subsequent criticism, by Popper ([1983] 2000), has led to a third approach, that of critical rationalism.

## *Functional Rationality: Relating Ends and Means*

The narrower definition, that of 'functional' rationality, involves, according to Mannheim (ibid., 53), 'a series of actions' that lead 'to a previously defined goal, every element in this series of actions receiving a functional position and role'. So defined, rationality can be operationalised and the

130  *Applying 'Reason' to Politics*

extent of rationality can be measured by two criteria 'a) ... with reference to a definite goal and b) a consequent calculability when viewed from the standpoint of an observer or a third person' (ibid.).

Subsequent planning theorists, notably those writing in the 1950s and 1960s, provide more detail. Banfield (1959) defined a rational decision as one that starts with an analysis of the situation and then proceeds in the following manner:

> (a) the decision-maker lists all the opportunities for action open to him; (b) he identifies all the consequences which would follow from the adoption of each of the possible actions; and (c) he selects the action which would he followed by the preferred set of consequences.

Likewise, Davidoff and Reiner (1962) defined planning 'as a purposive process, keyed to preferred, ordered ends'. Finally, McLoughlin (1969, 95) defined planning as a cyclic process with the following stages:

1. The environment is scanned and on the basis of values held by the individual or group needs or wants become apparent. ...
2. Goals are formulated in broad terms and perhaps at the same time certain more precise objectives (which must be reached in order to move toward goals) are identified.
3. Possible courses of action to reach the objectives and move towards the goals are identified.
4. Evaluation of these possible courses occurs by reference to the means available, the costs likely to be incurred in overcoming constraints on action, the benefits likely to be derived and the consequences of action, so far as can be seen.
5. Action is taken on the basis of these considerations. ... The environment continues to be scanned and new goals and objectives may be formed.

In discussions of rational planning, ends cover anything that planning seeks to achieve, including goals, aims and objectives. Goals, aims and objectives are typically distinguished by their level in a hierarchy of specificity, in which one sets the context for others. However, the literature is not always consistent in its use of language as to whether goals are more general than objectives and aims or *vice versa* or whether both are more general than aims. Whatever the term used, the specification of clear goals or objectives is commonly regarded as crucial. For example, a rationalist account of sustainable transport planning by Hutton (2013, 29) states:

> The definition of objectives is absolutely critical to effective planning; without them actions are merely blind fumbles in an attempt to do

something, no matter what, or much more likely, to be seen to being doing something.

In contrast, a pragmatic response would suggest that, while clear aims are essential to generate direction, these can be generated through analysis during the plan or policy-making process. Further, an insistence on the prior existence of clear goals or objectives is likely to limit analysis and evaluation to single, rather than double loop learning of the type that enables a questioning of aims, goals and objectives.

The information requirements of the rational model are potentially demanding, potentially very demanding indeed. Realistic accounts of rational planning must also involve a recognition that the information commonly available to make decisions is limited or 'bounded', to use the term used by Simon (1997). The bounds of knowledge are not static, however. Subject to the constraints of time and effort, a rationalist would argue that it makes good sense to expand the limits of knowledge, to collect more information and, as part of this, to apply systematic models. Moreover, the existence of limits to knowledge does not preclude learning as organisations encounter new situations or undertake new tasks (Simon 1991). Organisations can learn collectively through their existing staff or they can acquire new staff with different skills and experiences.

Recognition of the limitations of knowledge implies a degree of overlap with neoliberal critiques. However, neoliberals such as Hayek argue that the limits of knowledge show the impossibility of planning and that the price mechanism should always prevail. Economies are simply too complex to be planned. A rationalist position, following Simon, is more qualified (Fiori 2010). Centralised planning may indeed run into information problems. However, decentralised public planning is possible for exactly the reason that bounded rationality applies to both private and public agencies. In the case of public agencies, moreover, planning is likely to use 'devices other than prices for coordination' (March and Simon [1958], 1993, 229).

In principle, any realistic aim or end can provide a basis for plan making, policy and subsequent measurement. However, the typical approach is both utilitarian and growth oriented. The usual assumption in economic theory is to define rationality as the ability of actors, such as a firm or consumers, to maximise their 'utility', that is to say to maximise the achievement of their personal or organisational goals and demands (Simon 1986). Rational planning has commonly transferred that assumption to collective decision-making. The ultimate end of urban planning becomes the creation of a spatial framework in which firms can prosper and consumers can achieve a higher level of quantity and quality of material consumption, for example for travel or for new homes. This utilitarian orientation is, for example, implicit in the reference of McLoughlin (1969) to the identification of 'group needs or wants'. Planning forecasts economic activities and demands into the future and then involves the identification of alternative strategies to meet those forecasts.

Another related, economic definition of 'ends' comprises the 'three E's' of value for money—economy, efficiency, effectiveness. Economy means 'spending less' in terms of the resources of time and money; efficiency means 'spending well' to ensure the same or a better quality of service or product for less cost, time or effort; effectiveness means 'spending wisely' in relation to the achievement of a specified policy goal.[1] Planning, like other public services, one might argue from a rationalist position, has to be judged against the 'three E's'.

Not all situations and problems are easily reduced either to the three 'E's or to a simple, universal statement of objectives or aims, however. To provide some examples: tackling problems of traffic congestion in the long term might involve, *inter alia*, policies to reduce car use through parking controls or to build more roads or to change land use arrangements or to encourage and require employers to adopt supportive measures. Each policy measure defines the cause of the problem in a different way and has different policy implications. Likewise, the management of urban growth and decline is likely to break down into a multiplicity of local and specific problems, again including traffic congestion, house price inflation in areas of high demand and population loss in low demand areas in a way that rational analysis cannot prioritise of itself. The management of urban growth also raises other uncertainties, notably about the reliability of projections of population and economic activity that are uncertain, beyond say four or five years into the future.

Reducing traffic congestion and ensuring effective urban management are all aspects of 'value for money' in planning and more broadly in local government. They remain very general, however, and cannot be used to guide or evaluate practice without specification of the context, including their local policy context and history. Appeals to sustainable development are likewise too general and unspecific (Alexander 2009).

Traffic management, urban growth management and sustainable development are all examples of 'wicked' rather than 'tame' problems, to use the terminology of Rittel and Webber (1973). Wicked problems merit their description because an optimal solution cannot be defined unless the specific context is known and restrictive conditions and assumptions are imposed first. Every wicked problem comprises a unique combination of factors and may also be a symptom of another problem. The problem can as a result be explained and understood from a variety of different perspectives with different preferred solutions, many of which may be dependent on solutions to other related problems. In addition, wicked problems occur in a political context in which there is no objective definition of equity and where, in any case, it is impractical to define an optimal outcome.

Yet, the recognition of wicked problems does not completely undermine the use of the rational model. The distinction between a wicked problem and a tame problem is one of degree, rather than an absolute. Problems of housing shortages, traffic congestion and neighbourhood deprivation can at least be monitored to assess change over time. Equally, attempts can be made to assess the feasibility of policy initiatives in advance and to evaluate the impact of policies as implemented. Moreover, rational planning has, at least, the advantage of seeking out root causes, where these are known. In treating complex problems, therefore, a mixed approach is commonly preferable (Etzioni 1968, 282–309).

The concept of a wicked problem illustrates another related criticism, namely that functional rationality commonly assumes that the professional expert knows best, rather than the public. The defenders of a rational approach would no doubt respond that exactly the ability to work out the technical and scientific implications is its strength. Functional rationality, like other concepts of rationality, promotes knowledge and logic as the basis for making decisions and so promotes a sense of professionalism amongst practitioners (Baum 1996). Functional rationality also gives an impression of objectivity, at least within the relevant terms of reference (Owens et al. 2004). Partly for this reason, the basic principles of functional rationality—clarifying aims and objectives, identifying realistic alternatives, evaluating those alternatives—have proved durable and largely taken for granted in planning, policy-making and related forms of practice evaluation.

The durability and persistence of the rational model is almost certainly not attributable to any claim to objective knowledge, however. There are other models of scientific objectivity, including pragmatic models. Most likely, their durability is also attributable to the association between functional rationality and business-like methods and the continuing emphasis in public policy on economic calculation and on 'delivery', that is to say economy and effectiveness.

## *Substantial Rationality: Searching for 'Principia Media'*

The distinction between functional and Mannheim's second type of rationality, substantial rationality, has become largely forgotten. Most advocates and critics of rational planning have either assumed that the distinction is unimportant or have used administrative theories that, by definition, exclude substantial rationality. Other planning theorists (Alexander 2000; Verma 1996) equate Mannheim's concept of substantial rationality with another, looser concept of 'substantive rationality' that incorporates values, ideals and moral thinking.

Substantial rationality is neither functional nor substantive rationality, however. It is distinguished from the former by its strategic character and from the latter by its concern with social control rather than any specific issue or problem or value, other than the promotion of stability and the preservation of social order. For Mannheim ([1940] 1971, 55–8), substantial rationality is about self-observation, self-reflection and self-rationalisation, undertaken at both an individual and societal level. It involves individuals learning about the factors that determine their conduct and societies learning about the factors that determine their development so that they can exercise self-regulation and can control impulses. Substantial rationality amounts to the ability to make an 'intelligent insight into the inter-relations of events in a given situation' (ibid., 53).

In earlier historical periods, the enlightened self-interest of entrepreneurs and of an intellectual elite guaranteed the exercise of substantial rationality, according to Mannheim. In a complex modern society, substantial rationality can only be exercised through planning or to be more accurate and abstractly through 'thought at the level of planning' and operating through the exercise of power from key positions (ibid., 152–3). Substantial rationality, as exercised by planning, is therefore a means of adapting society to fundamental and inevitable drivers of change, *'principia media'*, to use his terminology (ibid., 174–84).

Like 'substantial rationality', the concept of *'principia media'* is rarely if ever used outside the work of Mannheim. These are 'middle principles' that mediate between abstract general laws and specific historical and local circumstances (Loader 2011, 483) They are, in the words of Mannheim, 'universal forces in a concrete setting as they become integrated out of the various factors at work in a given place at a given time'. Mannheim always refers to the plural *'principia media'* to suggest that different factors are likely to operate alongside each and to interact with one another. Together a 'large number of mutually related "principia media" form a structure' (Mannheim ([1940] 1971, 184). It is not possible, therefore, to read history from a single determinant, as for example is the implication of mainstream, 'scientific' Marxism with its emphasis on the workings of the economy. The same insistence on *'principia media'* in the plural also reduces the risk of oversimple solutions such as Jacobs (1964) and others noted were typical of modernist town planning in the 1950s and 1960s.

The identity and implications of these apparently inevitable principles does not figure in Mannheim's account, except for the tendencies that were the justification for planning itself. However, it is possible to think of examples, even if the same terminology is not used. Contemporary drivers of urban change might include demographic trends such as the simultaneous combination of an ageing population and continued immigration from overseas, globalisation, with this being understood as increased international economic integration, increased economic and social inequalities and deprivation, increased awareness of global environmental risks and the emergence of a rapidly changing, consumer society (see, for example, Amin, 2011; Ascher 2001; IDOX 2007, 8.)

The various trends are likely to interact with one another, so maintaining uncertainty about the direction of change in a specific city. Identifying the drivers of change still requires their application. Like functional rationality, substantial rationality is, moreover, vulnerable to the criticism of imposing a scientific narrative from above, so excluding politics. Even so, substantial rationality has the advantage of allowing double loop learning, placing events in context and working out a strategic, collective response in a way that functional rationality does not.

## Critical Rationalism: Planning as Hypothesis Testing

The third approach to rational decision making, that of critical rationalism, originated as a direct response to substantial rationality and, in particular, to its supposed weaknesses. The identification of *'principia media'* is an example of the application of induction or more accurately inductive reasoning. The social researcher observes patterns and trends and elaborates general principles on the basis of these observations whilst taking into account local circumstances. The assumption is that similar processes will operate into future.

In contrast, in the context of the great planning debate of the 1940s, Popper (1944) argued against the use of induction. The argument was partly based on the similarity between induction and the hated philosophy of 'historicism', where the identification of so-called laws of historical development is tied to social reconstruction and large-scale 'utopian social engineering'. However, the criticism of induction was also couched in terms of the philosophy of science. For Popper ([1976] 2002, 171–2):

> Sensible rules of inductive inference do not exist. ... The best rule I can extract from my reading of inductive literature would be something like this: 'The future is likely to be not very different from the past.' This, of course, is a rule which everybody accepts in practice; and something like it we must accept also in theory if we are realists. ... The rule is, however, so vague that it is hardly interesting. And in spite of its vagueness, the rule assumes too much. ...

Induction is a form of correspondence reasoning, based on the identification of patterns in a situation and assuming that these will continue either over time or elsewhere. Induction only allows limited predictions in Popper's view and has to be treated with caution.

Rather than induction, Popper ([1983] 2000, 33) argued for a method of 'critical rationalism' that involved data collection, deduction and falsification through hypothesis testing and the elimination of those hypotheses where observation and experiments indicate contrary results. Deduction is also not a foolproof method, as a hypothesis may work in one situation, but not in another. As a result, the concept of critical rationalism and its closely associated style of 'piecemeal social engineering' point to the need for the continuous monitoring and testing of policy and for a flexible policy response in the light of that monitoring.

So far, so good. Popper's concept of piecemeal social engineering implies a style of planning and policy making that is based on evidence, indicators and evaluation, as is a common theme in many statements on good practice (Faludi & Waterhout 2006) and is, in any case close to the implications of the rational decision model, as elaborated as a cyclic process, for example by McLoughlin (1969). Making a case for evidence and policy evaluation is not an aspect of practice where planners and policy researchers need to become involved in the intricacies of philosophy (Faludi 1983, 277). Searching for evidence and making evaluations, either of existing or likely impacts and outcomes, is a common theme in nearly all approaches.

The use of evidence, indicators and evaluation involves the testing of policy. Scientific falsification cannot be the whole test of policy, however, for a variety of reasons. Policies involve values that may be inherently good or bad and cannot be tested as such. Moreover, the aim of planning and policy is not to find some scientific generalisation, but to improve people's lives or to protect their quality of life in some way.

Further, piecemeal social engineering assumes a single 'planning subject' making decisions. It is not well adapted to a typical situation where decisions are the product of multiple institutional actors and are the outcome of deliberations and policy conflicts that have taken place over many years. It is also not suited to decisions with long-term implications that are difficult to reverse such as demolition or new development. The time to work out the implications of such long-term decisions is, in advance, not afterwards as an exercise in hypothesis testing. Finally, the emphasis on hypothesis testing looks cumbersome and unrealistic in the context of the uncertainties of practice, with, for example, varied levels of reliable evidence and multiple interpretations of that evidence.

To give an example of the complexities of multiple interpretations: an axiom of economic theory is that prices increase in the context of restrictions on supply. Therefore, as argued in the Barker (2003, 2004) review, house building rates in England and Wales should be increased. However, house prices are influenced by other factors apart from the availability of stock, including speculation and over-optimism. The relevant economic hypotheses may still be correct, but have to be qualified by the condition of 'all things being equal'. And this condition may not apply. The existence of housing shortages in Britain can, in any case, be shown by other means—for example, the number of homeless people, the number of sharing households who would prefer to live separately. It still makes sense to enquire about all the different potential blockages to house building and to find ways of removing those blockages. Complexity and uncertainty suggest, in other words, that Popper's concept of critical rationalism does not add much to the earlier concepts of functional and substantial rationality.

## Pragmatic Logics

The distinction between pragmatism and rationalism rests mostly in an effort to contextualise both the functional distinction between ends and means and, in addition, the reliance of substantial rationality on inductive methods. A pragmatic position does not reject functional rationality. It merely states that other, more flexible styles of action are possible. Functional rationality is, from a pragmatic perspective, no more than a potentially useful means of clarifying specific tasks and may be disregarded if it is unhelpful (Joas & Beckert 2002). In addition, the distinction between induction and deduction is considered as no more than overlapping elements in a continuing process of enquiry that involves other, alternative models of scientific reasoning. These alternative models are not just possible, moreover, but necessary to science as a creative process and therefore by analogy to planning a creative process.

### *Abduction and Retroduction*

This latter point may be explained in more detail. The distinction between induction and deduction remains common in introductions to the scientific method.[2] In contrast, for Peirce (1839–1914), the first to outline the alternative, pragmatic models, intellectual enquiry amounted to a combination, not just of induction and deduction, but of:

- 'abduction', involving the Latin '*ab*' meaning going away in an attempt to bring new elements into a reasoning process (Peirce [1903] 1998b, 224); and
- 'retroduction', from the Latin '*retro*' meaning going backwards to reanalyse events, facts and processes through the identification of a general idea (Peirce [1898] 1998a, 47) and therefore through the 'premises', that is to say the prior conditions that structure or allow a situation or phenomenon to exist.

An abductive explanation is about playing with ideas, broadening the interpretation of events and dealing with complex situations where analysis involves sorting through different possibilities and finding the best fit between multiple theoretical frameworks (Bajc 2012; Danermark et al. 2002, 89–92). An example concerns the use of energy in the home and its relation to the design of the home. No single explanation or understanding is capable of understanding the variety of factors that residents cite when discussing how they use and heat their home. Instead, analysis has to proceed pragmatically, citing different theories as and when they appear in the narrative (Goodchild et al. 2014).

Retroductive explanations, in contrast, are less about theory and more about the context of a pattern of behaviour. They commonly look for explanations outside the immediate situation and may also point to explanatory factors that people of which may otherwise be unaware. To provide an example: a retroductive explanation of levels of public transport and car use in a specific residential area might look at the overall population density, the reason being that high car use (and equally low public transport use) is associated with low densities and *vice versa* (Næss & Jensen 2002; Newman & Kenworthy 1989). It is unlikely, however, that direct questions to residents would elicit references to density or dispersion as factors that influence the use of a private car, rather than public transport. The residents would, most likely, not be aware of the impact of the context in which they live and that they mostly take for granted.

The difference between retroduction and abduction is not as large as their Latin roots would suggest. Sometimes the two terms are used interchangeably, both in Peirce's original writings and in subsequent discussions (Bertilsson, 2004; Chiasson 2005). Abduction is, in any case, the most characteristic feature of the pragmatic method. Pragmatism, notes Peirce ([1903] 1998b, 234) 'is nothing else than the question of the logic of abduction'.

More significantly, taken together, abduction and retroduction imply an extended enquiry in time and space, a process of experimentation and a circular process of coming and going that goes back to the original explanation and also advances other possibilities and that in doing so breaks down the distinction between induction, based on patterns, and deduction, based on hypotheses. Pragmatism assumes that both induction and deduction are sterile if pursued in isolation. Instead, the various types of reasoning—retroduction, deduction, abduction and induction, have to be mixed together in a circular process of reasoning and testing that allows the researcher to sift out explanations, to focus on that explanation that best suits the circumstances and that also tests the practical consequences in terms of impacts and outputs.

As is implicit in the reference to impacts and outputs, pragmatism may also be applied to policy-making and to informed political debate, as Dewey demonstrated. For Dewey (1938), the knowledge that underlies informed policy debate amounts to common sense rather than science, the latter term being reserved for abstract statements, quantitative relationships and a search for knowledge for its own sake. Absolute certainty and absolute truth are, moreover, unnecessary to achieve practical change or social improvement. Indeed, the search for absolute certainty and truth can divert attention away from human experience and denigrate some forms of practical knowledge in favour of more abstract, theoretical knowledge (Dewey 1929). Policy decisions always require an element of practical judgement about its consequences, a point that involves, in turn, the application of public values and public ethics, or morality to use Dewey's terminology.

Nevertheless, public policy may operate on similar principles to that of science, through experimentation and critical testing, in a way that facilitates collective problem solving. Indeed, democracy and pragmatic science are, for Dewey, complementary and closely related in that both have the potential to create objective knowledge based on human experience (Hildebrand 2011; Ray 2004). The main precondition is the creation of a public and the existence of some form of public debate. Conversely, the absence of a public means that policies are unlikely to be tested with any degree of rigour and the quality of democratic decision-making suffers (Dewey [1927] 2012).

Dewey's pragmatism, with its reference to common sense and suspicion of certainty, differs from that of Peirce. Peirce defined the truth of a statement through the extent that it conformed to an objective reality and was able to summarise accurately the characteristics of that reality. Truth, therefore, lies in abstract statements whose determination is, above all, a task for specialists. Dewey argued, in contrast, that truth, to the extent that it exists, emerges from the consequences of an action and, in the context of issues of collective interest, should involve debate from an educated public. Technical knowledge is, for Dewey ([1927] 2012), inadequate as it fails to promote public understanding and fails, therefore, to promote the ability of the public and ultimately of governments to confront problems. Given that the consequences of an action are, in any case, commonly uncertain or subject to interpretation, truth has a subjective aspect and involves judgements of value as well as fact.

The distinction between the objective, scientific pragmatism of Pierce and the common-sense, subjective pragmatism of Dewey is not total. Dewey did not use the methodological categories of abduction and retroduction, but also did not challenge these categories (Prawat 1999). Both Peirce and Dewey believed that scientific progress and innovation emerges from a situation of indeterminacy (a confusing, uncertain or conflicting situation) and, in addition, that scientific progress and innovation are about the transformation of an indeterminate into a settled, determinate situation (Dewey 1938, 108–9: Schön 1992). Further, Dewey sought to bridge the divide between objective, scientific knowledge and subjective positions by posing the existence of a process of interaction between the two. Science starts in common sense and, if scientific knowledge is to be applied, it has to return to common sense (Dewey 1938, 77).

Nevertheless, the distinction between Peirce and Dewey marks a persistent divide, suggesting for some critics (for example, Rescher 2012) that pragmatism is too indefinite and too multidimensional to constitute a single position and that it needs to be refined. However, for planning and many other forms of professional knowledge, the ambiguities of pragmatism pose less of a problem, as practice has to deal with both 'objective' knowledge (in the form of statistics and the projection of established trends) and 'subjective' knowledge that is socially constructed and sometimes associated with specific groups. The world of planning is 'ontologically diverse', to use the terminology of Schön (1988). It consists of multiple forms of knowledge, generated from both quantitative and qualitative methods and based on multiple sources that fit together or fail to fit together, as the case may be.

## Pragmatism in Planning Theory

As applied to planning, pragmatism links theory and action without giving primacy to either whilst also suggesting that action can itself generate ideas. As a result, pragmatism has the merit of recognising uncertainty, the possibility of correcting policy as events unfold and the possibility, as in Dewey's interpretation, of correcting policy through the democratic process. Pragmatism, therefore, allows a proliferation of different degrees of intervention in the property and labour markets. It does this, moreover, without becoming fixed on specific decisions and their rationality or otherwise. At the same time, both rational planning as envisaged by Mannheim and pragmatic social enquiry as envisaged by Dewey shared the assumption that social science or, to use the more qualified words of Dewey (1976–83, 37), 'an ethical science' offered a means of organising and reorganising the social world, much as the physical sciences had already achieved for the material world.

After World War II, Dewey's version of pragmatism became incorporated within US planning theory. Friedmann (1987, 193) comments:

> It was not difficult to be a faithful disciple. Dewey's message was of the simplest sort: only ideas that work matter; the scientific method points the way to human progress; one learns by changing reality.

The comments of Friedmann are one-sided. Harrison (2002, 160–1) and Schön (1983) both suggest that the dominance of positivist science, with its emphasis on laws and statistics, made the pragmatism of Dewey look 'unscientific' at exactly the time when the US planning profession was seeking to establish its scientific, rational character and legitimacy. Pragmatic planning and its close associate, social learning theory, evolved from the 1950s onwards either as a direct response to the complexities of practice or as an explicit alternative to the rational model, giving more emphasis to politics, institutions and ideas. Examples are illustrated in the following.

First, the theory of planning as the 'middle range' bridge, articulated by Meyerson ([1956] 1973), is an explicit attempt to promote the professionalisation of urban government in the US in the post-war years in conditions of weakly centralised power. Middle ground planning is neither exclusively long term nor exclusively short term, neither a comprehensive vision nor a specific project, but a bridge between these different time scales and levels. Hoch (1984, 338) comments that all the main conceptions of pragmatism are apparent in Meyerson's article: 'the identification of problems', 'the formulation and testing of alternative actions' and 'a reliance on education through democratic participation'.

Second, the so-called 'science of muddling through' articulated by Lindblom ([1959] 1973) concerns itself with how scientific evaluation, empirical analysis and democratic politics interact with one another to produce essentially a disjointed and incremental policy-making process. Lindblom's model is about learning from experience in conditions of fragmented power. It is close to Popper's concept of piecemeal, social engineering and amounts, in part, to an alternative to both scientific management and the models of long-term societal planning process associated with Mannheim and others. The science of muddling through is not an exercise in hypothesis testing, however. Hoch (1984, 338) comments that 'Lindblom refuses to separate the process of thinking from the context and experiences of decision making. ... Learning from human experience proceeds through the enactment of alternative actions that retain their meaning within the scope of that experience, i.e., at the margin.'

Third, the model of advocacy planning, advanced by Davidoff ([1965] 1973), envisages a plan-making process structured to reflect a dispersed pattern of power with different interest groups representing industry, real estate, the trade unions, social campaigners and local interests. Each plan and each position is then tested as to whether and to what extent its consequences are in the public interest. The advocacy planning model departs to an extent from pragmatism in accepting the inevitability and desirability of conflict. The language used to describe the process, advocacy, accepts that at some point a single plan will emerge, however. The concept of advocacy is taken from legal practice and, in particular, from legal practice in the US where legal representatives interact with one another as adversaries in a courtroom. Equally, legal practice and advocacy planning involves a judge who assesses the different viewpoints and comes to a single judgement. This process of judgement brings together the different contrasting views in an endorsement of one position rather than another.

Finally, though this goes beyond the list of examples given by Hoch (1984), the concept of 'social capital' takes the pragmatism of pressure group politics and advocacy in a distinctively communitarian direction. The promotion of social capital (and of relating themes such as community capacity) is about protecting community organization where it exists and promoting community organization in areas where the participation of individuals in voluntary activities is weak, for example in deprived neighbourhoods. Apart from the advantages for democracy, the promotion of social capital, particularly of 'bridging capital', is held to promote economic and social integration (Putnam 2000). Equally, however, pragmatic approaches to capacity building assume that, in the case of local programmes, the consequences of action should be tested as to its effects on community organization.

Pragmatic theories accept an optimistic assessment of the ability of planning and more generally of governments to tackle problems as and when they arise. Meyerson's theory is explicitly optimistic about the potential of planning as a profession. For Lindblom and Davidoff the optimism is implicit. In the words of Hoch (1984, 341),

> Would Davidoff ask planners to become advocates for the victims of injustice if he did not already believe that planners possess the capacity

to engage in such debate? Would Lindblom propose incrementalism if he did not already believe it would lead to better policy?

In other words, pragmatism assumes that something can be done and that a combination of analysis, advocacy and local programmes provides the best way forward.

By the 1970s, American planning theory had become widely cited in Britain and other English-speaking countries. Faludi's 'A Reader in Planning Theory', published in Britain in 1973, contains many of the key contributions by Meyerson, Lindblom and Davidoff amongst others. From the 1990s onwards, moreover, planning education and research became increasingly international, with numerous international conferences and other professional and political exchanges. For example, in Britain, the concept of social capital became particularly influential as part of the social investment programmes of the New Labour government from 1997 to 2010, again in conjunction with a pragmatic emphasis on community capacity building and 'on what works' (Coaffee and Headlam 2008).

The internationalisation of planning theory means that it has become increasingly difficult to brand pragmatic planning theory as distinctively American. Pragmatism has become widely accepted elsewhere in the world even if the word is not used and the relevant processes and policies operate on different political assumptions. Two examples of European pragmatic planning theory will suffice, by Healey and by Ascher. Both developed their ideas during the period from about 1990 to 2005 and, compared to the earlier US accounts, both amount to an attempt to restate the logic of modern town planning in response to neoliberal critiques with their emphasis on the market and, in addition, to postmodern critiques with their emphasis on fragmentation. Both have moreover received national honours. Healey received the honours of the OBE (Order of the British Empire) in 1999. Ascher received the French national town planning prize, *le Grand prix de l'Urbanisme*, for 2009.

The first example, that of Healey (1992, 1998, 1999) comprises the linked concepts of 'planning through debate' and 'collaborative planning'. The former concept of 'planning through debate' assumes that knowledge is not pregiven, but 'specifically created anew in our communication'. The aim of planning is not simply to inform people of their future, but to engage with them, explore alternatives and promote innovation. The latter, related concept, the collaborative style, is about creating a public interest through searching for agreement amongst different stakeholders—a public interest that responds to the specific concerns of these stakeholders and that also expresses a potential for learning (Healey 1998):

> Collaborative approaches to urban planning contribute to building up *institutional* capacity. ... They emphasise encouraging ways of thinking and ways of acting which generate an enduring capacity to discuss the qualities of places and to address the evident reality

of conflicts of interest in noncombative ways. Stakeholders come to place-making issues accustomed to the particular games of their own social worlds. Collaborative approaches to place making help to create arenas which can act as *learning* environments through which stakeholders learn new ways of relating to each other. (*Emphasis in the original.*)

Multi-agency interventions became common in Britain in the mid and late 1990s as urban regeneration policies sought to work with the market whilst undertaking social investment in deprived neighbourhoods (Stenson and Watt 1999). Local authorities were, as a result, required by a combination of legislative requirements and targeted spending programmes to work with other partners, not just other public sector agencies, but the voluntary sector, residents and business interests. Collaborative planning as elaborated by Healey (1998, 1999) is a product of this era of partnerships and regeneration, just as much as earlier US versions of pragmatism are a product of their political and economic circumstances. However, collaborative planning goes beyond any specific era in insisting that that place making invariably resists fragmentation, whilst involving an input from many different interested parties (Healey 2003, 104):

Taken together, concepts of planning through debate and collaborative planning amount to a distinctive style of 'communicative planning' that operationalises the general processes involved in democratic planning for multiple objectives with multiple partners. Communicative planning, as conventionally elaborated by Healey and others, is open to the criticism of neglecting the power of different stakeholders. It has survived as a theory of practice because in the words of one review (Bond 2011, 164), it establishes 'criteria against which empirical examples can be assessed, thereby lending insights into the democratic nature of decision-making in planning and governance processes'.

The second example of pragmatic planning, that of Ascher, provides an example of pragmatic planning adapted to conditions of uncertainty and also incorporating the lessons of the cyclic, rational decision-making process. As presented, 'The new principles of town planning', *Les nouveaux principes de l'urbanisme*, Ascher (2001, 80) assumes that a linear style of planning based upon the prior identification of needs or aims and the subsequent elaboration of a plan is obsolete. Planning has, instead, become an exercise in strategic urban management and as part of this an exercise in testing proposals. To cope with change and uncertainty, planning has to become:

- 'heuristic', that is to say based on specific criteria and provisional hypotheses about the feasibility of projects;
- 'iterative', based on successive and progressively more accurate approximations;

- 'incremental', based on a series of small steps within a strategy; and
- 'recurrent', based on a reflection of the implications of preceding steps.

This final characteristic means that Ascher's interpretation is about bridging between the short term and the long term, much like Meyerson's suggestions for US planning in the 1950s. In doing this, Ascher redefines the physical planning process as a continuous process of evaluation where plans and projects are refined over time. Planning is about mastering a new phase of urban development, ensuring that benefits flow from the situations so created and limiting possible negative consequences (ibid., 6).

To go slightly beyond Ascher's intention, strategic urban management is more than an exercise in rational decision-making or an exercise of technical regulation, following predetermined rules. It is, likewise, not simply an exercise in identifying and following a series of key trends, as in Mannheim's concept of *'principia media'*. It is an exercise in anticipating trends, in imagining possibilities and in using creativity as a resource for economic development and regeneration (Fagnoni 2011, 116–66).

'Mastering a new phase of urban development' to paraphrase Ascher is also close to market-oriented, entrepreneurial practice where local authorities seek to attract private investment through place marketing, cultural investments and the promotion of 'creative cities'. The scope for 'doing good' in entrepreneurial planning depends almost wholly on the private market. In places subject to development pressures, local authorities and other agencies are better able to pick and choose how to promote development and are able to negotiate with developers from positions of strength. In isolated towns and in depressed regions, in contrast, local authorities may still try to make choices, but these are likely to be more heavily constrained.

Ascher would respond that an effective planning practice has to be aligned with market trends, if it wishes to influence urban development without incurring major public expenses. Capitalism is too dominant and too pervasive to be ignored or avoided (Masboungi 2009, 33). However, in contrast to a neoliberal position, Ascher (1995, 156–7) also argues for a style of planning of a type that is based on citizenship, that is to say democratic involvement and, in addition, that maximises the collective benefits of urban development, rather than development that satisfies individual interests pure and simple. The implication of Ascher's analysis and this is also the implication of theories of communicative planning is an ambiguous decision making process which juxtaposes and partly integrates market mechanisms with citizen deliberation and voice.

## The Affinity Between Planning and Pragmatism

The relationship between pragmatism as a philosophy and planning practice, including in this context urban regeneration, is two-way. Pragmatism suits planning and urban regeneration because, like other forms of professional work, practice involves an exercise in sifting through large quantities of evidence and varied opinions and has to deal with the consequences of action. In particular, abductive reasoning is the typical method whereby professional workers of various kinds cope with uncertainty, for example detectives solving a crime (Eco 1983) or medical practitioners diagnosing illnesses against the reference of a typical 'frame' of indications (Eraut 1994; Maudsley and Strivens 2000) or, of obvious relevance to urban planning, designers framing a problem and then experimenting with different solutions to find the best fit (Schön 1988).

The relationship between pragmatism and planning is one of affinity, that is to say an inherent likeness, rather than any necessary direct influence. The affinity is apparent, moreover, in descriptions of the planning process, even in the absence of knowledge of pragmatism as philosophy. For example, 'Cities in Evolution' by Geddes (1915) has passages that endorse the interdependence of 'science with social action' and equally the interdependence 'of thought and deed' (ibid., 287), despite a reliance in other passages on induction—for example those passages dealing with the use of the survey method. The affinity between pragmatism and planning also means that pragmatic ideas—for example the ideas of learning, of common sense knowledge, of reflection, of assessing policies by its consequences, of involving the public in the assessment of those policies—are recurrent in studies of planning practice, even if the philosophical source of those ideas is not recognised.

Pragmatic contributions to planning theory say very little about ideal cities or urban form or about the long-term direction of cities. Pragmatism is, instead, about starting with cities as they exist in the here and now, albeit always with the hope of a better future and on the optimistic assumption that cities as they exist are open to improvement. The generally optimistic character of pragmatism leads, in turn, to a positive view of planning practice, as opposed to the limited ethical criterion of avoiding harm or avoiding negative externalities, as is the implication of neoliberalism.

Offering hope has, moreover, a particular importance for communities that otherwise lack hope for the future, for example low-income, declining or neglected communities. In this context, offering a better future is commonly interpreted as an exercise in empowerment, both of communities and of the individuals who live there (Beebeejaun et al. 2015). An emphasis on empowerment encourages communitarianism and favours a vision of a decentralised society and intervention in deprived neighbourhoods. Therein lies an obvious distinction with the rationalism of Mannheim and, by implication, with other rationalist theorists who favour the application of technical expertise. However, even communitarianism remains open as to how communities might use their powers. Pragmatism assumes that it is often undesirable to specify aims in advance, especially long-term rigid aims, and that these should emerge from an assessment of the potential and constraints, including the political potential and constraints, in a given situation.

In doing all this, pragmatism offers a third justification for planning, after that of Mannheim and the various neoliberal critics. Mannheim offers a wide-ranging justification for planning based on fundamental social tendencies and the adoption of rational methods in government. The neoliberals offer a very limited justification, based on another fundamental tendency, that of increased competition and the search for efficiency. Pragmatic interpretations justify planning, instead, as a means of promoting an ethical debate within society about its future.

## Notes

1 National Audit Office (NAO), 'Assessing value for money', consulted January 2014 at www.nao.org.uk/successful-commissioning/successful-commissioning-home/general-principles/value-for-money/assessing-value-for-money/.
2 See, for example, 'Foundations', Research Methods Knowledge Base, consulted July 2011 at www.socialresearchmethods.net/kb/intres.php; 'What are the differences between induction and deduction?', consulted July 2011 at http://answers.yahoo.com/question/index?qid=20060910164848AAo74Tw; 'Deductive and Inductive Arguments', Internet Encyclopedia of Philosophy, consulted July 2009 at www.iep.utm.edu/ded-ind/.

## References

Alexander, E. R. (2000). 'Rationality revisited: planning paradigms in a postpostmodernist perspective'. *Journal of Planning Education and Research*, 19:3, 242–56.

Alexander, E. R. (2009). 'Dilemmas in evaluating planning, or back to basics: what is planning for?' *Planning Theory & Practice*, 10:2, 233–44.

Amin, A. (2011). 'Urban planning in an uncertain world' in Bridge, G. and Watson, S. (eds.), *The new Blackwell companion to the city*. Chichester, Sussex: Wiley-Blackwell, 63–42.

Ascher, F. (1995). *Métapolis*. Paris: Odile Jacob.

Ascher, F. (2001). *Les nouveaux principes de l'urbanisme*. La Tour d'Aigues: Editions de l'Aube.

Bajc, V. (2012). 'Abductive ethnography of practice in highly uncertain conditions'. *The ANNALS of the American Academy of Political and Social Science*, 642:1, 72–85.

Banfield, E. C. (1959). 'Ends and means in planning'. *International Social Science Journal*, 11:3, 36–68.

Barker, K. (2003). *Review of housing supply: securing our future housing needs interim report – analysis*. London: HM Treasury.

Barker, K. (2004). *Delivering stability: securing our future housing needs: review of housing supply – final report – recommendations*. London: HM Treasury.

Baum, H. S. (1996) 'Why the rational paradigm persists: tales from the field'. *Journal of Planning Education and Research*, 5, 127–34.

Beebeejaun, Y., Durose, C., Rees, J. & Richardson, J. (2015). 'Public harm or public value? Towards coproduction in research with communities'. *Environment and Planning C: Government and Policy* 33, 552–65.

Bertilsson, T. M. (2004). 'The elementary forms of pragmatism: on different types of abduction'. *European Journal of Social Theory*, 7:3, 371–89.

Bond, S. (2011). 'Negotiating a "democratic ethos" moving beyond the agonistic–communicative divide'. *Planning Theory*, 10:2, 161–86.

Chadwick, G. F. (1971). *A systems view of planning: towards a theory of the urban and regional planning process.* Oxford: Pergamon Press.

Chiasson, P. (2005). 'Abduction as an aspect of retroduction'. *Semiotica* 153:1/4, 223–42.

Coaffee, J. and Headlam, N. (2008). 'Pragmatic localism uncovered: the search for locally contingent solutions to national reform agendas'. *Geoforum*, 39:4, 1585–99.

Danermark, B., Ekstrom, M., Jakobsen, L. & Karlsson, J. (2002). *Explaining society: critical realism in the social sciences.* London: Routledge.

Davidoff, P. (1973). 'Advocacy and pluralism in planning'. In: Faludi, A. (ed.), *A reader in planning theory.* Oxford: Pergamon, 277–96 (original 1965).

Davidoff, P. and Reiner, T. (1962). 'A choice theory of planning.' *Journal of the American Institute of Planners*, 28, 103–15.

Deleuze, G. & Guattari, F. (1987). *A thousand plateaus: capitalism and schizophrenia.* Translation and Foreword by Brian Massumi. Minneapolis, MN: University of Minnesota Press (French original 1980).

Dewey, J. (1929). *The quest for certainty: a study of the relations of knowledge and action.* New York: Minton, Balch and Co.

Dewey, J. (1938). *Logic: the theory of inquiry.* New York: Holt, Rinehart and Winston.

Dewey, J. (1976–83). *The middle works 1899–1924, vol. 3.* Carbondale, IL: Southern Illinois University Press.

Dewey, J. (2012). *The public and its problems.* University Park, PA: Pennsylvania State University Press (originally published 1927).

Eco, U. (1983). 'Horns, hooves, insteps'. In: Eco, U. & Sebeok, T. (eds.), *The sign of three: Dupin, Holmes, Peirce.* Bloomington, IN: Indiana University Press, 199–219.

Eraut, M. (1994). *Developing professional knowledge and competence.* London: Routledge Falmer.

Etzioni, A. (1968). *The active society.* New York The Free Press.

Fagnoni, E. (2011). *Culture et tourisme. Un jeu de construction de territoires entre Patrimoine et Création.* Mémoire présenté pour l'Habilitation à Diriger des Recherches Université Paris 1 Panthéon – Sorbonne.

Faludi, A. (1970). 'The planning environment and the meaning of "planning"'. *Regional Studies* 4:1, 1–9.

Faludi, A. (ed.). (1973) *A reader in planning theory.* Oxford: Pergamon.

Faludi, A. (1983). 'Critical rationalism and planning methodology'. *Urban Studies* 20, 265–78.

Faludi, A. & Waterhout, B. (2006). 'Introducing evidence-based planning'. *disP—The Planning Review*, 42:165, 4–13.

Fiori, S. (2010). 'Is HA Simon a theoretician of decentralized planning? A comparison with FA Hayek on planning, market, and organizations'. *Constitutional Political Economy*, 21:2, 145–70.

Friedmann, J. (1987). *Planning in the public domain: from knowledge to action.* Princeton, NJ: Princeton University Press.

Geddes, P., (1915). *Cities in evolution.* London: Williams and Norgate.

Goodchild, B., O'Flaherty, F. & Ambrose, A. (2014). 'Inside the eco-home: using video to understand the implications of innovative housing'. *Housing, Theory and Society*, 31:3, 334–52.

Harrison, P. (2002). 'A pragmatic attitude to planning'. In: Allmendinger, P. and Tewdr-Jones, M. (eds.), *Planning futures: new directions for planning theory.* London: Routledge, 157–71.

Healey, P. (1992). 'Planning through debate: the communicative turn in planning theory'. *Town Planning Review*, 63:2, 143–62.

Healey, P. (1998), 'Building institutional capacity through collaborative approaches to urban planning'. *Environment and Planning A*, 30:9, 1531–46.

Healey, P. (1999) 'Institutionalist analysis, communicative planning, and shaping places'. *Journal of Planning Education and Research*, 19, 111–21.

Healey, P. (2003). 'Collaborative planning in perspective'. *Planning Theory* 2:2, 101–23.

Hildebrand, D. (2011). 'Pragmatic democracy: inquiry, objectivity, and experience'. *Metaphilosophy*, 42:5, 589–604.

Hoch, C. (1984). 'Doing good and being right: the pragmatic connection in planning theory'. *Journal of the American Planning Association*, 50:3, 335–45.

Hoch, C. (2007). 'Pragmatic communicative action theory'. *Journal of Planning Education and Research*, 26:3, 272–83.

Hutton, B. (2013). *Planning sustainable transport*. London: Routledge.

IDOX plc (corporate author) (2007). *Delivering inspiring places: the role and status of planning*. London: The IDOX Group.

Jacobs, J. (1964). *The death and life of great American cities*. Harmondsworth: Pelican Books.

Joas, H. (1993). *Pragmatism and social theory*. Chicago: University of Chicago Press.

Joas, H. and Beckert, J. (2002). 'Action theory'. In: Turner J. H. (ed.), *Handbook of sociological theory*. New York: Kluwer Academic, 269–85.

Lassman, P. & Speirs, R. (1994). *Weber: political writings*. Cambridge, UK: Cambridge University Press.

Lindblom, C. E. (1973). 'The science of muddling through'. In: Faludi, A. (ed.), *A reader in planning theory*. Oxford: Pergamon, 151–69 (original 1959).

Loader, C. (2011). 'Karl Mannheim'. *The Wiley-Blackwell companion to major social theorists: classical social theorists*, volume I. Chichester, West Sussex: Wiley-Blackwell, 469–88.

McLoughlin, J. B. (1969). *Urban and regional planning: a systems approach*. Oxford: Pergamon.

Mannheim, K. ([1940] 1971). *Man and society in age of reconstruction*. London: Routledge and Kegan Paul (first published in English in 1940, partly based on a German original of 1935).

March, J., & Simon, H. A. (1993). *Organizations*, 2nd edition. Cambridge, MA: Blackwell (original 1958).

Masboungi, A. (ed) (2009). 'Organiser la ville hypermoderne'. *François Ascher Grand Prix de l'urbanisme 2009*. Éditions Parenthèses et Direction générale de l'Aménagement, du Logement et de la Nature (DGALN), Paris.

Maudsley, G. & Strivens, J. (2000). '"Science", "critical thinking" and "competence" for tomorrow's doctors: a review of terms and concepts'. *Medical Education*, 34, 53–60.

Meyerson, M. (1973). 'Building the middle-range bridge for comprehensive planning'. In: Faludi, A. (ed.), *A reader in planning theory*. Oxford: Pergamon, 127–38 (original 1956).

Næss, P. & Jensen, O. B. (2002). 'Urban land use, mobility and theory of science: exploring the potential for critical realism in empirical research'. *Journal of Environmental Policy & Planning*, 4, 295–311.

Newman, P. and Kenworthy, J. (1989). *Cities and automobile dependence: a sourcebook*. Brookfield, VT: Gower.

Owens, S., Rayner, T. & Bina, O. (2004). 'New agendas for appraisal: reflections on theory, practice and research'. *Environment and Planning A*, 36, 1943–59.

Peirce, C. (1998a). 'The first rule of logic'. In: The Pierce Education Project (collective author and editor), *The Essential Peirce, Volume 2 (1893–1913)*. Bloomington, IN: Indiana University Press, 42–56 (Original 1898).

Peirce, C. (1998b). 'Pragmatism as the logic of induction'. In: The Pierce Education Project (collective author and editor), *The Essential Peirce, Volume 2 (1893–1913)*. Bloomington, IN: Indiana University Press (Original 1903).

Popper, K. (1944). 'The poverty of historicism, II. A criticism of historicist methods'. *Economica, New Series*, 11:43, 119–37.

Popper, K. (2000). *Realism and the aims of science*. Abingdon, Oxon: Routledge (reprint: original 1983).

Popper, K. (2002). *Unended quest*. London: Routledge (original published in 1976).

Prawat, R. S. (1999). 'Dewey, Peirce, and the learning paradox'. *American Educational Research Journal*, 36, 47–76.

Putnam, R. (2000). *Bowling alone: the collapse and revival of American community*. New York: Simon & Schuster.

Ray, L. (2004). 'Pragmatism and critical theory'. *European Journal of Social Theory*, 7:3, 307–21.

Rescher, N. (2012). *Pragmatism: the restoration of its scientific roots*. New Brunswick, NJ: Transaction Publishers.

Rittel, H. W. J. & Webber, M. M. (1973). 'Dilemmas in a general theory of planning'. *Policy Sciences*, 4, 155–69.

Schön, D. A. (1983). *The reflective practitioner*. New York: Basic Books.

Schön, D. A. (1988). 'Designing: rules, types and worlds'. *Design Studies*, 9:3, 181–90.

Schön, D. A. (1992). 'The theory of inquiry: Dewey's legacy to education'. *Curriculum Inquiry*, 22:2, 119–39.

Shalin, D. N. (1986). 'Pragmatism and social interactionism'. *American Sociological Review*, 51:1, 9–29.

Simmel, G. (1997). 'The metropolis and mental life'. In: Frisby, D. and Featherstone, M. (eds.), *Simmel on culture*. London: Sage (German original 2003), [online] URL: https://core.ac.uk/download/pdf/11166961.pdf (consulted June 2016).

Simon, H. (1986). 'Rationality in psychology and economics'. *The Journal of Business*, 59(4), Part 2: The Behavioral Foundations of Economic Theory, S209–S224.

Simon, H. (1991). 'Bounded rationality and organizational learning'. *Organization Science*, 2:1, 125–34.

Simon, H. (1997). *Models of bounded rationality: empirically grounded economic reason*. Cambridge, MA: MIT Press.

Stenson, K. and Watt, P. (1999). 'Governmentality and "the death of the social"?: A discourse analysis of local government texts in South-east England' *Urban Studies*, 36:1, 189–201.

Verma, N. (1996). 'Pragmatic rationality and planning theory'. *Journal of Planning Education and Research*, 16: 5–14.

Wang, L. & Hoch, C. (2013). 'Pragmatic rational planning: comparing Shanghai and Chicago'. *Planning Theory*, 12:4, 369–90.

Weber, M. (1947). *The theory of social and economic organization* (Henderson, A. M. & Parsons, T., eds. & trans.) New York: Free Press.

# 6 Evaluation and Translation

Whether self-consciously rational or pragmatic, planning uses science and may also borrow aspects of the scientific method. It is not of itself a science, however. It is about the application of knowledge. Moreover, it differs fundamentally from professions such as engineering or medicine that rely heavily on a scientific or technical model of decision-making. In engineering and medicine, an individual works on an object or a system either alone or as a member of a group of specialists. The individual works outside the object or system being planned, designed or treated. In contrast, in the planning of urban areas and in the various ancillary exercises such as urban management and urban policy, the professional planner is only one actor amongst many with a potential influence on outcomes. The individual, whether working as a researcher or as a planner or in some other similar intermediate role, finds him or herself working within a process of change and a process of political debate, alongside others who may or may not be supportive, as the case may be, and who are likely to work on the basis of a mix of common sense and specialist, technical models of knowledge.

Working within a process rather than on an object or a system implies communication between all those involved in that process. Communication involves, in turn, a process of translation amongst multiple specialists and between those specialists and the public. The significance of translation has, moreover, almost certainly, increased over time, as is amply demonstrated by contrasting the most popular themes in planning theory in about 1970 to those in the 1990s and early 2000s. In the 1960s and 1970s, the most influential theories were derived from cybernetic systems and these treated communication as unproblematic. For example, McLoughlin (1969, 95) once noted that 'the control devices for any system have to be isomorphic' (of identical shape) 'with the system to be controlled, that is, they have to be in similar form'. In other words, the state, in the form of local or central government, has to fit, perfectly, the contours of the system to be controlled so that implementation proceeds automatically.

Systems approaches have persisted, notably through relatively new forms of socio-ecological and socio-technical systems theory that, respectively, have helped inform policies for environmental resilience and transitions.

## Evaluation and Translation 151

Planning in environmental systems theory is a means to an end, the end being reflexive governance in which societies anticipate the effects of their own development and learn to avoid any negative side effects (Voß and Bornemann 2011). Systems theories are no longer dominant, however, in planning and they offer, in any case, only general and abstract evaluation criteria, of which reflexiveness is an example.

Instead, the dominant concepts from the 1990s onwards have been about collaborative planning (Healey 1998) between public agencies, the private sector and interested voluntary and pressure groups; the existence of ad-hoc, flexible 'soft' spaces for governance (Haughton et al. 2013); and, for public administration, the emergence of 'fuzzy' jobs where employees have to negotiate across professional and organisational boundaries (Jeannot & Goodchild 2011). All these tendencies suggest a proliferation of agencies and equally a proliferation of efforts to cross the boundaries between one agency and another.

The shift towards collaborative, soft and fuzzy styles of planning is, moreover, more than a response, in words of Haughton et al. (2013), to 'turbulent institutional dynamics driven by neoliberal regulatory restructuring'. Globalisation and neoliberal, market-led development transform urban landscapes and require a flexible and differentiated response, both to adapt to and to counter market forces. However, the same pattern of flexible governance would most likely emerge in the context of any exercise that seeks to tackle multiple urban problems in a context of uncertainty, whilst also trying to determine the most effective solutions.

The proliferation of initiatives and 'fuzzy' approaches is, in any case, predicted by another branch of systems theory, linguistic systems theory, as developed by Luhmann (1995). Linguistic systems assume a continuing process of functional differentiation within modern society, with an increasing divergence between different institutions. The legal system exemplifies the processes, though the processes are not unique to the legal system. The law automatically grows in complexity as it attempts to cope with new elements and new requirements whilst retaining its old terminology (Bailey, 1997; Luhmann, 1989, 36–43, 145). Likewise, scientific specialisms proliferate, and politics tends to become specialised and separate from society, as does the economy. Moreover, each specialism and each functional element involves a different language for discussing the environment and the system to be controlled, whether this is an apparently natural environment or an urban environment.

In such circumstances, planning becomes the 'management of the interdependencies of systems, yet without a manager with a complete overview' (Van Assche and Verschraegen 2008, 280). Planning is therefore always imperfect, despite the best intentions and wishes of different agencies (Jacobs 2014) Planning becomes both more important as a coordinating mechanism, but also more difficult to undertake. The concepts of planning become 'fuzzy' and 'soft' as they are interpreted in a multitude of different ways by different institutional actors in different situations (Porter & de Roo 2007). Moreover, as the process of linguistic and functional differentiation proceeds, the need grows for the evaluation of practice and the effective translation and communication of perspectives from one institution and situation to others. The growth of information in scientific journals, in consultants' reports and on the Web and a proliferation of different pressure groups, with different perspectives, has much the same effect, increasing the importance of informed judgement.

## Classifying the Approaches

An exercise in classification is necessary, making sense of the many techniques and approaches that can be and are used in evaluation and translation. Discussions within planning theory commonly suggest a broad, long-standing distinction between prescriptive, professional theories on one hand and, on the other, theories that are derived from the main social research disciplines, such as economics or sociology and are commonly based on observation, interpretation and analysis. The distinction was first stated, in relatively crude terms, by Faludi (1973, 4) as a distinction between 'normative' rational decision-making and so-called 'positive' or behavioural theories. Normative theories, for Faludi, were typically concerned with procedures and the specification of a framework about how facts should be collected. Positive theories were concerned with the limitations that prevent rational decision-making. Later, Allmendinger (2002) distinguished between 'indigenous' theories that are specific to and guide planning practice and other theories that either frame planning practice or that are concerned with spatial and social processes or the philosophy of enquiry.

More recently, Leeuw and Donaldson (2015) have independently suggested a similar distinction in evaluation practice, between studies based on 'theories of policy makers, stakeholders and evaluators' and those based on 'scientific theories capable of contextualizing and explaining the consequences of policies, programs and evaluators' actions'. Leeuw and Donaldson (2015) add that the various theories and approaches have to be brought together in real-world situations and that two 'promising' methods are available to do this. 'Layering' is where evaluations mix theories that operate at different levels of generality, from the structural to the specific. 'Knitting' is where different complementary theories can be integrated with one another to define good practice.

The terminology is confusing. All theories and approaches to planning and evaluation are normative to some extent. They all have implications for how evaluation should be undertaken and, by extension, for how planning and urban policies should be organised, implemented and presented to different audiences. The reference to positive theories by Faludi (1973) and scientific theories by Leeuw and Donaldson (2015) is also misleading. Positive is usually defined as the opposite of 'normative', being concerned with facts rather than policies. The term comes from economics, where positive economics is concerned with making predictions about measurable trends and other factual phenomena (Friedman [1953] 2007). Positive and scientific are, as a result, interchangeable, and they both assume the possibility of distinguishing between scientific and unscientific in a way that is commonly unhelpful in applied forms of practice or applied bodies of knowledge, such as planning theory.

Putting the terminology to one side, however, the possibility of layering and weaving suggest that some other distinction might be more significant and easily applied. Evaluation in practice can layer or weave different theories together and has to do so to provide a credible account. To give an example, studies of impact have to mix procedural, 'how to' theories, with theories of the impact of environmental change on communities and theories of implementation and the political context. Separating out these theories provides only a limited understanding.

Actor-network theory assumes, in contrast, that the form and scope of scientific and professional enquiry is determined in part by the type of problem under enquiry. Actor-network theory sees the preparation and implementation of plans and projects as a series of moments of translation that start with the specific characteristics of the problem at hand and a review of how that problem has been tackled in the past and then involves the propagation of that proposal to a progressively wider set of networks (Boelens 2010; Callon 1999). The enquiry and its outcomes might be distorted by processes of linguistic specialisation and other factors. Practitioners have, in addition, to learn the relevant language and in the case of innovative and complex projects, teams of specialists have to be involved. However, the objective characteristics of the problem still count. Likewise, Alexander (2006), writing as a planning theorist, suggests that the form of plan and policy evaluation depends in part on its timing and object. Timing means whether evaluation is prospective or retrospective or ongoing during implementation. The object refers to a distinction between a social or economic programme or policy or a land use or physical plan.

It is not possible to give examples of all the potential variety of evaluation exercises relevant to urban planning. It is possible, however, to give contrasting examples of community programmes generally subject to evaluation during and after implementation and of evaluation in the preparation of land use plans of a type that looks forward, often over the long term. There are also hybrids—for example strategic projects in economic development or the preparation of local housing strategies—that can involve a combination of both prospective and retrospective evaluation. Evaluation methods have to be weaved together, as appropriate. Equally, they have to be assessed separately, given the distinctiveness of their objects.

# The Evaluation of Community-Based Programmes and Initiatives

Consideration of the evaluation of community programmes leads, in turn, to the so-called logic model/theory of change. Other, largely interchangeable names include 'result chains' (Picciotto 2005) and 'programme theories' (Chen 1994; Rogers 2008). The approach largely originated in the US in the 1970s and 1980s in attempts to evaluate educational, public health as well as community initiatives (Weiss 1997b). Later, it became used and popularised as an exemplary method in the drive towards the so-called evidence-based policy of the New Labour government elected in 1997 (Solesbury 2001; Wells 2011). Other uses include the evaluation and clarification of programmes of international development (Vogel 2012).

The logic model/theory of change is flexible in operation and in principle may be adapted to any initiative that seeks to improve life in a community or to change behaviour in a specific direction. It is a 'micro' model of evaluation that looks at local intentions and impacts in the light of policy intentions and aims as they are interpreted by practitioners. Much of the task is therefore to determine whether intervention is having the desired effect and, in addition, though this is not always explicit, whether intervention has avoided any undesirable, unexpected consequences.

Another approach, called a realist or critical realist approach by its supporters (Ho 1999; Pawson and Tilley 1997; Pawson et al. 2005), assesses the context with more emphasis on trends and objective indicators of community well-being such as unemployment levels, homelessness or educational attainment. For example, in the case of a policy for neighbourhood regeneration, a realist evaluation would focus on overall levels of deprivation and quality of life and their determinants and would be less concerned with the assumptions of policy.

However, realist evaluation is not necessarily incompatible with the logic model/theory of change, merely a way of exploring the context and outcomes in more depth through the process of layering. For example, the national, standardised framework for the evaluation of community empowerment in England has explicitly incorporated both contextual conditions as a starting point and the impact on the contextual situation as the final element in evaluation (Dickinson et al. 2009).

## Specification of a Logic Model/Theory of Change

The title 'logic model/theory of change' reflects a coming together of rationalism and pragmatism. The logic model is the rational element, concerned with monitoring activities undertaken in policy implementation. In effect, the logic model is about single loop learning. Theory, as used in the term 'theory of change', is the pragmatic element and equally the element that permits double and triple loop learning. The theory is 'grounded', as this term is understood by Glaser and Strauss (2012). The researcher immerses themselves in a situation in an attempt, amongst other things, to identify relevant working principles that are 'usable in practical applications' and give 'the practitioner understanding and some control of situations (ibid., 3). The theory of change is a 'plausible and sensible model' of how a policy initiative or programme is supposed to work (Bickman 1987; McLaughlin and Jordan 1999), the assumption being that this very exercise facilitates evaluation and helps provoke a process of reflection.

The specified theory can deal with the process of decision-making. Geddes et al. (2007), for example, have sought to define the theory of change of partnership working in local government in England, particularly the Local Strategic Partnership (LSP) established under the Local Government Act 2000. Though much depended on the external context, the specific arrangements of the LSP provide a framework that helps increase the capacity for strategic action and so lead to 'improved services and more inclusive local governance' (ibid., 101–2). Likewise, the theory can elaborate the assumptions of community involvement, with a specification of which groups and aspects of decision making this will benefit (Burton et al. 2006).

Equally, the theory of change can deal with the impact of community development or of environmental improvements. To provide some examples, local measures of crime prevention might draw on situational theories with their emphasis, *inter alia*, on manipulating the local environment to increase the difficulty of committing an offence, increase the risks of getting caught and reducing the available rewards.[1] Likewise, local measures in favour of sustainable consumption might draw on theories of community marketing or community education, using a combination of moral pressure, information dissemination and social networks to change behaviour (McKenzie-Mohr et al. 2012).

A theory of change does not have to be new and it does not have to offer a comprehensive explanation of a specific problem. Information about the theories incorporated or assumed in a policy or programme may be derived from either documents and policy statements or interviews with people, notably practitioners and funders, or from prior research on similar initiatives elsewhere or from logical reasoning (Weiss, 1997a). Whatever theory is adopted, it obviously has to be relevant and meaningful to those involved in policy-making and implementation (Eden & Huxham 1996). Connell and Kubisch (1998) suggest that a 'good' theory of change involves three criteria of plausibility, doability and testability. Plausibility is about the extent to which the 'evidence and common sense suggest that the activities, if implemented, will lead to desired outcomes'. A preliminary evaluation would, in this context, draw on the experience of similar initiatives elsewhere. Plausibility also means testing to see whether the theory of change has any inconsistent or contradictory elements. Doability is whether 'the economic, technical, political, institutional, and human resources' are sufficient to carry out the initiative, again given previous experience and the views of interested parties. Doability involves therefore an assessment of the feasibility of the partnership working and the commitment of various parties to a project. Finally, testability means asking whether the theory of change is 'specific and complete enough for an evaluator to track its progress in credible and useful ways' and whether as part of this relevant outcome criteria may be identified.

There is a potential objection and qualification. The advocates of the theory of change in the US in the late 1990s assumed the possibility of some unified sense of 'ownership' and support amongst all the relevant stakeholders and assumed therefore that all affected stakeholders should work together in defining an agreed theory of change (Sullivan & Stewart 2006). So defined, the theory of change is a method of communication and consensus building as well as evaluation.

However, it is commonly impossible to involve all the relevant stakeholders, even in favourable circumstances. It is commonly difficult, for example, to generate the interest of more than a minority of local residents in the processes of technical evaluation (Coote et al. 2004, 4). And the circumstances in Britain, especially in England, are generally not favourable to the mobilisation of support, given the centralised character of policy-making and the way that local stakeholders work within multiple, commonly fragmented funding regimes and policy guidelines over which they have little or no direct control.

In addition, the aim of evaluation has commonly not been just to help practitioners, but to exercise economic and policy control and to determine value for money (McEldowney 1997). Community programmes are based on an implied social contract between the community and some external agency or agencies. However, the contract places obligations on the various parties and is therefore an instrument of social control as well as a right or benefit. The community has to conform to a set of procedures and the practitioners have to ensure value for money if it is to survive and be extended.

In this context, the sense of ownership of the policy initiative may itself become part of the evaluation exercise, so triggering a range of supplementary questions (adapted from Mann & Schweiger 2009), for example: 'Is the policy supported by any particular branch of government or interest groups?' 'Was the policy introduced merely to take advantage of funding opportunities?' 'Is there a broad consensus that the best approach has been chosen?' Answering those questions in the context of centrally controlled initiative raises, in turn, potentially awkward ethical issues in relation to disclosure and confidentiality. Evaluation, like most forms of research, works best if respondents can be guaranteed confidentiality and once that guarantee is made, reports have to be written in such a way as to protect anonymity, even if this leads to a loss of relevant detail and even if the funding agency would prefer to know the detail.

The logic model, the rational element, provides a framework of means and ends. It is an exercise in matching activities against outcomes in the design of the policy using a standardised format that distinguishes, for example, between inputs, activities, outputs and outcomes.[2] In making these various distinctions, moreover, the logic model assumes a series of expected 'if-then' relationships. If staff are appointed, then relevant activities should follow. If the activities take place, then the likely outputs are as follows and so on. The theory of change adds a series of causal links to the logic model, so clarifying its impact or long-term impact.

## Examples and Implications

The combined logic model/theory of change provides therefore a 'road map' of linkages between the input of resources and their social and economic effects, as is shown in Table 6.1.[3]

The terminology needs to be explained. Following a standard interpretation (Jones et al. 2003), a logic model has five elements. *Inputs* refer to staff time, funding and the availability of supporting facilities and services. *Activities* refer to the specific services that are delivered in the project—analyses, buildings and exercises, meetings, exhibitions etc. *Outputs* represent the immediate achievements of the project, for example, various types of report, buildings completed etc. *Outcomes* refer to the changes and effects resulting from a project, such as increased satisfaction amongst residents or users, additional security, environmental improvements or improved awareness, knowledge and skills (Knowlton and Phillips 2012, 57; McLaughlin and Jordan 1999). Outcomes are generally measured through a combination of surveys and the collection of objective data, such as the number of people passing a test or the jobs lost or created. Finally, *impacts* or longer term outcomes include changes to practice and benefits from the project to society, including for example reduced unemployment, reduced crime levels or reduced energy consumption.

The relationship between inputs, activities and outputs is almost automatic, so long as the project is adequately financed and implemented. Investing in a place will, by definition, result in increased activities of different types, though the scale of that activity (for example, the number of meetings or events or properties treated) is itself a measure of value for money.

The relationship between outputs and outcomes, especially long-term outcomes, is more difficult to demonstrate. In the evaluation of an empty homes strategy, for example, the evidence base of local crime statistics is commonly not strong enough to allow a convincing analysis of whether this reduces vandalism or arson (Goodchild et al. 1997). However, residents and practitioners (housing managers, planners, the police) still generally support measures to 'fill' empty homes, either because of the amenity implications or because of the existence of local housing shortages. In addition, the insurance companies offer their support derived from separate internal records of the incidence of arson. In this latter case, therefore, local evaluation has to interpolate from non-local statistics. Similar considerations apply to the crime reduction impact of local regeneration projects such as the rebuilding

Table 6.1 Applying the Logic Model/Theory of Change

For an empty homes strategy

| Inputs | Activities | Early Outputs | Intermediate Outcomes | Impacts or Long-Term Outcomes |
|---|---|---|---|---|
| • Employment of specialist staff<br>• Selective grant aid<br>• Enforcement powers | • Inspection and monitoring of property<br>• Enforcement<br>• Engagement with property owners<br>• Working with social housing partners | • Established mechanisms for liaison with landlords<br>• Reduction in the number of long-term empty properties | • Greater awareness amongst owners of their responsibilities and opportunities<br>• Improved confidence amongst the owners of adjoining properties<br>• Increased availability of affordable housing | • Increased demand, raised house prices in depressed areas<br>• Reduced likelihood of arson and vandalism<br>• Greater reporting of problems, including crime.<br>• Continuing reduced vacancy levels |

Source: Barry Goodchild

For the rebuilding of a semi-derelict railway station

| Inputs | Activities | Early Outputs | Intermediate Outcomes | Impacts or Long-Term Outcomes |
|---|---|---|---|---|
| • Employment of specialist staff<br>• Community engagement from volunteers and professional companies<br>• Investment from interested parties | • Securing planning permission and other consents<br>• Building design<br>• External and internal building work<br>• Marketing<br>• Promotion of green technologies | • Building safeguarded and improved<br>• Derelict areas brought into use<br>• New spaces for small businesses<br>• Removal of signs of dilapidation<br>• Additional security and facilities for rail passengers | • Improved confidence and satisfaction amongst the users of public transport<br>• Improved reputation elsewhere in city<br>• Wider awareness of the potential of the station<br>• Reduced fear of crime | • Increased number of visitors to the area<br>• Increased property values in the locality<br>• Reduced crime rate<br>• Continued private investment and job creation |

Source: Unpublished documentation prepared by Yorkshire Forward and Groundforce Wakefield.

For neighbourhood regeneration and improvement

| Inputs | Activities | Early Outputs | Intermediate Outcomes | Impacts or Long-Term Outcomes |
|---|---|---|---|---|
| • Employment of specialist staff<br>• Community engagement from volunteers and public sector<br>• Investment from varied interested parties | • External and internal design and building works<br>• Enforcement of orders against anti-social behavior<br>• Promoting resident involvement<br>• Promoting local and social cultural activities<br>• The provision of training and educational opportunities<br>• Coordination of the activities of different agencies | • Improvements to the housing stock<br>• Environmental improvements<br>• More defensible space<br>• Derelict areas brought back into use<br>• Lower vacancies in the housing stock<br>• Better lighting<br>• Varied participation in events and programmes<br>• Establishment of community groups and cultural events | • Increased residential satisfaction<br>• Increased pride in the estate or neighborhood<br>• An increased sense of security<br>• Improved local leadership<br>• Improved confidence in talking to and working with neighbours<br>• Improved reputation elsewhere in city | • Improved social reputation<br>• Increased involvement in civic activities<br>• Improved physical and mental health<br>• Reduced crime<br>• Lower population turnover<br>• Stable or increased property values<br>• Increased private investment<br>• Reduced unemployment<br>• Reduced neighbourhood inequalities |

Sources: Adapted in part from Laprade and Auspos (2006, 147-48) and Cordero-Guzman and Auspos (2006, 176, 203).

160  *Applying 'Reason' to Politics*

of a semi-derelict railway station. This latter has other aims—the promotion of more rail travel, the creation of jobs and the promotion of pirvate investment—that are easier to measure, but may take many years before the full effects are known.

The New Deal for Communities, perhaps the most intensively researched of all recent community initiatives in Europe, offers another example of the difficulty of demonstrating long-term outcomes. The programme was in operation from 1999 to about 2009 and succeeded in improving the housing and environmental conditions in the project areas. However the programme had less obvious success in converting environmental and housing outputs into long-term outcomes, such as reducing inequalities or improving the life-chances of residents in relation to crime, education, health and worklessness (Lawless 2011).

The evaluation of long-term outcomes is made difficult partly because residents are moving in and out during the period of evaluation but also because not all residents participated in initiatives such as training or cultural activities. If the experience of users and other beneficiaries of a community programme is compared to non-users and non-beneficiaries, the outcomes may be more favourable, as was indeed the case for the New Deal for Communities. (Foden et al. 2010).

The significance of the beneficiary/non-beneficiary distinction suggests, in turn, that, as Montague (1996) and others have argued, the reach of policy interventions should be added as a variable to logic models, as is shown in Table 6.2.

By reach is meant the number of customers, clients or beneficiaries who are involved in policy implementation. Reach could also refer to the number of properties who are included within an improvement programme. Once reach is specified as a relevant criterion, the case for a small area-based initiative is weakened as the very process of drawing boundaries to the neighbourhood restricts the potential catchment. The counterargument is that concentration on small areas enables more community involvement than might otherwise be possible. In addition, a narrow focus may be justified if, as in the railway station example, the focus is directed towards a strategic problem whose resolution may have wide-ranging benefits or if the problem cannot be tackled any other way.

The specification of both outputs and outcomes requires the preparation of a baseline of conditions at the start of an initiative so that trends may be assessed over time. In addition, an estimation needs to be made of what would

*Table 6.2*  Including 'Reach' in a Logic Model

| Inputs | Activities | Reach ⟶ | Early Outputs | Intermediate Outcomes | Expected Impacts or Long-Term Outcomes |
|---|---|---|---|---|---|

happen anyway, to ensure that the additional impact of the policy or project is properly identified. In addition, an estimation needs to be made of the extent to which funds are diverted to recipients outside the programme- the concept of deadweight—and also of the extent to which the initiative has had any impact beyond what would have happened anyway—the concept of additionality. Identifying deadweight and additionality implies, in turn, the use of control samples or control areas where the policy and its effects are absent. However, if comparable controls cannot be identified or assessed, the views of relevant actors may still be of help in indicating what might have happened anyway (McEldowney 1997). In the absence of comparative cases, Danermark et al. (2002, 101), writing from the perspective of critical realism, argue for 'counterfactual thinking' where the researcher tries to imagine what would have happened in the absence of X or Y factor, using the researcher's experience and understanding of reality. There is no reason why such counterfactual thinking might not be combined with the logic model/theory of change approach.

Whether governments actually learn the lessons of evaluation exercises is another question. The quality of evaluation may be compromised for all manner of reasons, including a tendency for governments to standardise procedures through the imposition of rules and criteria that are set in advance. In addition, the evidence of formal evaluation exercises is not the only factor influencing either the retention of an initiative or the detail of its management. Policies can become overtaken by events, for example, by a change of government or by changed economic circumstances. Once designated as *passé*, moreover, initiatives are likely to become quickly forgotten other than by specialists in urban policy.

The lessons of community-based regeneration in England, such as the New Deal for Communities, again offer an example. The effectiveness of community-based initiatives was always open to challenge, mainly owing to the difficulty of demonstrating significant social and economic outcomes. However, as noted by a Select Committee of the House of Commons (HoC 2011), a change in national government in 2010 from Labour to a Conservative Coalition meant that the lessons of previous evaluation studies were lost. The incoming government introduced a series of new policies as though the previous evaluations did not exist. The desire of a new government for a new start swept everything away. Politics triumphed over reasoned evaluation, though the evaluation exercises have still left a body of knowledge that can be used in the future.

## Evaluation in Development and Spatial Plans

Where evaluation is undertaken in plan making and plan implementation, it is mostly prospective rather than retrospective. The past and future cannot be completely separated. Plan making also involves a review of the impact and appropriateness of previous and existing policies. The emphasis is, nevertheless, on the future. Many of those involved in planning would argue, in any case, that they are more interested in the future than in the impact of past policies.

The simplest forms of plan evaluation are based on a series of questions with a view to testing whether the various provisions are satisfactory or not on relevant criteria. In part, the criteria concern the context in which the plan is prepared and the extent to which the contents are aligned to its intended audience. These aspects of plan preparation refer to its external quality and also commonly raise issues that are best considered within a pragmatic philosophy. Other aspects are more technical and rational in character and refer to the plan's internal quality (Berke & Godschalk 2009).

To provide an example of external alignment: Hoch (2002, 66) has advocated an explicitly pragmatic approach to plan evaluation involving the following four questions:

1 Plausibility... : does the plan include alternatives that show potential consequences vividly and plausibly for the relevant stakeholders?
2 Similarity *(to the interests of stakeholders)*... : do relevant stakeholders use the plan, resist the plan, grudgingly submit or perhaps ignore it altogether? ...
3 Consensus... : does the plan propose or otherwise inspire consensus building measures?
4 Stewardship... : do the plan makers make their intentions known in ways that anticipate and include shared responsibility for plan consequences? (*Italics added.*)

As is apparent is the quotation, evaluation is linked to the likelihood of implementation and the interests and perspectives of stakeholders. That means, in turn, an exercise in consultation, notably with developers in the context of land use plans. Given the emphasis on external support, the plan is likely to emerge as a piecemeal adaption of existing and previous plans as practitioners look for precedents and models.

A complementary, but potentially more radical series of four questions is provided by the theory of practical judgement, or 'phronesis', as prompted by Flyvbjerg (2004, 289), as follows:

1 Where are we going with planning?
2 Who gains and who loses, and by which mechanisms of power?
3 Is this development desirable?
4 What, if anything, should we do about it?

Contrary to the interpretation sometimes made of phronetic methods in social policy (Fitzpatrick 2011; Spicker 2011), the assessment of direction (question 1) and of desirability (question 3) is not an anti-universalist, postmodern research strategy. It does not depend wholly on local criteria generated from within case studies and within the plan. Instead, the evaluation of where we are going assumes the existence of clearly established and widely accepted criteria of good practice. More accurately, the phronetic method involves an understanding of both the unique and the general characteristics of any situation, combined in addition with an appreciation of the dynamics of the operation of power as these exist in specific localities.

In relation who loses and who gains (question 2 in Flyvbjerg's list), Yiftachel (1998) has identified four main 'axes' of power:

1 a *territorial* dimension concerned with promoting or restricting land ownership (and by extension, though Yiftachel uses slightly different language, promoting or restricting rights in land, property and housing) by specific groups;
2 a *procedural* dimensional that includes or excludes groups from consultation exercises;
3 a *socio-economic* dimension whereby decisions distributes the benefits and disbenefits of economic development unevenly; and finally
4 a *cultural* dimension whereby decisions affect the cultural expression of specific groups, for example through banning the construction of minority places of worship.

All and any of these devices have the potential to create spaces and places that work for or against different interests and different groups and so help to determine whether a project is desirable (question 3). The researcher can compare interpretations of alternatives and can undertake this both retrospectively and prospectively.

The phronetic approach is not the only approach that emphasises judgement and power. The 'critical pragmatism' of Forester (1999) is similar, adding a concern with justice, injustice and empowerment as assessment criteria. It follows, therefore, that researchers (together with planners and others who undertake or commission research) should be aware of their political responsibilities, aware of the likely implications for different social groups and institutions and aware, in addition, of the political implications of the language of reports and planning documents. Moreover, in assessing the alignment between the plan and its context, attention has to be paid to those who lack power and who, therefore, cannot be regarded as stakeholders in the conventional sense of the word.

In relation to the internal quality of a plan, Berke and Godschalk (2009, 231) suggest that good practice involves, in principle, the following categories of issue:

> *Issue identification and vision*: Description of community needs, assets, trends, and future vision...
> *Goals*: Reflections of public values that express desired future land use and development pattern...

*Fact base*: Analysis of current and future conditions and explanation of reasoning Present and future population and economy: ...
*Policies*: Specification of principles to guide public and private land use decisions to achieve goals...
*Implementation*: Commitments to carry out policy-driven actions...
*Monitoring and evaluation*: Provisions for tracking change in community conditions ... Indicators of objectives to assess progress, e.g., annual percentage of residents within a quarter mile of transit stop...
*Internal consistency*: Issues, vision, goals, policies, and implementation are mutually reinforcing...

The categories are derived from a 'meta-analysis', that is to say a summary of previous published evaluations of plan adequacy and plan quality. The studies themselves are mostly drawn from the US, but include examples from New Zealand and the Netherlands. Good practice in land use planning involves a grounding in local needs, a reflection of the aims of intervention and on whether existing trends are consistent with those aims. It goes on to specify policies to achieve the desired aims and means of monitoring outcomes.

Meta-analysis is intended as a summation. Practice in specific cases does not necessarily follow the meta framework. For example, Carmona and Sieh (2005) have reported on the experience of an initiative in which English local authorities sought to measure performance in an effort to demonstrate value for money. They concluded that measures were 'fragmented and unbalanced in their selectivity' (ibid., 328). In addition, given the discretionary character of the planning system in Britain, local authorities commonly favoured indicators relating to the process of controlling development or the local authority planning service in general rather than the quality of the plan.

Alexander (2009) suggests, in any case, that the aims of planning are so varied that evaluation cannot proceed with asking the basic question: 'What is planning for?' There are indeed many types of plan—as a vision of the future, as a guide for developers, as a remedy to local problems, as the demonstration of a principle, as a condition for funding from some external body or as a product of a specific policy initiative. Each of these different purposes is likely to generate different evaluation criteria (Baer 1997). Moreover, a clarification of purpose is indeed helpful in establishing an evaluation framework. To insist, however, that the purpose of planning is defined beforehand goes too far in a rationalist direction, in the functional sense of the word. Both a Mannheimian and pragmatic position would, for different reasons, recognise the possibility that analysis and reflection can itself generate statements of purpose and aims.

Both the meta-categories of Berke and Godschalk (2009) and the pursuit of value for money criteria offer a means of evaluating the professional quality of the work undertaken in planning, rather than providing an evaluation of a plan or of a specific proposal. In their international review, Berke and Godschalk do not even mention the preparation of alternatives as an aspect of quality.

Alternatives are seldom prepared for a variety of reasons. Their preparation is commonly too expensive and time consuming; the contents of the plan are commonly determined by a mass of detailed local choices, rather than two or three strategic choices. Finally, acceptance of the plan is likely to proceed more smoothly if the experts involved can fix the strategy in a process that socio-technical theorists call 'closure' (Bijker 1995, 87–8).

In the absence of alternatives, plan evaluation may still involve the evaluation of impact, the assumption being that marginal improvements and changes are possible. Two basic methods are available:

1. economic methods of various types, including the planning balance sheet (also called community impact evaluation) (Lichfield et al. 1975); and
2. multi-criteria methods that combine economic and non-economic impacts.

Economic methods may, in turn, be divided into least cost method and various forms of cost/benefit analysis. Least cost methods are the most simple and probably the oldest. The development of any urban area is likely to encounter a combination of physical constraints caused by the local terrain as well as various limitations associated with the capacity of public utilities and services networks and the pattern of existing land uses. Analysis may therefore examine how development might proceed in a way that minimises costs and avoids crossing a threshold where further heavy investment is necessary to avoid deficiencies or underprovision (Hughes & Kozlowski 1968). Such analysis is not necessarily explicit or direct, however. Cost considerations can be identified through detailed knowledge of where development is the easiest to undertake and, in addition, through consultations with developers.

The economic benefits of land use planning are more ambiguous. The assessment of specific projects and other interventions is akin to the logic model/theory of change in which economic benefits such as job creation or infrastructure improvements are specified in advance and tested for their credibility and long-term outcomes. The assessment of general development plans involves, in contrast, tacit or general economic goals such as promoting economic growth. Evans (1969) has reviewed the scattered economic literature on town planning during the period in which blueprint styles predominated and suggests the existence of two benefits—on one hand, the minimisation of property rents (or more broadly property costs) and transport costs for occupants of all types and, on the other, the promotion of property values. Both criteria assume from the outset that adequate land is allocated for each use, as otherwise land values will be influenced by their scarcity rather than by location. The definition of adequate land release commonly remains, however, a point of contention in jurisdictions, notably the UK, that operate policies for urban containment and the protection of rural areas.

The twin aims of user cost minimisation and land value maximisation have limitations. Their impact is difficult to measure and predict. They are, in part, contradictory. They at least have the merit of simplicity, however and may be applied together. For example the economic evaluation of a rail investment might assess both time savings and the likely impact on local land values.

As is apparent from discussions such as Nijkamp et al. (1990), plan evaluation methods have, from the 1980s onwards, commonly favoured multi-criteria assessments that include some form of environmental impact assessment. And therein lies a dilemma. Given official concern with value for money and economic growth, a potential tendency exists for the quantified monetary outputs to be more influential than qualitative outputs. The typical environmental impact assessment consists of a discussion and where possible a prediction of future impact, both positive and negative, under a series of headings—for example, the impacts on biodiversity, air quality, water quality, noise, landscape and conservation, recreation and amenity and the socio-economic conditions in different communities (Glasson et al. 2005, 5). Given a choice between a multi-criteria environmental assessment and the apparent precision of an economic impact, governments may choose the latter. The official evaluation of road proposals has, in particular, been criticised for prioritising economics as expressed in the claimed time savings for motorists and delivery vehicles over environmental impact (Owens et al. 2004).

In response, specialists in environmental economics offer various ways of converting impact into monetary terms. A review by Gómez-Baggethun and Barton (2013) indicates the following: 'hedonic pricing' (modelling the extent to which different environmental attributes affect the price of a good or service, notably housing); savings in travel cost (for example, those savings achieved though having recreational space or the workplace near at hand); other avoided cost involving the loss of production, damage to business or physical damage; the avoided replacement cost of necessary amenities and public facilities; and the stated preferences of consumers, generated through questionnaire surveys amongst others.

However, it is arguable whether attempts to monetise environmental assets are either credible or can fully capture their value in use, to residents, workers or other users or their value as heritage. Some environmental attributes, for example biodiversity or natural beauty, have a value merely through their existence as contributing to the richness of the world and feelings of well-being, without having any short-term practical uses (Davidson 2013). Attributes of biodiversity and beauty also contribute to the identity of a place and, for conservation-minded pressure groups, merit safeguarding for this reason alone (Norton 1998).

Much depends on what is meant by the integration of criteria. Direct economic impacts on the property and labour markets can be monetised and quantified, albeit subject to forecasting uncertainties. Likewise, social impacts can be quantified under different headings (such as indices of health or well-being for example) and the value of heritage, including biodiversity and natural heritage, can be described in detail. Moreover, all these different aspects can be placed in the same document, detailing the impact of a proposed project or plan and providing a formal framework for integration, without however ending up with a single number or single estimated summation of the costs and benefits. A table might also be prepared showing various levels of achievement under different headings and aims, as was originally suggested by Hill (1968). Weaving different theories and different approaches together is not the same as blending them to the point that their distinctiveness becomes lost.

In any case, it is arguable as to whether a single integrated assessment is desirable. Nilsson (2005, 26–7) suggests, on the basis of interviews in the field of energy policy, that 'the assessments most useful for policy learning were those that explicitly accounted for and highlighted trade-offs. Fully integrated evaluation methods preclude that sense of trade-offs and close down discussion. They utilise 'black box' policy options, to use the language of actor-network theory, bundling together significant issues in a form that is opaque and inaccessible (Callon et al. 2009, 31).

There are further qualifications. Evaluation practice is commonly 'bounded' by time and resource limits. Plan evaluation may also become concerned with conformance to a fixed spatial pattern, rather than social and economic outcomes. The green belt, for example, is a fixed, doctrinal element of practice in England and therefore outside evaluation.

Moreover, whatever method is used, the assumptions of plan evaluation change over time in accordance with policy priorities. In particular, governments in Britain generally give the impression of being less concerned about the indicators of good quality planning, all of which allow for some local policy discretion and more about speed in making decisions and compliance with regional or national policies.

A succession of methods used in town planning in England provides an example. Here, the analysis of 'urban environmental capacity' became popular in the 1990s as local authorities sought to manage house building and urban development rather than meet housing demand. Later, in 2000, the principle of urban capacity studies was endorsed by the government in national planning guidance (Murdoch 2004). However, environmental capacity became less relevant once national policy turned to promoting housing supply, after the publication of the Barker review in 2004 (Bramley 2007, 228). Conversely, appraisal of the financial viability of schemes has become more and more relevant in the context from 2008 onwards as governments are eager to promote development in the context of a property market crisis and an economic recession. However, financial appraisal tests a proposal from the viewpoint of the developer only and is also essentially short term in character, saying for example little about the health impacts of any proposal (Town and Country Planning Association 2013, 14).

The shift from environmental evaluation to short-term financial appraisal provides a disappointing finale to a set of theories that seek to apply reason to politics and policy. '*Realrationalität*', the rationality of politics and political discourse, trumps the idealised rationality of planning, to paraphrase Flyvbjerg (1996), as has also happened in England in relation to the evaluation of community-based initiatives. Much depends on the level of expectation of rational planning, however. Planning theory generally assumes that analysis inevitably leads to or ought to lead to a set of recommendations based on that analysis and then to action. The concern with recommendations and action is implicit in the questions asked by Hoch, most of which are concerned with feasibility and support. The same concern is put explicitly by Flyvbjerg (2012, 169): 'Phronetic research results ("reason") are therefore results only to the extent they have an impact on practice ("action").'

Not all plans lead directly to implementation, however. Plans may be prepared as the demonstration of a principle, as has been the aim of some blueprint and master plans. Moreover, if the policy context is uncertain or potentially hostile, the analysis may not even lead to firm recommendations. Despite the difficulties, plan preparation can lead to a range of alternative scenarios. The alternatives can specify different urban growth strategies, as for example in the options generated a firm of consultants, Cambridge Architectural Research (2004) for South East England, outside London. They can also specify the type of town or type of countryside that might be envisaged in, say, 20 years, as has been documented in Denmark (Tress & Tress 2003)

In addition, the analysis may conclude with a statement of consequences, leaving the reader to determine the best course of action. Demonstrating consequences and sometimes issuing warnings on the basis of those consequences may itself be a sufficient research exercise (Jonas 1977). Warning, publicising and reporting is, at first sight, a departure from the optimism that characterises pragmatic interpretations of planning. A kernel of hope may remain, however, that an adequate policy response will still emerge. Pointing to the implications and consequences of a decision or trend promotes transparency in policy-making and is an ethical response, irrespective of whether it is welcomed by others. Evaluation, planning and implementation go together. But evaluation is worthwhile in its own right.

## Notes

1 'Twenty five techniques of situation crime prevention', available at the website of the Center for Problem-Oriented Policing, consulted January 2014 at www.popcenter.org/25techniques/.
2 Clark, H. & Anderson, A. (2004). 'Theories of change and logic models: telling them apart', presentation available at the website of ActKnowledge Theory of Change Community, consulted March 2011 at www.theoryofchange.org/library/presentations.html.
3 W. K. Kellogg Foundation (2004). Logic Model Development Guide, consulted May 2011 at http://ww2.wkkf.org/default.aspx?tabid=101&CID=281&CatID=281&ItemID=2813669&NID=20&LanguageID=0.

## References

Alexander, E. R. (2006). 'Evolution and status: where is planning evaluation today and how did it get here?' in Alexander E. R (ed.), *Evaluation in planning: evolution and prospects*. Aldershot: Ashgate, 3–16.

Alexander, E. R. (2009). 'Dilemmas in evaluating planning, or back to basics: what is planning for?'. *Planning Theory & Practice*, 10:2, 233–44.
Allmendinger, P. (2002). 'Towards a post-positivist typology of planning'. *Planning Theory*, 1, 77–99
Baer, W. C. (1997). 'General plan evaluation criteria: an approach to making better plans'. *Journal of the American Planning Association*, 63:3, 329–44,
Bailey, K. D., (1997). 'The autopoiesis of social systems: assessing Luhmann's theory of self-reference'. *Systems Research and Behavioral Science*, 14:2, 83–100.
Berke, P. & Godschalk, D. (2009). 'Searching for the good plan A meta-analysis of plan quality studies'. *Journal of Planning Literature*, 23:3, 227–40.
Bickman, L. (1987). 'The functions of program theory', In: Bickman, L. (ed.), *Using program theory in evaluation. New Directions for Program Evaluation no. 22*. San Francisco: Jossey Bass.
Bijker W. E. (1995). *Of bicycles, bakelites and bulbs: towards a theory of socio-technical change*. Cambridge, MA: MIT Press.
Boelens, L. (2010). 'Theorizing practice and practising theory: outlines for an actor-relational-approach in planning'. *Planning Theory*, 9, 28–62.
Bramley, G. (2007). 'The sudden rediscovery of housing supply as a key policy challenge'. *Housing Studies*, 22:2, 221–41.
Burton, P., Goodlad, R. & Croft, J. (2006). 'How would we know what works? Context and complexity in the evaluation of community involvement'. *Evaluation*, 12:3, 294–312.
Callon, M., (1999). 'Some elements of a sociology of translation: domestication of the scallops and the fishermen of St Brieuc Bay', In: Biagioli, M. (ed.), *the science studies reader*. London and New York: Routledge, 67–83 (first published in English in 1986).
Callon, M., Lascoumes, P. & Barthe, Y. (2009). *Acting in an uncertain world: an essay on technical democracy*. Cambridge, MA: The MIT Press (French original 2001).
Cambridge Architectural Research Ltd (collective author) (2004). *Housing futures: informed public opinion*. York. The Joseph Rowntree Foundation.
Carmona, M. & Sieh, L. (2005). 'Performance measurement innovation in English planning authorities'. *Planning Theory & Practice*, 6:3, 303–33.
Chen, H. T. (1994). 'Theory-driven evaluations: Needs, difficulties, and options'. *Evaluation Practice*, 15:1, 79–82.
Connell, J. P. & Kubisch, A. C. (1998). *Applying a theory of change approach to the evaluation of comprehensive community initiatives: progress, prospects, and problems*. Washington DC: The Aspen Institute, [online] URL: www.dmeforpeace.org/sites/default/files/080713%20Applying%2BTheory%2Bof%2BChange%2B Approach.pdf (consulted November 2015).
Coote, A., Allen, J. & Woodhead, D. (2004). *Finding out what works: understanding complex, community based initiatives*. London: King's Fund Publications.
Cordero-Guzman, H. & Auspos, P. (2006). 'Community economic development and community change'. In: Fulbright-Anderson & Auspos (eds.), *Community change: theories, practice, and evidence*. Washington, D.C.: The Aspen Institute, 195–268
Danermark, B., Ekstrom, M., Jakobsen, L. & Karlsson, J. (2002). *Explaining society: critical realism in the social sciences*. London: Routledge.
Davidson, M. D. (2013). 'On the relation between ecosystem services, intrinsic value, existence value and economic valuation'. *Ecological Economics*, 95, 171–77.

Dickinson, S., Prabhaker, M. & SQW Consulting (2009). *An analytical framework for community empowerment evaluations*. London: Communities and Local Government.

Eden, C. & Huxham, C. (1996). 'Action research for management research'. *British Journal of Management*, 7, 75–86.

Evans, A. W. (1969). 'Two economic rules for town planning: a critical note'. *Urban Studies*, 6:2, 227–34.

Faludi, A. (ed.) (1973). *A reader in planning theory*. Oxford: Pergamon.

Fitzpatrick, T. (2011). 'Response 2: social science as phronesis? The potential contradictions of a phronetic social policy'. *Journal of Social Policy*, 40:1, 31–9.

Flyvbjerg, B. (1996). 'The dark side of planning: rationality and *realrationalität*'. In: Mandelbaum, S., Mazza, L. & Burchell, R. (eds.), *Explorations in planning theory*. New Brunswick, NJ: Center for Urban Policy Research Press, 383–94.

Flyvbjerg, B. (2004). 'Phronetic planning research: theoretical and methodological reflections'. *Planning Theory & Practice*, 5:3, 283–306.

Flyvbjerg, B. (2012). 'Why mass media matter to planning research: the case of megaprojects'. *Journal of Planning Education and Research*, 32:2, 169–81.

Foden, M., Grimsley, M., Lawless, P. and Wilson, I. (2010). 'Linking interventions to outcomes in area regeneration: The New Deal for Communities Programme in England'. *The Town Planning Review*, 81:2, 151–71.

Forester, J. (1999). 'Reflections on the future understanding of planning practice'. *International Planning Studies*, 4:2, 175–93.

Friedman, M. (2007). 'The methodology of positive economics. Essays in positive economics'. In: Hausman, D. M. (ed.), *The philosophy of economics*. Cambridge, UK: Cambridge University Press, 145–79 (US original 1953).

Fulbright-Anderson K. & Auspos, P. (eds.) (2006). *Community change: theories, practice, and evidence*. Washington, DC: The Aspen Institute.

Geddes, M., Davies, J. & Fuller, C. (2007). 'Evaluating local strategic partnerships: theory and practice of change'. *Local Government Studies*, 33:1, 97–116.

Glaser, B. C. & Strauss, A. (2012). *The discovery of grounded theory: strategies for qualitative research*. New Brunswick, NJ and London: Aldine (seventh paperback printing: US original 1967).

Glasson, J., Thérivel, R. & Chadwick, A. (2005). *Introduction to environmental impact assessment: principles and procedures, process, practice and prospects*. London: Routledge.

Gómez-Baggethun, E. & Barton, D. N. (2013). 'Classifying and valuing ecosystem services for urban planning'. *Ecological Economics*, 83, 235–45.

Goodchild, B., Chamberlain, O., Dalgleish, K. & Lawrence, B. (1997). *Crime and the home front: the impact on crime and anti-social behaviour of housing people in town and city centres*. York: York Publishing Services

Haughton, G., Allmendinger, P. & Oosterlynck, S. (2013). 'Spaces of neoliberal experimentation: soft spaces, postpolitics, and neoliberal governmentality'. *Environment and Planning A*, 45:1, 217–34.

Healey, P. (1998). 'Building institutional capacity through collaborative approaches to urban planning'. *Environment and Planning A*, 30:9, 1531–46.

Hill, M. (1968). 'A goals-achievement matrix for evaluating alternative plans'. *Journal of the American Institute of Planners*, 34:1, 19–29.

Ho, S. Y. (1999). 'Evaluating urban regeneration programmes in Britain: exploring the potential of the realist approach'. *Evaluation*, 5:4, 422–38.

HoC—House of Commons Communities and Local Government Committee (2011). *Regeneration*. Sixth Report of Session 2010–12, Volume I: Report, together with formal minutes, oral and written evidence HC 1014. London: The Stationery Office.

Hoch, C. (2002). 'Evaluating plans pragmatically'. *Planning Theory*, 1, 53–75

Hughes J. T. & Kozlowski J. (1968). 'Threshold analysis–an economic tool for town and regional planning'. *Urban Studies*, 5, 132–43.

Jacobs, J. (2014). 'Spatial planning in cross-border regions: a systems-theoretical perspective'. *Planning Theory*, 15:1, 68–90, online first, [doi]1473095214547149.

Jeannot, G. & Goodchild, B. (2011). '"Fuzzy jobs" and local partnerships: case studies of urban and rural regeneration in France and England'. *Public Administration*, 89:3, 1110–27.

Jonas, H. (1977). 'Responsibility today: the ethics of an endangered future'. *Social Research*, 43:1, 77–97.

Jones, L, Taylor-Powell, E. & Henert, E. (2003). *Enhancing program performance with logic models*. University of Wisconsin-Extension, [online] URL: www.uwex.edu/ces/pdande/evaluation/evallogicmodel.html (consulted January 2015).

Knowlton, L. W. & Phillips, C. C. (2012). *The logic model guidebook: better strategies for great results*, 2nd edition. London and Thousand Oaks, CA: Sage.

Laprade, M. & Auspos, P. (2006). 'Improving a neighborhood's residential environment: pathways to physical and social change', In: Fulbright-Anderson and Auspos (eds.), *Community change: theories, practice, and evidence*. Washington, D.C.: The Aspen Institute, 141–94.

Lawless, P. (2011). 'Understanding the scale and nature of outcome change in area-regeneration programmes: evidence from the New Deal for Communities Programme in England'. *Environment and Planning C: Government and Policy*, 29:3, 520–32.

Leeuw, F. L. & Donaldson, S. I. (2015). 'Theory in evaluation: Reducing confusion and encouraging debate'. *Evaluation*, 21:4, 467–80.

Lichfield, N., Kettle, P. & Whitbread, N. (1975). *Evaluation in the planning process*, Oxford: Pergamon.

Luhmann, N. (1989). *Ecological communication*. Cambridge: Polity Press.

Luhmann, N. (1995). *Social systems*. Stanford, CA: Stanford University Press (German original 1984).

McEldowney, J. J. (1997). 'Policy evaluation and the concepts of deadweight and additionality: a commentary'. *Evaluation*, 3:2, 175–88.

McKenzie-Mohr, D., Lee, N., Schultz, P. W. &. Kotler, P. (2012). *Social marketing to protect the environment: what works*. Thousand Oaks, CA: Sage.

McLaughlin, J. A. & Jordan, G. B. (1999). 'Logic models: a tool for telling your program's performance story'. *Evaluation and Program Planning*, 22:1, 65–72.

McLoughlin, J. B. (1969). *Urban and regional planning, a systems approach*. Oxford: Pergamon.

Mann, S. and Schweiger, J. (2009). 'Using the objective hermeneutics method in policy evaluation'. *Evaluation*, 15:4, 445–57.

Montague, S. (1996). *The three R's of performance-based management*. Performance Management Network, [online] URL: www.pmn.net/wp-content/uploads/The-Three-Rs-of-Performance-Based-Management-A-Guide.pdf (consulted June 2016).

Murdoch, J. (2004). 'Putting discourse in its place: planning, sustainability and the urban capacity study'. *Area*, 36:1, 50–8.

Nijkamp, P. Rietveld, P. & Voogd, H. (1990). *Multicriteria evaluation in physical planning*. Amsterdam: North Holland.

Nilsson, M. A. (2005). *Connecting reason to power. assessments, learning, and environmental policy integration in Swedish energy policy*. Stockholm Environment Institute, [online] URL: www.sei-international.org/publications?pid=697 (consulted June 2016).

Norton, B. G. (1998). 'Evaluation and ecosystem management: new directions needed?' *Landscape and Urban Planning*, 40:1, 185-94.

Owens, S., Rayner, T. & Bina, O. (2004). 'New agendas for appraisal: reflections on theory, practice and research'. *Environment and Planning A*, 36, 1943-59.

Pawson, R., Greenhalgh, T., Harvey, G. & Walshe, K. (2005). 'Realist review – a new method of systematic review designed for complex policy interventions'. *Journal of Health Services Research & Policy*, 10:1, 21-34.

Pawson, R. & Tilley, N. (1997). *Realistic evaluation*. London: Sage.

Picciotto, R. (2005). 'The evaluation of policy coherence for development'. *Evaluation*, 11:3, 311-30.

Porter, G., & de Roo, G. (2007). 'The end has no merit'. In: Roo, G. de, & Porter, G., *Fuzzy planning–the role of actors in a fuzzy governance environment*. Hampshire: Ashgate Publishing Limited, 1–20.

Rogers P. J. (2008). 'Using programme theory to evaluate complicated and complex aspects of interventions'. *Evaluation* 14:1, 29-48.

Solesbury, W. (2001). 'The ascendancy of evidence'. *Planning Theory & Practice*, 3:1, 90-6.

Spicker, P. (2011). 'Generalisation and phronesis: rethinking the methodology of social policy'. *Journal of Social Policy*, 40:1, 1-19.

Sullivan, H. & Stewart, M. (2006). 'Who owns the theory of change?' *Evaluation* 12:2, 179-99.

Town and Country Planning Association (corporate author) (2013). *Planning healthier places – report from the reuniting health with planning project*. London: The T&CPA

Tress, B. & Tress, G. (2003). 'Scenario visualisation for participatory landscape planning—a study from Denmark'. *Landscape and Urban Planning*, 64, 161–178.

Van Assche, K. & Verschraegen, G. (2008). 'The limits of planning: Niklas Luhmann's systems theory and the analysis of planning and planning ambitions'. *Planning Theory*, 7:3, 263-83.

Vogel, I. (2012). *Review of the use of 'Theory of Change' in international development: review report*. Isabel Vogel Consultants, Eastbourne and UK Department for International Development, [online] URL: www.gov.uk/government/news/dfid-research-review-of-the-use-of-theory-of-change-in-international-development (consulted January 2014).

Voß, J., and Bornemann, B. (2011). 'The politics of reflexive governance: challenges for designing adaptive management and transition management'. *Ecology and Society*, 16:2, 9, [online] URL: www.ecologyandsociety.org/vol16/iss2/art9/ (consulted June 2016).

Weiss, C. H. (1997a). 'How can theory-based evaluation make greater headway?'. *Evaluation Review*, 21:4, 501-24.

Weiss, C. H. (1997b). 'Theory-based evaluation: past, present, and future'. *New Directions for Evaluation*, 76, 41-55.

Wells, P. (2011). *Evaluation: evidence based policy making and approaches to evaluation*, presentation given at Sheffield Hallam University, January 2011.

Yiftachel, O. (1998). 'Planning and social control: exploring the "dark side"'. *Journal of Planning Literature*, 12:2, 395-406.

# 7  Difference, Diversity and Dissent

Planning, noted Wootton (1945, 148), has to act within an agreed policy framework and it has to involve a process of 'discovering agreement prior to action'. Agreement might be elusive in some cases but the search is justified if the matters of interest are of public concern. Wootton's comments were part of an exchange between the advocates and opponents of central economic planning and were directed, in particular, at Hayek, who had accused the advocates of planning of 'manufacturing' and imposing agreement. The questions raised by that exchange have not disappeared. The very search for agreement raises continuing questions about how to cope with difference, multiple perspectives and multiple realities. Indeed, in some ways, the questions loom larger now than ever. For postmodern theorists, in particular, searching for a single plan, based on compromise and consensus, is futile and potentially damaging to minority groups and positions.

## Postmodernism

A clarification is necessary. Advocates of postmodernism, the anti-planning theorists of the 1940s and the neoliberals of later decades all offer a critique of the standardising effects of central planning and the state. They do this from different positions, however. The anti-planning and neoliberal theorists have always assumed that deregulation, the promotion of market processes and the promotion of economic growth are all in the public interest and they set themselves against public intervention of all types, except the most minimal. No further action and no targeting on specific groups is either necessary or desirable in the neoliberal world view. The postmodern critique, in contrast, cuts across the political divisions of Left and Right.

Postmodernism involves a cultural critique rather than political economy and in the most common interpretation by Lyotard ([1979] 1984) asserts the desirability of recognising multiple publics in opposition to both state and the market. For Lyotard, the all-encompassing, 'totalising' ideologies of Left and Right are no longer a source of progress and innovation. The old class-based ideologies, the 'grand narratives' of reform, have lost credibility, and the 'old poles of attraction', notably the nation-state have lost their attraction (ibid., 14, 37–41). In this context, change is provoked by the politics of reforming pressure groups and social movements and the 'little narratives', that is to say the discourses of policy and progress that these groups incorporate.

The 'little narratives' of postmodernism have a series of overlapping points of origin in the arts—architecture, literature—and in social philosophy, but these do not have much in common, other than as a critique of a unitary or universal concept of modernity. Postmodern urban planning, including urban regeneration and policy, has its own point of origin in a sense of disillusion with the results of the post-war reconstruction and new build programmes. This is its first meaning—postmodernism as reaction. Equally, however, postmodern urban planning can be understood through the lens of postmodern philosophy and literature. The latter strand provides a second meaning—postmodernism as storytelling. In addition, however, postmodern philosophy and literature leads to a third meaning—postmodernism as diversity. We take each meaning in turn.

## As Reaction: Breaking with the Past

Postmodernism as reaction can be understood as a failure of planning to meet its promises. The advocates of planning before World War II could always argue that planning had not been tried and that the failures of the laissez-faire industrial city were obvious. The 1960s, in contrast, were a period of exceptional activity in the development of planned new towns, in public sector and private house building completions and in the planned redevelopment of town centres and inner city slums. Indeed, some planning historians, notably the late Sir Peter Hall, have seen the late 1960s as the 'boom time' for planning in the UK, both in government and the universities—a high point in terms of delivery and practical impact.[1] Equally, however, the late 1960s, and even more so the 1970s, were a time of reaction.

Critiques of modern town planning in the 1960s and 1970s did not use the term 'postmodern'. This latter only entered planning theory later. The influence of Post-Modern architecture (spelt with a capital P and M) was one influence. Post-Modern architecture, as was explained by its leading advocate, Jencks (1977), assumed that architecture had to design for two audiences—for other architects and for popular tastes. Implicit in Post-Modern architecture was, therefore, a rejection of any assumption that a single standard of good taste was possible. In opening taste to the public, Post-Modern architecture admitted the possibility of multiple publics and so promoted the fragmentation of aesthetic criteria. Moreover, in accepting the relevance of the public's assessment, Post-Modern architecture involved an endorsement of speculative house building (Cowburn 1967;

Venturi 1976) and, above all in the US, an acceptance of commercial building and commercial advertising (Venturi et al. 1972)

The reaction against modernism was not mainly about architectural style, however. Equally, despite the arguments of architectural theorists (Jencks 1977; McCormac 1978), it was not the failures of tower blocks developed by local authorities and other social housing landlords. The reaction expressed instead a general sense of dissatisfaction with the type of city produced in the 1950s and 1960s.

To explain this, a brief historical digression is necessary. Jencks (1977) suggested a precise date for the start of Post-Modern architecture as being 15 July 1972 when the authorities blew up (or blew down, depending on the preferred terminology) a complex of high-rise homes at Pruitt-Igoe in St Louis in the US. The blocks were considered an irredeemable social failure and one that could not be rectified at a reasonable cost. Following the demolition of Pruitt-Igoe and of similar blocks elsewhere a standard story emerged in Britain as well as the US of how modern architecture in housing had failed to give people what they wanted. It had resulted it schemes that contributed 'to a process of social exclusion' (Brindley 1999, 42). The architectural profession had succeeded in imposing simple, unadorned styles and types of buildings, notably high-rises, that had never prevailed in dwellings built for sale. As a result, social rented housing and modern architecture had become almost synonymous in the public mind and the aesthetic of economy, which itself was also associated with the bureaucracy of local authority house building, had come to signify public tenancy with all its social problems (see, for example, McCormac 1978).

Yet, neither the failure of the blocks at Pruitt-Igoe nor the more general use of modern styles of architecture could be held as responsible for social exclusion, except as a contributing factor amongst many. In part, the demolition of Pruitt-Igoe was caused by a series of specific failures and by the subsequent failure of the housing authority to manage and maintain the blocks (Birmingham 1998). Much the same was, moreover, said about the experience of high-density, flatted estates in Britain (Anderson et al. 1985; Power 1984).

In any case, the reaction against modern architecture and modern town planning involved an exceptionally broad agenda. Other responses included 'non-plan', a consumer-oriented, populist approach to strategic planning, published in the journal *New Society* (20 March 1969); self-build and related anarchist approaches to housing as promoted by Ward (1976); flexible housing, otherwise known as open building as promoted by Habraken (1972); new types of design that would allow 'personalisation', the ability of users to stamp their identity on a place (Cooper Marcus & Sarkissian 1986, 63, Goodchild 1991); and finally various community-led approaches to urban regeneration that favoured improvement rather than mass demolition (Davies 1972; Goodchild 1997, 161–3; Hall 2002, 291;

Walters 2007, 73–4) All these initiatives assumed that, in different ways, modern architecture, modern town planning and mass, public sector building and rebuilding programmes were lacking in originality or responsiveness, too limiting in their scope, too dominated by technical criteria, too directive and too single-minded in searching to reconstruct the British city. The problem was therefore not style, but the excessive power exercised by professionals of all types.

As these examples suggest, the postmodern turn of planning and urban policy was a series of overlapping tendencies just as postmodernism in general involved different strands that stemmed from the arts and philosophy. The closer the ideas are examined, the more particular and varied is their history and implications.

In addition, because of the tendency of postmodern ideas to cut across conventional political divides, they became caught in a rerun of the double movement that Polanyi (1957) noted was a recurrent feature of public policy in Britain and other Western societies in the 19th and early 20th centuries. On one hand, reactions against modernism favoured market and consumer preferences, much as was later pursued in the 1980s and 1990s in Britain by the New Right. The 'non-plan' proposals published in *New Society* in 1968 were an obvious example of this, anticipating by about 12 years the Enterprise Zone idea. For the critics of neoliberalism, notably Harvey (1989), postmodernism represented the triumph of market-oriented urban design over social planning and was linked to other changes that amounted to a new phase of flexible (post-Fordist) capitalism. For others, the reaction against modern town planning and modern forms of organization favoured a different and more responsive, but not necessarily a weaker public sector. Whatever the interpretation however, all parties agreed that modern town planning had lost its public appeal and political allure and was now on the defensive.

### *As Storytelling: Favouring Minorities and Exceptions*

The debates in architecture and housing were further strengthened by the example of postmodern literature and social philosophy. For example, Hassan (1985) summarised trends in American literature in the 1970s as the unmaking of modern culture, this process being associated with a multiplicity of terms and tendencies, all of which carried the prefix 'dis' or 'de':

> deconstruction, decentering, disappearance, dissemination, demystification, discontinuity, difference, dispersion, etc. ... Such terms express an epistemological obsession with fragments or fractures, and a corresponding ideological commitment to minorities in politics, sex and language.

By implication, therefore, the trend towards a rational society, as noted by Simmel, Weber and Mannheim in the early and mid-20th century, had reached its limits, mainly because rationalisation implies a limited range of answers that fail to deal with a diversity of situations and groups.

Postmodern literature is a form of storytelling. Conversely, the postmodern turn in urban planning from the 1970s onwards is apparent in the way that Throgmorton (1996) and Sandercock (2003) amongst others have advocated 'persuasive' storytelling as a method of plan making and plan communication. Throgmorton (1996, 33) draws a parallel between energy planning and urban planning, comparing old-fashioned top-down energy planning where a monopoly supplier is able to determine policy without challenge and a current situation where energy suppliers have to negotiate and justify price rises and where, in addition, alternative visions of the future coexist with one another, including visions of decentralised energy production. The present situation therefore demands storytelling.

Storytelling gains strength from the way in which the plot and characters are likely to remain in the memory longer than any constituent detail and certainly more than a technical detail of say a population projection (Bruner 1991). Stories are central to accounts of social and personal identity, as for example in enabling a person to understand how they have come to live in a specific place and what this place means, both to the self and others. As a result, it is possible to apply the usual categories of literature, such as tragedy, romance, comedy and satire, directly to the personal accounts of workers or residents (Glaeser 1998; Goodchild et al. 2014). These have been called 'stories in planning' (van Hulst 2012), because they deal with personal and family experiences against a broader policy context. They also commonly relate to use values rather than either the abstractions of planning or the criteria of exchange values. Equally, stories can be constructed as 'stories of planning' to represent the fate of a collectivity, a neighbourhood, town or city, for the future as well as the past.

Merely insisting on the character of planning as storytelling is not enough, however. The same uncertainties that have produced an explicit emphasis on storytelling also raise questions about which models of storytelling are most appropriate.

The simplest approach is the fairy story, prefixed by 'once upon a time' or some similar form of words. The very terminology is intended to convey simplicity. Here are three examples taken from the Web, concerning cities and planning.

1 Mumbai, once upon a time, had its share of its dissipation spaces – wetlands, wastelands, mangroves and salt-pan lands, etc. that acted like sponges and took the pressure off high tides. In the past few years, these have been destroyed systematically.[2]

178  Applying 'Reason' to Politics

2 Once upon a time, all the talk … was of the end of suburbia. But what if we could create suburbs that are designed to function in harmony with their surroundings?[3]
3 Once upon a time, in the 1990s, Medellín, Colombia, was the 'murder capital of the world.' Then thoughtful architectural planning connected the slums to the city. Crime rates plummeted and, against the odds, the city was transformed. Well, yes and no.[4]

The fairy story is particularly suited to distinguishing the past or future from the present, for good as in the last example or ill, as in the first. In contemplating the future, the fairy story is also an invitation to use imagination in working out the implications of alternative lifestyles and technology. As the third example suggests, simple stories can become oversimple, however.

In any case, strongly contrasting stories, promising ambitious achievements or warning against severe consequences, are less likely to be accepted as credible, according to public opinion pollsters.[5] A variant of the fairy story, 'the hero story' (Janda and Topouzi 2013) of brave scientists and technological breakthroughs, is particularly vulnerable to concerns of exaggeration. A story is strictly speaking an exercise in credibility and plausibility rather than the scientific testing of hypotheses. Nevertheless, stories are commonly labelled as true or false.

Another approach to storytelling, advocated in particular by Throgmorton (1992, 19) is that that planning should be about promoting a sense of drama, should learn from films and novels and should, as a result, follow a series of simple rules:

- Build conflict, crisis and resolution into their narratives.
- Build characters into the narrative, characters who are interesting and believable, and whom readers … care about.
- Place the action in its rightful context. That means acknowledging the settings – regulatory commission hearing chambers, for example – in which those characters come into conflict.
- Adopt an appropriate point of view. To do so they (*the authors*) have to ask, both for themselves and their characters, who is standing where to watch the scene? Who is speaking? To whom? In what form?
- Use the imagery and rhythm of the language to express a preferred attitude toward the situation and its characters.

Some additional criteria of a convincing story may be identified. Visual imagery and not just the imagery of language is important—in catching the attention of an audience, illustrating themes, offering solutions and heightening the emotional impact of a story. Rational thinking and rational planning works through words and numbers. If the author of a plan wishes to appeal to the senses and to emotions, appropriate visual images have to be included (O'Neill 2013).

There are limits, however, to reducing storytelling to a formula. The subtlety of plots and the potential range and complexity of situations is too great. Further, the integration of quantitative information and qualitative criteria into the story does not necessarily make for a good read or a good drama, even if necessary for the sake of completeness and justification.

Above all, the analogy between plan making and drama is potentially misleading, if taken too far. Persuasive storytelling can itself go too far, drowning out dissenting views and treating opponents as figures of fun or hatred. The preparation of learning rather than persuasive stories might be a more neutral and also more useful exercise (Janda and Topouzi 2013). Likewise, the references to drama can go too far in the direction of a subjective approach to the production of knowledge. As is also the case for the fairy story, it is worthwhile remembering the ironic newspaper saying: 'Do not let an awkward fact get in the way of a good story.'

History provides a third model (after fairy stories and drama) of storytelling. History commonly involves the synthesis of different viewpoints and different personal stories into an account that unfolds over time. History is also an exercise in hermeneutics in which the accounts of different individuals and institutional actors are combined together to link the past, present and the future in an exercise that Gadamer (1989, 578) calls the fusion of horizons and that itself has the potential to trigger further debates and critical analyses. Like planning, moreover, history involves a mixture of subjective and objective information, including the consequences, if any, of an event. The overall account is subjective in that the historian or storyteller imposes his or her interpretation on events, but the account may use 'objective' supporting evidence. Historical accounts are also well suited to accounts that enable a consideration of alternatives and opportunities, as these have been defined and assessed in the past.

Studies of the historical method have drawn attention to the way in which the social position of the storyteller and the quality of the information sources influence the account (Alvesson and Sköldberg 2008). Historical narratives are, moreover, not necessarily new or postmodern. Historical accounts of urban development figure, for example, in the evolutionary approaches to plan making advocated by Geddes (1915). History only becomes postmodern if the sources reveal either a voice that is otherwise seldom heard, from a minority or excluded group, or an account that goes against an overarching, 'totalising' force or policy.

To grasp the full implications of postmodernism, it is best to return to literature and to a single work, *Invisible Cities* by Italo Calvino ([1972] 1997). *Invisible Cities* is treated as a classic of 20th century literature in the introduction to its current United Kingdom edition. It is also commonly regarded as a classic postmodern literary text, partly because it refuses any total understanding and any sense of a single reality (Hoffman 2005, 365), and partly because it involves a self-conscious and sometimes playful reflection on the process of reading.[6] It deserves detailed consideration, moreover, as the only postmodern 'classic' that treats cities and planning as central themes. *Invisible Cities* has been occasionally cited in the planning and urban studies literature (for example, Leandro 2005; Parker 2004, 159; Pinder 2002; Watson 1983), but only in relation to short passages that illustrate specific types of city or specific tendencies in utopian thinking.

The contents of *Invisible Cities* do not fall into the conventional fictional genres that people use to describe their own experience. There are only two characters, the explorer Marco Polo and his employer, the Chinese emperor Kublai Khan. Marco Polo is the traveller who experiences cities first hand and describes those cities and who, in effect, advocates a postmodern position. Kublai Khan, the emperor, sees cities from above as an autocrat and equally as a modernist planner.

The text has, moreover, no apparent story. It consists entirely of a series of short, precise contemplations on 55 different cities, presented by Marco Polo interspersed by a dialogue between Marco Polo and Kublai Khan. For example: Marco Polo describes 'Isadora', a city where desires are fulfilled, but only as memories; 'Tamara', where the visitor can only see signs rather than the reality; 'Phyllis', whose visible presence disappears in the routine of long-term residence; 'Chloe', where people glance at each other but never exchange a word or a touch; 'Adelma', a city inhabited by people that the visitor once knew but are dead; 'Octavia', a city suspended by a net over an abyss so that residents might be more aware of precarious nature of human existence; Berenice, the unjust city and so on.

As the text unfolds, Marco Polo remarks that he is not really describing different cities. He is, instead, repeatedly saying something about one city, his home city of Venice. In doing this, moreover, Marco is not just indicating that his home city has meanings and dimensions that are not immediately visible, for example to the tourist. He is also saying that all cites have multiple meanings and interpretations that resist generalisation. In one passage, the two protagonists give their contrasting views about how best to design an ideal city:

> 'I have constructed in my mind a model city from which all possible cities can be deduced,' Kublai said. 'It contains everything corresponding to the norm.' ...
>
> 'I have also thought of a model city from I which I can deduce all the others,' Marco answered. 'It is a city made of exceptions, incongruities, contradictions. If such a city is the most improbable, by reducing the number of abnormal elements, we increase the probability that the city really exists. ... But I cannot force my operation beyond a certain limit: I would achieve cities too probable to be real.'

Modern planning and modern urban design involved a choice between the model, the work of the architect and the visionary, and the rule, the work of public administration and bureaucracy (Choay 1996). Both may be interpreted as attempts to generalise and standardise planning as urban design. Planning by exceptions is a third, postmodern alternative that unmakes the generalisations of modernism, irrespective of whether these are based on rules or models. Planning by exceptions amounts to an ad-hoc and fragmented means of dealing with the varied and often unanticipated demands of multicultural identity politics (Piccolo and Thomas 2001; Qadeer 1997) and of informal or self-built settlements where it is impossible and undesirable to insist of modern standards (Roy 2005). A further use is dealing with aggrieved communities for whom some restorative or compensatory action is necessary. Sandercock (2004) has in particular suggested that the contemporary city requires a new style of planning that, amongst other things, is 'audacious' in 'daring to break the rules' and 'therapeutic' in resolving conflicts and changing public values.

Some qualifications are necessary, however. Planning by exceptions is impossible to conceptualise as a general principle. The possibility of an exception presupposes a general rule in the first place. In addition, Sandercock's reference to a 'therapeutic imagination' and to therapy is derived from a very specific type of relationship, namely that between counsellor and a patient. Moreover, applied to urban planning and to urban politics, the principle of therapy risks placing the onus on the so-called patient-the community-to come to terms with their fate (Schweitzer 2016). A pragmatic position would, in contrast, probably insist that the therapeutic imagination is too limited in its application and too paternalist. Likewise, those influenced by notions of social rights and social capabilities would argue that difference should not be prioritised over notions of social justice (Fainstein 2005).

*Invisible Cities* also provides some advice. The numerous cities described by Marco Polo include cases where the reader is invited to make judgements about issues of collective interest such as environmental pollution and injustice. Marco Polo's advice in such cases is to ignore the possibility of the ideal city and to recognise 'who and what in the midst of the inferno are not inferno.' In other words, give space and encouragement to progressive forces. *Invisible Cities* has therefore modernist as well as postmodern elements. It is not just about 'unmaking', but also about remaking. Indeed, the way in which *Invisible Cities* gradually moves towards a conclusion is one of the reasons why it is accessible and potentially instructive as a planning and not just as a literary text.

### *As Diversity: Reforming Planning Practice*

As is implicit in *Invisible Cities*, a repeated and exclusive emphasis on modern/postmodern contrasts gives a distorted impression. Identity politics may favour a sense of separateness in the way that local groups wish to protect and enhance the existing identity of their hometowns and neighbourhoods. However, different groups also share concerns – for example about local facilities and environmental quality. Moreover, in relation to the statutory planning system in England, consultation exercises do not generally involve a wide range of different publics. They tend instead to comprise another type of bipolar confrontation – between pro- and anti-development interests.

As a result, a fine division of the public into multiple groups by age, ethnicity and gender is commonly unnecessary. With the obvious exception of disabled people, different age and lifestyle groups can generally adapt the built environment to their wishes and needs. For example, ethnic and lifestyle diversity is commonly expressed in the furnishing and décor of a home, the type of shops present in an area and the use of distinctive signs on shop fronts and public buildings. Changes to the appearance of homes, the arrival of distinctive signs and ethnic shops eventually transform the landscape of a neighbourhood, but mostly through the details of a place, through moveable and decorative aspects of a building that are part of a spontaneous process that is generally independent of planning decisions.

The same emphasis on modern/postmodern contrasts also offers only a caricature of planning ideas in the twentieth century. Mannheim's concept of central planning fits the caricature of total solutions, However, Mannheim's concept also has the merit of tackling collective and structural issues that an emphasis of fragmentation neglects. In contrast, the pragmatic approach advocated by Dewey, itself a modern approach, envisages democratic politics as an open-ended learning process encompassing a variety of different futures.

Subsequent interpretations of pragmatism have, moreover, sought to show, moreover, how pragmatism allows an appreciation of difference without undermining the rationale for collective action and without, in addition, limiting collective action to specific, aggrieved communities. Rorty (1997) has, for example, reinterpreted Dewey, amongst others, to argue that an insistence of difference does not mean the end of political efforts to promote an enlightened society, characterised, for example, by tolerance and a commitment to reduce human suffering. Likewise Bridge (2005, x) has appealed to Dewey and other pragmatists to show how 'in myriad spaces of communication in the city, difference can still be brought into dialogue'. The public interest and a pragmatic rationale for planning may, therefore, be retained whilst recognising diversity.

The mainstream response in Anglo-American planning theory has followed the same pattern of seeking some combination of difference and the public interest. As Beauregard (1996, 227) stated of the situation in the US, planning occupies an uneasy middle ground 'between modernity and postmodernity'. In response to the postmodern challenge, a revision of working practices is necessary, but not too far.

## Difference, Diversity and Dissent 183

Though the modernist project in under attack, and seemingly less and less viable as a response to contemporary social conditions and intellectual tendencies, one should not propose too hastily that planners should resolve the confusion by unconditionally adopting postmodernist alternatives. The modernist project needs to be reconstructed in a way that takes into account its strengths – the focus on the city, the commitment to reform, the mediative role within the state – and eradicates its weaknesses – the outmoded view of the city, the lack of democracy, an illiberal attitude towards narratives and an insensitivity to the diversity of communities.

Likewise, Allmendinger (2001, 257) states of planning from a British perspective:

> Can we have a postmodern planning? No. ... Can we have a planning that is more open, sensitive to the needs of the many, radically challenges existing notions and actively seeks to encourage wider participation from those previously excluded in a continuously open discourse? Yes.

While both Beauregard and Allmendinger envisage a halfway house between modernism and postmodernism, there is a subtle difference. Beauregard sees changes in style being thrust on a planning process that still seeks to realise progress and consensus about specific aims. The boundary between modernity and postmodernity is, as a result, variable and capable of moving in either direction in a way, moreover, that is likely to remain unpredictable.

Allmendinger (2001, 233–4), in contrast, is more prescriptive and lists a series of administrative principles to which planning practice might aspire. The result is also a set of principles that might also reconcile postmodernism with the workings of a modern administration. The principles are as follows:

- 'transparency' (providing an assessment of who is likely to gain and who is likely to lose and whether any alternatives are available);
- 'accountability' (ensuring that specific groups can challenge decisions);
- 'targeting' (ensuring that intervention is relevant to a specific community);
- 'consistency' (over the area of a planning authority, but not necessarily between different authorities); and
- 'proportionality' (involving a presumption of 'no intervention unless it can be justified').

The principles look like common sense, but are not free of controversy. They have some similarities to the 'localism' policies supported in 2010 and 2011 in England and Wales by a coalition Conservative/Liberal government long after publication of Allmendinger's thoughts on postmodernism. Certainly, the combination of accountability, community targeting and proportionality are reminiscent of the localism measures, with their combined intent to downsize government intervention, whilst also decentralising decision-making. Reference to a presumption in favour of no intervention is, in particular, reminiscent of a presumption in favour of development and economic growth rather than sustainability. In 2011, amenity and heritage groups argued vociferously that any such presumption is likely to encourage development in the countryside or in places where the quality of the environment might be damaged.[7]

Consistency of application is another disputed principle, but also one that shows the limitations of postmodernism. Developers in Britain commonly argue that policy should be applied uniformly across the country rather than just consistently across a single local authority. As a result, they typically argue for restrictions on the ability of local authorities to impose controls or otherwise intervene in the market. Equally, however, for those arguing for a strong planning framework, consistency implies the application of design standards or of standardised decision-making techniques in a way that is clearly contrary to a postmodern search for flexibility and exceptions. Systematic techniques can incorporate a degree of flexibility through the application of different aims and objectives, but the very application of aims and objectives presupposes an agreed set of rules. As Beauregard and Allmendinger note, a purely postmodern planning is impossible.

## Thick Legitimacy

Difference implies conflicting expectations and raises questions about the ability of government to handle conflict. In this context a distinction may be made between 'thin' and a higher, more authentic and 'thicker' form of political and legal legitimacy (Black 2000, 2001). 'Thin' concepts of legitimacy mean that the actions of an individual or an institution are consistent in terms of the letter of the law and also in terms of some initial client brief, for example in a research or work contract or economic efficiency. Thick legitimacy, in contrast, involves some purpose or moral commitment that generally derives from extended deliberation amongst citizens. Deliberation means planning as debate and collaboration, but it also means a particular form of debate where those involved consider alternatives and come to a reasoned decision (Fearon 1998).

### The Logic of Deliberative Democracy

Deliberation can and does operate within government and within conventional political parties. Thick legitimacy means something else, however—a process whereby legitimacy is created and maintained through discussion with the representatives of different groups and interests consulted in multiple interactive forums that interact with one another, with the state bureaucracy and with elected representatives. In other words, thick legitimacy as opposed to thin legal legitimacy involves multiple, repeated exercises or 'moments' on consultation (Parkinson 2006, 174), rather than a few isolated instances. Political institutions have to become deliberative in general. Davies et al. (2012) have added that these multiple deliberative moments should not just be based on debate and decision-related meetings. They should include films and videos, online games, art and drama projects that might reach multiple audiences and that might also better relate to the material experience of urban life.

Deliberative democracy commonly involves the establishment of a public space, whether this is 'real' or media based or a network, that allows people to formulate and express their views and where citizens can discuss common affairs through the medium of talk, publications or electronic interactions (Fraser 1990). The public realm, through its reference to space, has therefore a direct and intimate relationship with planning as place making. Public space as a concrete entity is more than a shared encounter space, such as a park or street or town square. Instead, public space comprises an ever-changing landscape that is open to the public use (albeit subject to regulation) or the public gaze, as opposed to the private spaces associated with domestic and non-domestic property (Besse 2006). Equally, and this is its meaning in social philosophy, both the public realm and public space offers a metaphor for the organization of policy debates and politics. The reference to 'public' offers a means of emphasising the collective aspects of action and the dependency of the individual on the community, on collective relationships and on public policy (Pellegrino et al. 1990).

Deliberative methods are justified by the limitations of elected democracy and, in particular, the limitations of representative methods to deal with the complexities of a society that is more diverse, educated and less deferential than in the past. Deliberation enables policies and plans to capture the subtleties of different situations and the way that specific local considerations interact with one another. Deliberative methods are also favoured by those concerned with establishing social capital (Putnam 2000), that is to say local voluntary institutions, in deprived neighbourhoods. Social capital itself means the number and intensity of citizen involvement in civic institutions of all types.

Equally and less obviously deliberative methods are justified by the limitations of general public opinion as reflected in the press. General public opinion is too weak and open to manipulation by editorial judgements and by powerful interests that have access to the media. National newspapers in the UK sometimes mount campaigns that are relevant to planning. The 'Daily Telegraph', for example, has published many articles on the need to protect the countryside. However, there is no easy way of knowing the extent to which newspaper campaigns reflect public opinion.

In addition, local newspapers face financial and staffing constraints that limit their ability to undertake investigative and specialist journalism. Moreover, the most excluded social groups often fail to have their voice adequately represented in local newspapers owing to lack of knowledge, poor English language skills or other factors. Of course, to say that public debate in newspapers or other media is limited in its scope and depth is not to say that such public debate is irrelevant or futile, merely that it is not enough.

In some countries in Asia and Africa, civil society groups either have little or no ability to articulate and publicise an independent voice or otherwise have little influence on a policy debate that remains within the state apparatus (Watson 2008; Winkler 2011). Demonstrations and protests are nevertheless likely if residents feel sufficiently aggrieved. The demonstrations about the redevelopment of Gezi Park in Istanbul in 2014 provide an example. Here the lack of consultation on the redevelopment of the park came to summarise the faults of an autocratic regime and the protests became a means of pressuring wider democratic reforms (Kuymulu 2013).

Elsewhere, in the 'global north', the problem is not a lack of civil society bodies, but their abundance and fragmented character. Relevant groups in Britain include local companies (community businesses); very local elected councils (such as parish councils) with the ability to raise limited amounts of revenue through local taxation; area committees, made up of elected councillors and serviced by local government officers; formal partnerships that are part of wider governance arrangements; formal vehicles for consultation such as citizen's juries; and informal groups of residents established to tackle particular issues (see, for example, White & Dickinson 2006, 28). However, this very diversity of groups is itself justification for the use of deliberative approaches.

The extent to which deliberative methods depends in part on the local political context. A study of plan making in India (Vidyarthi et al. 2013) has shown for example how practice remains influenced by the elitist politics and central planning of the 1950s and 1960s and that, in addition, consultation varies greatly in both the breadth of efforts, that is its ability to reach a wide variety of different stakeholders, and in depth and intensity—for example the time devoted to consultation, the level of detail in the discussion and the stage at which consultation takes place. Each combination of depth and breadth in turn leads to a different style of planning (Vidyarthi et al. 2013). Broad, but shallow involvement is consistent with the principles of disjointed incrementalism, working with established pressure groups that are easy to reach. A combination of narrow and shallow involvement implies an unresponsive style dominated by the political elite, consistent with the principles of central planning. The opposite combination, that of broad and deep involvement, is consistent with the principles of communicative planning and deliberative democracy, but is obviously more demanding and more expensive. Finally, a combination of narrow reach, but deep involvement implies a situation where established elites co-opt a few key pressure groups.

The involvement of citizens may also be classified according to the extent to which power is delegated to citizen groups or committees. Arnstein (1969) has outlined a well-known ladder of citizen participation that ranges from cynical manipulation, degrees of tokenism and no public influence at one extreme to full community control at the other. The ladder was first worked out to clarify citizen participation in the model cities programme in the US in the 1960s, arguably the first attempt in any country to use participatory methods to improve the management and governance of deprived neighbourhoods.

Strictly speaking, however, the defining characteristic of deliberative approaches is the quality and reach of the discussion and not the delegation of power as such. Arnstein's language, notably the reference to 'degrees of tokenism', implies some right to or possibly some tendency towards citizen control that is outside the scope of deliberative democracy. The mere delegation of power, as represented by citizen control, would simply transfer the problem of legitimacy from a public bureaucracy to a community group that itself may be unrepresentative. Deliberative approaches, in any case, assume that urban management and governance is simply too big to be delegated or that delegation is unrealistic for other reasons, for example financial reasons in the case of housing management. The right to participate in deliberative democracy is therefore mostly about gaining a voice, at the level of partnership and consultation, rather than the delegation of power.

To an extent, the classifications of reach, quality and degree of participation are only a starting point. Power has a subjective aspect. Those involved in a participation exercise may feel that they are manipulated, even if this was not the intention. They may also feel that they have learnt little and their views were disregarded from the outset. Conversely, if participation is a two-way process, one might also enquire what information is provided, how it is selected, presented and interpreted and how responses of the 'audience' are used. Participation and consultation deserves evaluation, just as much as any plan.

The cost of undertaking the necessary work and the delays that this causes to decision-making or the implementation of policies is a major constraint. Legitimacy does not guarantee efficiency. Moreover, governments have to decide, in any specific case, where the priority should be and whether the search for legitimacy gets in the way of efficient policy implementation. Institutional analysis (Seo and Creed 2002; Buitelaar et al. 2014, 251) commonly regards the gap, contradiction or tension (depending on the preferred terminology) between legitimacy and efficiency to be endemic in public and private institutions and suggests that this is a source of instability, leading to recurrent, occasional change in one direction or another. In Britain, however, most of the recent changes have favoured efficiency. For example, in England and Wales, changes to infrastructure planning (the planning of roads, rail, ports and energy provision) from the Planning Act, 2008 Act onwards, have been motivated by exactly by a concern with speeding up decision-making rather than promoting democracy (Marshall 2013).

Given the various constraints, thick legitimacy is a demanding, perhaps impossibly demanding exercise, as has been widely noted (Fraser 1990; Huxley 2000; Tewdwr-Jones and Allmendinger 1998). At an abstract level, full legitimacy depends on the achievement of an 'ideal speech' situation according to Habermas (1970) in which, amongst other requirements, each person and each group has equal access. Yet specific groups are invariably over-represented in policy debates, whilst others are under-represented. For example, studies of community activism in Britain suggest that activists, whether involved in local party politics or in local environmental campaigning, do not generally come from the margins of society, for example from the dispossessed. They are commonly middle class, if measured by their occupation, and are relatively confident in their dealings with local bureaucracies and local politicians, partly because they share a common background (Pink 2008, 2009; Ray 2004).

The existence of a representative cross section of participants is, moreover, only the first of many demanding requirements. The ideal speech situation also assumes, *inter alia*, the following (Benhabib, 1986, 285):

- All who are potential participants must have equal rights to use speech acts in such a way that a discourse (or a plan or a policy) can be permanently open to claims and counter claims, questions and answers.
- All who participate in discourse must have an equal chance to present interpretations, and to make assertions, recommendations, explanations and corrections. (*In other words all participants have the right to set the agenda.*)
- Participants are honest to each other and make their intentions transparent.
- Participants have equal chances to order and resist orders, to promise and refuse, to be accountable for one's conduct and to demand accountability from others.

There is an irony in the concept of thick legitimacy, however. The concept is a dead-end, if considered as a set of impossible demanding standards. Yet planning does not have to involve the perfect understanding of the position of the various participants for decisions to be made. Decisions can and are made on the basis of imperfect knowledge and understanding. Moreover, in making decisions, a case for attempting to consult the public or involving the public in decision-making is likely to remain. The impossibility of a perfect or best solution does not prevent a search for improved procedures that might either strengthen legitimacy or at least improve the quality and effectiveness of the decision-making process, the concern of pragmatism and systems theory.

Put in slightly different language, thick legitimacy requires that legally authorised action is supported by 'communicative rationality', a term that is derived mostly from Habermas ([1981] 1987). Communicative rationality is rationality of a type that itself facilitates public debate and is distinct from technical rationality that is merely concerned with prediction and measurement. Yet a parallel may be drawn between communicative rationality and the concept of bounded technical rationality as defined by Simon (1997). Just as the existence of bounded rationality provides a spur to learning, further research and technical analysis within the constraints of time and other resources, so the limitations of communicative rationality encourages a constant striving towards more democracy, both as an end in itself and as a means of ensuring better quality decision making.

### Agonistic and Semi-Legal Alternatives

Deliberative democracy has also been criticised by those who favour so-called 'agonistic' approaches that attempt to use conflict in a constructive way that promotes good quality outcomes (McClymont 2011). For Mouffe (2000, 2002) and others (Brand & Gaffikin 2007, for example), difference requires the politics of agonism, the acceptance of opposition, rather than the politics of antagonism that seeks a general consensus that excludes any alternative. In the words of Mouffe (2000, 49), antagonistic politics are no more than 'the expression of a hegemony and the crystallisation of power relations.' Much better, it is suggested, to avoid closure in decision-making and to recognise democratic politics as a means of mobilising and expressing passions, rather than reason. 'A well-functioning democracy calls for a vibrant clash of democratic political positions' (ibid., 104).

Agonistic theory assumes that conflict is productive and facilitates social learning. The task of planning is therefore not just to mediate between interests, as is the interpretation in collaborative planning theory as is promoted by Healey (2003, 103). The task is, instead, to allow the full expression of different perspectives on the assumption that this facilitates negotiation, debate and politics. Agonistic theory also makes the good point that neither conventional democracy nor deliberation has proved capable of resolving tensions in divided, antagonistic societies. Mouffe (2002, 14), in particular, warns against the rise of intolerant, far right-wing political parties in Britain and other European countries.

However, combining learning and conflict assumes that the conflict does not become uncontrollable. The political passions of Mouffe are the passions of identity politics and difference (ibid., 6). Promoting difference pure and simple may simply freeze identities and exacerbate oppositions (Dryzek 2005, 221).

Further, the agonistic critique is more about a stereotype of deliberation as a philosophical ideal, rather than its application. Conflict is inevitable and the denial of conflict may indeed undermine the quality of deliberation (ibid.). Planning is, moreover, particularly prone to such denial owing to a continued reliance on technical presentations and, in some cases, comprehensive planning proposals that oversimplify the detail. However, the denial or acceptance of conflict is about the conduct of deliberative processes, rather than the principle. Deliberation does not exclude individuals and groups having strong feelings about a subject, just as it does not exclude conflict and disagreement. Moreover, as anyone who has attended a participation and consultation event will know, planning itself does not exclude strong feelings. People commonly feel strongly about where they live and about the environment. In any case, the very principle of deliberation assumes that citizens have the right to know about policies and proposals and the right to make comments. The difference between agonism and deliberative approaches is unclear, at least in relation to legal rights and the practical details of practice.

Finally, the critique of consensus is exaggerated. Consensus on basic democratic values is necessary, as Mouffe also recognises, to permit agonistic dissent. But if consensus on democratic values is necessary and desirable, why is consensus on policies impossible? The main argument is that consensus is impossible without coercion and that a democratic society should never involve the closure of debates about justice (Mouffe 2000, 32–3). Eventually decisions have to be made and implemented, however. In the words of Polanyi (1957, 266), 'No society is possible in which power and compulsion are absent'.

Agonism is nevertheless important in suggesting that the search for consensus is not enough and that governments have to exercise judgments between different positions. The question is how that judgement might best be undertaken. The pragmatic model of 'advocacy planning' (Davidoff [1965] 1973) recognised the crucial roles of judgements in planning and sought to organise the plan-making process around a judicial procedure. A weakness of 'advocacy planning' as a model is that it assumed the ability of different parties to prepare alternative plans. In addition, Habermas (1996, 440–1), who is best known for the concept of communicative rationality and the ideal speech situation, has called for 'institutional imagination' in government and as part of this called for the use of semi-legal procedures such as ombudsmen and ombudswomen, hearings and inquiries. These are formal devices that generally assume either an investigation or an adversarial model of argumentation and where a public agency has to show either that it has followed the relevant procedures, including adequate consultation, or that it incorporates the lessons of appropriate systematic evaluation and decision-making techniques or some combination of procedural correctness and substantive, systematic evaluation.

The investigations of ombudsmen and ombudswomen and the proceedings of public inquiries are therefore not based on the principles of communicative rationality. The language used can be highly technical and, for those not familiar with the procedures, they can be intimidating. They possess the same potential limitation as a reliance on legal procedures pure and simple—for example a tendency to favour those who can afford the best advice and a tendency to delay decision-making. Many public enquiries have poor levels of attendance, for example, other than from those with property interests or who feel strongly about an issue.

Yet semi-legal procedures also do not exclude communicative ideas, as expressed in earlier stages of public consultation or common sense interpretations of fairness. It is likely that those involved in formal deliberations will be aware of public opinion and the results of consultation exercises. They can moreover serve their purpose of opening up and testing proposals. Public inquiries in England, for example, 'have', in the words of one study (Owens & Cowell 2011, 71) 'brought together diverse groups, raised the profile of important issues and provided a forum for evidence, argument and critical challenge'.

In doing this, moreover, semi-legal procedures offer a means of testing the assertions made by the various participants and stakeholders. The critical comments raised by Flyvbjerg (2004) are relevant in this context. Even if they avoid outright deception, as Flyvbjerg suggests, stakeholders are likely to present evidence in a way that best suits their case and their interests. Their views should not be taken at face value and the process of planning and policy-making should not be treated as the equivalent of a cosy debating exercise.

Semi-legal procedures, above all public inquiries, also offer a means for the expression of different views, without the pretence of coming to an overall consensus. The conclusion to an inquiry is a decision favouring one party rather than another. Semi-legal procedures may therefore be interpreted as agonistic politics in practice (McClymont 2011), albeit a form of agonism that admits the relevance of technical information and reasoned debate and also admits some discussion has to stop at some point.

The coexistence in practice of participation, semi-legal procedures and within those procedures of debate and technical projections and evaluations is indicative of a general point. It is easy to look at the twin approaches of rationalism and pragmatism as polar opposites, especially if the reference point for pragmatism is the democratic philosophy of Dewey rather than the more scientific approach of, say, Peirce. The question is, however, not to choose one over the other, either rationalism or pragmatism, but to pursue both and find ways that they can be combined. Professional and technical expertise is inadequate alone. Decisions have to be debated and tested in public. Yet technical expertise also remains necessary to the testing of proposals and policies—necessary for example to providing relevant information and to understanding the strengths and limitations of different forms of evaluation (Owens et al. 2004). 'Good' planning, however that term is defined, involves a combination of more and higher levels of technical skills and expertise *and* more democracy.

## Notes

1 'Sir Peter Hall: reflections on a lifetime of town planning'. *The Guardian*, Wednesday 1 October 2014, consulted June 2016 at www.theguardian.com/cities/2014/oct/01/sir-peter-hall-reflections-on-a-lifetime-of-town-planning.
2 'Impact of climate change on urban areas in India', consulted October 2014 at http://base.d-p-h.info/fr/fiches/dph/fiche-dph-8632.html.
3 'How to build a permaculture suburb', at the website 'Global Possibilities', consulted October 2014 at www.globalpossibilities.org/how-to-build-a-permaculture-suburb/.
4 'Urban agriculture part III: towards an urban "agri-puncture"' from the website of arch-daily, consulted October 2014 at www.archdaily.com/239677/urban-agriculture-part-iii-towards-an-urban-agri-puncture/.
5 Presentation given by Matt Evans and Tim Silman (Ipsos MORI) at a Liverpool University Syposium, 'Keeping the flam alive? Climate change, the media and the public', held 30 May 2014.
6 'Italo Calvino' as discussed at the website 'Goodreads', consulted January 2010 at www.goodreads.com/author/show/155517.Italo_Calvino.
7 See, for example, 'Planning reforms will put "a house in every field"', *Daily Telegraph*, 22 October 2011, consulted November 2011 at www.telegraph.co.uk/earth/hands-off-our-land/8842422/Planning-reforms-will-put-a-house-in-every-field.html.

## References

Allmendinger, P. (2001). *Planning in postmodern times*. London: Routledge.
Alvesson M. & Sköldberg K. (2008). *Reflexive methodology*. London: Sage.
Anderson, R., Bulos, M. A. & Walker, S. R. (1985). *Tower blocks*. London: Polytechnic of the South Bank and the Institute of Housing.
Arnstein, S. R. (1969). 'A ladder of citizen participation'. *Journal of the American Institute of Planners*, 35:4, 216–24.
Beauregard, R. A. (1996). 'Between modernity and postmodernity'. In: Campbell, S. & Fainstein, S. S. (eds.), *Readings in planning theory*. Oxford: Blackwell, 265–87.
Benhabib, S. (1986). *Critique, norm and utopia: a study of the foundations of critical theory*. New York: Columbia University Press.
Besse, J.-M. (2006). 'L'espace public: espace politique et paysage familier'. *Rencontres de l'espace public*. Lille, France: Lille Metropole Communauté Urbaine, [online] URL: https://halshs.archives-ouvertes.fr/halshs-00191977 (consulted October 2015).
Birmingham, E. (1998). 'Reframing the ruins: Pruitt-Igoe, structural racism, and African American rhetoric as a space for cultural critique'. *Positions*, Issue 2, [online] URL: www.cloud-cuckoo.net/openarchive/wolke/X-positionen/Birmingham/birmingham.html.
Black, J. (2000). 'Proceduralising regulation: part I'. *Oxford Journal of Legal Studies*, 20:4, 597–614.

Black, J. (2001). 'Proceduralising regulation: part II'. *Oxford Journal of Legal Studies*, 21:1, 33–58.

Bridge, G. (2005). *Reason in the city of difference*. London: Routledge.

Brand, R. & Gaffikin, F. (2007). 'Collaborative planning in an uncollaborative world'. *Planning theory*, 6: 282–312.

Brindley, T. (1999). 'The modern house in England: an architecture of exclusion'. In: Chapman, T. & Hockey, J. (eds.), *Ideal Homes?* London: Routledge, 30–43.

Bruner, J. (1991). 'The narrative construction of reality'. *Critical inquiry*, 18:1, 1–21.

Buitelaar, E., Galle, M. & Sorel, N. (2014). 'The public planning of private planning'. In: Andersson, D. E. & Moroni, S. (eds.) (2014) *Cities and Private Planning*. Cheltenham, UK: Edward Elgar.

Calvino, I. (1997). *Invisible cities* (translated W. Weaver). London: Vintage Books (Italian original 1972).

Choay, F. (1996). *La regle et le modele*. Paris: Éditions du Seuil (original 1980).

Cooper Marcus, C. & Sarkissian, W. (1986). *Housing as if people mattered*. Berkeley, CA: The University of California Press.

Cowburn, W. (1967). 'Housing in a consumer society'. *Architectural Review*, 142:849, 398–400.

Davidoff, P. (1973). 'Advocacy and pluralism in planning'. In Faludi, A. (ed.), *A reader in planning theory*. Oxford: Pergamon, 277–96 (original 1965).

Davies, J. G. (1972). *The evangelistic bureaucrat*. London: Tavistock.

Davies, S. R., Selin, C., Gano, G. & Pereira, A. G. (2012). 'Citizen engagement and urban change: three case studies of material deliberation'. *Cities*, 29:6, 351–7.

Dryzek, J. (2005). 'Deliberative democracy in divided societies: alternatives to agonism and analgesia'. *Political Theory*, 33:2, 218–42.

Fainstein, S. S. (2005). 'Cities and diversity: should we want it? Can we plan for it?'. *Urban Affairs Review*, 41:1, 3–19.

Fearon, J. D. (1998). 'Deliberation as discussion'. In: Elster, J. (ed.), *Deliberative democracy*. Cambridge, UK: Cambridge University Press, 44–68.

Flyvbjerg, B. (2004). 'Phronetic planning research: theoretical and methodological reflections'. *Planning Theory & Practice*, 5:3, 283–306.

Fraser, N. (1990). 'Rethinking the public sphere: a contribution to the critique of actually existing democracy'. *Social Text*, 25/26: 56–80.

Gadamer, H. G. (1989). *Truth and method*, 2nd edition. London and New York: Continuum Publishing Group (German original 1960).

Geddes, P. (1915). *Cities in evolution*. London: Williams and Norgate.

Glaeser, A. (1998). 'Placed selves: the spatial hermeneutics of self and other in the postunification Berlin police'. *Social Identities*, 4:1, 7–38.

Goodchild, B. (1991). 'Postmodernism and housing: a guide to design theory'. *Housing Studies*, 6:2, 131–44.

Goodchild, B. (1997). *Housing and the urban environment*. Oxford: Blackwell Science.

Goodchild, B., O'Flaherty, F. & Ambrose, A. (2014). 'Inside the eco-home: using video to understand the implications of innovative housing'. *Housing, Theory and Society*, 31:3, 334–52.

Habermas, J. (1970). 'Towards a theory of communicative competence'. *Inquiry*, 13:4, 360–75.

Habermas, J. (1987). *The theory of communicative action: volume 2. Lifeworld and system: a critique of functionalist reason.* Boston: Beacon Press (German original 1981).
Habermas, J. (1996). *Between facts and norms: contributions to a discourse theory of law and democracy.* Cambridge, MA: MIT Press.
Habraken, N. J. (1972). *Supports: an alternative to mass housing.* London: Architectural Press (Dutch original 1962).
Hall, P. (2002). *Cities of tomorrow: an intellectual history of urban planning and design in the twentieth century.* Oxford: Oxford Blackwell (original 1988).
Harvey, D. (1989). *The Condition of postmodernity.* Oxford: Basil Blackwell.
Hassan, I. (1985). 'The culture of postmodernism'. *Theory, Culture and Society*, 2:3, 119–33.
Healey, P. (2003). 'Collaborative planning in perspective'. *Planning Theory*, 2:2, 101–23.
Hoffman, G. (2005). *From modernism to postmodernism: concepts and strategies of postmodern American fiction.* Amsterdam & New York: Editions Rodopi B. V.
Huxley, M. (2000). 'The limits to communicative planning'. *Journal of Planning Education and Research*, 19:4, 369–77.
Janda, K., & Topouzi, M. (2013). 'Closing the loop: using hero stories and learning stories to remake energy policy'. *Proceedings of ECEEE Summer Study, European Council for an Energy-Efficient Economy*, Presqu'île de Giens, France.
Jencks, C. (1977). *The language of post-modern architecture.* New York: Rizzoli.
Kuymulu, M. B. (2013). 'Reclaiming the right to the city: reflections on the urban uprisings in Turkey'. *City*, 17:3, 274–78.
Leandro, M. (2005). 'NET_CITY: A collaborative environment to promote the understanding of the contemporary city'. *Journal of Urban Technology*, 12:1, 21–47.
Lyotard, J.-F. (1984). *The postmodern condition: a report on knowledge.* Manchester: Manchester University (French original 1979).
McClymont, K. (2011). 'Revitalising the political: development control and agonism in planning'. *Planning Theory*, 10:3, 239–56.
McCormac, R. (1978). 'Housing and the dilemma of style'. *Architectural Review*, Vol. CLX III, No. 974, pp. 203–6.
Marshall, T. (2013). 'The remodeling of decision making on major infrastructure in Britain'. *Planning Practice & Research*, 28:1, 122–40.
Mouffe, C. (2000). *The democratic paradox.* London: Verso.
Mouffe, C. (2002). *Politics and passions the stakes of democracy.* London: Centre for the Study of Democracy, Westminster University.
O'Neill, S. J. (2013). 'Image matters: climate change imagery in US, UK and Australian newspapers'. *Geoforum*, 49, 10–9.
Owens, S., Rayner, T. & Bina, O. (2004). 'New agendas for appraisal: reflections on theory, practice and research'. *Environment and Planning A*, 36, 1943–59.
Owens, S. & Cowell, R. (2011). *Land and limits: interpreting sustainability in the planning process*, 2nd edition. London: Routledge/RTPI.
Parker, S. (2004). *Urban theory and the urban experience.* London: Routledge.
Parkinson, J. (2006). *Deliberating in the real world: problems of legitimacy in deliberative democracy.* Oxford & New York: Oxford University Press.
Pellegrino, P., Lambert, C. & Jacot, F. (1990). 'Espace public et figures du lien social.' *Espaces et Sociétés*, 62–3, 11–27.

Piccolo, F. L. & Thomas, H. (2001). 'Legal discourse, the individual and the claim for equality in British planning'. *Planning Theory & Practice*, 2:2, 187–201.

Pinder, D. (2002). 'In defense of utopian urbanism: imagining cities after the "end of utopia"'. *Geografiska Annaler, Series B, Human Geography*, 84:3–4, 229–41.

Pink, S. (2008). 'Re-thinking contemporary activism: from community to emplaced sociality'. *Ethnos: Journal of Anthropology*, 73:2, 163–88.

Pink, S. (2009). 'Urban social movements and small places, *City*, 13:4, 451–65.

Polanyi, K. (1957). *The great transformation*. Boston: Beacon Press. (UK original 1944).

Power, A. (1984). 'Rescuing unpopular council estates through local management'. *The Geographical Journal*, 150:3, 359–62.

Putnam, R. (2000). *Bowling alone: the collapse and revival of American community*, New York: Simon & Schuster.

Qadeer, M. A. (1997). 'Pluralistic planning for multicultural cities: the Canadian practice'. *Journal of the American Planning Association*, 63:4, 481–94.

Ray, L. (2004). 'Pragmatism and critical theory'. *European Journal of Social Theory*, 7:3, 307–21.

Rorty, R. (1997). *Truth, politics and post-modernism*. Assen: Van Gorcum Publishers.

Roy, A. (2005). 'Urban informality: toward an epistemology of planning'. *Journal of the American Planning Association*, 71:2, 147–58.

Sandercock, L. (2003). 'Out of the closet: the importance of stories and storytelling in planning practice'. *Planning Theory & Practice*, 4:1, 11–28.

Sandercock, L. (2004). 'Towards a planning imagination for the 21st century'. *Journal of the American Planning Association*, 70:2, 133–41.

Schweitzer, L. (2016). 'Restorative planning ethics: the therapeutic imagination and planning in public Institutions'. *Planning Theory*, 15:2, 130–44.

Seo, M. G. & Creed, W. D. (2002). 'Institutional contradictions, praxis, and institutional change: a dialectical perspective'. *Academy of Management Review*, 27:2, 222–47.

Simon, H. (1997). *Models of bounded rationality: empirically grounded economic reason*. Cambridge, MA: MIT Press.

Tewdwr-Jones, M. & Allmendinger, P. (1998). 'Deconstructing communicative rationality: a critique of Habermasian collaborative planning'. *Environment and Planning A*, 30, 1975–89.

Throgmorton, J. A. (1992). 'Planning as persuasive storytelling about the future: negotiating an electric power rate settlement in Illinois'. *Journal of Planning Education and Research*, 12:1, 17–31.

Throgmorton, J. A. (1996). *Planning as persuasive storytelling: the rhetorical construction of Chicago's electric future*. Chicago: University of Chicago Press.

van Hulst, M. (2012). 'Storytelling, a model of and a model for planning'. *Planning Theory*, 11:3, 299–318.

Venturi, R. (1976). 'A house is more than a home'. *Progressive Architecture*, August, 62–7.

Venturi, R., Scott Brown, D. & Izenour, S. (1972). *Learning from Las Vegas: the forgotten symbolism of architectural form*. Cambridge, MA: MIT Press.

Vidyarthi, S., Hoch, C. & Basmajian, C. (2013). 'Making sense of India's spatial plan-making practice: enduring approach or emergent variations?' *Planning Theory & Practice*, 14:1, 57–74.

Walters, D. (2007). *Designing community: charrettes, masterplans and form-based codes*. Oxford: Elsevier/Architectural Press.

Ward, C. (1976). *Housing: an anarchist approach*. London: Freedom Press.

Watson, S. (1983). 'Cities of dreams and fantasy: social planning in a postmodern era'. In: Freestone, R. (ed.), *Spirited cities*. Sydney: The Federation Press, 140–9.

Watson, V. (2008). 'Down to earth: linking planning theory and practice in the "metropole" and beyond'. *International Planning Studies*, 13:3, 223–37.

White, G. & Dickinson, S. (SQW Ltd) (with Miles, N., Richardson, L., Russell, H. & Taylor, M.) (2006). *Exemplars of neighbourhood governance*. London: Department for Communities and Local Government.

Winkler, T. (2011). 'Retracking Johannesburg: spaces for participation and policy making'. *Journal of Planning Education and Research*, 31:3, 258–71.

Wootton, B. (1945). *Freedom under planning*. London: G. Allen & Unwin.

# Part IV
# Environmental Risks, Urban Transitions

# 8 Managing Risks and 'Bad'

Does neoliberalism and the adoption of a combination of pragmatic and rational planning theory mark the end of proposals for long-term, social and economic planning, compared to say the period between about 1940 and the 1970s? To an extent, it does. Very few influential political figures talk about central planning. The language of politics has changed. Yet as Giddens (2008, 9) once noted, 'whenever we think about the future in a systematic way, in the sense of attempting to shape or guide it, planning of some sort is inevitable.' Concepts of planning come back into political discourse when governments start to think about the future, irrespective of whether those in power endorse previous planning exercises. From the 1980s onwards, moreover, thinking about the future came to the fore again in the form of a variety of increased environmental concerns, including a loss of biodiversity, a loss of natural habitats, pollution, the health and well-being of urban populations and most recently climate change.

To an extent, the growth of environmental concerns is compatible with pragmatic rationales for planning. Pragmatic approaches, as evidenced by the collaborative planning theory of Healey (1997, 1998), can work outwards from a problem and through debate and analysis produce co-ordinated environmental action across multiple disciplines, policy fields and interest groups. The supporters of sustainable development have, moreover, made similar pragmatic assumptions. For example, Brandon and Lombardi (2010, 21) refer to sustainable development 'as a process, not as an end goal or destination', a process that is 'open to further learning and adaptation' and to 'evolution as knowledge progresses'.

Once sustainable development is conceived as a process, the methods and theories of social research, including the categories of planning theory, become relevant. Friedmann (1987) distinguished between allocative, innovative and radical styles of intervention and each of these may be applied to sustainable development and related environmental issues. Allocative planning is about balancing different risks and the claims of different groups, whilst maintaining minimum standards and protecting what might be termed essential elements for the future. It is urban management, above all the management of risks to health and well-being in urban areas. Innovative and radical planning, in contrast, go beyond balance to pursuing aims and objectives that involve change. They are about changing cities through intervention in different sectors of the economy, both on the supply side through new production systems and on the demand side through changing behaviour, lifestyles and consumption practices.

The distinction between allocative planning on one hand and innovative and radical styles of intervention is sharpened by a related distinction, made by Jansson (2013), between ecology within cities and ecology of cities. This latter is as follows:

- Ecology within cities is about the web of factors that either pose a risk to or enhance the health and welfare of residents. Examples include the health risks associated with living in poor quality housing, with breathing poor quality air and with the stress caused by noise and the loss of green space, together with the damage and impact of catastrophic environmental events (for example flooding). Managing ecological processes within cities is therefore about promoting liveability, minimising health and safety risks to residents and visitors and maximising resilience to those risks, against the background of unstable and potentially damaging ecological processes.
- Managing the ecology of cities is instead about transition to a new sustainable relationship between the environment and processes of production and consumption. It is about minimising the impact of buildings, infrastructure and their users on the broader environment. It is concerned above all with minimising the external impact of cities and urban lifestyles, including the resource requirements, the global pollution caused by industrial and other processes and the generation of greenhouse gases. The focus of attention comprise the 'networks of agents interacting in a specific technology area' and covering both the supply side, the product and the demand side, such as consumption practices (Geels 2004).

Put slightly differently, allocative styles of intervention seek to sustain cities largely in their present form, managing risks and coping with change and problems as and when they occur. Innovative and radical planning are, in contrast, about changing cities and in relation to the environment, they are about transition to a different and new type of sustainable society. The various styles of planning are not contradictory to one another. Urban resilience, for example, is likely to be strengthened by a long-term transition to a less energy-intensive, more ecologically supported form of social organization (Ernstson et al. 2010). In addition, the various styles of intervention may be brought together in the physical planning models and rules that guide urban design and future urban forms. The concept of the 'green state' offers another way of bringing together the various approaches, in a way that addresses political questions. Discussion of urban transitions, models and rules and of the state can wait, however.

## Risk and Resilience

Risk and resilience are intimately tied together, though risk is the more fundamental concept. Issues of resilience would not apply, if people and places were not at risk in some way of disturbance. Resilience assumes that risks cannot be eliminated. As applied to environmental planning, it assumes that disruptive events will occur and that the task is essentially to ensure that communities, however this is defined, can cope with or recover quickly from some environmental misfortune or shock.

Both resilience planning and organised risk management are relatively novel concepts in the history of urban planning and urban policy. Concepts of resilience in planning have, in particular, emerged since about 2000. Wilkinson et al. (2010), for example, reports on the basis of discussions with practitioners in Stockholm, Glasgow and Melbourne that the concept of resilience has offered *'new metaphors* regarding the nature of structural change in linked and complex systems that prioritize change and uncertainty'. Wilkinson (2012) adds that concepts of resilience in urban planning are socio-ecological rather than engineering concepts. Socio-ecological concepts of resilience are about the ability of habitats or communities to cope with threats and adapt to change whereas engineering concepts are about the ability of materials and physical structures to resist and withstand stress. Engineering concepts are still relevant for specific projects, but risk management at a strategic level requires a mix of engineering and other initiatives intended to promote economic and community resilience. The use of engineering works is, in any case, commonly a very expensive option.

Metaphors, whatever their origin and application, take a concept from one context and apply it to another. The use of metaphors in resilience planning generally draws attention to the material base of intervention and applies that to policy. In relation to riverine flooding, for example, a socio-ecological approach would use the local catchment area as a basis for co-ordinated action, seeking to slow down the rate of water runoff from all the land before it reaches the flood plain or valley. Within the boundaries of the system, the emphasis would therefore be on generating a commitment to action amongst all relevant stakeholders (Innes & Booher 1999). Ecological systems theory also emphasises the unpredictable character of environmental systems, these being characterised by 'panarchy' and therefore by a tendency to teeter on the edge of chaos, without quite falling over the edge (Allen et al. 2014). Lack of predictability, in turn, draws attention to the risk that engineering resilience may, on occasion, be ineffective.

However, the repeated use of systems metaphors results in abstract accounts that cannot be easily related to issues of social integration and the close associate of social integration, politics. Systems operate impersonally and operate, in addition, in ways in which people are unaware. Systems integration or, its opposite, system tension, arises from the interaction between elements in society. They are therefore distinct from the processes of social integration and social conflict that arise from the interaction between people (Archer 1996; Lockwood 1964; Oliga 1996, 127).

Concepts of system integration and tension are separate from social integration and conflict, moreover, even if they are difficult to disentangle in practice. To give an example, the land use/transport system comprises different impersonal elements such as the pattern of spatial activities, the pattern of journeys, notably the journey to work, and the division between public and private modes of transport. Equally, however, any change to that system is likely to impinge on the varied interests of different individuals and groups—commercial interests, landowners, commuters and pedestrians. Co-ordinated action involves collective learning and collective learning has to accommodate both systems integration and social integration and their failures.

To go beyond metaphors and to identify recognisable social and economic processes, systems theory must be put on one side as too general and too limited. Attention has to be paid, instead, to the specific conditions that enable risks to be identified as such and that mould the policy response in favour of resilience. The practical definitions of risk and resilience, in any case, come from government and from the pressure groups that seek to influence government. It follows, therefore, that analysis should focus on how risks and resilience are treated in government and in the political discourses that support or oppose government, as the case may be.

In this context, two theoretical approaches may be identified. First, it is possible to identify organised risk management as the product of modern society, that is to say a 'risk society' where people and communities have become increasingly sensitised to danger and to threats to their well-being (Beck 1992). In a risk society, environmental problems and risks are no longer external to economic activities or to urban development. They are, instead, a central, unavoidable aspect of economic development and technological progress and are deeply implicated in the workings of modern society, with multiple implications for politics and policy. As a result, that risk management has become a common way of framing a wide variety of problems that characterise the contemporary city, going beyond the environment to include violence, crime and movement (Borraz & Le Galès 2010).

To say that risks in contemporary society are distinctive is not to dismiss the existence of continuities from earlier centuries, however. In contrast to risk society theory, with its emphasis on modernisation, the second theory or more accurately group of theories, associated with Douglas (1999), writing separately and with Wildavsky (Douglas and Wildavsky 1982), has offered a theory of continuity. Risk management, it is argued, is merely a new term for making judgements about the acceptability of various situations. As such, risk is best analysed through an analysis of the socio-cultural factors that influence its social construction and public perception. Socio-cultural theory, it should be noted in passing, is distinct from culturist, backward-looking theories in urban design. Socio-cultural theory is about perception, social communication and social integration, rather than physical planning practice.

Neither socio-cultural nor risk society theory is necessarily superior to the other. They have different uses in different contexts. Because socio-cultural theory is about universal or near universal processes and distinctions, it will be discussed first.

## Socio-Cultural Theory: Perceptions and Social Organization

Socio-cultural theory starts from the senses and the body. In relation to pollution, for example, attention is placed on the experience of physical dirt or soot in the home, smoke and fumes emitted from specific and proximate 'polluter' sources—either to the body or the home—which transgress the boundaries of personal or 'safe' space (Bickerstaff, 2004). Pollution is 'dirt out of place'. Pollution therefore depends on a set of conventions of an ordered environment as well as some transgression of those conventions (Douglas 1966, 36). By extension risk can be understood in the same way—a breakdown in the established order.

Thereafter, socio-cultural studies implicate a wide variety of factors that might influence the perception of risk as disorder. The studies postulate, for example, that people are less likely to recognise risks as significant if they are an everyday, routine occurrence (Douglas 2003 [1985], 30), as in the case of the danger from motor vehicles. Likewise, public support for safety regulations is reduced if this is likely to impinge on the lifestyles of ordinary people, as again illustrated by the example of traffic accidents and pollution from cars (Brenot et al. 1998, 736). Conversely risks are more likely to be recognised as significant if they relate to a situation or an organization that looks untrustworthy or novel or somehow unnatural. For example, people generally regard their own home or neighbourhood as safer than other neighbourhoods or areas in a city, even when this is palpably untrue in relation to the risk of crime (Warr 1990, 893).

The individual experience and perception of disorder is a minor theme in socio-cultural theory, however. The main direction and most distinctive aspect is an analysis of how the form of social integration influences how risks are perceived and environmental problems are managed to safeguard social order. Socio-cultural theory is therefore a conservative theory, one that enables an understanding of the stabilising aspects of environmental management but not those of change or even innovation.

## Grid and Group Dimensions

As developed by Douglas (1999), social integration operates along two main dimensions—the degree of integration (strong and weak) and whether integration involves informal (low grid) or formal (high grid) controls on action. Strong groups, whether they are composed of formal or informal rules and structures, are characterised by high levels of trust. Weak groups are characterised by low levels of trust.

The result is a four-way classification, as shown in Table 8.1.

The different styles have been used in part to classify the attitudes and worldviews of residents and citizens (Schwarz & Thompson 1990; Thompson et al. 1990; Mamadouh 1999). Different combinations of grid and group, it is suggested, make contrasting assumptions about the workings of nature and these assumptions are incorporated into the attitudes of individuals. For example, individualism assumes that nature is inherently resilient, without the need for human controls; fatalism assumes that nature is capricious and incapable of generating lessons about how it is best managed; hierarchical views assume that nature is tolerant, but only up to a point and that human activities need to be controlled; and finally, egalitarianism assumes that nature is vulnerable and needs to be respected by individuals and communities.

Were a stable clustering of attitudes to be demonstrated, it would suggest that the support or rejection of environmental policies is fixed in the human personality and cannot be influenced by evidence or debate. Different people would have different personality types that determined their view of environmental policy. The extent of clustering in attitudes and belief systems is open to doubt, however, as only a minority of the views expressed by individuals, for example 14 percent in one survey, fit consistently into

*Table 8.1* Managing Risk from a Socio-Cultural Perspective

|  | High grid |  |
| --- | --- | --- |
| Fatalism, isolated from groups or isolated in complex structure | | Hierarchies, strong groups with complex structures |
| **Weak groups, weak trust** | | **Strong groups, strong trust** |
| Individualism, weak incorporation and weak structures | | Egalitarian enclaves, strong groups with weak structures |
|  | Low grid |  |

Sources: Douglas (1999); Lodge (2009).

one category rather than another (Tansey & O'Riordan 1999). Considered merely as a classification of attitudes, grid/group theory says little.

In any case, the classification of attitudes misses the point. Grid/group theory is a theory of social integration, not of attitudes. It is, moreover, a heuristic device, that is to say, a means of mapping and classifying responses and a means of generating insights and hypotheses, rather than a full, deterministic explanation of variations in either perception or the organization of risk management and environmental management. The group/grid classification indicates, in the words of Douglas (1999, 411) 'four types of cultural bias' that are 'always potentially present in any group of persons, and that ... are at war with each another'. If some slight changes are made in the terminology, the relevance to planning becomes apparent. For bias, substitute 'discourse'. For group, substitute 'regime', a term that Douglas also uses for style of governance.

This being so, the four types of cultural bias become different styles of policy discourse and different ways in which governments react to environmental risks and issues as follows:

- Fatalist strategies stress the unpredictability of risks and so draw out a minimal *ad hoc* response from governments.
- Individualist strategies stress the role of individual trial and error learning via pricing or the actions of private agencies such as insurance companies.
- Hierarchical risk management is the risk management equivalent of centralised planning. It is about the application of technical expertise, consistent policy criteria and regulation.
- Finally, in opposition to positions based on hierarchy, egalitarianism favours working with local communities.

To examine each style in more detail: the grid/group classification suggests that fatalism arises where individuals are isolated and where, as a result, groups are incapable of acting collectively. For Douglas, the causal relationship is one way. Isolation leads to inaction. In the words of Douglas (1999, 412), 'the more that the persons are alone, the less can they predict or interpret what is going on'. Likewise, if individuals act in a wholly isolated manner from one another or they do not trust one another, they will fail to co-operate. Equally, one might argue that the relationship is reciprocal. Isolation and feelings of isolation may arise from a lack of support. Fatalism is not necessarily a result of apathy, understood as a process of letting events drift without consideration of the consequences. In some coastal areas in England, the owners of property have to abandon it to the sea, owing to a judgement by the state that protection measures are ether impractical or too expensive (Brown et al. 2005). Elsewhere in the world, especially in less affluent countries, fatalism is also associated with a belief that other pressing problems, rather than environmental risks, should be given priority (Faling 2012, 10).

In general, however, the very recognition of risk leads to some form of organised response. Fatalism becomes untenable as public policy once risks become subject to scientific measurement and prediction and once, in addition, the existence of these risks becomes discussed in public (Walker et al. 1999). Moreover, even where calamitous events cannot be predicted with any certainty—for example earthquakes—or only a short time in advance—for example destructive storms—measures are usually available to mitigate their impact and to improve the response of communities to their impact.

Of the various active forms of response, the distinction in socio-cultural theory between individualism and hierarches corresponds 'for all intents and purposes' to the distinction between markets and bureaucracies (Douglas 1999, 411). An individualised market-based approach would, if fully applied, provide individual owners and occupiers with detailed information about the risks involved in any given activity, but would enable them to make up their mind as to what they should do. Market-based approaches are, as usual, about promoting choice and minimising regulation.

Individuals may not always understand the implications of a risk, however. Voogd (2004) gives the example of a fireworks factory in the Netherlands where, at a consultation stage, the draft development permit received no adverse comment. Later, however, fireworks stored in the factory exploded, those affected looked to the state for help and the state itself felt obliged to help. Perhaps the risks could be emphasised through publicity campaigns. However, highlighting risk may simply serve to promote fear and sometimes unnecessary fear.

Insurance companies are a partial answer to the more predictable types of risk, but insurance is itself expensive and not always available for example to those living in the most vulnerable places or to less affluent households. Voogd's response, based on the experience of the fireworks factory, is partly to tighten planning controls, but also to encourage the preparedness, in other words, the resilience of the community for any future event.

Bureaucracy is the mechanism, *par excellence*, for controlling risks through regulation or through organised public works. It is simultaneously an instrument of power and an institution that encourages a public service 'ethos', that is to say a dispassionate orientation of public service workers in favour of their public responsibilities rather than sectional or personal interests (du Gay 2000, 35–60). Bureaucracy enables consistency in the application of criteria, for example those concerned with fire protection or flood control. It avoids policy being side-tracked or compromised by economic interests—for example those that wish to promote development on sites that might be unsuitable. In addition, centralised risk management provides a more effective means to use scarce professional skills and a more effective means to mobilise resources where these are needed, both to combat threats through investment in protective measures and to intervene in the case of catastrophic failure.

Bureaucracy has been commonly accused of being impersonal. Campbell and Marshall (1999, 470-1) write (citing the earlier work of Low 1991) that

> both bureaucracy and markets merely express the power structure of society, a structure with no intrinsic moral justification. ... Planners, therefore, find themselves inside the state but outside politics. (*Italics added.*)

As a result, it is suggested, bureaucracy discourages officials to think and act responsibly. Planners should supplement an awareness of procedures with a greater awareness of values and their implications.

A suitable response draws, in broad terms, on du Gay (2000, 35-60). The impersonality of bureaucracy means that decisions are made on the basis of criteria and offers an antidote to the personal and communal style of politics known as 'clientelism'. Here public office holders (politicians and senior officials) favour particular client groups linked to them by ethnic, geographic or party political ties and are able to ensure that these favours are delivered through the decisions they make. Clientelist politics may use the rhetoric of the public interest, but are essentially based on deals with private individuals and interest groups and as a result are likely to include deals of dubious ethical character and varying shades of illegality. In Europe, clientelism is most commonly associated with the Mediterranean countries, though petty clientelism is said to be wider than this (Borraz & Le Galès 2010). The operation of environmental policy in clientelist situations deserves more study (ibid). In principle, however, where clientelist politics prevail, the consistent application of environmental policies, including those concerned with safety, may prove impossible.

Land use planning regulations do not always prevent accidents and environmental disasters. Planning in England has arguably not done enough to stop building on floodplains. Procedures have been tightened over the years, but local authorities still allow house building in at-risk areas in a way that causes concern.[1] In Australia, failure to control house building has been implicated as a factor associated with the loss of property and life in bush fires (Buxton et al. 2011). The point is that the very process of regulating for safety involves an effective bureaucracy operating on relevant criteria and capable of resisting personal and group interests.

A related approach, undertaken either alongside or instead of a plan, is for the local authority or another similar agency to adopt the role of an 'honest broker' as advocated by Ingirige and Wedawatta (2014) and Pielke (2007) amongst others.[2] In this, each actor is advised on a range of actions that are consistent with the relevant policy objective and are given a range of choice as to which course action is adopted. The honest broker role implies a partnership between the public sector and the affected actors. For its supporters, therefore, this particular approach avoids the pitfalls of imposed, comprehensive solutions.

The role is well suited, moreover, to situations and sectors (for example small businesses) where individual actors are difficult to reach or to organise, where governments believe complete security is impossible and where, as a result, specific measures are necessary to safeguard property or personal safety. The role is also well suited to situations where property owners and householders do not know what to do. In a review of previous studies in England, Collingwood Environmental Partnership (2014, 75) noted 'there is some suggestion in the literature that people's confidence in their ability to choose and implement the right resilience measure can be a significant barrier to action'.

The 'honest broker' role depends on the ability of local agencies to provide advice and have sufficient numbers of staff to do so. In a context of expenditure cuts, the potential is often limited. The effectiveness of the advice also depends on the receptiveness of the audience and whether, for example, there is public awareness of the risk and a public memory of an event that requires action. Owners are unlikely to invest unless they are aware of the risks and see the consequences as real. And this awareness may be missing. Surveys in the US have shown, for example, that consumers often fail to adopt even low-cost protection against weather and other hazards (Kleindorfer & Kunreuther 2000).

The 'honest broker' involves a redistribution of responsibilities, away from the state and towards individuals, local groups and businesses, but takes place in a context where different actors have varied capacities. The variation for businesses is particularly marked. Factors such as the loss of infrastructure, population dislocation, income loss and pressure from larger companies can produce business failure long after the event (Zhang et al. 2009). There are limits, moreover, to how far responsibilities can be shifted away from public bureaucracies. Owners may lack the resources to invest. Likewise, residents and businesses, perceiving a lack of public support, may become angry and disillusioned with governing institutions and this, in turn, is likely to diminish opportunities for building constructive reciprocal relations (Butler & Pidgeon 2011).

The final style of response, based on egalitarian, cohesive groups, takes the same shift of responsibility a stage further in the hope of building a resilient community able to minimise the consequences of an environmental disaster and cope with the aftermath. High group solidarity is effectively a restatement of the concept of social capital. It means the existence of social networks that enable communication between most or all members of a community, so helping local communities to identify vulnerable individuals and to pool resources for building repairs and self-construction (Aldrich 2010; Munasinghe 2007). The 'honest broker' likewise assumes a degree of social capital and community involvement. Providing advice is easier and less expensive if individuals, families and firms can help and advise each other.

There is a major qualification, however. Community groups may be relatively egalitarian in their internal structure, but the context and policy impacts are not. Social capital in the sense of participation of residents in civic life and in social networks tends, in general, to be lower amongst lower income individuals and communities (Uphoff et al. 2013; Verhaeghe & Tampubolon 2012). Studies suggest that social networks in deprived areas still provide a buffer against adversity (Crisp & Robinson 2010; Uphoff et al. 2013). However, social capital is not a substitute for publicly provided support and safety networks for groups in need. In addition, of course, the scale of any disaster is relevant. Even the strongest local social network is unlikely to withstand a strong existential threat to a community.

Because each discourse and each style of risk management has its advantages and disadvantages, the management of environmental risks typically implies the weaving together of styles. Resilience requires a combination of styles—an element of fatalism for those sites where nothing can be done at reasonable expense (Hartmann 2011); community-based approaches that encourage local groups and firms to work out their own plans of action; hierarchical organization to allocate resources where they are most needed and to provide specialist staff and local efforts to help people and to provide flexibility of response; and finally engineering responses where the potential costs to property, economic activities and life are sufficiently high to justify substantial investment.

A commitment to resilience does not, as Douglas and Wildavsky (1982, 198) once stated, 'betray our bias towards the center (sic)', that is towards hierarchy. A combination of decentralised and centralised approaches is possible and likely. Resilience involves, instead, in the words of Douglas, 'clumsy solutions' and by extension 'clumsy' institutional learning that combines all the perspectives on what the problems are and how they should be resolved (Verweij, Douglas et al. 2006) and that recognise, in addition, no single solution, no single approach will suffice.

Institutional learning is particularly important because a variety of different bureaucracies are involved in environmental risk, those dealing with prevention and land use planning, those dealing with the financing and implementation of public works and those dealing with emergencies and recovery. However, political sensitivities still have to be addressed. The mix of solutions is likely to involve a trade-off between competing priorities and as part of this a trade-off between risk, costs and the maintenance of local communities and businesses.

In addition, in the aftermath of a disaster, the opposing requirements of speed and consultation may get in the way of each other. A primary need after a disaster is for a community to restart its economic life and for workers and residents to return to some form of routine. Equally different groups want a say in any rebuilding programme. Kitchen (2001) reports the experience of Manchester city centre after a bomb attack in 1996 where an up-to-date plan, prepared after consultation with interested parties, was available to facilitate recovery. Elsewhere, as in New Orleans after the much larger disaster of Hurricane Katrina in 2005, there existed neither a plan nor the social infrastructure for plan preparation such as community organizations, lines of communication and background documents (Olshansky et al. 2008).

## Conflicts Between the Centre and the Periphery

Bureaucracy (high grid, high group) and the market (low grid, weak groups) are the forms of organization preferred by mainstream planning theory with its focus on the political economy of urban development. Where socio-cultural theory is distinctive is in identifying tensions and conflict between government and marginalised pressure groups or, in the relevant language between centre and periphery. The centre means in this context any hierarchical governmental agency. In contrast, non-hierarchical organization is characteristic of peripheral groups, that is to say groups that are at the margin in terms of power relations or who feel that they are at the 'border', to use the term of Douglas and Wildavsky (1982) of conventional politics. Non-hierarchical organization is also typical of the groups that campaign on environmental issues, given the number, spread and often varied character of such issues.

The centre and the periphery are unlikely to agree on environmental issues, according to socio-cultural theory. The centre tends towards complacency. For different reasons, neither bureaucracy nor the market encourages critical thinking or radical change. They prefer instead business as usual. The periphery, in contrast, is alert to the failures of the centre, easily alarmed and well positioned to offer a critique of policy and more broadly of society.

The gap between the centre and the periphery can be bridged if the two parties trust each other. Local authorities and other similar agencies also offer a level of working where it is easier to gain the trust of local people (Bulkeley & Betsill 2005). However, when trust has been lost, say through negligence or deceit, it is not easy to restore and the consequent distrust is also likely to cast a shadow over other products or policies. For example, in the period from about 1999 to 2002, in the Byker district of Newcastle-upon-Tyne, the local authority faced hostile and ultimately successful opposition to the development of a combined heat and power plant, once it was discovered that the earlier spreading of ash on footpaths and allotments had led to high concentrations of dioxin contamination in local soils (Rootes 2013, 60). The history of previous contamination turned the local community against new proposals, even though the new development used different technology.

Socio-cultural theory therefore offers a means of conceptualising the relationship between environmental pressure groups and government. The depiction of environmental groups is, however, ambiguous and not, on balance, favourable. Environmental pressure groups may be a force for reform and for improved environmental protection. Equally, however, according to socio-cultural theory, they are also 'sectarian', characterised by 'exclusiveness, intolerance, narrow adherence to dissident doctrines and hostility to the outside world' (Douglas and Wildavsky, 1982, 114). Moreover the implication is that environmental groups cannot compromise or form alliances with others. The search for exclusiveness means upping demands just as the centre nears agreement. (ibid., 184).

It is unclear whether Douglas and Wildavsky (1982) are talking about all radical environmental groups or just all those with a completely flat, non-hierarchical structure or just one or two such groups such as the American branch of the Friends of the Earth. The counterargument, most closely associated with Deleuze and Guattari (1987) and their followers (for example Querrien 2007) is that campaigning groups, in particular, have to work through networks (or rhizomes in the terminology of Deleuze and Guattari) and have, therefore, to make external links if they wish to influence events. They cannot remain an exclusive, otherworldly sect. Another related counterargument is that contemporary forms of governance have to use networks of interested parties and have to be 'transactive' in a search to incorporate local knowledge and specialist knowledge in plans and policies (Certomà and Notteboom 2015).

The networks that link one group to others do not have to be strong to ensure a flow of new ideas and information. Campaigning groups can multiply their contacts and, in particular, nurture strategic contacts to 'brace' or strengthen the policy network. Kusakabe (2012) has provided a detailed example in which a group intent on protecting a lake in Japan, Lake Biwa, from dangerous algae blooms, used multiple networks, including strategic contacts, to change the regulations governing the make-up of soap—the main pollutant. Horizontal, rhizomatic campaigning helped change policy, but once policy was implemented, implementation proceeded through a bureaucratic hierarchy.

The so-called 'soap movement' from Japan may be no more typical than the exclusive US groups that are the subject of analysis by Douglas and Wildavsky. However, its very existence shows that more than one outcome is possible. Environmental risks can exacerbate conflict between the centre and peripheral groups, but they can also dissolve that conflict into multiple cross-cutting networks. Again 'clumsy solutions are likely to predominate— 'clumsy' in the sense that the outcome of pressure group politics is likely to produce a repeated redefinition of problems and solutions.

## The Risk Society

The concept of the risk society rests on a paradox. The residents and citizens of Western cities are almost certainly healthier and safer than at any point in their history. To give a specific example, in Britain, traffic accidents have declined steadily since the 1990s and are currently lower than at any time since the first statistics were collected in 1926.[3] The risk society thesis assumes, in contrast, that growing environmental insecurity and growing environmental concerns are fundamental trends in modern society and that these lead, in turn, to new forms of environmental politics.

## The Impact of Modernity and Modernisation

Why the heightened anxiety and concerns? Socio-cultural theory might point to the activities of peripheral groups, spreading alarm. But that does not explain why the message of alarm is credible. Another possible explanation, mentioned by Douglas and Wildavsky (1982, 11), but not fully explored or endorsed in their account, is that the more people have in the way of material possessions, the more they can lose and the more they are likely to want a pleasant environment. In this context, safety becomes 'another consumer good, part of general material advance'. One might go further and argue that the 'softer' environmental qualities such as a sense of place or the existence of green spaces are also a consumer good, tied to higher living standards and that, in general, planning and environmental standards are stricter in wealthier countries.

Other interpretations, including that of Beck et al. (2003), point to modernisation, meaning science, technological innovation and the search for ever greater efficiency as the main cause of uncertainty. Modernisation has become reflexive: it has turned on itself and started to erode its own foundations, causing all manner of problems that cannot be tackled through the production of more goods and services. Modernisation continues, but has encountered a multitude of unintended environmental consequences that call its rationale into question.

The increased circulation of information, on the web and through the mass media is part of this risk sensitive society. Public awareness of environmental risks, such as air and water pollution, and environmental problems, such as habitat loss, is no longer confined to those with direct experience. Instead, the problems are documented in specialist scientific journals and then made visible to a global public through the media, the print media and television (Beck 2011; Beck & Kropp 2007). Indeed, for environmental risks to become of public concern, they have to be articulated thought the media.

The changes associated with modernity are, moreover, unsettling. They disrupt the routines of daily life (Giddens, 1991, 167). They weaken and undermine the sense of order that Douglas (1966) suggests is at the root of cultural assessments of safety. The workings of the market economy and all manner of product innovations have the same effect. Individuals have to make choices amongst consumer products, but the very existence of multiple alternatives amounts to cultural disorder, destroying established patterns of response (Douglas, 1966, 95). Organisational and workplace innovations have a similar effect. People have to rely on their personal resources to prove themselves and make decisions rather than rely on tradition or established practices (Beck 2002).

Grid/group theory assumes that the individual acting outside an established group is likely to be apathetic and fatalist about the future. Trends towards greater personal autonomy and choice are, therefore, likely to promote fatalism. Theorists of the risk society provide, in contrast, a more nuanced account. Increased personal autonomy is, in the risk society, equated with individualisation—a force for change that itself has unintended consequences. At the same time, individualisation leads to a more fluid formation of political groups that seek to influence events, albeit only in a fragmented, piecemeal manner that is focused on specific issues and that involves the interaction between experts, pressure groups and politicians. The proliferation of consequences, both anticipated and unintended, leads to a politicisation of these consequences. As part of this, moreover, the environment has become politicised, albeit in a way that displaces the conventional politics of parties and elections in a process that Beck (1997) calls 'subpolitics'.

The risk society has been subject to varying evaluations in terms of its potential implications for urban planning and the future of cities. For Blowers (1997), the risk society suggests the unsustainability of modernity in its current form, but offers no more than 'a polemic', with 'no practical prescription or notion of how a transformation will proceed'. In contrast, for Davoudi (2000), the risk society has practical implications for the future of the planning system.

> Within risk society, planning has a pro-active dimension. It is ideological, socially responsive and interventionist. Here, planning is seen as an activity which is leading, rather than following, the state's policies. The planners' role is to defend the environment and local identities against the risk associated with contemporary economic processes. (ibid., 131)

On one hand, the risk society is a given. It is a product of impersonal processes that cannot be changed. We live in a particular type of risk-sensitive, environmentally sensitive society characterised by subpolitics rather than the big political questions of the past. From a very different starting point, therefore, the risk society endorses the 'end of the grand narrative', as promoted in postmodernism, albeit with the retention of a governmental process charged with managing environmental risks and managing the claims of different groups. To this extent, the risk society thesis presents an updated, globalised version of the analysis, undertaken by Mannheim ([1940] 1971, 193) in 'Man and Society', where the growth of dangerous technology and the demands of democratisation would lead to the introduction and maintenance of some form of central planning.

On the other hand, the concept of the risk society amounts to a plea to surmount the limitations of contemporary society, without specifying whether this might happen anyway. It remains, in particular, an open question whether subpolitics are capable of going beyond allocative planning, exactly because the various groups are on the periphery of conventional politics.

## The Politics of Community

Beck's analysis is framed within the concept of a global risk society. The analysis points to a level of global planning, based on international co-operation that is absent in 'Man and Society'. Equally, the risk society and the process of subpolitics can be related to communities and to local political campaigns that seek to avoid the nuisances and disamenities of day-to-day life. A suitable analysis, extending that of Beck, may be constructed as follows. The analysis is based specifically on the experience in England, but the underlying concepts apply in principle elsewhere.

The settled industrial working class communities of the mid-20th century, as for example documented in Britain by Young and Willmott (1957) in the Docklands of East London or by Dennis et al. (1956) in the Yorkshire coalfield, have either disappeared or become less common. Savage (2008) has, in particular, used a wide variety of survey sources, dating back to the 1940s, to distinguish between two forms of place attachment in Britain—a 'primordial attachment to place' that is largely taken for granted and an 'elective belonging' based on residential choice and the disposition of the resident. Though neither form can be said to be completely dominant at any time, the primordial form is associated with the traditional communities of the past. The latter form of attachment, 'elective belonging', is more individualised and more likely to involve a consciously developed narrative of the attractions or otherwise of a place. Elective belonging is, moreover, the contemporary elaboration of community, with the implication that community itself has become more about choice and constraint, rather than a backcloth to life.

Elective belonging and choice imply, in turn, two overlapping conceptualisations of community, derived respectively from notions of club consumption and interactionist theories that go by the name of the 'community of limited liability'. To summarise each approach, in turn:

- A club provides services to its members, including the opportunity to meet people for a price and subject to entry requirements (Webster 2001a, 2001b). The neighbourhood does likewise. The services are local facilities and amenities and the ability to socialise with other members. The price of entry comprises the price or rent of property. In social housing, there are also various non-financial entry requirements. The club analogy has been most commonly used as a means of understanding the growth of private neighbourhoods, including gated communities, that involve collective ownership and collective property rights (Manzi & Smith-Bowers 2005; Glasze 2005). The club analogy has a broader relevance, however, in suggesting that the services and amenities in a neighbourhood, including its environmental qualities, have an economic value that is worth defending and enhancing.
- The 'community of limited liability' (Hunter & Suttles, 1972; Janowitz 1951) is, in part, like a traditional community. It is 'a complex system of

friendship and kinship networks and formal and informal associational ties rooted in family life and on-going socialization processes' (Kasarda & Janowitz 1974, 329) The intensity of local social networks and more broadly of community is therefore likely to be dependent in part on the length of time that residents have lived together and on the extent of residential mobility. In addition, however, involvement in local organisations becomes based on specific social roles and contexts, for example being parents in a local school or being close neighbours, or on the fact that the area becomes subject to political and administrative decisions. At the same time, increased opportunities for longer distance communication mean that residents have more choice where, how and with whom they spend their time. As a result, the community of limited liability has a voluntary aspect. Residents are more able to pick and choose whether to become involved or not, though this ability is itself influenced by financial and other resources and by stage in the life-cycle. Adolescents are, for example, more dependent on the community for their friendships than working adults.

The club analogy rests on the neoliberal assumption of a natural social order arising from below. Community organisations are said to arise spontaneously and are then institutionalised into rules governing conduct, conflict and entry. It is a theory of the community as self-organization in which economically rational individuals get together for mutual advantage (Beito et al. 2002; Pennington 2003). In contrast, the community of limited liability defines the neighbourhood as a social construction, albeit one that is grounded in everyday life and, as part of this, as a product of the relationship between local residents and a wider society, either other community groups or relevant institutional actors (public service providers, planners, developers, local newspapers and so on).

The local, publicly provided school is a good example of the limitations of the club analogy. Different neighbourhoods lie in the catchment area of different schools, the quality of which typically varies substantially from one to another. Parents with children of school age or nearing school age will often pay a premium for access to a good quality school, with the result that the price of family houses is higher in those neighbourhoods where the schools have a good reputation (Cheshire & Shepherd 2004, F416). To this extent a school is a club with an entrance fee.

At the same time, the quality of schools and the terms under which children have access to those schools is not simply dependent on the workings of the local housing market or on some spontaneous upsurge of local activism. It is also dependent on policy decisions and on the allocation of funds. Education is a public good rather than a club good. Other neighbourhood issues, including environmental issues, can be understood in analogous terms. The neighbourhood has some of the characteristics of a club, but it also possesses the characteristics of a public good and these bring local people into contact with governments and so form the foundation for conflict and campaigning.

The 'community of limited liability' also implies a process of interaction and potential for conflict, except that it goes beyond the economic characteristics of the neighbourhood. People have an interest in their communities. Moreover, in pursuing that interest, a community as economic or social space is likely to become transformed into a community as political space—an active, politically conscious community—that is qualitatively different from a community as social space or economic space.

The distinction between a community as social and economic space on one hand and as political space on the other amounts to a reworking of the well-known distinction originally made by Marx ([1847] 2009) between a class in itself and a class for itself. A community in itself has no overall purpose or unity. It is the aggregate of individuals either merely living in an area with little contact with one another or merely involved in undirected sociability. In contrast, a community for itself is a community that seeks to change or manage events, to defend itself and promote local interests and identity. The community for itself is therefore an agent of 'place struggle', rather than class struggle and is concerned with liveability rather than economic inequality. Class remains relevant, however, in a broad sense as a summary of inequalities in culture and resources and, in addition, as a background factor, alongside other factors (such as ethnicity) that help determine the character of a neighbourhood, the ability of residents to choose where to live and the use of facilities.

In the context of urban planning, by far the most commonly discussed type of community for itself is the 'NIMBY' (Not In My Back Yard) group that objects to a proposal near their own community, but not elsewhere. The term 'NIMBY' itself, only widely used since the 1980s,[4] is typically used pejoratively, as a stereotype and a means of undermining the case of objectors to development proposals (Bedford et al. 2002). Stripped of the pejorative implications, however, NIMBY's summarise the reality of local environmental politics. Residents want the best of all worlds. They want the conveniences and lifestyles of modernity. Equally, they want to live somewhere without the negative aspects of contemporary life. The negative aspects include, moreover, not just environmental issues such as pollution and noise, but impersonal landscapes of electricity pylons, high-speed roads and rundown industrial estates. In the risk society, perceptions of risk are as important as the presence of danger. Landscapes of technology and, especially, impersonal, neglected and dilapidated landscapes are themselves a source of anxiety (Picon & Bates 2000).

There are ways in which public agencies might seek to influence the activities of NIMBY groups so that they do not disrupt or block development proposals. The methods might include those of neoliberal economics, that is to say using financial incentives and compensation, both for individuals and for the community as a whole. Negotiated planning agreements, such as Section 106 agreements, where developers provide social amenities, provide an example of compensation. The expected financial gains of taxing new development when completed provide another example, at least at the level of local government. Providing compensation raises the question, however, about how much is necessary to buy off entrenched opposition. The methods might also include those of hierarchical planning—the use of strategic plans and policies that bypass local communities; the use of policy agendas to frame local discussions; and detailed design in a way that might meet or soften local objections.

A broader point remains: who is to say that all NIMBY groups are contrary to the public interest, however that is defined? How might, for example, one assess a campaign against road widening or any similar measure to speed up traffic flows? Yes, it is likely to have been motivated by the parochial concerns of those living in adversely affected neighbourhood. Yet the concerns are real enough—increased risk of traffic accidents, increased vibration to buildings, increased noise and so on. Moreover, the critics, for example those representing car users living elsewhere or hauliers, are also likely to have relatively narrow concerns.

NIMBY-free spatial planning is unlikely. However, one might engage in a brief exercise in counterfactual thinking in imagining the characteristics of a NIMBY-free city. Most likely, such a city would be a city where local residents either do not care about the quality of the environment or more likely a city where they are denied a voice in maintaining environmental quality. A NIMBY-free city, one might anticipate, would be commercialised, ugly and polluted. The politics of liveability and community has its drawbacks, but it still serves to promote liveability and to counter neglect.

## Notes

1 'Why do we insist on building on flood plains?' *The Independent*, 3 February 2014, consulted November 2015 at www.independent.co.uk/environment/nature/the-more-the-experts-warn-against-the-more-we-build-on-flood-plains-9101710.html.
2 My thanks are due to Chris Hanson of Sheffield City Council for providing information on the 'honest broker' role.
3 'Reported road accident statistics' (October 2013). on the House of Commons Library website, consulted July 2014 at www.parliament.uk/briefing-papers/sn02198.pdf.
4 As reported in The Word Detective, 27 April 2002, citing the *Oxford Dictionary of New Words*, consulted March 2006 at www.word-detective.com/042702.html.

## References

Aldrich, D. P. (2010). 'The power of people: social capital's role in recovery from the 1995 Kobe earthquake'. *Natural Hazards,* [online] URL: http://works.bepress.com/daniel_aldrich/8 (consulted January 2013).

Allen, C. R., Angeler, D. G., Garmestani, A. S., Gunderson, L. H. & Holling, C. S. (2014). 'Panarchy: theory and application'. *Ecosystems* 17:4, 578–89.

Archer, M. (1996). 'Social integration and system integration: developing the distinction'. *Sociology*, 30:4, 679–99.

Beck, U. (1992). *Risk society: towards a new modernity*. London: Sage Publications (German original 1986).

Beck, U. (1997). 'Subpolitics: ecology and the disintegration of institutional power'. *Organization & Environment*, 10, 52–65.

Beck, U. (2002). 'A life of one's own in a runaway world: individualization, globalization and politics'. In: Beck, U. and Beck-Gernsheim, E. (eds.), *Individualization: Institutionalized individualism and its social and political consequences*. London: SAGE, 22–9.

Beck, U. (2011). 'Cosmopolitanism as imagined communities of global risk'. *American Behavioral Scientist*, 55:10, 1346–61.

Beck, U., Bonss, W. & Lau, C. (2003). 'The theory of reflexive modernization: problematic, hypotheses and research programme'. *Theory, Culture & Society*, 20:2, 1–33.

Beck, U. & Kropp, C. (2007). 'Environmental risks and public perceptions'. In: Pretty, J. & Ball, A. S. (eds.), *The handbook of environment and society*. London: Sage, [online] URL: www.researchgate.net/publication/263656251_Environmental_Risks_and_Public_Perceptions (consulted June 2016).

Bedford, T., Clark, J. & Harrison, C. (2002). 'Limits to new public participation practices in local land use planning'. *Town Planning Review*, 73:3, 311–32.

Beito, D., Gordon, P. & Tabarrok, A. (eds.) (2002). *The voluntary city*. Ann Arbor, MI: University of Michigan Press.

Bickerstaff, K. (2004). 'Risk perception research: socio-cultural perspectives on the public experience of air pollution'. *Environment International*, 30:6, 827–40.

Blowers, A. (1997). 'Environmental policy: ecological modernisation or the risk society?' *Urban Studies*, 34:5-6, 845–71.

Borraz, O. & Le Galès, P. (2010). 'Urban governance in Europe: the government of what?' *Métropoles*, 7, 2–12.

Brandon, P. & Lombardi, P. (2010). *Evaluating sustainable development in the built environment*. Chichester: John Wiley & Sons.

Brenot, J., Bonnefous, S. & Marris, C. (1998). 'Testing the cultural theory of risk in France', *Risk Analysis*, 181, 729–40.

Brown, K., Few, R., Tompkins, E. L., Tsimplis, M. & Sortti, T. (2005). *Responding to climate change: inclusive and integrated coastal analysis*. Tyndall Centre for Climate Change Research, Technical Report 24, [online] URL: www.tyndall.ac.uk/sites/default/files/t2_42.pdf (consulted February 2015).

Bulkeley, H. & Betsill, M. (2005). 'Rethinking sustainable cities: multilevel governance and the "urban" politics of climate change'. *Environmental Politics*, 14, 42–63.

Butler, C. & Pidgeon, N. (2011). 'From flood defence to flood risk management: exploring governance, responsibility, and blame'. *Environment and Planning C, Government and Policy*, 29:3, 533–47.

Buxton, M., Haynes, R., Mercer, D. & Butt, A. (2011). 'Vulnerability to bushfire risk at Melbourne's urban fringe: the failure of regulatory land use planning'. *Geographical Research*, 49:1, 1–12.

Campbell, H. & Marshall, R. (1999). 'Ethical frameworks and planning theory'. *International Journal of Urban and Regional Research*, 23:3, 464–78.

Certomà, C. & Notteboom, B. (2015). 'Informal planning in a transactive governmentality: re-reading planning practices through Ghent's community gardens'.

*Planning Theory*, online first: [doi] 10.1177/1473095215598177 (consulted October 2015).
Cheshire, P. & Sheppard, S. (2004). 'Capitalising the value of free schools: the impact of supply characteristics and uncertainty'. *The Economic Journal*, 114 (November), F397–F424.
Collingwood Environmental Partnership (2014). *Flood resilience community pathfinder evaluation rapid evidence assessment.* London: The Department for Environment, Farming and Rural Affairs.
Crisp, R. & Robinson, D. (2010). *Living through change in challenging neighbourhoods: a research project funded by the Joseph Rowntree Foundation.* Family, Friends and Neighbours: Research Paper No. 9, Centre for Regional Economic and Social Research, Sheffield Hallam University, [online] URL: http://research.shu.ac.uk/cresr/living-through-change/documents/RP9_FamilyFriendsandNeighbours.pdf (consulted December 2015).
Davoudi, S. (2000). 'Sustainability: a new vision for the British planning system'. *Planning Perspectives*, 15:2, 123–37.
Deleuze, G. & Guattari, F. (1987) *A thousand plateaus: capitalism and schizophrenia.* Translation and Foreword by Brian Massumi, Minneapolis, MN: University of Minnesota Press (French original 1980).
Dennis, N., Henriques, F. and Slaughter, C. (1956). *Coal is our life: an analysis of a Yorkshire mining community.* London: Tavistock.
Douglas, M. (1966). *Purity and danger.* London: Routledge and Keagan Paul.
Douglas, M. (1999). 'Four cultures: the evolution of a parsimonious model'. *GeoJournal*, 47: 411–5.
Douglas, M. (2003). 'Risk acceptability according to the social science'. *Collected works, volume XI.* Abingdon, Oxon: Routledge (original 1985).
Douglas, M. & Wildavsky, A. B. (1982). *Risk and culture: an essay on the selection of technical and environmental dangers.* Berkeley, CA: University of California Press.
du Gay, P. (2000). *In praise of bureaucracy.* London: Sage.
Ernstson, H., van der Leeuw, S. E., Redman, C. L., Meffert, D. J., Davis, G., Alfsen, C. & Elmqvist, T. (2010.) 'Urban transitions: on urban resilience and human-dominated ecosystems'. *AMBIO: A Journal of the Human Environment*, 39:8, 531–45.
Faling, W. (2012). 'Translating disaster resilience into spatial planning practice in South Africa: challenges and champions'. *Proceedings of the AESOP 26th Annual Congress*, METU, Ankara.
Friedmann, J. (1987). *Planning in the public domain: from knowledge to action.* Princeton, NJ: Princeton University Press.
Geels, F. W. (2004). 'From sectoral systems of innovation to socio-technical systems: insights about dynamics and change from sociology and institutional theory'. *Research Policy*, 33, 897–920.
Giddens, A. (1991). *Modernity and self-identity.* Cambridge: Polity Press.
Giddens, A. (2008). *The politics of climate change.* London: The Policy Network.
Glasze, G. (2005). 'Some reflections on the economic and political organisation of private neighbourhoods'. *Housing Studies*, 20:2, 221–33.
Hartmann, T. (2011). *Clumsy floodplains: responsive land policy for extreme floods.* Farnham: Ashgate.
Healey, P. (1997). *Collaborative planning: shaping places in fragmented societies.* Basingstoke: Macmillan.

Healey, P. (1998). 'Building institutional capacity through collaborative approaches to urban planning'. *Environment and Planning A*, 30:9, 1531–46.

Hunter, A. J. & Suttles, G. D. (1972). 'The expanding community of limited liability' in Suttles, G. D. (ed.), *The social construction of communities*. Chicago: The University of Chicago Press, 41–82.

Ingirige, B. & Wedawatta, G. (2014). 'Putting policy initiatives into practice: adopting an "honest broker" approach to adapting small businesses against flooding'. *Structural Survey*, 32:2, 123–39, [online] URL: http://eprints.aston.ac.uk/23756/1/Adapting_small_businesses_against_flooding.pdf (consulted June 2015).

Innes, J. E. & Booher, D. E. (1999). 'Consensus building as role playing and bricolage'. *Journal of the American Planning Association*, 65:1, 9–26.

Janowitz, M. (1951). *The community press in an urban setting*. Chicago: University of Chicago Press.

Jansson, A. (2013). 'Reaching for a sustainable, resilient urban future using the lens of ecosystem services'. *Ecological Economics*, 86, 285–91.

Kasarda, J. D. & Janowitz M. (1974). 'Community attachment in mass society'. *American Sociological Review*, 39:3, 328–39.

Kitchen, T. (2001). 'Planning in response to terrorism: the case of Manchester, England'. *Journal of Architectural and Planning Research*, 18:4, 325–40.

Kleindorfer, P. R. & Kunreuther, H. (2000). 'Managing catastrophe risk'. *Regulation*, 23, 26–31, [online] URL: www.cato.org/pubs/regulation/regv23n4/kleindorfer.pdf (consulted January 2016).

Kusakabe, E. (2012). 'Social capital networks for achieving sustainable development'. *Local Environment*, 17:10, 1043–62.

Lockwood. D. (1964). 'Social integration and system integration'. In: Zollschan, G. & Hirsch, W. (eds.), *Explorations in social change*. Boston: Houghton Mifflin.

Lodge, M. (2009). 'The public management of risk: the case for deliberating among worldviews'. *Review of Policy Research*, 26:4, 395–408.

Low, N. (1991). *Planning, politics and the state: political foundations of planning thought*. London: Unwin Hyman.

Mamadouh, V. (1999). 'Grid-group cultural theory: an introduction'. *GeoJournal*, 47:3, 395–409.

Mannheim, K. ([1940] 1971). *Man and society in age of reconstruction*. London: Routledge and Kegan Paul (first published in English in 1940, partly based on a German original of 1935).

Manzi, T. & Smith-Bowers, B. (2005). 'Gated communities as club goods: segregation or social cohesion?' *Housing Studies*, 20:2, 345–59.

Marx, K. (2009). *The poverty of philosophy: answer to the 'Philosophy of Poverty' by M. Proudhon* (original published in French in 1847, new translation 2009), at the website of the Marxists Internet Archive, [online] URL: www.marxists.org/archive/marx/works/1847/poverty-philosophy/index.htm (consulted June 2010).

Munasinghe, M. (2007). 'The importance of social capital: comparing the impacts of the 2004 Asian tsunami on Sri Lanka and Hurricane Katrina 2005 on New Orleans'. *Ecological Economics*, 64:1, 9–11.

Oliga, J. C. (1996). *Power, ideology, and control*. New York & London: Plenum Press.

Olshansky, R. B., Johnson, L. A., Horne, J. & Nee, B. (2008). 'Planning for the rebuilding of New Orleans'. *Journal of the American Planning Association*, 74:3, 273–87.

Pennington, M. (2003). 'To what extent and in what ways should governmental bodies regulate urban planning? A response to Charles C. Bohl'. *Journal of Markets & Morality*, 6:1, 213–26.

Picon, A. & Bates, K. (2000). 'Anxious landscapes: from the ruin to the rust'. *Grey Room*, 01, 64–83, [online] URL: www.mitpressjournals.org/toc/grey/-/1 (consulted June 2016).

Pielke, R. A. (2007). *The honest broker: making sense of science in policy and politics*. Cambridge, UK: Cambridge University Press.

Rootes, C. (2013). 'More acted upon than acting? Campaigns against waste incinerators in England'. In: Rootes, C. & Leonard, L. (eds.), *Environmental movements and waste infrastructure*. London: Routledge, 53–80.

Querrien, A. (2007). 'Faire rhizome en passant en revue'. *Le Portique*, 20, [online] URL: http://leportique.revues.org/index1358.html (consulted December 2009).

Savage, M. (2008). 'Histories, belongings, communities'. *International Journal of Social Research Methodology*, 11:2, 151–62.

Schwarz M. & Thompson M. (1990). *Divided we stand: redfining politics, technology and social choice*. Hemel Hempstead: Harvester Wheatsheaf.

Tansey, J. & O'Riordan, T. (1999). 'Cultural theory and risk: a review'. *Health, Risk & Society*, 1:1, 71–90.

Thompson M., Ellis R. & Wildavsky A. (1990). *Cultural theory*. Boulder, CO: Westview Press.

Uphoff, E. P., Pickett, K. E., Cabieses, B., Small, N. & Wright, J. (2013). 'A systematic review of the relationships between social capital and socioeconomic inequalities in health: a contribution to understanding the psychosocial pathway of health inequalities'. *International Journal of Equity in Health*, 12:54.

Verhaeghe, P. -P. & Tampubolon, G. (2012). 'Individual social capital, neighbourhood deprivation, and self-rated health in England'. *Social Science & Medicine*, 75:2, 349–57.

Verweij, M. Douglas, M., Ellis, R., Engel, C., Hendriks, F., Lohmann, S., Ney, S., Rayner, S. & Thompson, M. (2006). 'Clumsy solutions for a complex world: the case of climate change'. *Public Administration*, 84:4, 817–43.

Voogd, H. (2004). 'Disaster prevention in urban environments'. *European Journal of Spatial Development*, 12, 1–20, [online] URL: www.nordregio.se/EJSD/.

Walker, G., Simmons, P., Irwin, A. & Wynne, B. (1999). 'Risk communication, public participation and the Seveso II directive'. *Journal of Hazardous Materials*, 65:1, 179–90.

Warr M. (1990). 'Dangerous situations: social context and fear of victimization'. *Social Forces*, 68, 891–907.

Webster, C. J. (2001a). 'Gated cities of tomorrow', *Town Planning Review*, 72:2, 149–70.

Webster, C. J. (2001b). 'Contractual agreements and neighbourhood evolution'. *Planning and Markets*, 4:1.

Wilkinson, C. (2012). 'Social-ecological resilience: Insights and issues for planning theory'. *Planning Theory*, 11:2, 148–69.

Wilkinson, C., Porter, L. & Colding, J. (2010). 'Metropolitan planning and resilience thinking: a practitioner's perspective'. *Critical Planning*, 17: 2–20.

Young, M. & Willmott, P. (1957). *Family and kinship in East London*. London: Routledge & Kegan Paul.

Zhang, Y., Lindell, M. K. & Prater, C. S. (2009). 'Vulnerability of community businesses to environmental disasters'. *Disasters*, 33:1, 35–57.

# 9 Transition Management

In some ways, it is only a short step from risk management and the risk society to transition management. To give a specific example, carbon reduction is long-term risk management, based on the knowledge that carbon dioxide emissions and other greenhouse gas emissions will promote climate change and eventually cause very serious disruption and threats to life and property. The role of human action in climate change is admittedly still disputed by some, but the possible long-term consequences are too serious to ignore. Transition is more than risk management, however. It involves a shift towards more sustainable systems of production and consumption. Moreover climate change, though crucially important, is not the only environmental consideration.

## The Logic of Transition

As presented by its main advocates (Geels 2005, 11; Kemp et al. 2007; Loorbach 2010), transition involves a multiple, multi-level passage from one state to another of a socio-technical system comprising networks of producers, consumers, intermediaries and technology. Transition is a structural and systemic process, guided by government in a process of co-production and partnership. Transition management is distinct from the transition town movement, which is a series of local, place-based initiatives of which Totnes in Devon is the best-known British example.[1] The common use of the term 'transition' reveals, nevertheless, that the movement to a sustainable society, the process of transition, should not be tied too closely to a single 'school' or group of theorists. Transition management is, in any case, not the first theory of its type. It has emerged partly as a reaction to and partly as an extension of predecessors whose characteristics, limitations and strengths are also relevant to current debates.

### Antecedents, Related and Alternative Theories

The earliest, at least the earliest widely cited predecessor, can be summarised under the heading of 'Small is Beautiful' as stated by Schumacher (1973).

Economic policy needed a new start and needed to abandon 19th- and 20th-century concepts of modernity, it was argued. Governments needed to promote a human scale and needed, in addition, to reject all manner of large-scale organisations, including the big city, in favour of local self-sufficiency. Exactly how governments were supposed to downsize big cities was not stated, however. Moreover, the concept of economic self-sufficiency looked utopian, except in limited market sectors—for example seasonal food produce.

In the 1980s, in response to growing concern about industrial pollution, a group of social scientists in Berlin elaborated a more easily applied interpretation of environmental policy in the form of what was called 'ecological modernisation' (Mol & Spaargaren 1993). This latter involved an extension of modernity in a sustainable direction, rather than its rejection. A sustainable society was therefore not an end point, for example a series of small communities or a fixed level of consumption. It was, instead, a society characterised by a continuous process of reflection on its environmental impact and a continuous process of change in minimising that impact.

Reflection on environmental impact offers parallels with the concept of reflexive modernisation as stated by Beck (1992). Both Beck and the theorists of ecological modernisation would agree that some form of environmental action and protection is necessary and inevitable, that governments have to be alert to unintended consequences and that modernisation itself involves an increasing social entanglement of rules, regulations and policies all with intended and unintended consequences.

Otherwise, the implications of the two approaches stand in contrast to one another. Ecological modernisation is essentially an optimistic planning theory, whereas the risk society is a pessimistic critique of modernity and technology, as out of control, following its own trajectory and logic. Modernisation theorists would probably respond to Beck along the lines once suggested by Ascher (2001, 72–5). Modern technology does indeed increase risks, but it also increases the capacity to monitor those risks, control them and avoid adverse consequences. Technology has therefore not become out of control.

Ecological modernisation has also been criticised from a 'deep green' position for being overcautious, too close to industry, for seeing capitalism as the saviour of environmental problems, rather than a cause and, finally, for ignoring the way in which modernisation is itself a contested concept (Blowers 1997; Hajer 1995; Latour 1997). A particular criticism of ecological modernisation has been its use of a narrative of 'win-win' to generate political support. Win-win means that the adoption of green technologies would itself create jobs and increase national competitiveness in comparison with other countries. There are, admittedly, examples of win-win measures—the wind turbine industry in Denmark, the solar panel industry in Germany and the district heating and combined heat and power installations manufactured in Germany and Austria. Win-win arguments continue, moreover, to be promoted by international bodies, such as the OECD and the European Union, under the heading of 'green growth'.[2] Growth and green policies both involve public investment. They can be combined together and, in doing so, create new industries and become incorporated into local development strategies. Lissandrello and Grin (2011) have, for example documented the formulation of a spatial strategy for the port of Rotterdam based on the concept of a green technology hub.

For all the cases of green growth, however, there are others where energy-intensive or polluting industry has suffered and lost jobs as a result of environmental regulation (Jänicke 2008). The losers, one might add, have included the local communities whose livelihood depended on these industries. Moreover, the emphasis on commercial products may lead to the development of standardised urban neighbourhoods, as has been a criticism of the export-drive urban design strategies used in Sweden (Hult 2015). In response, the supporters of ecological modernisation and its popular equivalent 'green growth' would argue that, for all its limitations, their policy agenda offers a more feasible political strategy than a more confrontational or restrictive, deep green alternative (Jänicke 2008). Refusing to work with industry or commerce is only likely to stiffen political resistance.

The same distinction between 'deep green' positions and ecological modernisation arises in a related debate about economic growth. Global environmental pressure groups such as Greenpeace and Friends of the Earth are concerned with changing social values, encouraging people and institutions to live in harmony with nature and ensuring that the values of sustainable development are fully recognised through political changes. Economic growth, including claims of 'green growth', is either opposed or treated as a side issue in comparison with the scale of environmental problems.

In some countries, mostly in continental Europe, environmental activism overlaps the 'degrowth' movement, actively hostile as its name implies to the pursuit of economic growth. This latter had its first international convention in Paris in 2008.[3,4] However, it is possible to find similar oppositional ideas in the critiques of earlier generations of economists and environmental theorists. Typical critiques have pointed to the existence of some form of physical, resource limit to consumption (Meadows et al. 1972), to the inherent social scarcities and social limits (Hirsch 1977) involved in market-based production and to the apparent failure of material economic growth to promote a sense of well-being or satisfaction with life (Scitovsky 1976).

Conventional economists would probably argue, in reply, that resource depletion will not be a sudden process and that, in the meantime, higher resource costs and prices will stimulate alternative supplies and alternative technologies. They would probably add that social limits to growth are imaginary in that growth helps fund greater choice for individuals and their families or, in the social democratic version, helps fund higher quality social services of all types. The argument about social limits, as presented by Hirsch (1977), is mostly about a loss of moral capital, the glue that enables the functioning of civilised society. Hirsch's critique is aimed at the commercialisation of ordinary life, rather than growth as such. Finally, conventional economics would probably add that 'degrowth', economic stagnation and unemployment would certainly not increase and would probably decrease satisfaction with life.

A further issue and further uncertainty is whether 'degrowth' can be achieved through voluntary means and planning as argued by Kallis (2013), rather than imposed on individuals and economic actors through the force of events, as argued by Sorman and Giampietro (2013). If the latter, degrowth will be organised through the market and is more likely to come from an economic crisis rather than a conscious policy choice. Degrowth as crisis is, moreover, likely to discourage investment in renewable and low carbon technologies, as well as investment in the built environment. Indeed, evidence exists that investment in renewable energy in continental Europe declined in 2012 and 2013, exactly as a result of economic recession and the pursuit of austerity (Frankfurt School et al. 2014).

Economic growth is not a cure-all. However, the policy choice is not confined to the bleak options of degrowth on one hand and uncontrolled growth on the other. The growth/degrowth distinction is, in any case, irrelevant to poorer countries. Growth is best considered, as Lefèbvre ([1973] 1976, 10–119) once argued, as a means to a variety of specific tangible aims, including the promotion of employment and the maintenance of public services, rather than an end in itself. The implication is to retain these specific aims, whilst seeking to avoid the negative aspects of growth.

Transition management and its associated theories are the successor to ecological modernisation and the earlier debates about economic growth, without, however, displacing the old terminology. Transition management was, in part, a response to the criticism of overcaution as directed against ecological modernisation. As a distinct form of environmental policy, it originated, in the Netherlands, in the 'Fourth National Environmental Policy Plan', published in 2001, and sought to reinvigorate ecological modernisation to tackle the problem of climate change and continuing environmental degradation (Smith & Kern 2007). Like ecological modernisation, transition management involves relatively light touch state intervention. It is about helping societies to transform themselves in a 'gradual, reflexive way' towards sustainable development in a process of 'co-evolutionary steering' (Kemp et al. 2007). Unlike ecological modernisation, which was almost wholly concerned with industry and pollution, transition management deals with a wide variety of issues, including urban infrastructure, greenhouse gas emissions, the use of resources and ecological systems. Through a reference to multi-level interventions, transition management also recognises the value of small-scale, local initiatives, as well as large-scale structures.

Thereafter, despite continuing criticisms that, as applied, it is also too close to business and insufficiently concerned with local democracy, transition management has come to offer a loose set of conceptual tools and assumptions for analysing any long-term, innovative national environmental strategy. In the European Union, the elaboration of national energy plans after 2010 has made transition management especially relevant, though the theory itself has a broader application than energy alone. Transition management theory, its supporters would argue, has not and cannot make either energy or environmental policy any less contested or any less complex. Its contribution is to offer a framework for analysis and, in doing so, to offer a means of improving the effectiveness of that analysis.

## The 'S' Curve

As commonly envisaged, transition proceeds through an S-shaped curve, illustrated in Figure 9.1. The curve shows how innovations in sustainable technologies, products and practices become established and spread over time until they become commonplace. In the simplest representation, expansion proceeds smoothly from one stable, locked-in system to another through take-off, acceleration, breakthrough and then stabilisation into another locked-in system.

Transition is of different sizes and speeds, but may last decades. Sometimes, full transition requires a repetition of the 'S' curve as the 'system' lurches from one plateau to another, stabilises and then moves on. The IEA (2013, 220)

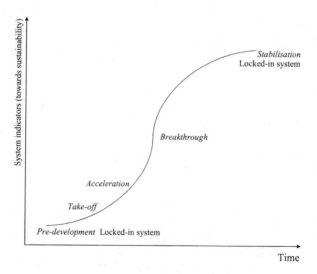

*Figure 9.1* Transition Represented as a Simplified 'S' curve
Source: Adapted from Rotmans and Kemp (2003).

gives, for example, three plateaus in the adoption of low-carbon building standards, an initial experimental plateau, another plateau where adoption is facilitated by quality labelling of various types and a final plateau near to universal adoption facilitated by regulation.

The vertical dimension, that of 'system indicators', is open to more interpretations than the horizontal dimension of time. Economic and business interpretations use the 'S' curve to refer merely to market penetration, for example the proportion of households who possess a new product or technology. In transition management, systems indicators may also mean the take up of new technology, but in the direction of a sustainable system and measured either by broad environmental indicators or by carbon emissions. As policies have unfolded over the past few years, the latter, narrower range of carbon reduction and energy savings indicators have tended to predominate (Béal & Pinson 2014; While et al. 2010).

In seeking to apply the 'S' curve, the advocates of transition management commonly point to various historical examples, drawn largely from the 19th and early 20th centuries and especially from the Netherlands. However, it is arguable where earlier shifts in technology offer a direct parallel to the contemporary and future experience of ecological transitions. The spread of technological innovations was not, at this time, a product of a search for sustainability, as this is currently understood. Instead, the adoption was either motivated by public health concerns or by concerns of speed, comfort or convenience.

*Cities in Evolution* by Geddes (1915) provides another way of understanding the context or 'landscape' of technological change, to use the language of transition management in the early 20th century. Geddes is best remembered as an advocate, theorist and practitioner of urban planning. Equally, however, Geddes grasped processes that were operating independently of any move towards planning. The previous industrial age, the 'palaeotechnic', was ending. The 'palaeotechnic' was the age powered by steam power and coal. A new 'neotechnic' age was about to commence, powered by a plentiful supply of gas, oil and electricity (ibid., 60), with the potential to change the fabric and pattern of cities and remove much of the previous drudgery of daily life. For Geddes, the life-enhancing potential of the neotechnic would only be realised through planning or civic design to use the relevant language, but the shift in patterns of energy production was likely to ocur anyway.

It is possible that governments could have directed technological innovation more actively if they had wished to do so. Through the 20th century central heating systems gradually became more widespread, much in the way predicted by the 'S' curve. Central heating can be provided either through small boilers in each home or building or through collective district heating networks. The latter have been widely used in continental Europe, whereas their development in Britain was frustrated by the indifference and occasional hostility of mainstream energy providers and central government

(Hawkey et al. 2013; Russell 1993). However, the development of local heat networks was also part of a trend towards more comfort and convenience in the home (Rybczynski 1987; Shove 2003). The direction was set, even if the means could have been varied.

Just as much as the neotechnic offered a new era for urban development, so does the present emphasis on energy consumption and renewable energy. There is potential for governments to act, in promoting catch-up and in changing technologies. However, the scope of that potential and even more so the scope for demand reduction and behaviour change is uncertain, exactly because it is without historical precedent.

## Backcasting, Targets and Progress

Innovative and radical forms of planning are about setting an agenda rather than following trends. In transition management, agenda setting commonly involves an exercise in 'backcasting' in which a specific set of targets or a scenario is specified as necessary and the means to achieve those targets or scenario are worked out later (Dreborg 1996; Höjer & Mattsson 2000). Backcasting, as opposed to the more common exercise of forecasting, offers a means of creating an alternative future, when current trends are part of the problem and are unsustainable.

There are various interpretations of how backcasting is best applied, whether for example the starting point should be expressed in the form of quantitative goals or how much emphasis should be placed on public involvement. Backcasting can refer to a specific target or measure or to a broad set of criteria, depending on the context. It may, for example, refer to establishing sustainable levels of energy consumption, as in the UK carbon delivery plan (DECC 2011). Equally, backcasting can start from a broadly based urban vision that shows how sustainable levels of energy might be represented in space and time (Höjer et al. 2011).

In principle, however, backcasting does not require the elaboration, in advance, of a detailed set of measures for its creation. Instead, for its supporters, backcasting is useful exactly because it forces policy-makers and governments to innovate, to discover potential means of implementation of a type not previously considered (Höjer & Mattsson 2000). It offers a willed, rather than a predicted future. Progress is made and targets are realised through the selection of short-term tactical measures or opportunities, based on a combination of material levers of change, negotiation, networking and institution building. Situations of opportunities might, for example, include a major regeneration project or a transport investment or a major review of organisational structures and policies (Svane 2008).

Whether backcasting is fully feasible as a political strategy is another matter. The critics of rational planning, notably Lindblom ([1959] 1973) have, for many years, insisted that democratic governments have to pursue disjointed policies to satisfy the demands of different groups and that long-term planning is a misnomer. Exactly the same criticism is applicable to backcasting and, more generally, transition management (Hendriks 2009), including the attempts to implement a transition plan in the Netherlands (Smith & Kern 2007). The need to maintain political alliances, to avoid mistakes and to cope with adverse external conditions such as recession may supersede the long-term environmental strategy (Heiskanen et al. 2009; Paredis 2008). Further, the long-term character of climate change processes may encourage scepticism about the scale and speed of impacts if nothing is done, so weakening public support (Poortinga et al. 2011).

Other complications involve conflict within government and within the transition strategy itself. Governments are large heterogeneous institutional actors. Other policy agendas, for example dealing with education or medical care, may well have a larger, electoral impact, certainly a larger impact in the mass media. Moreover, energy policy is itself subject to contradictory policy priorities that are not directly related to carbon reduction but that cause uncertainty and so hinder investment. The policy priorities of competition and energy price freezes provide an example, as these do nothing to encourage the take-up of renewables which require a long-term commitment and long-term payback periods.

A related criticism concerns the selective effects of an opportunist, tactical approach. Identifying opportunities helps promote cost-effective action in the short term, but also leads to missing transitions where governments fail to act or do little (Shove & Walker 2007). The treatment of transport and building reveals the point. The UK national carbon delivery plan (DECC 2011) states in relation to transport, excluding international transport (where no targets are set):

> By 2050 the transport system will need to emit significantly less carbon than today. (ibid., 47)

In contrast, for the building sector, mostly comprising consumption in the home:

> By 2050 the emissions footprint of our buildings will need to be almost zero. (ibid., 30)

The target for transport is vague and much less stringent than for the building stock, the main reason being that 'transport is an enabler on other economic activities and its restraint might have a negative impact of economic growth (DECC 2010, 60).

The difference between the treatment of domestic energy consumption and that of transport also involves different assessments of the so-called 'rebound' effect whereby consumers increase consumption as technology becomes more fuel-efficient. The national carbon delivery plan accepts the logic of the rebound effect for transport but not for buildings. Yet a rebound effect does exist in relation to the building stock and in particular to the housing stock. Estimates of the rebound effect in relation to home insulation measures suggest a reduction of anywhere between 10 percent in potential savings in energy consumption and 65 percent or 100 percent for low-income households (Sorrell et al. 2009). The direct rebound effect is therefore, on average, higher for lower income households. For lower income households, moreover, the achievement of higher temperatures within the home is also likely to have positive implications for their welfare and health (Hong et al. 2009). The rebound effect may have beneficial consequences, albeit in public health and social policy rather than energy.

Trends in UK energy consumption follow the same distinction as noted in the carbon delivery plan. National statistics are available to monitor progress in relation to domestic energy and road transport consumption. Domestic energy consumption covers all type of energy consumption in the home, but not, of course, other types of building. The pattern since 2000 is shown in Figure 9.2.

The pattern shows a gradual decline in domestic energy consumption over the past fifteen years, with variations caused by cold and less cold winters. Between 2000 and 2014, for example, domestic energy consumption per person fell by about 19 percent in the context of an increase of 12 percent in the number of UK households and a 9.7 percent increase in the UK population (DECC 2015, 5). In contrast, for road transport, the trend is flat, suggesting that recent policy and technological innovations have had little or no impact whatsoever.

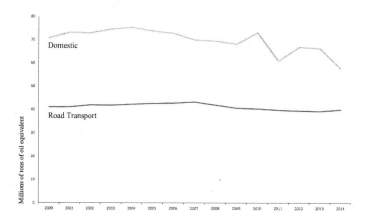

*Figure 9.2* Selected Trends in UK Energy Consumption

Source: Department of Energy and Climate Change, Digest of UK Energy Statistics, Annex, Tables 2.01 and 3.01. Consulted September 2015 at www.gov.uk/government/collections/energy-consumption-in-the-uk.

The decline in domestic energy consumption is associated with a long list of technical innovations—improvements in the design of central heating boilers, increased insulation in the roof cavity and elsewhere, increased use of double glazing, improved efficiency in household appliances and lighting and so on, all of which can be represented as an 'S' curve in terms of market penetration (DECC 2013, 93; Shorrock 2003; Shorrock et al. 2005, 67). These improvements and innovations, incorporated into the existing stock as well as new builds, have stayed ahead of the rebound effect and the increases in the number of households and population. The decline in energy consumption is not enough to ensure, by itself, the achievement of the delivery plan target of a housing stock approaching zero carbon by 2050, however. Moreover, overall improvements in energy efficiency conceal major variations between old and new property, between homes in different tenures and between affluent and poorer households.

In contrast, technological innovation in motor vehicles has been insufficient to counter an increase in traffic levels of 7 percent during the same period from 2000 to 2014.[5]

Carbon reduction is not the same as a reduction in energy sources. Governments can shorten transition time through a reliance on decarbonised electricity production. Decarbonisation is not straightforward, however, given the dependence in the UK on petrol and diesel for road transport and on gas central heating for buildings. It remains debateable therefore whether carbon reduction targets can be achieved without further measures to reduce energy demand and, as part of this, without further measures for increased energy efficiency, in the use of energy in buildings and elsewhere. In any case, some of the decarbonised technologies, for example nuclear and the proliferation of wind turbines, raise other objections. Further, carbon reduction is not the only indicator of sustainability and not the only aspects of an ecological transition to which energy demand reduction and changed patterns of consumer behaviour are relevant.

## Transition Pathways

Backcasting, like other aspects of transition management, runs into ambiguities about politics and political institutions. Conceptualising a different future still requires a consideration of who and how this future will be realised in terms of existing institutions and policy instruments (Wangel 2011). Once, moreover, the focus of attention switches away from 'S' curves and trends to institutions and assuming, in addition, that governments do indeed have to consider energy efficiency in buildings, demand reduction and changes in consumption, the theoretical frame has to shift accordingly, to processes of governance and to how governments can seek to influence behaviour. That, in turn, means an initial exercise in classification, mapping the pathways, that is to say the main lines of change and how these relate to one another.

## Mapping and Classifying the Field

Moving away from the 'S' curve means, in turn, moving away from some other concepts of conventional transition management. It means abandoning, or at least heavily modifying, a tripartite classification between 'niches' (areas of experimentation), 'socio-technical regimes' (policy networks that promote innovation) and 'landscape' (the context) (Geels 2002; Loorbach and Rotmans 2010). The niche/regime/landscape distinction refers to the stages of product innovation and diffusion from the small-scale to the global. However, niche merely refers to an abstract economic space that is protected from the market rather than an actual space or place (Coenen et al. 2012) or unit of government. Regimes and processes of governance, just as much as niches, can be local. Landscape is another, residual problematic category of transition management, at least if the aim of analysis is to identify pathways. Landscape is 'the overall societal setting in which processes of change occur' (Loorbach & van Raak 2005, 3). It is the context for policy, 'something around us that we can travel through and metaphorically as something that we are part of' (Geels & Schot 2007).

A classification undertaken for the French ministry of sustainable development (MEEDM 2010) offers a more concrete starting point. The MEEDM classification recognises the difference between levels whilst referring to the typical levels of government—decentralised, centralised and international (or global). Global, as presented by MEEDM (2010), refers to a level that is outside day-to-day policy but is nevertheless a level of international trade and also a practical level of decision-making where governments meet to define a common position and come to an agreement. At the same time, the MEEDM classification recognises that different political values many be applied at any level of government, given the varied emphasis of mainstream and deep green groups.

The MEEDM classification is therefore based on a double distinction as follows:

- first, between levels of decision-making; and
- second, between policies that seek to bring the economy into environmental questions (economising ecology) or *vice versa*, bring the environment into economic decision-making (ecologising the economy).

The second dimension in the MEEDM classification, between economising ecology and ecologising the economy, deserves more scrutiny. Economising means understanding and explaining socio-technical assemblages as functioning markets and also using the knowledge so gained to reconstruct assemblages as markets (Çalışkan & Callon 2010). As an extension, therefore, economising means using the various instruments of economic policy, such as the provision of incentives and cost penalties, to change assemblages, using economic expertise to do so and thereby also giving policy measures a degree of scientific legitimacy amongst economic experts (Rumpala 2004). The Stern report is an example of the economising approach, *par excellence*. Stern (2007, v) redefines climate change as, in economic terms, an externality, admittedly an unusual and severe type of externality and equivalent therefore from an analytical viewpoint to a local problem such as air pollution or a noise nuisance.

Reference to an economising logic does not mean, however, that all relevant economic measures are applied. Some measures remain missing. Treating climate change as an economic externality implies the use of carbon taxes as a means of discouraging emissions and these are either weak or completely absent in most countries.

Ecologising means bringing ecological considerations directly into policy making. The concept does not, however, give full justice to the variety of different strategies, especially those that seek to change lifestyles and behaviour. A parallel distinction between 'economic' or mainstream and alternative approaches as made by Mourik & Rotmann (2013) on behalf of the International Energy Agency provides a richer, more detailed account.

The conventional economic models focus, *inter alia*, on individuals and individual companies; they treat individuals and companies as economically rational actors and commonly focus on a combination of technological innovation and a transformation in the pattern of demand, achieved through consumer choice. Even technological solutions require that consumers are made aware of the potential. As a result, conventional demand reduction measures tend to regard information deficits as an important cause of non-rational behaviour. They favour green labelling of products and smart metering that tells users the amount of energy and cost of the energy as used at any time. The conventional model also commonly focuses on once-off financial incentives, on pricing and the taxation of non-renewable fuels and on marketing in favour of pro-environmental behaviour. Consumers, it is assumed, choose one product rather than another. The question is to influence that choice.

In the conventional model, the marketing and information strategies are sometimes called exercises in 'nudging', after the book of the same name by Thaler and Sunstein (2008). Nudging comes from behavioural economics, the economics of how markets actually work rather than from an idealised interpretation of how they work. Nudging is a 'soft' policy instrument that is less expensive than 'hard' strategies based on the development of new technologies or the redevelopment and construction of a city and less controversial than measures based on the imposition of higher prices or higher taxes or on prescriptive rules.

However, nudging is not the only 'soft' way to promote pro-environmental behaviour. 'Alternative' models include measures to promote collaboration between different institutional actors. Examples include the preparation and implementation of voluntary agreements such as work-based travel plans and the promotion of trust amongst different parties such as householders, their landlords and local authorities. Alternative models use multiple definitions of success, for example the existence of health benefits (from walking in the case of transport planning or warmer homes in the case of housing policy); they are concerned with recycling and environmental protection as well as energy reduction; they involve regulation and other forms of institutional change that focus on lifestyles; and they allow participation and consultation. In addition, alternative models of change assume that behaviour change will be achieved only through changes in collective customs and behaviour rather the rational choices of individuals (Schwanen et al. 2012). Economic measures, especially if pursued in isolation, are likely to have a limited impact.

How might behaviour change best be achieved? Design can physically prevent or facilitate forms of behaviour. For example, the occupants of a building can be prevented from misusing heating or cooling systems through various devices such as the installation of automatic temperature limits in the control mechanisms or through use of non-openable windows. Likewise, the use of a car can be prevented in specific places by closing and pedestrianizing roads.

Equally, behaviour can be influenced by the symbolism of a physical artefact. The relevant concept, borrowed from actor-network theory (Latour 2009), is that of a 'script' where an artefact materialises the intention of its designer and 'tells' the user how it should be used. A speed bump has, for example, the script 'slow down when you approach me', a plastic cup, 'throw me away after use' (Verbeek 2006, 58). Likewise an eco-home may announce through its design its special role in reducing energy consumption. Whether through physical interference or through scripts, radical changes to design amount, therefore, to a social change in their own right.

There are qualifications to the logic of a script, however. The script for reduced energy use is less easy to understand than say the scripts for a speed bump or a disposable coffee cup, which is of course not very sustainable. Reduced energy is achieved in a variety of different ways and depends largely on how space and technology is used, both space within buildings and, in the case of transport, external urban space. It is an ethereal, rather than a concrete, specific act tied to a specific product.

'Practice theory' offers a series of further distinctions to help understand and change the workings of consumption. The theory involves a distinction between practices as entity and practices as performed (Warde 2005: 134). Practice as entity is a combination of practical understandings, rules and motivational factors. It includes specific activities associated with the home or elsewhere—for example cooking, cleaning, heating or gardening—as well as the activities involved in moving around a city—walking, driving a car and cycling. Performance is the carrying out of those practices. The material fabric and equipment of the built environment, its technology and its location affects the ability to undertake performances and, partly through this mechanism, influences the various practices as entities. The materiality of space and the built environment is, therefore, a means of supporting, preventing or discouraging practices, as the case may be, as well as providing the background to those practices.

Practice theory offers an antidote to conventional economising approaches as it emphasises how patterns of consumption are rooted in the routines of daily life, rather than in individual preferences or attitudes (Shove 2010). Practices are 'bundled activities' (Schatzki 2002, 71) that operate through 'the horizontal circulation of elements' and 'multiple relations (rather than hierarchical levels) of reproduction across different scales' (Shove & Walker, 2010, 474). In practice theory, change can only occur through changing the routines of daily life. Suggested mechanisms for change commonly include micro-political activities such as local campaigns; the creation of 'communities of practice' where people are involved in experiments or exposed to new practices (Sahakian and Wilhite 2014); and direct influence and neighbourhood networks (Bartiaux et al. 2014). In addition, the bundled activities of practice theory are influenced by externally set rules and by manipulating the context of daily routines. Regulation, physical planning and design are, therefore, potential means of policy implementation.

Taken literally, the emphasis in practice theory on horizontal circulation would deny the potential of governmental action. The question of horizontal rather than multiple levels of intervention is a side issue, however. Practice theory offers an apparently simple theory of change, irrespective of the question of levels. Change the design of the built environment so that it encourages behaviour in one direction rather than another. Change the technology so that it is either more efficient or directly encourages energy savings. Provide some form of practical understanding. Set appropriate rules and motivate people to use the technology in a sustainable manner. Make all these changes simultaneously and consumption will change in a sustainable direction.

Behaviour change is not that simple. The character of the practice is sometimes unclear. People may say, for example, that they are going shopping when they mean that they merely want to get of the house or undertake some leisure-related activity. Shopping and leisure overlap but raise different environmental and spatial issues. In addition, the context in which practice is undertaken is relevant. Practices become entwined with cultural assumptions—for example about what is clean and healthy (Shove & Walker, 2010, 472-3) or masculine or feminine. Further, consumption objects—for example expensive cars or a large house—sometimes acquire a social status or contribute to a social identity in a way that itself hinders change. Consumption is about social communication as well as practice and communicative function can get in the way of energy savings (Goodchild et al. 2014).

Given these constraints, judgements have to be made about what is possible. In the case of collective consumption products such as transport systems, users may lobby to ensure that any such proposal is not implemented or they may protest in some other way if they do not like what they see. In the case of individually consumed products such as domestic technologies, potential users may refuse to buy what is offered—a fatal or near fatal weakness in a consumer economy. If unpopular consumer objects are imposed, without the possibility of choice, users may also attempt to maintain existing behaviours and lifestyles in a way that defeats the logic of design.

There are 'green' consumers willing to purchase green products. In addition, a Swedish study by Jansson et al. (2010) suggests that, once a consumer has bought a green product, they are more likely to do so again. Once established, green patterns of consumption may therefore become self-perpetuating. Practice theory predicts such a pattern. However, the number of green consumers is probably small. Surveys suggest that most of those who engage in energy saving behaviour or purchase energy saving devices do so for financial reasons (Whitmarsh 2009)—a point that supports the use of multiple strategies of change.

### An Outline of the Pathways

Given all this, a possible classification of measures and initiatives is as shown in Table 9.1.

*Table 9.1* Pathways for Environmental Transition

|  | Favoured level of intervention | | |
|---|---|---|---|
| Focus | Decentralised pathways | Centralised pathways | Global |
| Economising (based on the individual, technology and choice) | Organisational and technical innovation in 'niches' | Incentivised technological change | Geopolitical and economic change |
| Ecologising or 'alternative' (based on culture and collectivities) | Social change | Directed change | Geocultural change |

Sources: Adapted from MEEDM (2010); Mourik & Rotmann (2013).

To summarise, there are three main pathways for change, each with a mainstream, economising and alternative variant and each using a variety of strategies to influence behaviour. These comprise:

- decentralised pathways: organisational and technical operating either through a small or local network or through agencies that promote social change such as local government or a community;
- centralised pathways: institutional and technical change operating through a regime—the governmental structures, policy fields and their associated regulatory functions; and finally
- global and international pathways: geopolitical, geoeconomic and geocultural change that provide the context both for regimes and local networks of actors.

There is risk that the identification of pathways suggests a degree of clarity and organisation that is absent. Intervention may proceed independently at any single level or, as is a repeated theme in statements of good practice in transition (Geels 2011) simultaneously at two or three. Governments may and commonly do work through local authorities in a way that ensures central control at a distance. Other agencies and intermediate levels of government may also become involved. Transition, like risk management, consists of overlapping initiatives and also involves a degree of experimentation as governments determine the effectiveness of different measures in reaching the backcasting targets, whilst also pursuing numerous other objectives, including the promotion of economic growth and the avoidance of regulation. As a result, transition poses repeated questions of co-ordination and the alignment of objectives (Bulkeley & Betsill 2013).

For the sake of simplicity, however, a tripartite distinction between three levels of pathways—decentralised, centralised and global—will suffice. Examples may be given of each pathway, as they appear in a cool, damp climate such as Britain, again emphasising those that involve buildings, transport or the urban infrastructure.

Local authorities provide an obvious means of implementing decentralised pathways and commonly have relevant experience dating back to the 'Local Agenda 21' policy agenda in the period from about 1992 to the early 2000s (Voisey et al. 1996). Local authorities have extensive assets, both human and property. They act as service providers and implementing agencies, for example for waste management. They provide a means of coordinating measures at the local level, in conjunction with partnership arrangements of the type established for other reasons such as neighbourhood regeneration and economic development. They therefore act as enablers or intermediaries between the various agencies, the state and members of the public. In some cases, other, semi-independent agencies might also act as intermediaries, loosely coordinating local green initiatives. There is no set pattern.

A European Commission–funded study provides an optimistic, albeit qualified account of the role of local authorities based on the experience of five European cities where the transition management approach has been used as a framework to tackle climate change. The project, named 'MUSIC' (Roorda et al. 2014, 51) suggests that the adoption of an explicit transition management approach had enabled, amongst other advantages, institutional 'actors … to enter new roles' as well as new ways of sustainable working. It is also possible to find specific, self-contained local projects that have at least made some limited progress. The schools retrofitting initiative of 'Green Suffolk' in the east of England provides an example.[6]

On other hand, Moloney and Horne (2015) have applied the transition model to what might be considered a failed transition in the city of Melbourne. Multi-level interventions were either fragmentary or in conflict with one another. Experimental niches were ad hoc and confined to those associated with local government. For example, local policies to reduce car use were not supported by national policies. In addition, Vandevyvere and Nevens (2015) have tested the model against practice in the towns and cities of Belgian Flanders. Their conclusion is that the niche model provides a kind of half-truth. Initiating a transition programme at a local level can promote discussion, but implementation remains problematic. The reasons were various but were broadly consistent with practice theory. Transition 'entails a reconsideration of aspects such as values and norms that underlie deeply entrenched routines of consumption, living and building, eating, etc.'

This latter study included the experience in Ghent, a city also covered in the more optimistic European Union study, so suggesting that in the promotion of sustainable development, different interpretations of the same phenomenon are possible. Where Vandevyvere and Nevens (2015) and the European-funded study would agree, however, is that transition is open-ended, experimental process.

The provision of adequate resources is a prerequisite for effective policy implementation. Local authorities in the UK and many other European countries would almost certainly say that at times of austerity, concerns of financial caution are likely to predominate. There is another constraint, moreover. Sustainable development is about accountability to future generations. Future generations have no voice and no vote. As a result, local authorities may be torn between democratic responsiveness and promoting 'green' issues. An international review, undertaken by Bai (2007), drawing on numerous other studies, suggests that local authorities are most effective where they tackle problems or grasp opportunities that they would face in any case. The limitations of local authorities have long been recognised in Britain in other fields such as housing policy (Malpass and Murie, 1982, 178) and have led to the use of many measures—legal obligations, inspection regimes, performance targets, agreed or approved plans, financial incentives and grant aid—to ensure a consistent and strong response.

National governments must, in other words, support and encourage local action if a substantial shift in policy is to be achieved.

Local authorities are able to span both conventional economically driven transition pathways, based on markets and incentives, and their alternative, collective alternatives, based on local groups and communities. Much depends, however, on whether the policy is a broadly based exercise in promoting sustainable development or a concern with climate change and carbon reduction alone. Community groups are well adapted to a broad policy agenda in favour of sustainable development. They may take an interest in recycling, healthy eating and healthy lifestyles, countering fuel poverty and managing local green space as well as climate change. They can also become involved in projects in schools or demonstration projects of renewable or energy-saving technologies and so contribute to a long-term culture change. In doing all this, moreover, community groups can serve as a bridge between energy policy, infrastructure measures and policies for neighbourhood regeneration. Some community initiatives, for example, the promotion of healthy lifestyles in terms of walking and cycling, promote energy savings and carbon reduction, either directly or indirectly. Others, such as reducing fuel poverty or recycling, do not.

National transition programmes raise again questions about their scope—whether they are only concerned with carbon reduction rather than sustainable development, writ large. The carbon delivery plan (DECC 2011) has, for example, a relatively narrow focus and makes no reference to community initiatives other than to the former Community Energy Savings Programme intended to stimulate home improvements in deprived neighbourhoods. This latter was a relatively small programme that was run by the energy companies and that failed to reach its carbon savings targets, as was noted in the national evaluation of the policy (Ofgem-eserve 2013). The programme was not controlled or initiated by local communities and, by virtue of its business orientation, was arguably not a community programme at all.

Pathways that involve incentives, labelling, regulation or nudging all involve governmental actors. These pathways are generally set by the national government, because they seek to influence markets that are national or international, rather than local. Moreover, private investors dislike local variations as these increase transaction costs and fragment their efforts. Co-evolution in the language of transition management means essentially central government working with manufacturers and investors. Co-evolution is not easily applied either to the production or the upgrading of the built environment owing to the very large number of potentially relevant actors. Even so, government can still lay down a framework for transition.

The various measures include the voluntary adoption of environmental standards, adoption through regulation and the use of private/public sector methods of financing. In the conventional pathway, innovation in technology is sufficient, so long as the consumer is aware of the advantages and is given adequate financial incentive to adopt that technology. In the alternative pathway, innovation follows policy, through the direct intervention of government, including regulation.

Green labelling is arguably the most common method of encouraging voluntary adoption. Green labelling 'nudges' both consumer decisions and producers in the direction of environmental sustainability. They make the environmental impact of consumer and investment choices visible and have a potential educative function, so long as the rationale of the label is transparent. Since green labelling covers energy consumption, for example of energy goods, they also tell consumers and the public when they can expect savings in running a home (Thaler & Sunstein 2008, 194).

For new urban development, the labels include codes for different types of non-residential buildings (in the UK, the BREEAM rating system)[7] and housing (the former Code for Sustainable Homes [CfSH] [CLG 2008] in England and Wales). The labels provide a degree of assurance that the claims made about sustainability have been undertaken in a consistent and responsible manner. Sustainability labels in housing and building do not guarantee quality in relation to convenience or liveability, however, and this is a disadvantage from the viewpoint of consumers. For this reason, in housing schemes, environmental code levels have rarely if ever been used as a selling point by developers. In the case of non-residential buildings, the labels are generally used for prestige schemes.[8]

Adherence to the standards included in a code implies a higher quality of product and therefore a higher cost. Over time, the additional costs associated with low energy, low carbon and sustainable housing are likely to diminish as developers and the construction industry become more familiar with the relevant techniques. Evidence cited by the House of Commons (HoC 2013), for example, suggests that, in the UK, in relation to higher levels of the former Code for Sustainable Homes, costs were already starting to diminish. Costs had also declined for the related, zero carbon house building standard (Zero Carbon Hub 2014).

The cost differences of higher quality building are unlikely to disappear completely, however. Moreover, the ability of the land market to absorb higher building costs is dependent on local land values and these vary substantially from place to place and region to region (Goodchild & Walshaw 2011). In addition, for lower value development, including low-cost housing and non-for-profit schemes, a reallocation of costs towards land owners may be impractical, irrespective of location. In such circumstances, the additional costs are more likely to fall on consumers and the viability of projects may be affected. Concern about costs and the complexity of the CfSH was a reason why the government announced in 2013 that it was minded to downgrade its role in England and Wales, effectively removing the ability of local authorities to impose any level of the code on developers (HoC 2013). Concern about costs also led to a progressive dilution of zero carbon housing standards until the relevant policy commitments were scrapped in the summer of 2015.[9] Increased regulation is a powerful way of changing development and building practices. Arguably, it is the only sure way in the context of a fragmented building industry. The absence of effective regulation is therefore likely to hinder the achievement of the carbon reduction targets, as expressed for example in the UK national carbon delivery plan (DECC 2011).

Even if all new homes and all new buildings were regulated to the highest possible standards, the question remains about how to upgrade and modernise the existing urban fabric. Contrary to an assessment by Killip (2013), the technology of energy upgrading can still be improved—for example the bulkiness of insulation material in lining the interior of a home or the form and efficiency of solar panels. Technology remains a constraint. Equally, however, non-technological social and economic constraints are also significant.

In particular, Stern (2007, 412) predicted that property owners of all types would not generally be interested in financing unsubsidised energy upgrades owing to the long time-spans over which any financial benefits are likely to materialise. Trends in domestic energy consumption, as shown in Figure 9.2, suggest that owners at least undertake piecemeal improvements, for example as elements of a property, say the boiler or the window frames, come to the end of their life or have to be replaced for other reasons. However, piecemeal improvements to elements do not amount to extensive remodelling. The experience of energy retrofitting amongst home owners in Germany (Galvin 2014) and in the context of the loans offered in England and Wales under the short lived 'Green Deal' policy (2013–15) have shown suggest disappointing rates of investment (Marchand et al. 2015).[10] The Green Deal also showed that the same lack of interest applies to private landlords. In rented property, and this would also include commercial property, owners are likely to consider whether they can recoup the cost of investment through higher rents or possibly through an expanded market. If they cannot charge higher rents, the economic case for investment disappears.

Given the reluctance of owners to invest, some external stimulus is necessary and in terms of economic measures these can be divided broadly into those that raise awareness such as energy performance certificates and those that provide some form of financial help such as investment grants or subsidised feed-in tariffs. Lund (2007) suggests that, in general, measures to promote awareness are more cost effective to the public purse, but have less impact in delivering results. The constraints will almost certainly require more direct, local contact between renewal agencies and the owners, including landlords and occupiers, as is the implication of practice theory.

Nudging can also make some difference to energy consumption, even in the absence of building improvements. For example, a social housing initiative in Camden is reported as having secured a saving of 9 percent in energy consumption through combining a positive message about energy saving with relevant information about good practice. In this case, the positive message consisted of providing additional information about the savings achieved by other households in the same estate, the implication that any laggardly households could do the same.[11] A savings of 9 percent is significant in terms of energy bills or energy use at peak times. For example, in the electricity sector, such a savings, if permanent, would avoid the provision of additional generating capacity. It is not enough to achieve ambitious carbon reduction targets, however. It is also unclear whether the change was temporary or permanent.

A similar range of energy savings is apparent from 'soft' measures in the transport sector. Soft measures have been defined by Cairns et al. (2008) to include workplace travel plans, car sharing, teleworking, school travel plans, teleconferencing, online grocery shopping, local collection points, personalised travel planning, public transport information and marketing travel awareness campaigns and car clubs. All of these are likely to involve a combination of local and national initiatives, but given their scale are likely to be initiated by the central government.

The impact, this same study shows, depends on their intensity—that is to say on the level of expenditure—and on whether they are combined with hard measures such as physical improvements to transport infrastructure or operations, control of road space and economic measures such as changes in price or travel costs. The authors comment (ibid., 598):

> with lower intensity application, and/or without support from complementary hard measures, there was scope for soft measures to reduce traffic levels, but not very much: perhaps 4% or 5% at the National level, with a range around this according to local circumstances. With higher intensity application (and emphasizing the importance of supportive hard measures either by assumption or explicitly), the estimated potential for soft factor interventions was to reduce traffic levels by 10–15% as a national average, and 15–20% in favourable local conditions.

The recognition of a mixed strategy is well taken. Soft measures involve voluntary change and the promotion of travel choices and, as practice theory insists, the promotion of choice is ineffective once routines become habitual and part of daily life. For example, when consumers in Britain are asked in surveys how they have responded to the threat of climate change, the most commonly cited measures are those that involve 'little effort or sacrifice' (Whitmarsh 2009, 21), measures such as switching off lights or undertaking waste recycling. Abandoning the private car is not one of the more commonly mentioned, easy to achieve, popular measures. In terms of popularity, it also lags behind measures to improve domestic energy efficiency.

Global and international pathways are more general and abstract in character. Within Europe, the European Commission acts as a supranational state within defined spheres of competence. Promoting the use of renewable energy sources and, by extension, promoting energy efficiency are, moreover, major themes of European policy, being, for example, incorporated into EU directive 2009/28/EC and the national energy action plans that are associated with that directive.[12] Outside Europe, however, international agreements are either weak or absent or are still in the early stages of their development and application.

The question remains, therefore, about how far a single national state can be expected to go in the direction of green policies, if this involves a sacrifice for the local population. The experience of ecological modernisation points to the pressures of international competition as a constraint on industrial pollution controls (Jänicke 2008) and by extension on the use of carbon taxes for energy intensive industry. Fears about job losses and a loss of growth can be greatly overdone, however. For such issues as reduced domestic energy consumption and reduced personal car use, the impact on international competitiveness is almost certainly limited and perhaps non-existent. The Nordic countries possess highly competitive cities with an energy efficient housing stock by international standards and, commonly, extensive public transport networks. Likewise, examples can be found in Asia of wealthy, highly competitive cities with low levels of car use (Olszewski 2007).

In any case, an absence of formal agreements does not prevent a start being made. (Ostrom 2010). Nation states, including groupings of nation states such as the European Union, may still be prepared to go some way to initiate relevant policies in the expectation of reciprocal action by others. Further, even apart from the concern about global warming, fears about the security of fuel supply offer a reason why governments might wish to reduce dependency on fossil fuels in favour of renewable sources and reduced energy consumption (Jamasb & Pollitt 2008). However, the expectation of reciprocal action and the search for energy security are weak arguments, compared to the ethical case for action. Pollution and the emission of greenhouse gases, many of which are generated by unsustainable forms of production and consumption, already cross boundaries. All countries, but especially the richest countries with the highest levels of consumption, have therefore an extended responsibility that includes, but goes beyond, the local and national (Roy 2011).

## Notes

1 'Transition Town Totnes', consulted February 2016 at www.transitiontowntotnes.org/.
2 'OECD work on green growth', available on the OECD website, consulted March 2010 at www.oecd.org/document/10/0,3343,en_2649_37465_44076170_1_1_1_1,00.html.

3 'Décroissance: un "mot-obus" contre le consensus', at the website of GoodPlanet. info, consulted February 2011 at www.goodplanet.info/Economie/Decroissance/Decroissance/%28theme%29/2386.
4 'Parti pour la décroissance', consulted February 2011 at www.partipourladecroissance.net/?cat=10.
5 Calculated by the author from Table TRA8904 of the traffic statistics of the UK Department of Transport, consulted January 2016 at www.gov.uk/government/collections/road-traffic-statistics.
6 My thanks are due to Jonathan Mobbs, an MSc student at Sheffield Hallam University for providing information on 'Green Suffolk'.
7 Building Research Establishment (collective author) Homepage of BREEAM as updated, [online] URL: www.breeam.com/index.jsp (consulted June 2016).
8 'Environmental assessment methods workshop: from buildings to communities'. Report of a workshop held at the University of Reading, 17 July 2013, in collaboration with the Building Research Establishment, consulted March 2014 at www.reading.ac.uk/CME/NewsItems/2014/cme-news-Environmental-Assessment-Methods-what-can-we-learn-Report-published.aspx.
9 'Scrapping zero-carbon homes is senseless policy vandalism', at the website of 'The Conversation', consulted November 2015 at http://theconversation.com/scrapping-zero-carbon-homes-is-senseless-policy-vandalism-44723.
10 'Government kills off flagship green deal for home insulation', *The Guardian*, 23 July 2012, consulted January 2016 at www.theguardian.com/environment/2015/jul/23/uk-ceases-financing-of-green-deal.
11 'Can nudges help to cut household energy consumption?' *The Guardian Professional Network*, 27 January 2012, at the website of *The Guardian*, consulted February 2012 at www.guardian.co.uk/sustainable-business/behaviour-change-energy-consumption.
12 Official Journal of the European Union: 5.6.2009: Directive 2009/28/EC of the European Parliament and of the Council of 23 April 2009, 'National Action Plans', at the website of the European Commission, consulted March 2015 at http://ec.europa.eu/energy/en/topics/renewable-energy/national-action-plans.

## References

Ascher, F. (2001). *Les nouveaux principes de l'urbanisme*. La Tour d'Aigues: Editions de l'Aube.
Bai, X. (2007). 'Integrating global environmental concerns into urban management. The scale and readiness arguments.' *Journal of Industrial Ecology*, 11, 15–29.
Bartiaux, F., Gram-Hanssen, K., Fonseca, P., Ozoliņa, L. & Christensen, T. H. (2014). 'A practice–theory approach to homeowners' energy retrofits in four European areas'. *Building Research & Information*, 42(4), 525–38.
Béal, V. and Pinson, G. (2014). 'From the governance of sustainability to the management of climate change: Reshaping urban policies and central–local relations in France'. *Journal of Environmental Policy & Planning*, 17:3, 402–19.
Beck, U. (1992). *Risk society: towards a new modernity*. London: Sage Publications. (German original 1986).
Blowers, A. (1997). 'Environmental policy: ecological modernisation or the risk society?' *Urban Studies*, 34:5–6, 845–71.
BRE—Building Research Establishment (collective author) (2013). *BREEAM international technical manual*. Watford: The BRE, [online] URL: www.breeam.org/page.jsp?id=109.

Bulkeley, H. & Betsill, M. (2013). 'Revisiting the urban politics of climate change'. *Environmental Politics*, 22:1, 136–54.

Cairns, S., Sloman, L., Newson, C., Anable, J., Kirkbride, A. & Goodwin, P. (2008). 'Smarter choices: assessing the potential to achieve traffic reduction using "soft measures"'. *Transport Reviews*, 28:5, 593–618.

Çalışkan, K. & Callon, M. (2010). 'Economization, part 2: a research programme for the study of markets'. *Economy and Society*, 39:1, 1–32.

CLG—Department for Communities and Local Government (2008). *The code for sustainable homes: setting the standard in sustainability for new homes.* London: DCLG.

Coenen, L., Benneworth, P. & Truffer, B. (2012). 'Toward a spatial perspective on sustainability transitions'. *Research Policy*, 41:6, 968–79.

DECC—Department of Energy and Climate Change (corporate author) (2010). *2050 pathways analysis call for evidence: part 2 – detailed sectoral trajectories,* [online] URL: https://econsultation.decc.gov.uk/decc-executive/2050_pathways/ (consulted March 2015).

DECC—Department of Energy and Climate Change (corporate author) (2011). *The carbon plan: delivering our low carbon future.* Presented to Parliament pursuant to Sections 12 and 14 of the Climate Change Act 2008. Amended 2 December 2011 from the version laid before Parliament on 1 December 2011. London: Crown Copyright.

DECC—Department of Energy and Climate Change (corporate author) (2013). *The future of heating: meeting the challenge.* London: DECC, [online] URL: www.gov.uk/government/publications/the-future-of-heating-meeting-the-challenge (consulted June 2016).

DECC—Department of Energy and Climate Change (corporate author) (2015). *Energy consumption in the UK,* [online] URL: www.gov.uk/government/uploads/system/uploads/attachment_data/file/449134/ECUK_Chapter_3_-_Domestic_factsheet.pdf (consulted June 2016).

Dreborg, K. H. (1996). 'Essence of backcasting'. *Futures*, 28:9, 813–28.

Frankfurt School—UNEP Centre/BNEF (collective author) (2014). *Global trends in renewable energy investment.* (Report updated annually) Frankfurt School of Finance & Management gGmb, [online] URL: www.unep.org/pdf/Green_energy_2013-Key_findings.pdf (consulted June 2016).

Galvin, R. (2014). 'Why German homeowners are reluctant to retrofit'. *Building Research & Information*, 42:4, 398–408.

Geddes, P. (1915). *Cities in evolution.* London: Williams and Norgate.

Geels, F. W. (2002). 'Technological transitions as evolutionary reconfiguration processes: a multi-level perspective and a case-study'. *Research Policy*, 31:8, 1257–74.

Geels, F. W. (2005). 'Processes and patterns in transitions and system innovations: Refining the co-evolutionary multi-level perspective'. *Technological Forecasting and Social Change*, 72:6, 681–96.

Geels, F. W. (2011). 'The multi-level perspective on sustainability transitions: Responses to seven criticisms'. *Environmental Innovation and Societal Transitions*, 1:1, 24–40.

Geels, F. W. and Schot, J. (2007) 'Typology of sociotechnical transition pathways'. *Research Policy* 36, 399–417.

Goodchild, B. & Walshaw, A. (2011). 'Towards zero carbon homes in England? From inception to partial implementation'. *Housing Studies*, 26:6, 933–49.

Goodchild, B., O'Flaherty, F. & Ambrose, A. (2014). 'Inside the eco-home: using video to understand the implications of innovative housing'. *Housing, Theory and Society*, 31:3, 334–52.

Hajer, M. A. (1995). *The Politics of environmental discourse: ecological modernization and the policy process*. Oxford: Oxford University Press.

Hawkey, D., Webb, J. & Winskel, M. (2013). 'Organisation and governance of urban energy systems: district heating and cooling in the UK'. *Journal of Cleaner Production*, 50, 22–31.

Heiskanen, E., Kivisaari, S., Lovio, R. & Mickwitz, P. (2009). 'Designed to travel? Transition management encounters environmental and innovation policy histories in Finland'. *Policy Sciences*, 42:4, 409–27.

Hendriks, C. (2009). 'Policy design without democracy? Making democratic sense of transition management'. *Policy Sciences*, 42:4, 341–68.

Hirsch, F. (1977). *The social limits to growth*. London: Routledge and Kegan Paul.

HoC—House of Commons Environmental Audit Committee (collective author) (2013). *Eighth report: code for sustainable homes and the housing standards review*, HC192. London: House of Commons.

Höjer, M. & Mattsson, L. -G. (2000). 'Determinism and backcasting in future studies'. *Futures*, 32:7, 613–34

Höjer, M., Gullberg, A. & Pettersson, R. (2011). 'Backcasting images of the future city – time and space for sustainable development in Stockholm'. *Technological Forecasting and Social Change*, 78:5, 819–34.

Hong, S. H., Gilbertson, J., Oreszczyn, T., Green, G. & Ridley, I. (2009). 'A field study of thermal comfort in low-income dwellings in England before and after energy efficient refurbishment'. *Building and Environment*, 44(6), 1228–36.

Hult, A. (2015). 'The circulation of Swedish urban sustainability practices: to China and back'. *Environment and Planning A*, 47:3, 537–53.

IEA—International Energy Agency (2013). *Transition to sustainable buildings: strategies and opportunities to 2050*. Paris: IEA/ OECD, [online] URL: www.iea.org/publications/freepublications/publication/Building2013_free.pdf (consulted March 2015).

Jamasb, T. & Pollitt, M. (2008). 'Security of supply and regulation of energy networks'. *Energy Policy*, 36:12, 4584–89.

Jänicke, M. (2008). 'Ecological modernisation: new perspectives'. *Journal of Cleaner Production*, 16, 557–65.

Jansson, J., Marell, A. & Nordlund, A. (2010). 'Green consumer behavior: determinants of curtailment and eco-innovation adoption'. *Journal of Consumer Marketing*, 27:4, 358–70.

Kallis, G. (2013). 'Societal metabolism, working hours and degrowth: a comment on Sorman and Giampietro'. *Journal of Cleaner Production*, 38, 94–8.

Kemp, R., Loorbach, R. & Rotmans, J. (2007). 'Transition management as a model for managing processes of co-evolution towards sustainable development'. *International Journal of Sustainable Development & World Ecology*, 14:1, 78–91.

Killip, G. (2013). 'Transition management using a market transformation approach: lessons for theory, research, and practice from the case of low-carbon housing refurbishment in the UK'. *Environment and Planning C: Government and Policy*, 31:5, 876–92.

Latour, B. (1997). *Nous n'avons jamais été modernes*. Paris: Éditions La Découverte.
Latour, B. (2009). 'A collective of humans and non-humans following Daedalus's labyrinth'. In: Kaplan, D. M. (ed.), *Readings in the philosophy of technology*. Lanham, MD: Rowman & Littlefield Publishers, 156–68.
Lefèbvre. H. (1976). *The survival of capitalism: reproduction of the relations of production*. London: Frank Bryant (French original 1973).
Lindblom, C. E. (1973). 'The science of muddling through'. In: Faludi, A. (ed.), *A reader in planning theory*. Oxford: Pergamon, 151–69 (original 1959).
Lissandrello, E. & Grin, J. (2011). 'Reflexive planning as design and work: lessons from the port of Amsterdam'. *Planning Theory & Practice*, 12:2, 223–48.
Loorbach, D. (2010). 'Transition management for sustainable development: a prescriptive, complexity-based governance framework'. *Governance: an International Journal of Policy, Administration, and Institutions*, 23:1, 161–83.
Loorbach, D. & Rotmans, J. (2010). 'The practice of transition management: examples and lessons from four distinct cases'. *Futures*, 42(3), 237–46.
Loorbach, D. & van Raak, R. (2005). 'Governance in complexity: a multi-level policy-framework based on complex systems thinking'. Paper for the conference *Lof der Verwarring*. Rotterdam, [online] URL: www.drift.eur.nl/?p=260 (consulted April 2014).
Lund, P. D. (2007). 'Effectiveness of policy measures in transforming the energy system'. *Energy Policy*, 35:1, 627–39.
Malpass, P. & Murie, A. (1982). *Housing policy and practice*. London: Macmillan Press.
Marchand, R. D., Koh, L. S. C. & Morris, J. C. (2015). 'Delivering energy efficiency and carbon reduction schemes in England: lessons from Green Deal Pioneer Places'. *Energy Policy*, 84, 96–106.
Meadows, D. H., Meadows, D. L., Randers, J. & Behrens III, W. W. (1972). *The limits to growth: a report for the Club of Rome's project on the predicament of mankind*. New York: Universe Books.
MEEDM—Ministère de l'Ecologie, de l'Fnergie, du Développement durable et de la Mer (collective author) (2010). *Appel a propositions de recherches prospectives: programme transition(s) a long terme vers une economie ecologique?*, [online] URL: www.developpement-durable.gouv.fr/spip.php?page=article&id_article=16574 (consulted March 2014).
Mol, A. P. J. & Spaargaren, G. (1993). 'Environment, modernity and the risk-society: the apocalyptic horizon of environmental reform'. *International Sociology*, 8:4, 431–59.
Moloney, S. & Horne, R. (2015). 'Low carbon urban transitioning: from local experimentation to urban transformation?' *Sustainability*, 7:3, 2437–53.
Mourik, R. & Rotmann, S. (on behalf of the International Energy Agency Demand Side Management Group) (2013). *Closing the loop – behaviour change in DSM: from theory to practice, Task 24 final report*, [online] URL: www.ieadsm.org/ViewTask.aspx?ID=17&Task=24&Sort=0 (consulted March 2014).
Ofgem-eserve (collective author) (2013). *The final report of the Community Energy Saving Programme (CESP) 2009–2012*. London: Ofgem, [online] URL: www.ofgem.gov.uk/ofgem-publications/58763/cesp-final-report-2013final-300413.pdf.
Olszewski, P. S. (2007). 'Singapore motorisation restraint and its implications on travel behaviour and urban sustainability'. *Transportation*, 34:3, 319–35.

Ostrom, E. (2010). 'Polycentric systems for coping with collective action and global environmental change'. *Global Environmental Change*, 20:4, 550–7.

Paredis, E. (2008). *Transition management in Flanders: policy context, first results and surfacing tensions*. Centrum voor Duurzame Ontwikkeling/Centre for Sustainable Development Working Paper 6, Universiteit Gent/Ghent University, Belgium, [online] URL: https://biblio.ugent.be/input/download?func=downloadFile&recordOId=908600&fileOId=908606 (consulted October 2012).

Poortinga, W., Spence, A., Whitmarsh, L., Capstick, S. & Pidgeon, N. F. (2011). 'Uncertain climate: an investigation into public scepticism about anthropogenic climate change'. *Global Environmental Change*, 21:3, 1015–24.

Roorda, C., Wittmayer, J., Henneman, P. Steenbergen, F. van, Frantzeskaki, N. & Loorbach, D. (2014). *Transition management in the urban context: guidance manual*. Rotterdam: DRIFT, Erasmus University Rotterdam.

Rotmans, J. & Kemp, R. (2003). *Managing societal transitions: dilemmas and uncertainties: the Dutch energy case-study*. OECD Workshop on the Benefits of Climate Policy: Improving Information for Policy Makers. Paris: OECD ENV/EPOC/GSP(2003)15/FINAL.

Roy, A. 2011. Commentary placing planning in the world – transnationalism as practice and critique. *Journal of Planning Education and Research*, 31:4, 406–15.

Rumpala, Y. (2004). 'Expertise économique et gestion publique des problèmes environnementaux: mobilisation et utilisation d'un savoir particulier dans un champ de l'univers politico-administratif français'. *L'Année de la régulation*, 8, 2004–2005. Paris: Presses de Science-Po, 77–108.

Russell, S. (1993). 'Writing energy history: explaining the neglect of CHP/DH in Britain'. *British Journal for the History of Science*, 26:1, 33–54.

Rybczynski, W. (1987). *Home: a short history of an idea*. New York: Penguin USA.

Sahakian, M. & Wilhite, H. (2014). 'Making practice theory practicable: towards more sustainable forms of consumption'. *Journal of Consumer Culture*, 14, 25–44.

Schatzki, T. (2002). *The Site of the Social. A Philosophical Account of the Constitution of Social Life and Change*. University Park, PA: Pennsylvania State University Press.

Schumacher, E. E. F. (1973). *Small is beautiful*. New York: Harper & Row.

Schwanen, T., Banister, D. & Anable, J. (2012). 'Rethinking habits and their role in behaviour change: the case of low-carbon mobility'. *Journal of Transport Geography*, 24, 522–32.

Scitovsky, T. (1976). *The joyless economy*. Oxford: Oxford University Press.

Shorrock L. (2003). 'A detailed analysis of the historical role of energy efficiency in reducing carbon emissions from the UK housing stock'. Paper presented at the *European Council for an Energy Efficient Economy 2003 Summer Study*, La Colle sur Loup, 295–302, [online] URL: www.eceee.org/conference_proceedings/eceee.

Shorrock, L. S., Henderson, J. & Utley, J. I. (2005). *Reducing carbon emissions from the UK housing stock*. The BRE, DEFRA, [online] URL: http://projects.bre.co.uk/PDF_files/ReducingCarbonEmissionsHousingv3.pdf.

Shove, E. (2003). 'Converging conventions of comfort, cleanliness and convenience'. *Journal of Consumer Policy*, 26:4, 395–418.

Shove, E. (2010). 'Beyond the ABC: climate change policy and theories of social change'. *Environment and Planning A*, 42:6, 1273–85.

Shove, E. & Walker, G. (2007). 'CAUTION! Transitions ahead: politics, practice, and sustainable transition management'. *Environment and Planning A*, 39:4, 763–70.

Shove, E. & Walker, G. (2010). 'Governing transitions in the sustainability of everyday life'. *Research Policy*, 39:4, 471–76.

Smith A. & Kern, F. (2007). *The transitions discourse in the ecological modernisation of the Netherlands*. WP 160, SPRU, University of Sussex, Brighton, [online] URL: www.sussex.ac.uk/spru/documents/sewp160.pdf (consulted March 2014).

Sorman, A. H. & Giampietro, M. (2013). 'The energetic metabolism of societies and the degrowth paradigm: analyzing biophysical constraints and realities'. *Journal of Cleaner Production*, 38, 80–93.

Sorrell, S., Dimitropoulos, J. & Sommerville, M. (2009). 'Empirical estimates of the direct rebound effect: a review'. *Energy Policy*, 37, 1356–71.

Stern, N. (2007). *The economics of climate change*. London: HM Treasury and Cambridge, UK: Cambridge University Press.

Svane, Ö. (2008). 'Situations of opportunity – Hammarby Sjöstad and Stockholm City's process of environmental management'. *Corporate Social Responsibility and Environmental Management*, 15:2, 76–88.

Thaler, R. and Sunstein, C. (2008). *Nudge* New Haven, CT: Yale University Press.

Vandevyvere, H. & Nevens, F. (2015). 'Lost in transition or geared for the S-curve? An analysis of Flemish transition trajectories with a focus on energy use and buildings'. *Sustainability*, 7:3, 2415–36.

Verbeek, P. P. (2006). 'Acting artefacts'. In: Verbeek, P. P. & Slob, A. F. (eds.), *User behavior and technology development: shaping sustainable relations between consumers and technologies*. Dordrecht, The Netherlands: Springer, 53–60.

Voisey, H., Beuermann, C., Sverdrup, L. A. & O'Riordan, T. (1996). 'The political significance of Local Agenda 21: the early stages of some European experience'. *Local Environment*, 1:1, 33–50.

Wangel, J. (2011). 'Exploring social structures and agency in backcasting studies for sustainable development'. *Technological Forecasting and Social Change*, 78:5, 872–82.

Warde, A. (2005). 'Consumption and theories of practice'. *Journal of Consumer Culture*, 5:2, 131–53.

While, A., Jonas, A. E. G. & Gibbs, D. (2010). 'From sustainable development to carbon control: eco-state restructuring and the politics of urban and regional development'. *Transactions of the Institute of British Geographers*, 35:1, 76–93.

Whitmarsh, L. (2009). 'Behavioural responses to climate change: asymmetry of intentions and impact'. *Journal of Environmental Psychology*, 29:1, 13–23.

Zero Carbon Hub (collective author) (2014). *Cost analysis – meeting the zero carbon standard*. London: Zero Carbon Hub, [online] URL: www.zerocarbonhub.org/recent-publications (consulted June 2014).

# 10 Sustainable Urbanism

Whatever the details, collective forms of planning amount to a regime, as understood in transition management as a governing network of actors (Eames et al. 2013). However, urban planning is distinct from transition management as it is not based on sectors of the economy or on classifications of energy users. Instead, urban planning, like spatial planning in general, is a distinctive type of multi-criteria regime that co-ordinates a variety of different sectors within a defined area and that, amongst environmental criteria, covers resilience, risk avoidance and environmental protection as well as energy reduction.

Despite the repeated references to sustainable development in UK planning guidance and policy statements, international reviews of environmental transitions either say little or nothing about urban planning or they complain about the tendency of governments to ignore the potential role of either urban planning or of closely related forms of planning as a co-ordinating mechanism (Mickwitz et al, 2009; BMVBS 2010; Roggema 2010, 57). Transition management operates through a multiplicity of different themes and policy fields of which spatial planning is only one and commonly only a minor element of national and local energy action plans. The way that planning in Britain has become defined as a regulatory exercise only also limits its apparent relevance. The issue then becomes one of obtaining planning permission for the installation of renewable energy sources or for changes to the building stock and road layout and dealing with the local effects.

Partly because of this passive, short-term orientation, professional planning is also sometimes said to have lost confidence and to be incapable of long-term imaginative thinking in relation to carbon savings and related policy agendas (Ratcliffe & Krawczyk 2011). Such assessments ignore the potential of staff to use their imagination, if encouraged to do so. Spatial planning has, moreover, a particular role in transition exactly because it deals with local issues and has the potential to act as an educational device showing the implications of climate change and sustainable development for a community.[1] The preparation of plans, even idealised demonstration plans, shows that alternatives are possible, helps to visualise those alternatives and helps to show how towns and cities can construct and present themselves as responsible institutional actors. In the words of an OECD report: 'Part of the cost associated with low carbon, climate resilient projects comes from the lack of knowledge, awareness and capacity from the private and consumer sector' (Corfee-Morlot et al. 2012, 51).

Conceptualising and envisaging environmental alternatives implies, in turn, the existence of some form of 'sustainable urbanism'. The latter term 'urbanism' means essentially physical planning, without the association with either statutory town planning or economic intervention. Green urbanism is another possible label (Beatley 2000; Beck 2013). Whatever the label, however, sustainable urbanism is distinct from 'new urbanism', a term of US origin that indicates a concern with urban design and the visual and aesthetic aspects of place making.

Admittedly, sustainable urbanism and new urbanism overlap each other. Both share a dislike of 20th century urban and especially suburban forms, for example. Interviews with international consultants, undertaken by Rapoport (2014), suggest, in addition, that commercial interpretations of sustainable urbanism have to incorporate conventional notions of marketability, liveability and quality as a means of appealing to commercial and political clients who remain interested in economic growth. Local and national consultants are unlikely to be different, if only because they also have to sell their product to clients, including government. The emphasis in sustainable urbanism remains distinct, however, as it poses a series of new questions about environmental impacts, energy use and the behaviour of city users of all types. Though always constrained and always subject to concern about the adequacy of measures, the balance of policy priorities has, in any case, already shifted. Concern about climate change has started to stimulate measures for energy efficiency and, to some extent, demand reduction in relation to motor traffic, of a type that would have seemed impossibly radical in, say, the 1980s.

## Models and Rules Reconsidered

'Urbanism', whether new urbanism or green urbanism, means, in turn, a revival and reconsideration of the long-standing distinction between models and rules. The former, model-based planning, involves spatial patterns and distinct urban forms. The latter, rule-based planning, involves criteria, standards and procedures. The former has the advantage of facilitating the creation of images of the good city. The latter, the elaboration of rules, has the advantage, in principle, of flexibility to a specific case.

To an extent, and despite their differences, the model and the rule can be converted into one another. Models can also be converted into a series of criteria and standards, once the basic characteristics are established. The application of rules will also generate a model, so long as the criteria and weighting systems remain constant. Equally, models and rules can be applied separately and in various combinations—a characteristic that also makes their presentation read, on occasion, like a catalogue of alternatives and considerations. Nevertheless, at an analytical level, the two approaches remain distinct.

## Model-Based Planning: The Compact City and Its Alternatives

Sustainable development emerged in part as a reaction against overconsumption of resources and as part of this involved a reaction against the excessive use of land in the form of urban sprawl. Discussions in physical planning followed suit and sought a compact alternative to the 20th-century city. Most of the early debates about sustainable development, certainly before about 2000, were dominated by support for compact urban forms and this was also reinforced by considerations of urban design and place making. (See, for example, the 'Green Paper on the Urban Environment' by the European Community [as the European Union was then called] [CEC 1990], the Congress for New Urbanism established in the US in 1993[2] and in Britain the Urban Task Force [UTC 1999]).

The compact city continues, moreover, to be promoted in the international planning literature, notably by the OECD (2012) in a study that shows that some form of compact city policy is now the conventional wisdom in economically advanced countries. This latter is notable, in addition, for a call to find ways of transforming compactness as a spatial model into measures that would permit urban sprawl to be monitored, with national and international statistics being presented on a comparable basis. The monitoring of urban sprawl and the evaluation of the impact of compact cities is notable by its absence in most countries and the use of consistent, international measures of compactness are completely absent.

In contrast, from about 2005, the compact city in Britain became overtaken by other models and other priorities, notably in the past few years by proposals to revive the concept of the garden city and to apply this to the development of suburban extensions (CLG 2014).[3] Reasons for the shift away from the compact city, or to use the name of the relevant policy, the shift away from 'Urban Renaissance', has seldom been explicitly discussed, but is probably linked to concerns about marketability and image and the influence of an entrepreneurial, growth-oriented policy climate, in other words the same economic and political forces that have led to the demise of the Code for Sustainable Homes and the zero carbon housing standard in England.

In addition, the Urban Renaissance policy agenda had a specific limitation in that, in Britain, it triggered the overdevelopment of flats outside of London, this being exacerbated by local property speculation (Goodchild 2013; URBED 2014, 6). In England, excluding London where special factors apply, a house with a garden remains the preference of families with children (Bramley et al. 2009; Goodchild 2008, 210–14). The land savings of urban containment, in any case, mostly arise through the prevention of low densities, say less than 30 dwellings per hectare, a figure consistent with the use of terraces and semis, rather than through requiring the development of higher densities of low or high rise flats. Moreover, the risk of a proliferation of low-density housing development has been greatly reduced by continued inflation in land prices

The high and increasing cost of land in and around major cities also works against another interpretation of sustainable urbanism—the dispersed, green, self-reliant city (Eames et al. 2013) characterised by a combination of autonomous or semi-autonomous neighbourhoods (Scoffham & Vale 1996); autonomous housing (Vale & Vale 1975) with *in situ* technology able to generate energy (from solar cells, wind turbines and ground source heat pumps) and filter waste (through reed beds); extensive areas of parkland (Beatley 2011); and the promotion of local food production (Hopkins 2000). However, high land costs are not the only objection to dispersed green urbanism. Irrespective of the workings of the land market, high levels of land consumption are inconsistent with the necessity of accommodating a growing urban population as is characteristic of most countries in the world, including those in Britain.

There are, moreover, objections in principle to proposals for an autonomous or semi-autonomous house and neighbourhood. Existing energy and transport networks are already in place and are exceptionally useful to consumers. Energy networks can, moreover, be converted to the use of renewable energy. Transport networks are more difficult to convert, owing to the dominance of vehicular traffic. However, searching for some notion of local or neighbourhood autonomy does not easily square with the requirement of people to work and travel elsewhere. On a more general point, the principle of autonomy is also flawed in suggesting that individuals and communities might prosper if isolated.

The compact city has, in principle, two main advantages for environmental sustainability—a spatial advantage in promoting compact cities, so reducing the impact on the countryside and preventing the fragmentation of landscapes and habitats, and a transport advantage in discouraging car use. Discouraging car use is likely to lead to reduced energy demand, but is also important in promoting the safety of pedestrians in urban areas and in reducing noise and pollution. A third, claimed advantage, namely that compact cities produce higher density, more energy-efficient building forms is less easily demonstrated. We take each aspect in turn, starting with the spatial.

To an extent, planning in Britain has long promoted compact cities. For example, the green belt dates to 1955, the date of the first national green belt policy, with local initiatives in London and Sheffield and probably elsewhere dating from the 1930s. Over time, the green belt policy has become an exceptionally well-known and supported aspect of planning in Britain, with areas around all the main urban centres. Green belts were initially conceived as a means of keeping different settlements separate and preserving their identity (Hall et al. 1973, 72–80; Prior & Raemaekers 2007). Over time, green belts have also come to serve other functions, including those of promoting recreation and of encouraging urban regeneration. The term itself is sometimes a misnomer, given the patchy character of urban development around many cities. It is, however, widely used and endorsed in many policy statements.

The contrary argument comes from econimists. To cope with a modern economy, Barker (2006a, 2006b) and Monk et al. (2013), amongst others, argue that the compact city and its associated green belts have to be converted into a dynamic concept, capable of decline and growth. Monk et al. (2013) in particular quote varied international examples where governments have promoted higher urban densities, whilst also promoting the development of more housing and, most importantly, providing the infrastructure for that development to take place. They argue for planning as growth management rather than as urban containment and, as part of this, they argue for the flexible operation of green belts with regular reviews of their boundaries. Exactly the same argument applies, of course, to commercial and industrial development.

The complaints of the economists are well taken. Mere adherence to urban containment in conditions of growth, whether this is population growth, the growth of economic activity or both, is likely to push up land prices and densities to a point that is unnecessary in terms of land savings and is likely, in addition, to frustrate consumer wishes for a house with a garden. Most surveys in England, in particular, show that the hosue with a garden remains a popular ideal outside of London, where special factors apply (Goodchild 2008, 210–17). Further, in areas of rapid growth, the application of rigid green belt policies may be self-defeating as it encourages further dispersal of development beyond their boundaries, with longer distance commuting. However, urban growth management is not simply about relaxing controls on greenfield development. Depending on the opportunities, growth management is also about about promoting the development of infill housing and removing the barriers to such development. In any case, acceptance of continued urban development, including in Britain higher levels of house building, also means ensuring that urban development conforms to the highest environmental standards—a point that is easily ignored if the aim is to encourage either economic development or house building as an overriding priority.

The case for growth management, rather than urban containment, is supported by statistical evidence, generated from the census, that, in medium-sized English cities, higher urban densities involve disbenefits of reduced living space and a lack of affordable housing (Burton 2000). The empirical material is sufficiently old, dating from the 1990s, to justify a repeat analysis. Disbenefits of reduced living space and decreased housing affordability are to be expected if local planning exercises have restricted the supply of housing development sites over a long period or if they have sought to stop, rather than manage, urban growth.

The distinction between urban containment and urban growth management is also a distinction between the types of space. The pursuit of growth management is likely to transform green belts into a flexible, fluid spatial designation rather than as at present a hard, inflexible designation 'in perpetuity'. Moreover, in changing the designation, existing green belts would become merged into concepts of 'green infrastructure' with its implication of a patchwork of green and built-up areas, green networks and corridors linking neighbourhoods (Thomas & Littlewood 2010). Likewise, the compact city is itself likely to be transformed into an urban form that Jenks et al. (1996, 298) once called 'decentralised concentration', comprising a series of centres and subcentres within a discontinuous urban area. In some European countries, decentralised concentration also goes by the name of an 'urban archipelago', as it consists of islands of development in a green or blue (watery) matrix with a shared infrastructure.[4] Since Jenks et al. wrote, moreover, the requirements of 'making space for water' has reinforced the case for discontinuous urban areas, with the retention or creation of areas that serve as a means of retaining water and slowing down water runoff at times of heavy rainfall.

Whether green belts will be relaxed or transformed is another question. The retention of existing green belts commonly features as a priority in local exercises in public consultation and is supported by influential pressure groups, notably the Campaign for the Protection of Rural England.[5] In addition, for areas of critical landscape and ecological value, some of which may be close to urban areas, strict development controls would be justified for other reasons. Most likely, therefore, and whatever the policy language (green belts, green infrastructure, sites of scientific or ecological interest etc.), the pattern of spatial designations will comprise a mixture of hard, inflexible, 'in-perpetuity' no development areas and soft, flexible areas being applied in different locations.

Growth management at least allows some overall control over urban form. The compact city is more difficult to implement in the context of population decline. The OECD (2012, 22) suggests, mainly based on the experience in Japan, that the compact city is poorly adapted to regions with a shrinking population owing to 'fears of weakened competitiveness and accelerated hollowing out of the population'. Instead, the OECD suggests the use of financial incentives, though these too are likely to be less effective in areas with low demand from developers.

The experience in Liverpool and Leipzig, two declining European cities, as documented by Couch et al. (2005), reinforces the limitations of urban containment in the context of decline. In particular, in Liverpool in the period 1971 to 2002, economic development and employment creation took priority over environmental protection, including building in the green belt. Housing development remained subject to strict controls and, for most of the period, grants were available to cover the additional costs of building on brownfield sites. But the various measures did not prevent continued population decline in the central city, the replacement of high-density by low-density suburban housing and the emergence of increased areas of derelict land or temporary parks. In principle, population decline offers the opportunity to create dispersed green cities, with reduced congestion and increased green space. Dispersed green urbanism is a possible option in areas of population decline in a way that is precluded in areas of growth. In practice, however, political priorities get in the way, especially given the costs of managing decline and dereliction.

Density is the key measure of the compact city and the key to understanding and predicting its impact on energy consumption. Density is a measure of intensity of use of land and urban space and is a result directly linked to the compact city. However, there is more than one type of density and a distinction may be made between net residential density and overall population density. This latter refers to the number of people living within the whole of an urban area and is the most relevant measure in relation to the energy consumption involved in urban transport.

Many studies have shown the existence of a relationship between higher urban population densities and a reduced dependency on cars (Ewing et al. 2013; Fouchier 1997; Næss & Jensen 2002; Newman & Kenworthy 1989). The compact city promotes a more supportive spatial framework for public transport and for walking, whilst still permitting the use of the private car and also allowing variations in car use to emerge on the basis of lifestyle and income group. In Copenhagen, for example, Jensen et al. (2014) have shown a general association between higher densities and lower energy consumption, but with the exception of a wealthy inner city suburb where higher densities were associated with higher income households and higher levels of car ownership.

In the past, higher energy costs were expected to cause a concentration of new development around public transport hubs (Ascher 2008), as consumers reduced their dependence on road vehicles. There is no evidence, however, of a trend towards higher energy costs, except where taxation is used for the purpose. A reliance on market mechanisms alone is likely either to lead to a continued emphasis on greenfield and suburban development or to encourage higher value development around urban hubs rather than affordable housing.

The promotion of development around public transport hubs will therefore mostly have to proceed though the planned shaping of local property markets and, in addition, through discouraging traffic in urban areas.

Discouraging and slowing down traffic is itself likely to change the balance of advantages between the private cars and other forms of transport. A variety of relevant measures are available, including small-scale, segregated 'car free' residential zones and town centres, car parking restrictions, traffic calming, bus and public transport lanes and reduced speed limits (Grant-Smith et al. 2012; UNICEF 2012, 71; Whitelegg 2015). Such measures are very common, though they are seldom presented as part of a co-ordinated, strategic programme to reduce vehicular traffic. Attention to the detailed ease, safety and simple pleasantness of pedestrian movement and cycling is another consideration. In the case of pedestrian movement, access to all types of facility including public transport is not just influenced by the actual distance, but by the number of road crossings, traffic conflicts and number of ascending steps (Olszewski & Wibowo 2005).

A strong version of the compact city, the car-free city, is conceivable (Crawford 2000). This latter literally throttles and stops the use of motor vehicles, but is only of limited use in designated areas. Even apart from the likely adverse political reaction, the car-free city is impractical owing to the disruption to lifestyles and commercial goods delivery and the impact on emergency vehicles. However, recognising the impossibility of the car-free city does not mean acceptance of any trend towards more and more reliance on road transport.

Buildings, rather than transport, remain the largest single source of energy consumption in most cities in the world (IEA 2013), as is in any case demonstrated by UK energy statistucs (see Figure 9.2). Compared to transport, however, the impact of density is less clear and more conditional on the circumstances. High-density, compact cities have the disadvantage of hindering the installation of renewable energy technologies in individual buildings, mostly because they offer less space. They are also largely irrelevant in warmer climates, as here higher densities contribute to uncomfortable local heat islands and a higher dependence on air conditioning. In Hong Kong, for example, local planners take care to ensure that the construction of apartment blocks does not block cooling sea breezes (Ng 2009). Conversely, however, flats and terraces have a more favourable ratio of internal floor area to external wall and roof area—the main sources of heat exchange in both cool and warm climates. They are also better suited to district heating and cooling networks.

Studies of the impact of urban design on energy consumption in buildings are relatively recent. A relatively early study of energy use in London by Steemers (2003), using a variety of largely secondary and theoretical sources, came to no real conclusions of the relative merits of high-density and low-density housing for energy consumption. The arguments for and against densification were finely balanced and probably depended on the type of energy infrastructure, for example, whether district heating was in operation in higher densities. For office buildings, however, the main influence was whether the block incorporated air conditioning or natural ventilation, with the latter involving much less energy use.

A survey of eight contrasting residential areas in Greater Oslo by Holden and Norland (2005) is probably the most extensive and systematic European study of the impact of density on energy consumption. The survey shows that high-density, inner-city housing generally involves the consumption of less energy per person, but that the difference is more marked for older property. The difference between high and low density is, moreover, likely to diminish or disappear in the future, as building standards improve. Modernisation rather than densification is the most effective long-term strategy. A complication is that apartments are commonly smaller than houses with gardens and their heating consumes less energy for that reason. However, even the impact of floorspace is likely to diminish as building standards improve. Moreover, the higher embodied energy consumption of flats, especially high flats, that is to say the energy expended in the construction of the blocks, must also be considered, alongside the higher operational energy consumption of communal services in flats, for example in the running of lifts (Jensen et al. 2014; Perkins et al. 2009). For all these reasons, higher density schemes should not be assumed as necessarily delivering lower levels of consumption in buildings.

The importance of building standards, rather than design, in determining energy use in turn throws doubt on proposals to maintain or increase occupancy rates, as has been proposed in the sustainable development scenarios prepared by Höjer et al. (2011) for Stockholm. Growth in floorspace per person is a cause of increased energy consumption for heating—hence the argument to increase occupancy rates. However, domestic energy consumption is also dependent on building standards and there are, in any case, no easy mechanisms that would both control dwelling size (including size of dwellings in the existing stock) and ensure the equitable allocation of floorspace to different individuals. Further, though the evidence is fragmentary, house sizes in Britain have not grown (and housing occupancy rates have not declined) as much as elsewhere in Europe (Morgan & Cruickshank 2014).

Transport costs and energy consumption and domestic energy consumption may also interact with one another. Holden and Norland (2005) suggest on the basis of their survey results that decentralised concentration is the most energy-efficient urban form as the presence of greenery near the home provides an alternative locale for leisure activities and discourages leisure travel. They also suggest that living in a house with a garden provides similar advantages. This is the only study to report such results and needs to be treated with caution, especially as energy use and in particular energy use connected to leisure and travel are influenced by income.

The broad implication is to endorse the principle of suburban expansion, so long as the densities are not too low (which is, in any case, unlikely owing to high land costs around most larger cities), the housing stock is sufficiently varied for demand and the building stock is of a high quality and so long, in addition, as development is accompanied by measures to control traffic and encourage other forms of transport. Subject to qualifications, about the need for urban growth management and for green infrastructure, the compact city remains a relevant model against which proposals may be tested. Suburban development and the compact city can coexist with one another so long as the compact city is not conceived as a frozen, static urban form. However, decentralised concentration is likely to remain a feature both of existing urban patterns and proposals to change those patterns.

### *Rule-Based Planning: Eco-Cities and Eco-Rating*

As an alternative to the compact city, discussion has sometimes focussed on the concept of 'eco-cities'. As summarised by Jabareen (2006, 47),

> The distinctive concepts of the eco-city are greening and passive solar design. In terms of density and other concepts, the eco-city might be conceived as a 'formless' city or an ecoamorphous city. There are some approaches that emphasize the passive solar design. … There are others that emphasize the concepts of greening and passive energy design.

The 'eco-city' is, in principle, indifferent to density and to any specific urban form. Its core idea is use of a series of detailed environmental criteria, without any long-term considerations of urban form. It is doubtful whether eco-cities or another type of city or neighbourhood could be conceptualised wholly without reference to some model. Even so, eco-cities reflect the second approach to planning, based on rules.

The Building Research Establishment (BRE), through their label 'BREEAM Communities' (BRE 2013), provides an example of a detailed statement of the rules for sustainable planning, at least in relation to a relatively simple neighbourhood project. Like other BREEAM tests, BREEAM Communities is intended to offer a mark of international best practice and involves accreditation by a third party and the payment of a fee for accreditation to take place. For BRE, 'BREEAM Communities' provides a common framework for stakeholders and a means of 'facilitating and supporting collaboration between professionals'.[6] The common framework itself consists of a series of questions about the impact under five dimensions—governance (this being determined by the extent of local community involvement), social and economic well-being, resource and energy, land use and ecology and finally transport and movement. Like other BREEAM labels, 'BREEAM Communities' measures sustainability on a cumulative points basis, with regard to multiple standardised criteria and weights. Five ratings are available—pass, good, very good, excellent and outstanding.

'BREEAM Communities' is paralleled by other assessment tools developed since about 2000 in other countries—in the US, Japan, Australia and Europe. An international review (Sharifi & Murayama 2014) suggests that while they all share a common general approach, the weighting given to different factors and the detailed application vary substantially. The dependence of these systems on weights is itself a limitation, as there is no *a priori* way in which it is possible to say the different factors contribute to sustainability to the same extent.

In addition, each evaluation tool has specific omissions, compared to others. For example, compared to other neighbourhood evaluation labels, 'BREEAM Communities' places more emphasis on community involvement and social and economic well-being. Conversely, BREEAM gives no credit to internal ecological greenways, whereas this is recognised in the main Japanese system (CASBEE-UD). Again, the US system (LEED) has an urban design dimension in giving points to the number of street connections in a neighbourhood—the more the better. BREEAM gives no such recognition to street connections, partly no doubt because of an apparent conflict between maximising street connections and controlling access for security, itself an urban design criterion within BREEAM. Another omission of BREEAM, compared to its Japanese equivalent, is the absence of any recognition of efforts by employers to discourage car use for the journey to work.

The limitations of existing evaluation systems lead in two directions. One way is to amalgamate the strong points of different national systems and for governments to encourage their use. Without government encouragement and without being embedded into existing planning procedures, the international experience suggests that neighbourhood evaluation tools are not commonly used (Sharifi & Murayama 2014). The contrary view is that standardised neighbourhood systems have inherent limitations. They are commonly complex in terms of information requirements, delay decision-making, duplicate the work of local planning authorities and, given their limitations and dependence on a context, do not of themselves guarantee high-quality sustainable design. As a result, the most effective approach to rule-based planning is to work out piecemeal improvements to the variable local systems and methods that planning authorities already deploy in assessing neighbourhoods (Jensen & Elle 2007; Garde 2009).

## Urban Upgrading and Retrofitting

A distinctive consequence of effective transition management is to make the existing urban fabric potentially obsolete. The adoption of ever-higher building standards and higher standards of protection against extreme climatic events, and an insistence on the use of renewable energy, all make the existing urban fabric inadequate in some way. The application of compact urban forms, if pursued with any vigour, is likely to have a similar effect,

# Sustainable Urbanism 261

leading to pressures for higher densities around public transport nodes, for example.

The terminology requires a brief explanation. Upgrading covers both abatement (or mitigation), meaning making cities more resilient to environmental disturbances when these occur, and avoidance, meaning reducing the carbon emissions whose consequences involve climatic disturbances in the long term. Upgrading a building for carbon reduction is commonly called retrofitting. The term itself is misleading as retrofitting implies merely the fitting of new equipment, say a new efficient central heating boiler or a solar hot-water system. In most cases repairs to the building fabric are also necessary. Repairs and minor improvements are, in any case, pervasive within the urban building stock. Undertaken *en masse*, retrofitting of buildings becomes urban retrofitting and involves strategic planning and strategic measures to upgrade both the building stock and the space between buildings and to deal with a combination of issues—climate change, resilience, the liveability of cities and biodiversity (Dixon & Eames 2013: Eames et al. 2013).

A report from the International Council for Local Environmental Initiatives (ICLEI) offers one interpretation of how a strategic upgrading exercise might be organised. ICLEI is, according to its website, 'a powerful movement of 12 mega-cities, 100 super-cities & urban regions, 450 large cities, 450 small & medium-sized cities & towns in 85 countries dedicated to sustainable development'.[7] The report (ICLEI 2011) suggests, as a starting point, a detailed survey and classification of different areas and sites. The report (ibid., 25–6) cites in this context an earlier study by Moon et al. (2009, 2–4), also undertaken for ICLEI.

> Climate change related urban adaptation decisions require a rational characterization of urban structural landscapes according to risk relevant features. Urban structure types, block size, and form are dependent upon the transportation or surface water networks that frame the block, as well as the formal or informal nature of the building typologies, their individual forms, their connections as well as their interconnections to adjacent structures. ... Other differentiations are made based upon land uses, orientation, structure density and building and sealing material.

The survey allows, in turn, an integrated focus on overall risks, development conditions, and local area performance and therefore an assessment of priorities for upgrading (ICLEI 2011, 4).

The method itself is worked out with reference to Ho Chi Minh City in Vietnam, but is neither innovative nor distinctively un-European or un-Western. It involves a revival and restatement of the methods of the comprehensive blueprint type of modern town planning. To be specific, the ICLEI method suggests a combination of the comprehensive survey method of

Abercrombie (rather than the looser, more qualitative approach of Geddes) and the technical, functional modernisation of the Athens Chart of 1932. The ICLEI method bears little resemblance to the 'clumsy solutions' favoured by socio-cultural theory or the multiple, multi-level solutions favoured by transition management, both of which favour a Baroque concept of planning, oriented towards the specific context.

A Baroque concept implies, in turn, the multiple use of appropriate models and rules. The compact city may, for example, be identified in the abstract as a broad model for the future. However, it still needs to be qualified by the claims of the alternative model of deconcentrated concentration, as this is better suited to the provision of greenery and water within an urban area. The models of the compact city and decentralised concentration are therefore not in opposition, but in a process of repeated interaction. Further, whatever model is used, it has to be applied in a way that conforms to local expectations and requirements and also meets relevant environmental rules, of which there are different interpretations. Unless accompanied by a rigidly top-down approach, the models used in urban remodelling correspond to the description of Deleuze and Guattari (1987, 20) as 'perpetually in construction or collapsing, and of a process that is perpetually prolonging itself, breaking off and starting up again'.

Economic considerations are also relevant. A systematic, comprehensive approach to urban restructuring is impractical with the long life of the urban infrastructure and built form and the very large scale of fixed capital invested in their construction (Hommels 2005). Houses are commonly said to have a maximum life expectancy of sixty years (Needleman 1965, 1969). The period is derived from the borrowing terms of social housing in the early and mid-20th century and is almost certainly a general understatement of life expectancy before demolition. The life of other aspects of the urban infrastructure, such as roads and drainage systems, is longer still, up to 200 years (Corfee-Morlot et al. 2012, 12). A long life in turn implies selective interventions and successive improvements over time.

Given the cost and long life expectancy of infrastructure and given, in addition, the multitude of actors involved, systematic comprehensive replanning of existing cities has been seldom attempted in Western countries. The housing modernisation programmes of the period from about 1955 to 1980 are the closest approximation in Britain, at least at a time of peace rather than war, though these only treated residential areas. The lessons are mixed. Local authorities showed that they are able to ensure the long-term upgrading of even the most intractable parts of the housing stock. However, the programmes sought to impose higher, modern standards on households who commonly had lower expectations and for many years the programmes relied almost wholly on demolition. The programmes amounted to forced modernisation and were, in part, responsible for the reaction against the methods of modern town planning in the late 1960s and 1970s

(Goodchild 2008, 103–8). They were, moreover, repeatedly characterised by delays and setbacks, in a way that inconvenienced and disrupted the daily lives of residents. In the meantime, as the programmes were delayed, residents lived in deteriorating properties as the very announcement of clearance rendered repairs unworthwhile from an economic viewpoint and also prevented sale to private buyers.

Later, in the 1970s, the programmes became more reliant on improvement of various types, including in Scotland the use of locally controlled housing associations that purchased tenement blocks with the agreement of owners. Reviews at the time suggested that these community housing associations were better able to secure the cooperation, rather than the opposition, of residents (Goodchild 1997, 161–3; Robertson 1996). Dedicated, special purpose vehicles, to use contemporary language (Vandevyvere & Nevens 2015), succeeded after multi-purpose local authority intervention had failed. Even so, the experience of the various housing programmes of the 1960s and 1970s suggests that the issue of clearance—a subject wholly off the current policy agenda—does not disappear.

Previous programmes also show that intervention has to rely on a combination of minimum (socially intolerable or unfit) and target (or improvement) standards and that, over time, the standards may be progressively raised in a way that also implies revisiting a property, say after 10 years. For energy efficiency, appropriate regulatory standards do not as yet exist in Britain in relation to the existing stock. Whatever the definition, however, the minimum socially intolerable or unfit standard cannot, at any single time, classify more than a small proportion of stock as unsatisfactory, say 5 percent, if the programme is to remain manageable and if in addition extensive property blight is to be avoided. Once a property is deemed either uninhabitable or unsaleable, the effect is to place an obligation on the state to cope with the consequences.

The installation of district heating (and possibly cooling) networks offers an alternative, complementary strategy to the very long-term and difficult process of improving and replacing the existing building stock (Lund et al. 2010). Collective systems are not necessarily more efficient than boilers or air conditioning devices installed in individual homes or buildings. Performance in use varies substantially. The advantage lies, instead, in their ability to use a diverse range of energy-efficient sources, including combined heat and power, biomass and other renewable sources and waste heat from industrial processes. Collective energy systems can therefore promote flexibility in sources of supply and resilience in the face of disruptions to supply (Jamasb & Pollitt 2008) and in the case of multi-source networks they can also optimise energy efficiency through using different sources at different times of the day and year (Faninger 2000).

The proportion of total heat demand served by district systems varies substantially between different countries. Nordic cities such as Helsinki and Copenhagen offer examples where a very high proportion of the total heat load is supplied by district heating. In Copenhagen, for example, 98 percent of homes have access to a district heating network (Hildyard 2011). In London, in comparison, the equivalent figure is about 5 percent with an even lower average elsewhere in Britain (ibid.). The Copenhagen figure is probably unattainable in Britain, given competition from an established gas network. Most financial assessments suggest that district heating currently only becomes viable in locations with a high density of energy demand (Pöyry 2009) and preferably in locations with end users such as hospitals or universities that have a relative stable demand. Where district heating is impractical, small-scale renewables and air- and ground-source heat pumps offer other alternatives. All these technologies depend, however, on a favourable economic context and, in the UK, have to compete with existing gas network.

The availability of finance is a further constraint. There are no obvious magic revenue sources, no new sources of finance. The sources will be same as for social housing and for other, conventional infrastructure, that is to say a mixture of government loans and grants, private financing and borrowing for projects with commercial potential, together with impact fees and similar charges generated through the statutory planning system. The difficulty of funding 'green infrastructure' is compounded, moreover, by competing demands for investment, including investment such as that in roads, with more easily demonstrated advantages for job creation and economic growth and a more favourable ratio between economic benefits and public sector costs.

There are some proposals for innovative funding sources. Vandevyvere & Nevens (2015) have suggested that densification may provide a means of funding the retrofitting of low-density suburban areas, the logic being that, say, the development of two new zero-carbon homes built on the site of a single old home is likely to be a commercially viable proposition. The commercial rationale is likely to vary substantially from town to town and from site to site, however. Moreover, any such scheme will have to ensure the agreement of all parties and this is likely to raise the setup costs. The measure is feasible in principle, but probably only of limited applicability.

In addition, an OECD report (Merk et al. 2012, 27) recommends the adoption of site value taxation as a green source of taxation. Site value taxation is a tax on the use of land, rather than buildings and was once, in the 19th century, suggested as a universal tax and replacement for income tax, notably by Henry George ([1879] 2006). According to its supporters, site value taxation remains a useful source of public revenue and counts as a green tax because it encourages higher densities and discourages urban sprawl. Taxing the value of a site encourages the maximum development of that site and does not penalise owns who make improvements to their properties.

Site value taxation exists in a variety of countries, including parts of the US, New Zealand and Australia (Merk et al 2012; Dye and England, 2000, 16). It is not without its limitations, however. A recent proposal to introduce site value taxation in Ireland came to nothing, after a negative review by a national 'Commission on Taxation' (2009, 158). The information requirements to assess site values were substantial and would take time to complete. Further, the report (ibid., 171) continued, the establishment of the tax would 'involve a long and sustained challenge for policy-makers to inform the community of its benefits and to implement the proposal'. The tax itself would not necessarily be seen as fair as larger houses were likely to be charged at the same rate as smaller houses in the same locality, so long as they occupied the same ground area.

Assuming, however, that the taxation obstacles are overcome, is site value taxation a green tax? A site tax is indifferent to whether a site is vacant or occupied and indifferent, in addition, to the number or height of buildings on a site. It is therefore likely to encourage owners to develop vacant sites, including undeveloped sites with planning permission, and to build more densely to maximise their income. The tax paid on an apartment in a high-density block will, for example, be less than that paid for a detached house of equivalent market value. However, site value taxes will only discourage urban sprawl in the context of urban containment and other land use planning policies that restrict the development of agricultural sites. The Australian experience, for example, does not suggest that site value taxation has much impact on urban sprawl and the basic financial incentives to develop greenfield sites would remain unaltered. In any case, as is another recommendation in the Irish Commission report, specific recurrent taxes can be levied on the value of vacant sites with planning permission, in an effort to stop land hoarding and promote development.

Given financial constraints, one possibility implicit in the ICLEI report is that policies will focus on health, safety and resilience rather than carbon reduction. It is in the interest of every local authority and every national government to take measures to adapt the built form to the risks of climate change and to promote the resilience of local communities. The effects of flooding, for example, are place specific and the effects are also sensitive to the type of extreme rainfall events whose frequency is expected to increase in the future (RCEP 2007, 61). In contrast, the advantages of carbon emissions circulate worldwide and are not specific. As a result, the balance between local costs and benefits favours resilience alone, unless, and this still seems problematic, innovative building and renewable energy sources can lead to such significant energy cost savings that they generate private investment. In the long term, however, as Stern (2007) has argued at length, achieving resilience is likely to become more and more expensive, unless the underlying issue of global warming is also tackled.

Another possibility is that the cost of future proofing may deter investment. Different levels and agencies of government and different financial institutions may enter into a game of brinksmanship. Here one or more of the various parties—central government with its access to income tax and other national revenues, local government with its access to local taxes, land-related sources of revenue and private agencies such as insurance companies or developers—delay or refuse a financial contribution to the point that this approaches the limits of safety. ICLEI and other supporters of strategic urban upgrading would almost certainly reply that the risk of brinksmanship demonstrates the importance of strong partnerships and of political determination to overcome the obstacles.

At the cost of saying the obvious, urban upgrading is a complex process that is influenced by numerous and sometimes-conflicting interests. The regeneration and development programme pursued along both banks of the Thames Estuary from 2004 to its partial dismantling in 2011 and 2012 provides an example. The Thames gateway project was not about climate change. It merely suggests the complexities of what Ascher (2001) would call hypermodern planning, in which planning policy and policy statements become embedded in other policy statements and constraints. For example, in seeking to pursue an 'integrated' programme, Brownill and Carpenter (2009) have noted how the various agencies have had to resolve multiple tensions and dilemmas, not just about funding, notably between:

- governability, in the sense of maintaining a combination of consistent long-term objectives and flexibility in dealing with different situations;
- economic competitiveness, social inclusion and sustainability as policy aims; and
- openness in the sense of open to consultation and closure in the sense of maintaining a political commitment.

In managing the tensions, three possibilities are apparent, none of which is exclusive and all of which may merge into the other two. The first is outright conflict in which the preparation of strategic plans provides a focus for debates between environmentalists and the supporters of growth, between the advocates of compact cities and their opponents and between the supporters of traffic calming and the advocates of road building (Coutard and Rutherford 2010). A second possibility is an uneasy compromise and blending, with a mixture of policies in different areas, with green neighbourhoods promoted as a marketing measure, but employment creating activities subject to little or no intervention (Béal 2015; Bramley & Kirk 2005). A third possibility, which is very close to the critiques of transition management theory, is one of gradual exhaustion in the face of multiple obstacles (Vandevyvere & Nevens 2015). It might also be possible to trace a sequence of stages, from conflict through compromise and then exhaustion, at least until the climate change policy agenda and the more general sustainability agenda again come to the fore.

Urban upgrading and retrofitting is a form of urban planning, However, statutory forms of town planning and land use planning are commonly inadequate for the full range of tasks involved in this. Statutory systems are generally more concerned with conservation of specific areas than with setting targets for pollution or the reduction of greenhouse gases; they also lack financial incentives of the type that might aid implementation (Jänicke & Jörgens 1998, 47). In addition, political debates about town planning tend to become polarised into pro-development and anti-development positions in a way that ignores both the quality of new development and even more so the quality of the existing building stock.

For all these reasons, lack of policy coordination is a recurrent complaint in accounts of environmental planning, as is shown in both the British (RCEP 2002) and the international literature (Chaker et al. 2006; Hilding-Rydevik & Bjarnadottir 2007). The complaints have, in turn, led to suggestions that the statutory planning system be turned into an explicitly environmental planning system (Meadowcroft 1997; RECP 2002, 4). That is not easy to reconcile with the detailed legal features associated with a typical planning system, including that in Britain, and is probably not necessary if the statutory system is given clear environmental policy priorities.

The issues go beyond administrative co-ordination. The modern Western state, notes Polanyi (1957 [1944], 132), is marked by a double movement towards both economic freedom, the market and the recognition of property rights on one hand and collective responsibility, environmental protection and planning on the other, albeit with a shifting balance between the two depending on the circumstances. The tensions implied by the double movement have become exacerbated over time by the conflict between global competition and neoliberalism on one hand and, on the other, the growing issues summarised under the heading of environmental risks, environmental sustainability, climate change and carbon reduction. The campaigns of local amenity groups have, moreover, further exacerbated the tension, though mostly with an emphasis on amenity and liveability.

## Towards the Green State?

To look forward beyond current preoccupations, a longer term political perspective is required. The various editions of the leading textbook *Readings in Planning Theory* limit planning theory to the context of a capitalist political economy (Fainstein & DeFilippis, 2016, 2). In contrast, the emergence of theories of economic and social planning in the 1930s led to a new concept of the 'planning state' as well as a reaction in the form of a restatement of the principles of a minimal liberal state. The planning state, developed by Mannheim ([1940] 1971) and others, and its opposite, the liberal and neoliberal state, were, at the time of their first formulation, normative concepts that involve political values, counterfactual thinking and the exercise of imagination. In the past, therefore, those interested in planning and interested in its role in society have not confined their analysis to practices within existing economic and political arrangements.

By the same token, if taken seriously, the pursuit of sustainability points towards a new type of state, a 'green state' as, for example, proposed by Eckersley (2004) and others. Such a state cannot be described in any detail. It is too hypothetical. Its broad contours may, however, be sketched out.

A green state is one 'that places ecological considerations at the core of its activity' (Meadowcroft, 2005:3) or similarly adopts 'environmental conservation' as a core imperative (Dryzek et al 2003: 164–5) or, again, integrates '"ecological" evaluations into the public mind so that they become as "natural" as those "economic" criteria presently applied'. (Lundqvist 2001, 455). Ecological considerations have to be normalised and considered as routine and universal.

The definitions say little about the green state having distinctive institutional structures. In many ways, it would not. For example, environmentalists seldom if ever challenge the conventions of an ideal liberal democracy—a commitment to the rule of law, to the maintenance of civil and political rights and to open political debate (Eckersley 2004). Though green theorists seldom make the point explicit, a commitment to civil rights also means a respect for the principle of property rights, albeit in a way that emphasises the avoidance of harm and the responsibilities of property owners. In any case, planning and the maintenance of property rights can and do coexist in different forms and to different degrees, as is amply shown in the different legal arrangements in different countries.

There is also little or no explicit or open support in the green literature either for cities without markets on the old Soviet model or for the highly centralised, but democratically-controlled forms of planning associated with Mannheim. Concepts of ecological modernisation and socio-transition are, for example, about working with industry and the private sector in a process of co-evolution. More radical, 'alternative' versions are about the promotion of deliberative democracy and of local groups. Conventional electoral democracy, based on competitive parties, may be adequate, it is argued, for the liberal and neoliberal state, but not for the complexities, multiple criteria and priorities involved in the practical application of environmental policy making (Dryzek 1999, 36–7; Hajer 2003; Lafferty 2004, 1–2; Sneddon et al. 2006).

However, co-evolution and decentralisation still raise the question of direction and effective implementation. The ideal, which is easier to say than to implement, is to combine central coordination with flexibility and sensitivity to the realities of everyday life. Lundqvist (2001) uses the memorable term 'a green fist in a velvet glove' to describe such an arrangement. In doing so Lundqvist (2001) also provides a reminder that, in a green state, neither localism, nor diversity nor deliberative democracy are aims in themselves and that all will have to operate within an appropriate policy brief.

Given a concomitant commitment to behaviour change, the green state may prove to be more centralised than is currently realised and also closer to the vision set out by Mannheim ([1940] 1971). However, Mannheim's vision was criticised at the time as being too centralised and, in any case, belongs to an era when the failures of the economy and the waging of mass warfare encouraged a strong trend towards centralised government. Another way forward is to emphasise the interaction and reciprocal relationship between central and local government and between, in addition, the centre and 'peripheral' environmental groups, as Douglas and Wildavsky (1982) would call them, in the hope that the resulting learning process would have positive, creatve outcomes.

The philosophy of desire of Deleuze and Guattari (1987, 20) offers one way of thinking about processes of interaction within a green state, as their models and distinctions are institutional as well as spatial. The distinction between an arborescent, that is to say a tree-like hierarchical model, and a rhizomatical, horizontal model offers contrasting but not opposing models. They are 'dualisms'. They exist to challenge one another and 'to arrive at a process that challenges all models'. The ideal types of planning and the market as posed by Kornai (1971, 1979) offer another relevant way of thinking. Kornai's analysis shows that the ideal types of each are unworkable and that practical processes of economic development have to incorporate elements of both. In making a distinction between planning, above all central planning as 'resource-constrained' and markets as 'demand constrained', Kornai (1979) also touches on the substantive aspects of a green state, as well as its form. Planning in a green state would limit the consumption of resources and would provide limits that go beyond those of price, but should also include appropriate mechanisms to avoid shortages, notably of human necessities such as decent housing.

The substantive aspects of a green state are important in another way. As is commonly recognised, policies for sustainability will have to address issues of social justice, if these are to prove socially acceptable (Campbell 1996; Gunder 2006). People who feel that they are being singled out unfairly are less likely to support climate change and other environmental measures. Moreover, policies for sustainable development and carbon reduction impact on social justice in numerous ways—through higher fuel costs whose burden falls disproportionately on those with lower incomes, through a loss of jobs as industry becomes transformed (Jänicke 2008), through green urbanism becoming a tool for gentrification, so displacing low income households (Checker 2011), and through low income households being pushed around by insensitive demolition programmes (Allen 2008).

At the same time, issues of social justice and environmental justice arise from social and economic inequalities. Environmental problems, environmental risks, social inequalities and social exclusion go together, at least in relation to the 'ordinary' risks where people interact routinely with their surroundings (RCEP 2007, 34). There are many, many examples of this, but two will suffice. The wealthy and the affluent can choose to live in neighbourhoods with less pollution, to the benefit of both themselves and their family (Mitchell & Dorling 2003). In Newcastle-upon-Tyne, for example, 'the most deprived wards in the city with the ... larger incidence of respiratory illnesses receive a higher level of traffic-related air pollution, compared with the least deprived wards' (Davoudi & Brooks, 2012, 41). Further, those with sufficient resources to choose where they live can avoid the problems and risks of poor quality housing, the physical problems such as dampness, insect infestation, the use of lead paint and so on and can avoid, in addition, the psychosocial problems associated with the loss of well-being, security and self-esteem associated with living in an excluded neighbourhood (Clark & Kearns 2012; Gibson et al. 2011).

Environmental and housing inequalities are long standing. However, they have almost certainly been exacerbated by growing inequalities, associated with for example variations in income, education, occupational status, migrant status and so on (European Commission 2010). The relationship between economic and environmental, including housing, inequalities is therefore reciprocal. Inequalities in socio-economic conditions are a basic cause of environmental and housing inequality but these in turn reinforce social and economic disadvantage and a differential exposure to environmental risks of all kinds (WHO 2010).

Merely addressing the issue of social justice in the abstract is not enough. Specifying a series of ethical principles for professional planners is likewise not enough. The potential impact of sustainability is too varied and too unpredictable for a single policy or equity criterion to be useful. Further, opening up the planning process and making communities more aware of inequalities is not enough. Recognising the rights of communities to information and consultation is almost certainly necessary in attempts to counter environmental inequalities and is also consistent with the various theories of collaborative planning and planning as learning. Opening up the planning process to communities does nothing, however, directly to counter inequalities. In addition, the problems of poor quality housing and of urban deprivation are not generally amenable to mere defensive political campaigns, such as those pursued by NIMBY groups. Such problems can only be tackled through various forms of publicly funded support—the provision of good quality affordable housing, community-based programmes of investment and supply-side planning to co-ordinate those programmes. And mention of such wide-ranging measures leads inevitably to a consideration of the welfare state.

Neoliberal and weak welfare states are able to undertake environmental regulation. Measurement of performance through targets, adherence to defined principles and financial and policy transparency are all themes that are consistent with efficient, minimal government. Pennington (2008) has argued, in particular, that neoliberal political principles offer a way of reconciling disputes between those who favour centralised solutions and those, such as the advocates of deliberative democracy, who favour decentralisation. Pennington appeals to classical liberalism but in a contemporary context classical liberalism is, in effect, neoliberalism. According to such a classical liberal view, the green state would comprise a framework of 'polycentric' environmental laws whilst preserving the spontaneous order of the market based on voluntary agreements and private action.

The magnitude of the problem of climate change and the consequent scale of intervention is such, however, as to suggest the irrelevancy of classical 19th century liberalism and to imply, in addition, a weakening over time of neoliberal ideologies. 'Polycentric' laws and initiatives can also be read as fragmented laws and initiatives that reinforce inequality. Strong welfare states are more likely to impose the high levels of taxation necessary to finance urban upgrading and retrofitting; are generally better inclined to help industry undertake industrial innovation; and are also likely to be committed to an ethic of care that can be extended to the environment.

An affinity exists therefore between the welfare state and strong environmental measures (see, for example, Eckersley 2004; Hildingsson & Khan 2013.) It is, for example, no coincidence that the lead countries in environmental policy in northern Europe have been the Nordic countries, together with Germany and the Netherlands, all of whom have relatively strong systems of personal protection. These same countries also rely more heavily on direct public intervention in the land market and have, for this reason, been better able to resolve the tensions between environmental protection and the land supply for new housing (Adams & Watkins 2014, 29). No doubt many reasons are responsible for the use of direct intervention in these countries, but one reason is surely a political culture that facilitates stronger public policy measures and essentially amounts to a distinct political culture for planning (Nadin & Stead 2008). A preference for a strong welfare state is, nevertheless, subject to various caveats.

First, the concept of the welfare state, as applied to northern Europe, is merely shorthand for a state with strong welfare services. The state still operates in a competitive global economy and is subject to a wide range of forces including the demographic changes associated with an aging population and changing social expectations. The response of governments to the various pressures has typically been to shift the pattern of state expenditure towards education, health and individual welfare payments and away from the housing, neighbourhood and other measures that are associated with supply-side planning and a community-based urban policy. Financial austerity since 2008 has reinforced the tendency as it has forced governments to prioritise spending in one policy field rather than another. As a result, most European states are more limited in their ability to influence land and housing markets than, say, in the 1950s and 1960s (Burrows & Loader 1994; Tsenkova 2008) and less able, in addition, to influence the quality of life in deprived neighbourhoods.

Secondly, the provision of welfare services, including social housing, is not a panacea. For example, the history of housing in the city of Glasgow, especially in the 1970s and 1980s onwards, offers a warning that deep segregation and deprivation can coexist alongside extensive public ownership of housing (Clapham & Kintrea 1986; Damer 1974). A welfare state provides a potential means of policy implementation, but is not of itself sufficient.

Finally, the welfare state operates on the principle of social rights and this is a right to possess something or have access to something. In contrast, the ethic of a green state is about the responsibility of all to care for the environment for its own sake, irrespective of social rights (Groves 2009). The welfare state and the green state have overlapping characteristics, but their rationale is not the same. Much the same qualification applies to related concepts of the right to the city and use value. In the past, as promoted by Lefèbvre (1991, 1998), the right to the city has been unqualified and treated as the right for an urban population not just to enjoy access to urban spaces but to pursue private lifestyles as they see fit. In contrast, to the extent that rights exist in a green state, these are qualified by an ethic of global environmental care that implies limits to consumption and limits to the use of space. For these reasons, the green state is unlikely to emerge without continued political effort and commitment.

## Notes

1 See the website of Soka Klima, consulted September 2014 at www.soko-klima.de/#. Soka Klima is a Berlin-based educational charity that specialises in explaining the implications of climate change through town planning.
2 Congress for New Urbanism website, consulted August 2012 at www.cnu.org/history.
3 'Garden City Principles', The Town and Country Planning Association, consulted June 2014 at www.tcpa.org.uk/pages/garden-cities.html; 'Wolfson Economics Prize 2014', at the website of the Policy Exchange, consulted September 2014 at www.policyexchange.org.uk/wolfsonprize/item/wolfson-economics-prize-2014.
4 The Sibbesborg Archipelago, presented on the website of the deep green design alliance of Finland, consulted July 2013 at www.dgda.com/sibbesborg-archipelago/single-gallery/14881060; Olofsdotter, B., Björnberg, K., Chang, H. W., Kain, J. -H., Linn, E. and Scurrell, B. (2013). *Synthesis report: competing for urban land*, on the website of Urban-Nexus, consulted July 2013 at www.urban-nexus.eu/www.urban-nexus.eu/index.php?option=com_content&view=article&id=31&Itemid=28.
5 'Green Belt: are we valuing it enough?', an opinion piece taken from the website of the Campaign to Protect Rural England, consulted October 2014 at www.

cpre.org.uk/magazine/opinion/item/3745-green-belt-are-we-valuing-it-enough?highlight=WyJncmVlbiIsImJlbHQiLCJncmVlbiBiZWx0Il0=.
6 'Introductory brochure to BREEAM communities', consulted April 2014 on the website of BREEAM, consulted April 2014 at www.breeam.org/page.jsp?id=372.
7 The website of ICLEI, consulted September 2013 at www.iclei.org/.

## References

Adams, D. & Watkins, C. (2014). *The value of planning*. London: The Royal Town Planning Institute.
Allen, C. (2008). *Housing market renewal and social class*. London: Routledge.
Ascher, F. (2001). *Les nouveaux principes de l'urbanisme*. La Tour d'Aigues: Editions de l'Aube.
Ascher, F. (2008). 'Effet de serre, changement climatique et capitalisme cleantech'. *Esprit*, février, 150–64.
Barker, K. (2006a). *Barker review of land use planning interim report*. London: HM Treasury.
Barker, K. (2006b). *Barker review of land use planning final report – recommendations*. London: HM Treasury.
Béal, V. (2015). 'Selective public policies: sustainability and neoliberal urban restructuring'. *Environment and Urbanization*, 27:1, 303–16.
Beatley, T. (2000). *Green urbanism: earning from European cities*. Washington, DC: Island Press.
Beatley, T. (2011). *Biophilic cities*. Washington, DC: Island Press.
Beck, U. (2013). 'Risk, class, crisis, hazards and cosmopolitan solidarity/risk community-conceptual and methodological clarifications'. *HAL – Archives Ouvertes*, [online] URL: https://halshs.archives-ouvertes.fr/halshs-00820297/ (consulted November 2015).
Bramley, G. & Kirk, K. (2005). 'Does planning make a difference to urban form? Recent evidence from Central Scotland'. *Environment and Planning A*, 37:2, 355–78.
Bramley, G., Dempsey, N., Power, S., Brown, C. & Watkins, D. (2009). 'Social sustainability and urban form: evidence from five British cities'. *Environment and Planning A*, 41, 2125–42.
BRE—Building Research Establishment (collective author) (2013). *BREEAM Communities, Technical Manual*: SD202 Issue Date: 21/02/2013. Watford: The BRE, [online] URL: www.breeam.org/page.jsp?id=372 (consulted June 2016).
Brownill, S. & Carpenter, J. (2009). 'Governance and "integrated" planning: the case of sustainable communities in the Thames Gateway, England'. *Urban Studies*, 46, 251–74.
Burrows, R. & Loader, B. (eds.) (1994). *Towards a post-Fordist welfare state?* London: Routledge.
Burton, E. (2000). 'The compact city: just or just compact? A preliminary analysis'. *Urban Studies*, 37, 1969–2001.
BMVBS—Federal Ministry of Transport, Building and Urban Development (Germany) (collective author) (2010). *National strategies of European countries for climate change adaptation: a review from a spatial planning and territorial development perspective*. BMVBS-Online-Publikation, No. 21/2010,

[online] URL: www.bbsr.bund.de/nn_21168/BBSR/EN/Publications/BMVBS/Online/2010/ON212010.html (consulted June 2016).

Campbell, S. (1996). 'Green cities, growing cities, just cities?' *Journal of the American Planning Association*, 62:3, 296–312.

CEC—Commission of the European Communities (corporate author) (1990). *Green paper on the urban environment*. Brussels: CEC.

Chaker, A., El-Fadl, K., Chamas, L. & Hatjian, B. (2006). 'A review of strategic environmental assessment in 12 selected countries'. *Environmental Impact Assessment Review*, 26, 15–56.

Checker, M. (2011). 'Wiped out by the "greenwave": environmental gentrification and the paradoxical politics of urban sustainability'. *City & Society*, 23:2, 210–29.

Clapham, D. & Kintrea, K. (1986). Rationing, choice and constraint: the allocation of public housing in Glasgow. *Journal of Social Policy*, 15:1, 51–67.

Clark, J. & Kearns, A. (2012). 'Housing improvements, perceived housing quality and psychosocial benefits from the home'. *Housing Studies* 27:7, 915–39.

CLG—Department for Communities and Local Government (2014). *Locally-led garden cities*. London: CLG, [online] URL: www.gov.uk/government/publications/locally-led-garden-cities-prospectus (consulted June 2014).

Commission on Taxation (Ireland) (collective author) (2009). *Report*. Dublin: The Stationery Office.

Corfee-Morlot, J., Marchal, V., Kauffmann, C., Kennedy, C., Stewart, F., Kaminker, C. & Ang, G. (2012). *Towards a green investment policy framework*. OECD Environment Working Papers, No. 48, OECD Publishing.

Couch, C., Karecha, J., Nuissl, H. & Rink, D. (2005). 'Decline and sprawl: an evolving type of urban development – observed in Liverpool and Leipzig'. *European Planning Studies*, 13:1, 117–36.

Coutard, O., & Rutherford, J. (2010). 'Energy transition and city–region planning: understanding the spatial politics of systemic change'. *Technology Analysis & Strategic Management*, 22:6, 711–27.

Crawford, J. H. (2000). *Carfree cities*. Utrecht, The Netherlands: International Books.

Damer, S. (1974). 'Wine Alley: the sociology of a dreadful enclosure'. *The Sociological Review*, 22:2, 221–48.

Davoudi, S. & Brooks, E. (2012). *Environmental justice and the city: full report*. Newcastle University, [online] URL: www.ncl.ac.uk/sustainability/news/item/environmental-justice-and-the-city-report-now-available (consulted May 2014).

Deleuze, G. and Guattari, F. (1987). *A thousand plateaus: capitalism and schizophrenia*, translation and Foreword by Brian Massumi, Minneapolis, MN: University of Minnesota Press (French Original 1980).

Dixon, T. & Eames, M. (2013). 'Scaling up: the challenges of urban retrofit'. *Building Research & Information*, 41:5, 499–503.

Douglas, M. & Wildavsky, A. B. (1982). *Risk and culture: an essay on the selection of technical and environmental dangers*. Berkeley, CA: University of California Press.

Dryzek, J. (1999). 'Transnational democracy'. *The Journal of Political Philosophy*, 7:1, 30–51.

Dryzek, J. S., Downes, D., Hunold, C., Schlosberg, D. & Hernes, H. -K. (2003). *Green states and social movements: environmentalism in the United States, United Kingdom, Germany, & Norway*. New York: Oxford University Press.

Dye, R. F. & England R. W. (2010). *Assessing the theory and practice of land value taxation*. Cambridge, MA: Lincoln Institute of Land Policy.
Eames, M., Dixon, T., May, T. & Hunt, M. (2013). 'City futures: exploring urban retrofit and sustainable transitions'. *Building Research & Information*, 41:5, 504–16.
Eckersley, R. (2004). *The green state: rethinking democracy and sovereignty*. Cambridge, MA: MIT Press.
European Commission, Directorate-General for Research (collective author) (2010). *Why socio-economic inequalities increase? Facts and policy responses in Europe*. Report no EUR 24471 E, European Commission, Brussels, [online] URL: https://ec.europa.eu/research/social-sciences/pdf/policy_reviews/policy-review-inequalities_en.pdf (consulted December 2015).
Ewing, R., Hamidi, S., Nelson, A. C., & Grace, J. B. (2013). 'Combined effects of compact development, transportation investments, and road user pricing on vehicle miles traveled in urbanized areas'. *AESOP-ACSP Joint Congress*, 15–9 July, Dublin.
Fainstein, S. S. and DeFilippis, J. (2016). *Readings in planning theory*, 4th Edition, Chichester, West Sussex: John Wiley.
Faninger, G. (2000). 'Combined solar–biomass district heating in Austria'. *Solar Energy*, 69:6, 425–35.
Fouchier, V. (1997). *Les densités urbaines et le développement durable*. Paris: Édition SGVN/La Documentation Française.
Garde, A. (2009). 'Sustainable by design? Insights from US LEED-ND pilot projects'. *Journal of the American Planning Association*, 75:4, 424–40.
George, H. (2006). *Progress and poverty*. New York: The Robert Schalkenbach Foundation (Original 1879), [online] URL: www.henrygeorge.org/pcontents.htm (accessed June 2016).
Gibson, M., Thomson, H., Kearns, A. & Petticrew, M. (2011). 'Understanding the psychosocial impacts of housing type: qualitative evidence from a housing and regeneration intervention'. *Housing Studies*, 26:04, 555–73.
Goodchild, B. (1997). *Housing and the urban environment*. Oxford: Blackwell Science.
Goodchild, B. (2008). *Homes, cities and neighbourhoods*. Hampshire: Aldershot.
Goodchild, B. (2013). 'Flats, higher densities and city centre living: a response to Evans and Unsworth'. *Urban Studies*, 50:14, 3036–42.
Grant-Smith, D., Edwards, P. & Johnson, L. (2012). 'Mobility in the child (and carer) friendly city: SEQ vs. Stockholm'. *Proceedings of the AESOP 26th Annual Congress*, METU, Ankara.
Groves, C. (2009). 'Future ethics: risk, care and non-reciprocal responsibility'. *Journal of Global Ethics*, 5:1, 17–31.
Gunder, M. (2006). 'Sustainability: planning's saving grace or road to perdition?' *Journal of Planning Education and Research*, 26, 208–21.
Hajer, M. A. (2003). 'A frame in the fields: policy making and the reinvention of politics'. In: Hajer, M. & Wagenaar, H., *Understanding governance in the network society*. Cambridge, UK: Cambridge University Press, 88–110.
Hall, P., Gracey, H., Drewett, R. & Thomas, R. (1973). *The containment of urban England, volume two: the planning system*. London: George Allen & Unwin.
Hilding-Rydevik, T. & Bjarnadottir, H. (2007). 'Context awareness and sensitivity in SEA implementation'. *Environmental Impact Assessment Review*, 27:7, 666–84.

Hildingsson, R. & Khan, J. (2013). 'Greening the welfare state'. A paper presented at the annual conference on Nordic Environmental Social Science: *Welcome to the Anthropocene*, Copenhagen, Denmark.

Hildyard, L. (2011). 'Decentralised energy and the Danish model'. In: *Decentralised energy: could London emulate Copenhagen?*, [online] URL: www.ucl.ac.uk/london-2062/documents/DecentralisedEnergy (consulted December 2014 at the website of London 2062).

Höjer, M., Gullberg, A. & Pettersson, R. (2011). 'Backcasting images of the future city – time and space for sustainable development in Stockholm'. *Technological Forecasting and Social Change*, 78:5, 819–34.

Holden, E. & Norland, I. T. (2005). 'Three challenges for the compact city as a sustainable urban form: household consumption of energy and transport in eight residential areas in the greater Oslo region'. *Urban Studies*, 42:12, 2145–66.

Hommels, A. (2005). 'Studying obduracy in the city: toward a productive fusion between technology studies and urban studies'. *Science Technology Human Values*, 30:3, 323–51.

Hopkins, R. (2000). 'The food producing neighbourhood'. In: Barton, H. (ed.), *Sustainable communities*. London: Earthscan, 199–215.

ICLEI—International Council for Local Environmental Initiatives (corporate author) (2011). *Financing the resilient city: a demand driven approach to development, disaster risk reduction and climate adaptation*. Bonn: ICLEI.

IEA—International Energy Agency (2013). *Transition to sustainable buildings: strategies and opportunities to 2050*. Paris: IEA/ OECD, [online] URL: www.iea.org/publications/freepublications/publication/Building2013_free.pdf (consulted March 2015).

Jabareen, Y. R. (2006). 'Sustainable urban forms their typologies, models, and concepts'. *Journal of Planning Education and Research*, 26:1, 38–52.

Jamasb, T. & Pollitt, M. (2008). 'Security of supply and regulation of energy networks'. *Energy Policy*, 36:12, 4584–89.

Jänicke, M. (2008). 'Ecological modernisation: new perspectives'. *Journal of Cleaner Production*, 16, 557–65.

Jänicke, M. & Jörgens, H. (1998). 'National environmental policy planning in OECD countries: preliminary lessons from cross-national comparisons'. *Environmental Politics*, 7:2, 27–54.

Jenks, M., Burton, E. & Williams, K. (1996). 'A question of sustainable urban form: conclusions'. In: Jenks, M., Burton, E. and Williams, K. (eds.), *The compact city. A sustainable urban form?* London: E & FN Spon, 297–300.

Jensen, J. O. & Elle, M. (2007). 'Exploring the use of tools for urban sustainability in European cities'. *Indoor and Built Environment*, 16:3, 235–47.

Jensen, J. O., Christensen, T. H. & Gram-Hanssen, K. (2014). 'Sustainable urban development – compact cities or consumer practices?' *Tidsskrift for Kortlægning og Arealforvaltning*, 46:1, 50–64.

Kornai, J. (1971). *Anti-equilibrium*. Amsterdam: North Holland Publishing.

Kornai, J. (1979). 'Resource-constrained versus demand-constrained systems'. *Econometra*, 47:4, 819.

Lafferty, W. M. (2004) (ed.). *Governance for sustainable development*. Cheltenham, UK & Northampton, MA: Edward Elgar.

Lefèbvre. H. (1991). *The production of space*. Oxford: Blackwell (French original 1974).

Lefèbvre. H. (1998). 'Le droit a la ville'. In: Ansay, P. and Schoonbrodt, R. (eds.), *Penser la ville*. Brussels: AAM Éditions (extract from an original published in 1968).

Lund, H. Möller, B., Mathiesen, B. & Dyrelund, A. (2010). 'The role of district heating in future renewable energy systems'. *Energy* 35:3, 1381–90.

Lundqvist, L. J. (2001). 'A green fist in a velvet glove: the ecological state and sustainable development'. *Environmental Values*, 10, 455–72.

Mannheim, K. (1971). *Man and society in age of reconstruction*. London: Routledge & Kegan Paul (first published in English in 1940, partly based on a German original of 1935).

Meadowcroft, J. (1997). 'Planning for sustainable development: insights from the literature of political science'. *European Journal of Political Research*, 31, 427–54.

Meadowcroft, J. (2005). 'From welfare state to ecostate'. In: Barry, J. & Eckersley R. (eds.), *The state and the global ecological crisis*. Cambridge, MA: MIT Press, 3–23.

Merk, O., Saussier, S., Staropoli, C., Slack, E. & Kim, J. -H. (2012). *Financing green urban infrastructure*. OECD Regional Development Working Papers 2012/10, OECD Publishing, [online] URL: www.oecd.org/gov/regional-policy/WP_Financing_Green_Urban_Infrastructure.pdf (consulted November 2014).

Mickwitz, P., Aix, F., Beck, S., Carss, D., Ferrand, N., Görg, C., et al. (2009). *Climate policy integration, coherence and governance*. Helsinki: Partnership for European Environmental Research.

Mitchell, G. & Dorling, D. (2003). 'An environmental justice analysis of British air quality'. *Environment and Planning A*, 35:5, 909–29.

Monk, S., Whitehead, C., Burgess, G. & Tang, C. (2013). *International review of land supply and planning systems*. York: Joseph Rowntree Foundation.

Moon, K., Downes, N., Rujner H. & Storch, H. (2009). 'Adaptation of the urban structure type approach for vulnerability assessment of climate change risks in Ho Chi Minh City'. In: *E-Proceedings: 45th ISOCARP Congress 2009, 'Low Carbon Cities'*. The Hague: ISOCARP.

Morgan, M. & Cruickshank, H. (2014). 'Quantifying the extent of space shortages: English dwellings'. *Building Research & Information*, 42:6, 710–24.

Nadin, V. & Stead, D. (2008). 'European spatial planning systems, social models and learning'. *disP-The Planning Review*, 44:172, 35–47.

Næss, P. & Jensen, O. B. (2002). 'Urban land use, mobility and theory of science: exploring the potential for critical realism in empirical research'. *Journal of Environmental Policy & Planning*, 4, 295–311.

Needleman, L. (1965). *The economics of housing*. London: The Staples Press.

Needleman, L. (1969). 'The comparative economics of improvement and new building'. *Urban Studies*, 6:2, 196–209.

Newman, P. & Kenworthy, J. (1989). *Cities and automobile dependence: a sourcebook*. Brookfield, VT: Gower.

Ng, E. (2009). 'Policies and technical guidelines for urban planning of high-density cities–air ventilation assessment (AVA) of Hong Kong'. *Building and Environment*, 44:7, 1478–88.

OECD (2012). *Compact city policies: a comparative assessment*. OECD Green Growth Studies, OECD Publishing.

Olszewski, P. & Wibowo, S. S. (2005). 'Using equivalent walking distance to assess pedestrian accessibility to transit stations in Singapore'. *Transportation Research Record: Journal of the Transportation Research Board*, 1927, 38–45.

Pennington, M. (2008). 'Classical liberalism and ecological rationality: the case for polycentric environmental law'. *Environmental Politics*, 17:3, 431–48.

Perkins, A., Hamnett, S., Pullen, S., Zito, R. & Trebilcock, D. (2009). 'Transport, housing and urban form: the life cycle energy consumption and emissions of city centre apartments compared with suburban dwellings'. *Urban Policy and Research*, 27:4, 377–96.

Polanyi, K. (1957). *The great transformation*. Boston: Beacon Press (UK original 1944).

Pöyry, with Faber Maunsell (collective authors) (2009). *The potential and cost of district heating networks*. Oxford: Pöyry Energy, [online] URL: www.gov.uk/government/policies/increasing-the-use-of-low-carbon-technologies/supporting-pages/heat-networks (consulted January 2015 at the website of the UK Department of Energy and Climate Change).

Prior, A. & Raemaekers, J. (2007). 'Is green belt fit for purpose in a post-Fordist landscape?' *Planning Practice & Research*, 22:4, 579–99.

Rapoport, E. R. (2014). *Mobilizing sustainable urbanism: international consultants and the assembling of a planning model*. Doctoral thesis, UCL (University College London), [online] URL: http://discovery.ucl.ac.uk/1449528/ (consulted December 2015).

Ratcliffe, J. & Krawczyk, E. (2011). 'Imagineering city futures: the use of prospective through scenarios in urban planning'. *Futures*, 43:7, 642–53.

RCEP—Royal Commission on Environmental Pollution (2002). *Twenty-third report: environmental planning*. Cm 5459. London: Crown Copyright.

RCEP—Royal Commission on Environmental Pollution (2007). *Twenty-sixth report: the urban environment* Cm 7009. London: Crown Copyright.

Robertson, D. & Bailey, N. (1996). *Review of the impact of housing action areas*, Research Report 47. Edinburgh: Scottish Homes.

Roggema, R. (2010). *Adaptation to climate change: a spatial challenge*. Berlin: Springer.

Scoffham, E. & Vale, B. (1996). 'How compact is sustainable – how sustainable is compact'. In: Jenks, M., Burton, E. & Williams, K. (eds.), *The compact city: a sustainable urban form*. London: E&FN Spon, 66–73.

Sharifi, A. & Murayama, A. (2014). 'Neighborhood sustainability assessment in action: cross-evaluation of three assessment systems and their cases from the US, the UK, and Japan'. *Building and Environment*, 72, 243–58.

Sneddon, C., Howarth, R. B. & Norgaard, R. B. (2006). 'Sustainable development in a post-Brundtland world'. *Ecological Economics*, 57:2, 253–68.

Steemers, K. (2003). 'Energy and the city: density, buildings and transport'. *Energy and Buildings*, 35:1, 3–14.

Stern, N. (2007). *The economics of climate change*. London: HM Treasury & Cambridge, UK: Cambridge University Press.

Thomas, K. & Littlewood, S. (2010). 'From green belts to green infrastructure? The evolution of a new concept in the emerging soft governance of spatial strategies'. *Planning, Practice & Research*, 25:2, 203–22.

Tsenkova, S. (2008). *Housing policy reforms in post socialist Europe*. Springer.

UNICEF (2012). *Children in an urban world: the state of the world's children 2012*. New York: United Nations Children's Fund (UNICEF), [online] URL: www.unicef.org/uganda/SOWC_2012-Main_Report_EN_13Mar2012.pdf (consulted August 2013).

URBED (2014). *Uxcester Garden City: Wolfson Economics Prize submission 2014*, [online] URL: www.urbed.com/wolfson-economic-prize (consulted September 2014).

UTC—Urban Task Force (collective author) (1999). *Final report: towards an urban renaissance*. London: Department of the Environment, Transport and the Regions, E&FN Spon.

Vale, B. & Vale, R. J. D. (1975). *The autonomous house*. London: Thames & Hudson.

Vandevyvere, H. & Nevens, F. (2015). 'Lost in transition or geared for the S-curve? An analysis of Flemish transition trajectories with a focus on energy use and buildings'. *Sustainability*, 7:3, 2415–36.

Whitelegg, J. (2015). *Mobility: a new urban design and transport planning philosophy for a sustainable future*. Church Stretton, Shropshire, UK: Straw Barnes Press.

WHO—World Health Organisation Europe (corporate author) (2010). *Environment and health risks: a review of the influence and effects of social inequalities*, [online] URL: www.euro.who.int/__data/assets/pdf_file/0003/78069/E93670.pdf (consulted November 2015).

# Index

'A Reader in Planning Theory' (Faludi) 142
abduction 137–9, 145; *see also* science philosophy/scientific method
Abercrombie, P. 46, 63
accountability to future generations 237
actor-network theory 25–6, 81, 153, 234
additionality 161
advocacy planning 141, 190
agonistic approaches 189–91
agreement 173
Alberti, L. B. 51
alethic hermeneutics 30–1
Alexander, E. R. 153, 164
Allmendinger, P. 16–17, 24–5, 27, 152, 183–4
allocative planning 96–115; housing market impacts 107–15; non-residential property markets and 102–7; risk management and 199–200; styles of 98–102
Alvesson and Sköldberg 7, 13, 27, 30–31, 179
amenities 104–5
American Institute of Certified Planners 22
American Planning Association 22
analytical debate 17–18
anarcho-capitalism 85
Andersson, D. E. 81, 85
Antwerp, Belgium 64
arborescent growth 43, 269
Ascher, F. 142, 143–4, 223
assemblage theory 50–1, 63, 65
'Athens Chart' (1932) 52, 262
Augustine, St. 53
autonomy of planning 92

backcasting 228–31
Banfield, E. C. 130
Barcelona, Spain 54, 56
Barker, K. 47, 108, 112–14, 136
Baroque planning 49, 57–64, 62, 262
Barton, D. N. 166
Bates, K. 10
Beard, V. A. 118
Beauregard, R. A. 117, 182
Beck, U. 212, 213, 214, 223
behaviour change: nudging 233–4, 241–2; practice theory 234–6
behavioural theories 152
Berke, P. 163–5
Bickenbach, J. 23
black-box policy options 167
blueprint planning 49; historical development 46–9; Mannheim's establishment concept 78; Romantic and Baroque distinction 49, 57–64; rules and models distinction 49–57; use value and exchange value distinction 49–50, 64–9
Boelens, L. 64
BREEAM Communities 259–60
Bridge, G. 182
British house building *see* house building trends (UK)
Broadacre City 53
Brundtland report (1987) 97
building codes and standards 240–1
Building Research Establishment (BRE) 259
bureaucracy and risk management 206–7

Callon, M. 15
Calvino, I. 179–81
Cambridge Architectural Research 168

Cameron, David 88
Campbell, H. 207
Campbell, S. 18–19, 20
carbon delivery plan 228–30, 239, 241
carbon reduction policies 32; building upgrading or retrofitting 261; UK national carbon delivery plan 228–30, 239, 241
Carmona, M. 164
case studies 8, 9–10
central heating systems 227–8
central planning, Eastern European model 82
centre and periphery conflict 210–11
Chandigarh, India 55
Cheshire, P. C. 105
Cheshire, UK 110–11
China 58, 83–4
Choay, F. 51, 53
*Cities in Evolution* (Geddes) 227
citizen participation 187; *see also* stakeholder involvement
City Beautiful movement 58
'City of God' (Augustine) 53
City of Tomorrow 53
clientelism 207
'club' analogy 214–16
codes and standards 240–1
Cohen, S. S. 15, 91, 92
Cole, G. D. H. 78
collaborative planning 9, 101–2, 142–3, 151, 199
collective planning 77
command planning, allocative planning styles 98, 101
commercial property values 105–7
Commission for Architecture and the Built Environment (CABE) 103
communicative planning 21, 143
communicative rationality 189, 190–1
community, risk society and politics of 214–17
Community Energy Savings Programme 239
community housing associations 263
community of limited liability 214–16
community-based programmes and initiatives, evaluation of 154–61
compact city model 252–9, 262
competition: planning as partial alternative to 82; planning for 87
complexity theory 9
comprehensive planning 91–2

conceived space 65
conflict: advocacy planning model and 141; agonistic and semi-legal alternatives 189–91; centre versus periphery 210–11; 'cooperative' 101; planning as partial alternative to 82
Connell, D. J. 20
Connell, J. P. 155
consensus, critique of 190
Conservative Party 88
consumer good, environmental quality as 212
cooperative conflict 101
co-operative planning 100
Copenhagen, Denmark 256, 264
Coppens, T. 64
corporate planning 100–1
cost/benefit analysis 165
costs of planning 87
critical areas 97–8
critical hermeneutics 13
critical pragmatism 163
critical rationalism 135–6
critical realist approach 154
critical theory 17
cybernetic systems 150

Davidoff, P. 141–2
Davoudi, S. 213
*De re aedificatoria* (Alberti) 51
deadweight 161
Dear, M. 30
decentralised concentration 255, 262; *see also* compact city model; sustainable urbanism
decentralised transition pathways 237–9
deception 28
deconstruction 30
deduction 135, 137; *see also* science philosophy/scientific method
DeFilippis, J. 24, 32
degrowth movement 224–5
Deleuze, G. 42, 45, 47, 49, 50, 127, 211, 262, 269
deliberative democracy 184–9, 269
demand-side interventions 89–91
democracy, deliberative 184–9, 269
democracy and the green state 268–9
democratisation 80
density 256
deregulation 88, 111
design quality 103–4
deterritorialisation 42–3

development plans, evaluation in 161–8; *see also* plan evaluation
Dewey, J. 128, 138–9, 140, 182
difference: agonistic and semi-legal alternatives 189–91; deliberative democracy 184–9; pragmatic appreciation of 183–4
dissent, agonistic and semi-legal alternatives 189–91
district heating 263–4; *see also* heating networks
diversity, postmodernism as 181–4
Donaldson, S. I. 152–3
'double hermeneutics' 7–8
double loop learning 12
Douglas, M. 203, 204, 205, 209, 210–13, 269
drawing and mapping 44–6
du Gay, P. 207
Durkheim, É. 7

eco-cities 259–60
ecological modernisation 223–5, 268
ecological planning 52–3
ecological systems theory 201
ecological transition management 32; *see also* transition management
ecologising the economy 232–3
ecology of cities 200
ecology within cities 200
eco-modernist approach 52–3
economic growth: allocative planning and 102–5; degrowth movement 224–5; pillars of sustainable development 97
economic impacts, plan evaluation 165–7
economic planning 77; indicative planning 91; innovative planning 115–17; Mannheim and 77–82; planning as ideal type 81–6; state role in 78–9; town planning distinction 78; value for money 132, 164
economising ecology 232–3
Eco-Village network 118
egalitarianism 204
Egan review (2004) 5–6
elective belonging 214
empirical studies 15
empty homes strategy 157, 158–9*t*
energy action plans 116
energy consumption model 25

energy consumption trends 230–1, 241–2, 257–8
energy retrofitting 241
environmental capacity 167
environmental impact assessment 166–8
environmental planning: allocation/control of 'bads' 96; policy coordination issues 267; as resource allocation 82; *see also* planning styles; sustainable urbanism; transition management
environmental pressure groups: centre-periphery conflict 211; economic growth and 224; planning flexibility considerations 47
environmental quality, as consumer good 212
environmental risk *see* risk management
environmental systems theory 151
establishment 78
ethical principles 22–4
European Commission 243
European Union national energy plans 226
'European Urban Charter' (1992) 67
evaluation *see* plan evaluation
Evans, A. W. 165
exchange value 49–50, 64–9

Fainstein, S. S. 18–19, 20, 24, 32
fairy story 177–8
false consciousness 29
Faludi, A. 49, 57, 142, 152–3
fatalism 204, 205–6, 213
fictitious commodities 65, 69
flexibility 47
fluid space 48
Flyvbjerg, B. 15, 28, 162, 168, 191
folded surfaces 59
Forester, J. 163
Foucault, M. 28, 30, 59–60
Freiburg, Germany 54
Friedmann, J. 14–15, 18, 79, 96, 98, 100, 115, 140, 199
functional interdependence 80–1
functional rationality 129–33, 137
funding urban upgrading 265–6
future, knowledge of 21
future generations, accountability to 237
future orientation in plan evaluation 161–2
fuzzy jobs 9, 151

Gadamer, H. G. 11, 179
garden city 48, 53, 54, 62, 252
Geddes, P. 62–3, 145, 227
Gezi Park, Istanbul 186
Ghent, Belgium 237
Giddens, A. 7, 27, 199
Glasgow, Scotland 272
globalisation, deterritorialisation 43
goals and objectives 130–1
Godschalk, D. 163–5
Gómez-Baggethun, E. 166
'Good City Form' (Lynch) 52
great planning debate 14–15, 16, 77
green belts 55, 253–4
'Green Deal' policy (2013-2015) 241
green growth 224
green labelling 240
green space 104
green state 200–1, 267–72
green taxation 264–5
green urbanism 251; see also sustainable urbanism
grid/group theory 204–10, 213
grounded theory 8–9, 11; logic model/theory of change 154; pragmatism and 13
growth: allocative planning and 102–5; arborescent or rhizomatic 43, 269; green 224; see also economic growth
growth management, sustainable urbanism 254–6
Gruber, J. 8–9
Guattari, F. 42, 45, 47, 49, 50, 127, 211, 262, 269
Gunder, M. 29

Habermas, J. 188, 190
Hall, P. 107, 108, 174
Harrison, P. 140
Hassan, I. 176
Haughton, G. 151
Haussmann 58, 61
Hayek, F. 14, 32, 85, 86–7, 131, 173
Healey, P. 48, 115, 142, 143, 189
heating networks 116, 227–8, 263–4
hedonic pricing model 166
Helsinki, Finland 263
Hendler, S. 23
Hermant, E. 81
hermeneutics 7–8; alethic 30–1; correctly posed questions 11; critical 13; deconstruction 30; defining the questions 13–24; objectivist 31; phenomenology distinction 10–11; power considerations 27–9; pragmatism and 12–13
hermeneutics of suspicion 27–30
heterotopia 59–60
hidden agendas and processes 28–30
Hilber, C. A. 102, 105, 111
Hillier, J. 29, 44
Hirsch, F. 106, 225
historical method 179
Ho Chi Minh City, Vietnam 261
Hoch, C. 54, 127–8, 140–1, 162, 168
homeland society 18
honest broker role 207–9
Hong Kong 83–4, 257
house building trends (UK) 55; allocative planning impacts 107–14; density and energy consumption 257–8; explaining housing shortages 136; Section 106 agreements 84, 90
house with garden ideal 253, 254
housing: British practices 55; density and energy consumption 257–8; explaining British shortages 136; life expectancy of 262; market impacts of planning 107–15; modernisation programmes 262–3
Houston, Texas 88
Howard, Ebenezer 53
Hudson, B. 14–15, 18
human rights 66–7
hurricane Katrina 210
Hutton, B. 130–1

ideal cities 61
ideal type see planning as ideal type
indicative planning 91
individualism 204, 206, 213
induction 135, 137; see also science philosophy/scientific method
industrial cities 53
information requirements 131
Innes, J. E. 8–9
innovative planning 96, 115–17, 200
institutional analysis 187
institutional learning 209
insurance companies and risk management 206
international applications of planning theory 32–3, 142
International Council for Local Environmental Initiatives (ICLEI) 261–2
international transition management pathways 243

interpretative methods 24; deconstruction 30; defining planning 41–2; hermeneutics of suspicion 27–30; positivism and postpositivism 24–7; *see also* hermeneutics
*Invisible Cities* (Calvino) 179–81
Irish Republic 114
Istanbul, Turkey 186

James, William 128
Jansson, A. 200
Japan 211
Jencks, C. 174–5
Johannesburg Declaration of 2002 97

Keeble, L. 47
knowledge and power 28–9
knowledge limitations 131
Kornai, J. 82–3, 91, 107, 269
Kubisch, A. C. 155
Kusakabe, E. 211

labour theory of value 64
Lai, L. W.-G. 83–4
land use planning: economic impacts 165–7; good practice in 163–4; zoning 88
land value: allocative planning impacts 107; fictitious commodities 65, 69; greenery and 104; sustainable urbanism considerations 253; *see also* property values; *see also* site value taxation
Latour, B. 81
layering 152–3
le Corbusier 53, 55
Le Dantec 63–4
learning theory 12–13; *see also* social learning
least cost methods 165
Leeuw, F. L. 152–3
Lefèbvre, H. 65, 225, 272
legal system 151
legitimacy 5; deliberative democracy 184–9; 'thick' and 'thin' 184; *see also* thick legitimacy
Leibniz, G. W. 59
Leipzig, Germany 255
libertarianism 85, 100
Lindblom, C. E. 140–2, 228
linguistic systems theory 151
lived space 65–6
Liverpool, UK 255–6

'Local Agenda 21' 237
local authorities and transition management 237–41
Local Strategic Partnership (LSP) 155
localism 68
logic model/theory of change 154–61
London, UK: commercial property values 105–7; deregulation impacts 88; district heating 264; planning impacts on housing market 112; Plans for Greater London 46; Wren's reconstruction plan 58
London Docklands UDC 107
long-term outcomes, evaluation of 160
Lord, A. 10
Luhmann, N. 151
Lukes, S. 29
Lundqvist, L. J. 268–9
Lynch, K. 52
Lyotard, J.-F. 173

McFarlane, C. 50, 63, 65
McLoughlin, J. B. 127–8, 130, 136, 150
'Man and Society' (Mannheim) 77–82; *see also* Mannheim, K.
Manchester, UK 65, 210
Mannheim, K. 14–15, 32, 77–82, 86, 91, 108, 128, 129, 133–4, 146, 182, 214, 267, 269
mapping 45–6
mapping exercises 14–17
Marcuse, P. 23
market economy, as utopian project 65
market shaping 98–100
market-based approaches, sociocultural perspective for risk management 206
Marshall, R. 207
Marxist theory and approaches 17; community in itself/community for itself 216–17; false consciousness concept 29; use value/exchange value concepts 64
'material turn' of planning theory 25
Mead, G. H. 128
means and ends 19; functional rationality 129–33
MEEDM 232
meta-analysis 164
Meyerson, M. 140–2
middle ground planning 140
minarchism 85
models 49, 53–7; sustainable urbanism 251–9

modernisation: ecological modernisation 223–5, 268; innovative planning 115–17; risk society and impact of 212–14
modernism 52–3
Moore Milroy, B. 56
More, Thomas 53
Moroni, S. 81, 85
Mouffe, C. 189

national carbon delivery plan 228–30, 239, 241
national energy plans 226
negotiated planning agreements 84, 90
neighbourhood regeneration and improvement strategy 157, 158–9t
neoliberalism 14–15, 17, 85–6, 173; critique of planning as ideal type 85–9; green state considerations 271; justification for planning 146; on knowledge limitations 131; social justice perspectives 21
Netherlands 49
Neuman, M. 19–20
New Deal for Communities 160, 161
New Orleans, Louisiana 210
New Right policies 117–18
new urbanism 251
'New Vision for Planning' (2001) 22–3
Newcastle-upon-Tyne, UK 210
newspapers and deliberative democracy 185–6
Nijkamp, P. 166
NIMBY (Not In My Back Yard) 216–17, 270
Norbert-Schulz, C. 10
normative theories 152–3
'Northern Way' plan (2004) 48
nudging 233–4, 241–2

objectivist hermeneutics 31
ombudsmen 191
organization development 15
Oslo, Norway 258
outsourcing 87
ownership 81; plan evaluation and 156

Paris, France 58, 61, 64
Peirce, C. S. 128, 137, 138, 139
Pennington, M. 271
phenomenology 10–11
philosophical synthesis 14–15, 16
phronetic methods 162–3

Picon, A. 10
piecemeal social engineering 135–6, 141
plan evaluation: changing assumptions over time 167; classifying the approaches 152; of community-based initiatives 154–61; in development and spatial plans 161–8; environmental impact assessment 166–8; future orientation 161–2; internal quality of plan 163–4; layering and weaving 152–3; logic model/theory of change 154–61; of long-term outcomes 160; normative and positive distinction 152–3; ownership and stakeholder involvement 156; phronetic methods 162–3; realist approach 154; rules and models 56–7
planning, as profession 150
planning, defining 3, 14, 24, 41–2; drawing and mapping 44–6; goals and objectives 130–1; Mannheim and 77–8; social/historical contexts and 21; spatial assemblages 42–4
planning as growth management 254
planning as ideal type 81–2; economic attributes 82–5; neoliberal critique 85–9; political planning 91–2; styles 96; supply-side and demand-side interventions 89–91; see also planning styles
planning as mapping 45–6
planning as process 77
planning as strategic drawing 44–5
planning by exceptions 180–1
planning state 267–8
planning styles 8–9, 96–7; soft and fuzzy 151–2; see also allocative planning; innovative planning; planning theory; radical planning
'planning tax' model 105–6
planning theory 3–5; defining the questions 13–24; grounded theory 8–9, 11; hermeneutics and pragmatism 12–13; input or output 8–11; intellectual traditions 14–16; internationalisation of 32–3, 142; logic model/theory of change 154–61; 'material turn' 25; normative and positive distinction 152–3; pragmatism in 140–4; public interest and ethics 21–4; questions-first approaches 17–24; restating

the questions 24; significance of translation 150; social learning 12–13; theory/practice gap 5–8; uses or functions for 19–20; *see also* hermeneutics; interpretative methods; pragmatism; rational planning
'Planning Theory' (Allmendiger) 16–17; *see also* Allmendinger, P.
planning through debate 142
Plans for Greater London 46
pluralist society 18
Polanyi, K. 65, 69, 176, 267
policy statements, allocative planning styles 98–100
political influence-based planning style 8
political planning 77; ideal type 91–2; Mannheim and 77–82; radical planning 117–19; state role in 78–9
politics of community 214–17
pollution 203
Popper, K. 79, 129, 135–6, 141
population decline 255–6
population density 256
population growth 102
positive or behavioural theories 152–3
positivism 24–7
Post-Modern architecture 174–5
postmodernism 173–4; deconstruction 30; as diversity 181–4; historical method 179; neoliberalism versus 173; as reaction 174–6; as storytelling 176–81
postpositivism 24–7
power 18; agonistic approaches 189; allocative planning styles 98; hermeneutics of suspicion 27–9; phronetic methods 163; right to the city 66–8
practice theory 234–6
pragmatism 32, 127–8, 137; abduction and retroduction 137–9; affinity with planning 144–6; appreciation of difference 182; collaborative planning 142–3; combining rationalism 191; critical 163; hermeneutics and 12–13; plan evaluation approach 162; in planning theory 140–4; sustainable development and 199
'*principia media*' 134
'Principles and Practice of Town and Country Planning' (Keeble) 47
privatisation 81
procedural debate 17–18

professionalisation and professionalism 9, 140
programme theories 154; *see also* logic model/theory of change
project plans 49
project-based approach 48
property markets 26
property markets (non-residential), allocative planning and 102–7
property markets (residential) *see* housing
property rights: green state and 268; right to the city 66–8
property tax 62
property values: allocative planning and 102–7; design quality and 103–4; *see also* land value
Pruitt-Igoe, St. Louis, Missouri 175
psychoanalysis in planning 30
public awareness of environmental risks 212
public interest 21–4
public opinion and deliberative democracy 185–6
public space 185
public transport hubs 256–7
Pudong, China 58

quality of design 103–4
quasi-objects 25–6
questions-first approaches 17–24

radical planning 15, 16, 96, 117–19, 200
rational planning 128–9; critical rationalism 135–6; functional rationality 129–33, 137; goals and objectives 130–1; information requirements 131; substantial rationality 133–5; utilitarian orientation 131–2; wicked problems 132–3
rationalism 15, 16, 21, 127–8; combining pragmatism 191; communicative rationality 189, 190–1; neoliberal critique 86
Reade, E. 5
'Readings in Planning Theory' 18–19, 267
realist approach 154
reason 127
regulatory policies: allocative planning styles 98–100; building codes and standards 240–1

resilience 201, 209–10; cost of achieving 265; risk and 201–3
resource allocation 82
result chains 154
retroduction 137–9; *see also* science philosophy/scientific method
retrofitting 241, 260–7
rhizomatic growth 43, 269
Richardson, T. 28
Ricoeur, P. 27, 30
right to the city 66–9
risk management: grid/group theory 204–10, 213; honest broker role 207–9; market and bureaucracy distinctions 206–7; public awareness of environmental risks 212; risk and resilience 201–3; socio-cultural theory 203–11; transition management and 222
risk society 202–3, 212; impact of modernity/modernisation 212–14; politics of community 214–17
Rittel, H. W. J. 132
Robinson, N. A. 97
Romantic planning 49, 57, 60–4
Rorty, R. 182
rules and models 49–57; sustainable urbanism 251, 259–60

'S' curve 226–8
Sandercock, L. 52
Schön, D. A. 6, 51, 140
'science of muddling through' 140–1
science of opinions 7
science philosophy/scientific method 150; abduction and retroduction 137; induction and deduction 135, 137; normative and positive distinction 152–3; positivism and postpositivism 25
scientific management 78–9
scripts 234
Section 106 agreements 84, 90
semi-legal approaches 190–1
'Shaping the Future" (2010) 22–3
Sieh, L. 164
Simmel, G. 129
Simon, H. 131
single loop learning 12
site value taxation 264–5
Sköldberg, K. 30
social capital 141, 142, 185, 208–9
social contract 68, 156

social engineering 135–6, 141
social housing 68
social justice: green state considerations 269–70; planning perspectives and 21
social learning 12–13, 61; assemblage theory 50–1, 61, 63
social mobilization 15, 16
social movements-based planning style 8–9
social rights 66–8
social theory 6–7
socio-cultural theory 203–11; centre-periphery conflict 210–11; grid/group theory 204–10, 213
socio-ecological systems theory 150, 201
socio-technical systems theory 150
soft measures 242
soft spaces 151
spatial assemblages 42–4
spatial planning and transition management 250–1; *see also* transition management
spatial plans, evaluation in 161–8
stakeholder involvement: deliberative democracy 184–9; evaluation and 156; politics of community 214–17; postmodernism as diversity 181–4
standards and codes 240–1
state role in planning 78
Stern report (2007) 233
'store' metaphor 4
storytelling 176–81
strategic drawing 44–5
substantial rationality 133–5
substantive rationality 133
supply-side interventions 89–91, 114–15
surveying 45
surveying before planning 62–3
sustainable development: accountability to future generations 237; compact city model 252–9; planning styles 97; planning theory reorientation 24; pragmatic assumptions 199; as process 199; social justice considerations 269–70; three pillars of 97; *see also* sustainable urbanism
sustainable urbanism 251; compact city model 262; eco-cities and eco-rating 259–60; funding and investment 265–6; growth management 254–6; land costs and 253; model-based

planning 251–9; rule-based planning 251, 259–60; upgrading and retrofitting 260–7
symmetry 25–6
systems theory 9, 150–1; cybernetic 150; ecological 201; linguistic 151; risk and resilience 201–2; socio-ecological 150, 201; socio-technical 150, 232–3

taxation, site value 264–5
technical/bureaucratic planning style 8
territorialisation 42–3
Tewdwr-Jones, M. 27
theory *see* planning theory
theory of change/logic model 154–61
thick legitimacy 184; agonistic and semi-legal alternatives 189–91; deliberative democracy 184–9
Throgmorton, J. A. 177, 178
Toronto, Canada 56
town planning: economic planning distinction 78; historical development 46–9; modernist 52–3; as resource allocation 82; rules and models 49–57; *see also* blueprint planning
Town Planning Institute 46
transaction cost theory 87
transition management 222, 225–6; backcasting 228–31; carbon reduction policies 32; economising and ecologising 232–3; global and international pathways 243; local authorities and decentralised pathways 237–41; mapping and classification 232–6; nudging 233–4, 241–2; pathways 231–43; practice theory 234–6; related and alternative theories 222–6; retrofitting 241, 260–7; risk management and 222; 'S' curve 226–8; soft measures 242; spatial planning and 250–1; urban fabric inadequacies 260
transition town movement 222
translation 150; actor-network theory 153; classifying the approaches 152; *see also* plan evaluation
transport infrastructure and development 256–7

triple hermeneutics 27
triple loop learning 12–13

UK energy consumption patterns 230–1
UK house building trends *see* house building trends (UK)
UK national carbon delivery plan 228–30, 239, 241
Unwin, R. 61–2
upgrading and retrofitting 260–7
urban archipelago 255
urban design quality 103–4
urban environmental capacity 167
urban form debate 18
urban functions 52
urban growth management 254–6
urban planning and transition management 250; *see also* transition management
urban planning, defining *see* planning, defining
Urban Renaissance 252–3
urban resilience *see* resilience
urban rights 67
urban upgrading and retrofitting 260–7
urbanism 251; *see also* sustainable urbanism
use value 49–50, 64–9
'Utopia' (More) 53
utopias 61
value for money 132, 164

Vancouver, Canada 54
Vermeulen, W. 102, 111
voluntary planning 100–1

Wang, L. 128
Webber, M. M. 132
Weber, M. 82, 129
welfare state 68, 271–2
wicked problems 132–3
Wildavsky, A. B. 203, 209, 210–12, 269
Wilkinson, C. 201
win-win arguments 223–4
Wooton, B. 80, 173
Wright, Frank Lloyd 53

Yiftachel, O. 17–18, 21, 24, 163

zoning 88